AN INCREDIBLE DREAM

AN INCREDIBLE DREAM

Ralph Roberts

and the

Story of Comcast

WILLIAM NOVAK

People often ask me, "When you started in Tupelo with a few hundred customers, did you ever think that some day you'd have the largest cable company in the country?"

And I always answer with a straight face, "Of course I did!"

— RALPH ROBERTS

I went to Ralph's office a few years ago and said, "Ralph, you've got to write a book so we can capture all the things you've done."

He said, "Look at all the books on my shelf. I don't need a book about me."

"Maybe you don't," I said. "But we do."

— MARTHA SOEHREN, CHIEF LEARNING OFFICER

Contents

Contents

Contents

Contents

AN INCREDIBLE DREAM

Foreword

Brian Roberts

For my entire adult life, I have had the joy of working side by side with my father.

Ralph Roberts has had a remarkable life, and a consistent one, too. In every setting—whether in the office, over dinner at his favorite greasy spoon, or painting a schoolhouse wall during Comcast Cares Day—he has always been optimistic, warm, and encouraging.

For years I asked him to consider writing a book about his life and especially the creation of Comcast. And for years his answer was always the same: "Other than you, Brian, why would anyone care?" But I've seen the look in people's eyes when he describes the origins of the company, or explains how it grew to where we are today. Eventually, with the encouragement of family, friends, and colleagues, he agreed to talk about his life and about Comcast.

It all began with Ralph and his two earliest colleagues, Dan Aaron and Julian Brodsky, huddling together in a humble office in Bala Cynwyd, Pennsylvania, to figure out this new business known as community antenna television. They were a great team, with a knack for seeing around corners, and for being a tad smarter, a bit quicker, and often a lot bolder than the competition. Ralph, the patient, unassuming gentleman, kept a steady hand on the wheel as they made a series of brilliant bets on the future.

When he chose to work with Dan and Julian, my father set a pattern that continued through his career. He surrounded himself with fine and talented people who shared his love and loyalty for the company they were working so hard to build. In this regard, as in so many others, I have tried to emulate him.

Ralph wanted every employee to feel that his business was also their business. Even as we kept growing larger, he worked to retain the family feeling that inspired people to dedicate a big part of their lives to the company. With the culmination of our acquisition of NBC Universal in 2011, Comcast took its place among the global leaders in communications and entertainment.

A great story deserves a skilled writer, and Bill Novak has masterfully brought our history and some of its key personalities to life. He learned about Comcast not only through the eyes of Ralph, Dan, and Julian, but also from hundreds of employees from every period of our history.

This book does more than tell our story. It shows what a single entrepreneur can accomplish. When you focus relentlessly on new products and services, when you create jobs, and when you give employees and their communities the opportunity to share in your growth, you can change people's lives.

As I read this book, I reflected on the gift of a unique father-son business partnership. I have also been so blessed with my own family, as well as a wonderful mother and four terrific siblings and their loving spouses and children. But life is unpredictable. Late in 2011 we lost our charismatic and beloved youngest brother, who died suddenly at fifty-one. There has been nothing sadder in our lives, and we miss him terribly.

Over the years, I have been fortunate enough to watch my dad build this company and see it flourish. It has been a dream come true for him—and also for me.

As he has had honors and recognition heaped upon him, he has accepted them with gratitude and humility. And almost every time, he says the same thing: "Only in America." Whenever I've seen him at the podium with his self-effacing smile, I've had the same thought: Sometimes the good guys really do finish first.

Pops . . . thanks for sharing your journey.

Preface

William Novak and Ralph Roberts

This book began in a slightly roundabout way. Most of my work consists of helping prominent people write their memoirs, and the path that led me to Ralph Roberts, a founding father of cable television, began with Barbara Walters, a founding mother of broadcast television. Back in 2005, after we'd had a couple of good meetings about working together on her life story, her agent, Mort Janklow, called to say that Barbara had decided to work with another writer, a woman I knew and respected, because they were neighbors in New York. (I live in Boston.) I was disappointed, but what could I do?

Then Mort told me that Ralph Roberts, the founder of Comcast, was also looking for a writer. "You may not know his name," he said, "but I promise you'll like him." So I flew to Philadelphia and had lunch with Ralph, and of course I liked him. Who doesn't like Ralph?

But liking a potential book partner isn't enough. Having teamed up with people like Lee Iacocca, Tip O'Neill, Tim Russert, Oliver North, and Magic Johnson, I knew it was easier to work with celebrities who enjoy being the center of attention and holding forth about themselves. And Ralph was nothing like that.

I've interviewed many people over the years, and while most of them have treated me well, Ralph was especially considerate. He never kept me waiting, and during our afternoons together, there wasn't a single interruption—except when his wife, Suzanne, or one of their children or grandchildren called.

Both of us enjoyed our conversations, and we laughed often. Ralph, whose favorite word is *family*, loved to tell me about his childhood, his parents, his sister, and especially his brother, Joseph; and later, as we moved along chronologically, about Suzanne and their children, and the families those children have created. He happily recalled his various jobs before Comcast, and especially his years during the 1950s in the men's accessories business, where he was able to draw upon his visual, design, and marketing talents.

When we came to the Comcast era, he was a little more reticent. Here he gently shifted the attention away from himself and on to his earliest colleagues, Dan Aaron and Julian Brodsky, his son Brian, and the other leaders who have helped him guide and grow the company.

After a number of conversations with Ralph, I called Brian to propose a different kind of book: "As you know, your father doesn't like to focus on himself. But I'd love to keep working with him, and I'm getting some good material. Instead of a memoir, what if I wrote a history of Comcast with as much about Ralph as he'll tell me?"

Brian welcomed the idea. So did Ralph and David Cohen, who was in charge of the project, although none of us realized how big an undertaking it would be. But one advantage became clear immediately: in a book *about* Ralph, rather than by him, it was much easier to portray who he really is. He might be hesitant to talk about himself, but a great many other people couldn't wait to tell me how much they loved and respected him.

I wasn't sure how to write the story of Comcast, but I knew what I wanted to avoid. Instead of presenting a compendium of facts, dates, numbers, and job titles, I preferred to write a more personal book, with in-depth portraits of the individuals who have helped Ralph and Brian transform a tiny cable system into a world-class media company. Here I was fortunate: Comcast's decision makers have been people of ability, ideas, and substance. And, as you'll see, they have also been good talkers.

I noticed early on that the top executives were unusually supportive of one another. Most of them preferred appreciating their colleagues to describing their own accomplishments, which is very much like Ralph. Sometimes this was frustrating: how could I do justice to an event or a decision if everyone wanted to give the credit to the next guy?

I also wondered how I could get a little closer to the corporate culture. Ralph made that possible when he suggested that I attend the closing dinner for that year's ELF class. (ELF, I soon learned, is the unfortunate acronym for Executive Leadership Forum, the high-level leadership program sponsored by Comcast University, the company's training and development arm.) Earlier in the day, six teams of young executives from different parts of the country had each presented a detailed, thought-out proposal for the company that they had been working on all year. Their audience consisted of Comcast's leaders, who asked tough questions and took these recommendations seriously.

It sounded so interesting that I impulsively asked Brian Mossor, who co-directed the program, if I could join the new, incoming class as an observer. And as I hoped, ELF provided a terrific window into the company. I also attended several Spirit of Comcast sessions for employees from the field, and various other events, including the CommTech Jeopardy finals in Charleston, South Carolina—the culmination of a series of competitions celebrating the expertise of Comcast's technical employees. In 2008, at the company-wide management conference in Arizona, I was able to meet and talk with employees from across the country.

At all of these events, I saw that the values I kept hearing about seemed to be genuine. The company's leaders were accessible. The senior people really did welcome ideas from their junior associates. Ralph's kindness and ethical concerns really did permeate through the ranks.

Because values seemed to be so important at Comcast, I was surprised that nobody had ever sat down to figure out exactly what they were. I decided to fill that vacuum, and to conclude the book with a chapter in which employees from different parts of the company, and different periods of its history, described these values as if they were all participating in one big conversation—which in a sense they were.

From the start, I thought this book should be released by Comcast itself, rather than a commercial publisher. But even a privately printed work imposes certain restrictions. To limit the book to a single volume, and to respect the family's privacy, I stopped writing about Ralph's family life after 1942, the year he and Suzanne were married. Had it been up to Ralph, there would have been a hundred more pages about Suzanne—and they would have been easy to fill. Their relationship, and their marriage of almost seventy years as we go to press, could be its own book. Suzanne's loving support of Ralph every step of the way makes her an integral part of the Comcast story as well.

And if Ralph had his way, and time allowed, I would have interviewed just about every employee. But we both recognized that I had to limit myself to about three hundred—an ambitious number, but just a tiny fraction of the workforce. Please forgive me if you weren't one of them—or if you were, and your name doesn't appear in the book. (That's one reason there's no index.) The original version was even longer, and I had to make some painful cuts.

I spent most of my time talking with, and writing about, employees at the company's corporate headquarters in Philadelphia, and before that, in nearby Bala Cynwyd. So you wouldn't know from reading this book that the real business of Comcast, the work that keeps the wheels turning, goes on every day (and in many cases, around the clock) in offices, call centers, headends, warehouses, and payment centers across the country—to say nothing of a major broadcast network, a good number of cable channels, a movie studio, theme parks, websites, and the list goes on.

In keeping with the culture of Comcast, I have referred to the four main characters—Ralph Roberts, Dan Aaron, Julian Brodsky, and Brian Roberts—mostly by their first names, which is how they have been thought of by most employees in the corporate office. I refer to everyone else by the informal names by which they are actually known at work—Art Block, rather than Arthur; Steve Burke, rather than Stephen.

I am enormously grateful to the many people who helped me by sharing stories, checking facts, and offering comments and corrections in person, over the phone, and via e-mail. I am especially indebted to the individuals I turned to again and again; if I started naming names, the book would be even longer and I would invariably leave someone out. But I must thank Julian Brodsky and Art Block, whose continued engagement and patience were especially valuable. Back in Boston, the talented Michael Shiner helped with some of the interviews, and the meticulous Johanna Ehrmann was my trusted copy editor. And in Philadelphia, Patty O'Brien reviewed the proofs with great care and was indispensable in helping us get the book to press.

As part of my research, I drew upon an unpublished history of the company from 1996 by the Winthrop Group and on the many interviews they conducted, and on the writings of Professor Thomas Eisenmann of the Harvard Business School. And I reviewed some of the many transcripts of interviews with cable executives that are available online from the Barco Library at The Cable Center in Denver.

Because it's clear that I came to admire the people I was writing about, some readers may conclude that I wrote this book wearing rose-colored glasses. But as my wife knows all too well, I am not a natural optimist. It's just that hundreds of enjoyable and often stimulating conversations with the company's leaders and employees have persuaded me that Comcast is pretty much as they describe it—a really good place to work.

This has been a dream assignment. True, the book took years to research and to write, and it was a challenge to capture the history of a company that hasn't stopped growing. But if any book had to take a long time, I'm glad it was this one. There were many days when I didn't want it to end.

Arrivals

Charisse Lillie; Art Block

When a recruiter called him in the spring of 2006 about moving to Comcast, Michael Angelakis wasn't really interested. As a managing director at Providence Equity Partners, a private equity firm specializing in media and telecommunications, Angelakis already had a terrific job.

But he listened politely as Howard Fischer, the head of an executive search firm, explained why he was calling. Larry Smith, one of Comcast's two co-CFOs, was thinking of retiring, and Brian Roberts, the company's CEO, wanted to know whether Angelakis had any thoughts about who might make a good replacement, or whether he might even consider taking the job himself.

Because private equity executives are very highly compensated, and because Providence Equity, in Providence, Rhode Island, had an unusually warm corporate culture, nobody at Comcast was surprised when Angelakis said he was happy where he was, thank you.

And he *was* happy, except for all that travel, which was increasingly taking him out of the country. And although he didn't mention this to Howard Fischer, there was a spark in him that rather liked the idea of getting involved in operations again. During the 1990s he had loved running a small cable company in Maine. He respected Comcast and its leaders, and because he and his colleagues at Providence Equity examined something like three hundred potential new investments every year, the idea of spending all his time on a single company held a certain appeal.

A week later, Steve Burke, Comcast's chief operating officer, called Angelakis on another matter. They already knew each other, and Angelakis had once tried to get Burke to join him at Providence Equity. "By the way," Burke said at the end of their conversation, "I think you're making a big mistake by not talking to us."

"I've been wondering about that," Angelakis said.

When Burke told him that John Alchin, Comcast's other co-CFO, was also considering retirement, Angelakis realized there might be a bigger opportunity at the company than he had thought.

"Do you think I'd be a good fit?" he asked Burke.

"Absolutely."

"The hook is in," Burke told Brian Roberts, who in turn called Angelakis and invited him to Philadelphia. "Come down for coffee," Brian said, trying to make the visit sound casual.

Brian and his colleagues knew Angelakis as an experienced and talented deal maker who understood the cable business. But that wasn't the only reason they liked him. They also *liked* him. "In the end," says Howard Fischer, "it's personality, values, and cultural style that will make or break a hire." When Angelakis asked Burke if he would fit in at Comcast, it was a question his future colleagues had already asked and answered.

Angelakis, who had expected to talk with Brian for an hour or so, ended up spending the entire day at Howard Fischer's office in downtown Philadelphia as the Comcast leaders came by to meet him. On their way out, they all told Fischer the same thing—that Angelakis was their first choice.

One of those executives was Ralph Roberts, the eighty-six-year-old founder of Comcast and Brian's father. Angelakis was excited to meet this industry legend, whom he thought of as the Sam Walton of the cable business. But when they sat down together, Ralph didn't ask a single question about business, cable, or even finance. Instead, he asked Angelakis about his family, and he spoke about his own family, especially Brian. Even when Angelakis asked Ralph what he considered his greatest accomplishment, Ralph gave a personal answer, not a business one: "All five of my children speak to me frequently, and my wife and I have been happily married for more than sixty years."

Angelakis was impressed. He had met plenty of older entrepreneurs who were blustery, self-centered, and aggressive, but this man was different. He was moved by Ralph's ability to speak from the heart and also to listen, and he was surprised to feel so kindly toward somebody he had just met.

That night, after Angelakis returned home, Brian called to continue the conversation. They spoke again on Saturday—twice—and scheduled a fourth call for Sunday morning, which ran from seven thirty until ten, when Angelakis drove his kids to Sunday school. When they spoke again that night, Angelakis asked, "How serious is this? Are you down to just three or four candidates?"

"We were," said Brian. "But now it's just you."

Christine Angelakis wasn't thrilled that her husband was thinking about a move, but she wasn't surprised, either. When Michael mentioned that he was going to Philadelphia for coffee with Brian Roberts, she could tell from his voice that this was more than an exploration. "I knew before he did," she says.

On Monday Angelakis returned to Philadelphia for dinner with Brian, followed by breakfast the next day with Steve Burke and a flight to California with Larry Smith for a board meeting that both men were attending.

Christine, an at-home mother, was willing to move on one condition: "If the Comcast job means I'll see you one minute less than I do now," she told her husband, "we're not going. But if it means more time with the family, that's a deal I'll make any day." On Saturday they flew to Philadelphia and explored the city. On Sunday they visited with Steve and Gretchen Burke in the morning. Then they all drove over to Brian and Aileen's house, where Brian was hoping to close the sale.

Over lunch, sensing that Angelakis was already on board, Brian turned his attention to Christine. Gretchen Burke told her that Steve was home for dinner almost every night, and that she, too, had at first resisted moving to Philadelphia. Christine liked what she was hearing. If this was the culture they would be part of, it was worth moving for.

"We're in," Angelakis told Brian on the phone that night. It took them only a few minutes to settle on terms.

Michael Angelakis was the first partner to leave Providence Equity. He still has friends there, but he is enjoying the new challenges at Comcast. He travels less than he used to, and most nights he tries to be home for dinner.

When Angelakis came to Comcast, Charisse Lillie had been with the company for about two years. As one of Philadelphia's top labor and employment attorneys at the prestigious law firm of Ballard Spahr Andrews & Ingersoll, she had been handling cases for Comcast for several years when Al Peddrick, the head of Human Resources, called in 2005 to ask if she would have lunch with Steve Burke. "I'm going to retire," Peddrick said, "and we're thinking of hiring you for my job."

This sort of thing happened regularly to Lillie. A journalist once wrote that her résumé was as long and winding as the Delaware River, because early in her career she had taken a new position every two years. Her grandparents used to worry that she couldn't keep a job, and they continued to worry even after she assured them that every new position represented another promotion.

She grew up in Houston, where she attended a segregated elementary school. Her father, Richard, was a jazz musician who had toured with B.B. King. He practiced his horn daily, including many days when he was in the hospital dying of cancer in his early fifties, and his commitment to his craft was obvious to his two daughters. Their mother, Vernell, was a high school drama teacher who quit her job and moved the family to Pittsburgh to earn her doctorate in English literature at Carnegie Mellon. She then began a second career as a professor of African American Studies at the University of Pittsburgh, where she started a repertory company. Unable to find a script about the great gospel singer Mahalia Jackson, she wrote her own. "The can-do spirit I have today," Charisse Lillie says, "is because I grew up with can-do parents."

When Charisse was a girl, one of her role models was Barbara Jordan—a family friend, a lawyer, and the congresswoman who gave a memorable keynote address at the 1976 Democratic National Convention. When Charisse told her third-grade teacher that she, too, wanted to become a lawyer, the teacher said, "Women aren't lawyers. Women are teachers." But Charisse knew better.

At Wesleyan University in Connecticut, she majored in history and government and graduated in three years. After Temple University law school and graduate work at Yale, she served, among other jobs, as city solicitor of Philadelphia. And while practicing law at Ballard Spahr, she chaired the board of the Federal Reserve Bank of Philadelphia—the first African American woman to hold that position.

Over lunch with Steve Burke at a nearby Marathon Grill, she became excited about his vision for a more inclusive and diverse Comcast. Then she met with Ralph Roberts, who told her how he felt about Human Resources: "You will be making sure conditions are right for members of my family," he said, "and my family is huge now, with over sixty thousand people."

Lillie, who already knew some of the other executives, felt an immediate connection to Ralph. "Every time I've been in his presence," she says, "he has acted consistently with what he told me when we first met. People adore him, and he loves them right back. I'd follow that man into a burning building."

Lillie wasn't eager to give up her law practice or her leadership position at Ballard, where she had recruited a number of women and minority lawyers and was a mentor to some of them, but she could see that Comcast was determined to create a more diverse workforce, especially at the executive level, and that was an endeavor she wanted to be part of.

In 2008 Lillie was asked to head up both the Comcast Foundation and the company's community investment programs—to take charge of a variety of corporate giving, employee contributions, and employee volunteer projects. "Community investment at Comcast is a three-hundred-million-a-year enterprise," says executive vice president David Cohen, "and with Charisse's experience, her connections in the community and to our offices all over the country, and her passion for investing in the community, she was the obvious choice."

A couple of years earlier, in the summer of 2003, D'Arcy Rudnay was wishing she had never heard of Comcast. Months before, a recruiter had suggested that she apply for a position as vice president of corporate communications. Rudnay, who held a similar job at Lincoln Financial Group in Philadelphia, was happy there, and she had heard that Comcast executives worked insane hours, which didn't sound appealing. But a few years earlier, she had used her year-end bonus to buy Comcast stock. It was the first time she had ever invested on her own, and she held on to those shares even when her broker urged her to sell. The investment worked out nicely, and now she wondered whether it might have been a sign that she should apply for the job. She knew that was silly, but surely there was no harm in talking.

Nobody had told Rudnay that Comcast could be painfully slow when it came to hiring new executives. Later, she would learn that this deliberate, unhurried approach was one reason the company generally ended up with the right people and experienced so little turnover, but while she was going through the hiring process, it just made her angry. She had met twice with Brian; three or four times with David Cohen, who would be her boss; twice with John Alchin; and once each with Steve Burke and Dave Watson from the cable division. These meetings had gone well, and for six or seven months, Rudnay reminded herself that she, too, was in no rush. But eventually, her patience ran out. And it didn't help that Comcast and Lincoln Financial had their headquarters in the same building at 1500 Market Street. Every time she stepped into the elevator for another meeting at Comcast, she was afraid one of her colleagues would notice.

When a full year had passed, she expressed her annoyance to the recruiter. Comcast had finally made her an offer, but by now the process had dragged on so long that Rudnay wasn't sure she still wanted the job. If this was how slowly the company moved, maybe she should stay where she was.

Seeing that it was time to close the deal, David Cohen asked Rudnay to meet with Ralph. When she walked into his office, the first thing she noticed was a huge photo of Suzanne Roberts on the wall, part of a collage of pictures showing Ralph and his wife in a variety of locations. As Rudnay took it all in, Ralph stood with her, and soon they were talking about his favorite subject—his family. "Whether he knew it or not," Rudnay says, "he pushed all the right buttons."

To her surprise, Ralph didn't mention the job, its responsibilities, or her qualifications. And she soon felt comfortable enough to raise a question that bothered her even more than the slow hiring process: Would this job keep her at the office for such long hours that she wouldn't see much of her husband or their daughters?

Ralph looked at her kindly and said, "My wife and our five children are the most important people in my life. All the years I was building this company, I was home most nights for dinner. We would never ask you to neglect your family."

Rudnay was reassured by how Ralph talked about families—both his own family and his corporate one—and she took the job. He had made the sale by showing her that the company had the same values she did.

In 1991 Dave Watson, the head of marketing at Metrophone, a Philadelphia-based regional cell phone company, picked up the phone to find his boss on the line. "Dave, are you sitting down? Comcast just bought the company and they're on their way over to meet us."

Metrophone had been on the market for a while. A few months

earlier, when Comcast had tried to hire Watson to be head of marketing for its own cell phone division, he had declined because he had promised to stay at Metrophone for another year to respond to due diligence inquiries from potential bidders. The Comcast executive who wanted to hire him had not taken this well.

Metrophone was in Valley Forge, about half an hour from Philadelphia, which didn't leave Watson much time. He called his wife and said, "Comcast just bought us, which is probably not good for me because I turned them down." He was still talking when he saw a blue van pull into the parking lot. Then his boss came in and said, "They're here. We'll meet in the conference room in five minutes, but Ralph Roberts wants a moment with you first."

That's a nice touch, thought Watson. He's going to fire me in person.

When they were introduced, Ralph said, "I know you turned us down, but there are no hard feelings. The wireless business is still new to us. We're building our management team, and we admire what you and your group have done. When this deal closes, we'd love you to stay with us."

Watson came to Comcast as head of sales and marketing for the cellular division, and later became the division's president. In 1998, when Comcast sold its cellular operations to Southwestern Bell, the new owners assumed that the division's senior executives were part of the sale. But Brian Roberts refused to let Watson go. Although his entire career had been in cellular, and he knew nothing about cable, Dave Watson struck Brian as someone who knew how to operate in a competitive environment. With satellite companies making inroads into cable's turf and phone companies about to jump in, Watson was too valuable to lose. He became the cable division's head of marketing, and in 2004, after Steve Burke was made chief operating officer of Comcast, Dave Watson became head of operations for Comcast Cable, and later, its chief operating officer.

Ralph didn't always close the sale; sometimes he sealed it after the deal was done. In 1990, soon after Gene Shatlock was hired by the

Comcast system in West Palm Beach, Florida, he flew to Philadelphia for a meeting of marketing executives from around the country. At the opening dinner, Shatlock, who didn't know anyone, took a seat at one of the round tables, where, a moment later, an older man sat next to him. Only when Shatlock heard somebody wave and say, "Hi, Ralph," did he realize that he was sitting next to Ralph Roberts. Ralph asked about his job, and his family, and how he liked working for Comcast. Shatlock found him easy to talk to, but he couldn't believe he was sitting next to the founder. He hadn't expected that Ralph Roberts would be there at all, and if he was, he would surely be sitting at the head table with other senior executives.

Why is he talking to *me*? Shatlock wondered. "But I finally got it," he says. "I understood why everyone here was so committed. Ralph cared about me not just as an employee, but also as a person. Those few minutes set me up for my career. I knew what company I wanted to stay with."

When Brad Dusto graduated from Cornell with a degree in electrical engineering, he went to work building power plants. "Extreme engineering," he calls it. "You weren't supposed to talk to anyone—just work."

Dusto wasn't sure what he was looking for, but it wasn't that. After earning a business degree, he ended up at a division of RCA, where he became an expert in digital communications and satellite broadcasting. In the late 1970s, when content providers were starting to use communications satellites to distribute their programs to cable companies, Dusto knocked on doors all over the country to sign up customers for RCA's satellite division. He had some success with Showtime, ESPN, and The Movie Channel, but it was a slow process, a classic chicken-and-egg dilemma. Cable companies were reluctant to buy expensive receiving dishes because there wasn't enough programming to justify the cost, while programmers didn't want to pay for satellite time because not enough people were watching.

He was working for a small cable operator in upstate New York when a recruiter called in late 1990 about an opening at Comcast.

Dusto was wary. Comcast had a fine reputation in the industry, but Dusto knew what D'Arcy Rudnay hadn't—that the company was known for long, time-consuming job interviews, after which, people said, they often hired somebody from within. Still, he drove down for interviews with Tom Baxter and Mike Tallent, who ran Comcast's cable division.

After what felt like a long time, he was invited back for a meeting with Ralph and Brian Roberts in Ralph's office. Brian, who had recently been named president of Comcast, did all the talking and started firing questions at Dusto: "What's your cash flow? What's your churn? How do you do this? What about that?"

Dusto had an answer for every question, and the interview was going well. When Brian left to take a phone call, Dusto thought the meeting was over. Ralph still hadn't said a word, but as Dusto got up to leave, Ralph asked if he would stay a little longer. Then he said, "Tell me about your work ethic."

Dusto felt a moment of panic. He thought he was about to be hired, but this was a question he hadn't anticipated. All right, he decided, I'll tell him the truth. "I work all week," he told Ralph, "and I try to leave weekends for my family and my church. I'm also a Boy Scout leader. But I'll come in during budget season or any time you need me."

Ralph was silent.

Oh great, thought Dusto. I just lost the job.

"You know," Ralph finally said, "we think a lot about families here. We like people who are family oriented, and we hope you'll join the company."

The offer came the next day, and Brad Dusto became vice president of the Northeast Region. When Frank Ragone, the head engineer, announced his retirement, Dusto was persuaded to take his job. He agreed to try it for three years, but he stayed for ten and was named chief technology officer of the whole company. Among other things, Dusto was responsible for the massive fiber-optic rebuild of Comcast's network infrastructure during the 1990s that provided the foundation for digital cable, digital phone, and high-speed Internet.

"He knows the cable business cold," Julian Brodsky says. "He understands everything from end to end about the network, and top to bottom about our customers."

In 2003, after Comcast bought AT&T Broadband, Steve Burke asked Dusto to return to cable operations and move his family to Denver to head up what is now the West Division. Younger executives are often asked to relocate, but such requests are rare at Dusto's level. It wasn't an easy decision, and there may have been a little arm-twisting, but Dusto, who was free to say no, said yes.

In 1980, when the partner heading up the Comcast account at the Philadelphia law firm of Wolf, Block, Schorr and Solis-Cohen was too sick to accompany Ralph to a meeting in New York, he asked if a young associate named Arthur Block could go in his place. Ralph could have requested another partner, but he said that Block, whom he had never met, would be fine. (Arthur Block was not related to the Block in the law firm's name.)

Block was nervous, because he had never been on a business trip with a client. He was even more nervous when, on the train to New York, he admitted to Ralph that he had been practicing law for just over a year. By the time they pulled into Penn Station, Ralph had learned that his young traveling companion was completely unfamiliar with the city; although Block had grown up in Philadelphia, he had never seen Central Park. He hadn't even been in a taxi.

At the meeting, which concerned a possible joint cable venture with the family of Estée Lauder, Ralph liked the way Block spoke up to protect the Comcast name. Back at Penn Station, before their train to Philadelphia was announced, Ralph went over to a vendor and bought an "I ♥ New York" T-shirt, which he presented to Block as a souvenir of his first business trip to the city. Instead of being angry about Block's lack of experience, Ralph had chosen to celebrate it.

A few years later, Stanley Wang, the first lawyer hired at Comcast, invited Block to join the company. Block was tempted, but his father, a door-to-door furniture salesman, had died young, and it was his mother's dream that her son would make partner at the law firm, so he stayed. Two years later, in 1988, Wang called again: "Arthur, you're still our first choice for a deal attorney, but the train is leaving the station."

Block, who was now a partner, felt like part of the Comcast family. When a deal closed, he was up all night with Julian Brodsky and the financial team. The company had even presented him with a five-year service award as if he actually worked there.

When he met with Ralph, Block mentioned that coming to Comcast would mean he'd have to take a pay cut. "Here's what I'd like you to do," Ralph told him. "Take a pay cut for now to help us fit you into our salary structure and to show some confidence that we'll treat you fairly. In January, we'll give you a raise so you'll be earning the same as what you'd be making at the law firm."

"I would have come anyway," Block says, "but this helped. Ralph wanted me to make a sacrifice to come here, but he was willing to meet me halfway."

Art Block went on to become general counsel of Comcast. "He was a great addition," says Julian. "He came around the same time as Bob Pick and Mark Coblitz, when we decided to beef up our brainpower. Some lawyers go by their own perception of what's important, but Arthur has always understood what really matters around here."

Stanley Wang, who hired Block, was not your typical lawyer. Tom Nathan, who worked for him, noticed right away that instead of composing long, fancy, legal memoranda, Wang limited his memos to two simple paragraphs. But these short memos included something that those beautiful legal memoranda did not provide: answers.

Stanley Wang was the practical voice of common sense. Appearances didn't matter; what counted was substance. His enjoyment of the law came from solving the real problems of real people, which is why there was always a steady stream of employees seeking his counsel on all kinds of issues, both professional and personal.

He had learned about the cable business as a lawyer in New Jersey during the late 1970s, when a newspaper publisher named Guy Savino bought seven unbuilt franchises in the Meadowlands and hired Wang to help him. Wang soon found himself trying to mollify the communities Savino had agreed to serve, who were frustrated that Savino was taking so long to deliver the cable service he had promised. In 1978, when Comcast bought Savino's franchises, Ralph was so impressed with Stanley Wang, who represented the seller, that he hired him to represent Comcast in its legal battle with one of the towns, whose leaders were so impatient with Savino that as soon as Comcast took over, they revoked the franchise.

A year into the case, Ralph asked Wang if Comcast could start building the system while the litigation was still going on.

"Go ahead," said Wang. "We're going to win this case. And if we don't, you can probably sell it to the next guys."

Wang won the case, which took three years and went all the way to the New Jersey Supreme Court. That gave Ralph more than enough time to know him, and on several occasions he offered Wang a job. "Come down and join us," he would say. "We need a fourth person." (For years, Comcast was run by Ralph and his two earliest associates, Dan Aaron and Julian Brodsky.)

"I tried to recruit him for operational jobs," Julian recalls, "but Ralph had a better idea, that Stanley should become our first general counsel."

But Wang turned him down, telling Ralph there wasn't enough work at Comcast to keep him busy. Years later, he was more candid: "I was happy in my law firm and did not want to leave for this unknown company whose headquarters consisted of a card table and a fishbowl in an unpronounceable town, Bala Cynwyd."

Ralph kept trying. He assured Wang that cable had a great future and introduced him to Brian, who Ralph said might be president of the corporation in ten years. "I can imagine working for *you*," Wang told Ralph, "but Dan is too finicky and Julian is too bombastic."

"That won't be a problem," Ralph said. "You'll be your own boss, and there will be plenty of work to keep you busy."

"It was that casual," Wang said later. "And before long, Dan and Julian became my best friends. I loved all three, even if I didn't want to work for two of them."

As Comcast's first general counsel, he did a little of everything—human resources, labor law, employee benefits, public relations, franchise deals, insurance, and regulatory issues. Until Art Block arrived to provide some relief, he also handled the legal work for the company's various acquisitions. He was a problem solver, an advice giver, and a model of integrity. "There are a million little things a lawyer can do for you," says Ralph, "and Stanley did them all."

After twenty-eight years at Comcast, he was scheduled to retire on June 30, 2008. As much as he loved the company, he was looking forward to the next stage of his life, when he'd have more time to ride his bike and to travel with Pola, his wife. But on June 13, two and a half weeks before his last day of work, Stanley Wang was killed in a bicycle accident.

At the funeral, Tom Nathan spoke lovingly of his friend and mentor: "He was about as far from an egotist as it is possible to be," Nathan said, "and he took pleasure in needling those who were." Shortly after the AT&T Broadband merger, Wang had been asked by an AT&T executive whether Comcast would be sending a helicopter or a limousine to bring him from New York to a meeting in Philadelphia. Wang replied that the Comcast limousine was spelled A-M-T-R-A-K.

And Art Block recalled that Wang had done things that are not normally done in the corporate world, such as giving up the position of general counsel because he thought it was time Block had the job. In 2003, when he moved from full-time to part-time, he gave Block his corner office. "He was comfortable in his own skin," Block said, "and he never needed to impress anybody or make anyone else feel less important. That's why receptionists and secretaries were crying when they heard the news."

Dick McCaffery also arrived in 1980. He had previously worked for *Time* magazine, and in the early days of HBO he ran its Philadelphia office, which was in the same building as Comcast. That wasn't a coincidence: McCaffery wanted to be there because even though Comcast was a small company, it was clear to the executives at HBO that it wasn't going to remain small for very long.

He liked the Comcast people and they must have liked him; Ralph hired him as vice president of marketing and programming. When a few weeks had passed with no sign of McCaffery, Ralph called him: "Dick, I thought we had hired you. What's the holdup?"

McCaffery explained that he had been negotiating with Dan Aaron's deputy, but that they still hadn't come to terms.

"What are you doing tomorrow?" Ralph asked.

When McCaffery said he was free in the morning, Ralph asked him to come to the house at eight thirty.

"Have you had anything to eat?" Ralph asked when McCaffery showed up.

When McCaffery said he hadn't, Ralph whipped up a batch of scrambled eggs. Then they sat at the kitchen table and worked out the terms over breakfast.

Late in 1966 a young man named Larry Reese was living in Tupelo, Mississippi, after his family moved there from Fort Worth. Looking for work, he walked into the office of the local cable company and asked Harold Null, the manager, about a job. Ralph, who had bought the system three years earlier, was visiting from Philadelphia, and he told Reese about community antenna television, as cable was known in those days. Reese listened carefully, because all of this was new to him; nobody back in Fort Worth, or any other big city, received television signals through a wire. In its early years, cable was an exclusively rural phenomenon. People in big cities, who required only a rooftop antenna to pick up signals from nearby stations, had never even heard of community antenna television, which was commonly known as CATV.

Ralph must have had a good feeling about Reese, because he turned to Null and said, "Harold, go ahead and hire this young man. I believe he'll stay with us."

Larry Reese was only twenty. The minimum wage in those days was $1.25 an hour, and many businesses in the South paid new employees exactly that. Reese, who became an installer, started at $1.40. "I never did know why," he says. "An extra fifteen cents an hour may not sound like much, but it was a lot back then, and I was happy to have it. It made me feel like they cared."

More than forty years later, Larry Reese was still working for the Comcast system in Tupelo.

Reese was one of the company's first employees. Dan Aaron arrived at the very beginning, and Julian Brodsky showed up a few weeks later. Ralph, of course, was there even before the beginning. In 1962 he owned and operated a small, diversified company that had nothing to do with cable television until a chance encounter changed his life—and, over time, the lives of many other people.

Ralph was forty-three when he took the first step toward establishing Comcast. Although he was new to cable, he had already learned a lot about business, and about the things that matter more than business. To understand Ralph Roberts and his values, it helps to know where he came from, and the world in which he grew up.

2

The Entrepreneur

Ralph Roberts

When his grandchildren were very young, Ralph Roberts would sit on the floor as they crawled around the room. A generation earlier he had learned that a child's first spoken word is often "No," and he wanted to nudge these kids in a different direction. At eye level with the little ones, he would smile at them and nod.

"Yes!" he would tell them, moving his head up and down. "Yes," he would repeat, so they could hear and absorb that wonderful word and keep it at the front of their minds. "Yes!" he would tell them again and again. "Yes! Yes! Yes! Yes! Yes!"

He grew up in a bountiful world of Yes. Enhanced by his resilient and buoyant personality, the love and security he experienced during his formative years would always stay with him. Like many middle children, he became adept at forming relationships and responding to the feelings and needs of those around him. And yet, except for close family members, Ralph has never really needed other people. It's a paradox that often points to success, and also to leadership—the man with superb social skills who enjoys and appreciates his fellow human beings but is essentially self-sufficient. This may be why it is easier to love Ralph Roberts than to know him well.

He entered this world on March 13, 1920, the second son of Robert and Sara Roberts, Russian Jewish immigrants who had come to America as teenagers and now lived on Riverside Drive on Manhattan's Upper West Side. Ralph's beloved brother, Joseph, was born three years earlier; Shirley, his sister, was two years younger.

Ralph's most powerful and poignant memory from his earliest years is of little Shirley coming down with scarlet fever, a dangerous but common infection at that time. As was often done, the family moved out of their apartment for a few weeks, leaving Shirley, who was seriously contagious, in the care of a nurse. Ralph can still recall standing on the sidewalk and looking up at his sister through the window, wondering if he would ever play with her again. Fortunately, she recovered.

In another scene from those early years, five-year-old Ralph climbed into his father's parked car and calmly coasted down the hill from West End Avenue to Riverside Drive. He doesn't recall this event, but in view of his later drive and determination, his cousin Deborah's recollection isn't hard to believe.

Later that year, the family moved to New Rochelle, a prestigious and affluent suburb on Long Island Sound in nearby Westchester County, New York, that was immortalized in the George M. Cohan musical *Forty-Five Minutes from Broadway*. Known as Queen City of the Sound, New Rochelle was stylish and sophisticated but still dotted with farms. Its rural flavor linked it to an earlier era, when its most famous citizen was the colonial revolutionary Thomas Paine, whose statue stood in the center of town and whose story was known to every schoolchild. When Ralph's family arrived, New Rochelle was full of artists and illustrators, including the immensely popular

Norman Rockwell, whose cover drawings for the *Saturday Evening Post* live on today as icons of a more innocent America—the one in which Ralph grew up. Ralph wished he could draw; he still remembers how the boy sitting next to him in art class sketched a birthday cake that looked so real, "you could have lifted it off the page and eaten it." A lifelong doodler and would-be illustrator, Ralph has always loved art and architecture, and has a fondness for design—and a flair for it, too.

It wasn't only artists who flocked to New Rochelle. Other Manhattanites who migrated to New York's premier suburb included Broadway producers, corporate executives, lawyers, judges, and successful businessmen like Ralph's father.

Robert M. Roberts had gone to City College of New York—where the student body showed such a hunger for learning that it was sometimes known as the poor man's Harvard—and then to pharmacy school. He had a talent for business and eventually owned a small chain of Manhattan drugstores before he began investing in commercial real estate. Early on his entrepreneurial ambition captured his son's imagination. "Instead of working for someone else," Ralph notes, "my father was driven to have his own business, to become somebody in this new country."

There were other influences in that direction. Ralph's maternal grandmother had been running her late husband's leather business until she left for America. And her brother, Ralph's Uncle Albert, started out selling inexpensive jewelry to factory girls and went on to become a successful diamond merchant.

Ralph intended to follow in their footsteps. As far back as he can remember, he was determined to run his own business. He wanted to be important—not as a lawyer, politician, or scholar, but as an independent businessman. "That came from my father," he says. "I admired him so much that I wanted to emulate him."

He has never been much inclined to look back or to explore his family's roots. "My parents never spoke of their past," he says, and intentionally or not, Ralph has followed a similar course. "I've noticed that," says Brian. "His focus has always been on the future."

• • •

In the late 1920s, life was idyllic for the Roberts children of 33 Rose Hill Avenue, a broad, tree-lined street filled with large, elegant homes. (Their own house included a two-car garage, which was unusual for that time.) Beyond their material wealth, the family had something far more precious: "I don't know anyone who has happier memories of his childhood," says Suzanne Roberts of her husband's early years. As Ralph describes it, "I picked up a family feeling that's carried me all the way through my life. And because I grew up in a happy family, I wanted to create a happy family when I started a business. It wasn't a conscious decision, but when I started Comcast, I wanted it to be a family group."

When Ralph was young, he recalls, "Children were allowed to be children. I never had any pressure that I couldn't handle." Unlike some of his contemporaries, who delight in describing their long, arduous treks to school along steep, snowy roads that somehow ran uphill in both directions, Ralph and his siblings were shuttled to the local elementary school, six blocks away, by Willy, the family's driver. In nicer weather the children would walk, with Willy driving slowly beside them. The family also employed a cook, and a feisty nanny, Nora Murphy, who promised to protect the kids. "Nobody will hurt you," she assured Ralph in the spring of 1932, when the whole country was buzzing about the kidnapping of the Lindbergh baby, "and if anyone tries, I'll fight them off."

Ralph was close with Joe and Shirley, and the three of them rarely fought. "We were brought up to love each other," he says, "and we really did." After school they played outside, often with Jimmy, their frisky Scotch terrier, and sometimes they helped their mother make jam from the apple and peach trees in the backyard.

The children grew up with positive role models. "My parents were madly in love with each other," Ralph says, "and that was always clear to us." He can still sing a long-forgotten popular song, "Goodbye My Lady Love," with which Bob Roberts would serenade his wife:

Goodbye, my lady love,
Farewell, my turtledove,
You are the idol and darling of my heart,
But someday you will come back to me,
And love me tenderly,
So goodbye, my lady love, goodbye.

When Ralph was sick, which wasn't often, he was allowed to spend the day in his parents' bed, listening to their radio. A new program began every fifteen minutes, and the boy, showing an early fondness for organization, liked to draw up a schedule of the times and stations of his favorite shows—especially *Buck Rogers, Amos 'n' Andy*, and *The Shadow*: "Who knows what evil lurks in the hearts of men? The Shadow knows!"

The residents of New Rochelle took great pride in their public schools, and Ralph enjoyed and appreciated his education, especially the art and music classes. He looked forward to Fridays, when the whole school would listen, through loudspeakers in every classroom, to classical music selections on the popular radio broadcast *NBC Music Appreciation Hour*. Conductor Walter Damrosch, whose national audience included some seven million students, opened each program with his signature greeting: "Good afternoon, my dear children!"

New Rochelle was a big yachting center, and although Ralph's parents didn't sail, they belonged to the Westchester Yacht Club, where the kids and their friends would venture out in little single-mast sailboats, known as catboats. Sometimes they sailed around *Corsair*, an imposing, black steam yacht that belonged to the financier J. P. Morgan and was so large and powerful that the navy had used it for anti-submarine warfare in World War I. The youngsters were always hoping to spot its elusive owner, but the world's most famous banker never appeared.

Ralph had little interest in organized sports, either as a participant or a fan, although he played football with his friends and ran cross-country in high school. And he happily recalls a trip with his father to Yankee Stadium, where they sat behind first base and saw Babe Ruth hit one out of the park. Three-quarters of a century later, when Comcast owned both the Philadelphia Flyers and the 76ers, Ralph would be briefed by his driver on his way to the office so he'd know just enough about the teams to carry on a conversation.

He preferred to spend his time reading in a house that was filled with books, riding his bike with the neighborhood kids, skating on the frozen lake in front of the high school, and—surprisingly, given his amiable temperament as an adult—getting into scraps with other boys. "I liked to mix it up a little," he says. "There were fights in the schoolyard, and every now and then I would get beat up." He pauses and adds, "And once in a while I'd beat up somebody else."

There were also lessons in elocution, piano, horseback riding (a big part of the Westchester scene and a lifelong passion of Ralph's), and both tap and ballroom dancing. "I was the best dancer around," he says with a twinkle. "I still am." (Dancing is pretty much the only thing he brags about.) His mother was a fan of the enormously popular French singer Maurice Chevalier, and one year, for the annual show at the yacht club, young Ralph, wearing a straw hat and tap shoes, sang and danced his way through Chevalier's accented version of "Mimi," one of the singer's biggest hits. (Years later, Suzanne would present her husband with a giant poster of Chevalier. And in 2005, at Ralph's eighty-fifth birthday party, his son-in-law Anthony took the stage in a straw hat and a cane to sing a Chevalier tune for the guest of honor.) Although Ralph enjoyed performing, that wasn't his only motivation. "My mother loved Chevalier," he explains, "and I loved my mother."

Did he ever! Their closeness was critical to the person Ralph would become. "If a man has been his mother's undisputed darling," Freud famously observed, "he retains throughout life the triumphant feeling, the confidence in success which not infrequently leads to real success." Ralph admired his father and was certainly influenced by him, but he had a deeper and more loving attachment to Sara, almost a spiritual bond.

"I was a mama's boy," he says without embarrassment. "I thought I was her favorite, although my sister and brother probably felt the same. She was kind and generous, and I grew up taking goodness for granted." Sara had an interest in art, fashion, color, and interior design, and so did her adoring son.

He was an expressive child who left tender notes on his mother's pillow on nights when his parents went out, letting her know what had happened during his day. With her nurturing and support, Sara imbued her son with optimism and self-assurance, and taught him, above all, to believe in his own abilities. "She was a sensational mother," he says, "and probably the only real mentor I ever had. She told me I could do anything if I worked hard enough, which is why I was never discouraged and never felt incompetent. No matter what I was doing, I don't ever remember being afraid of failing."

Suzanne Roberts concurs: "His mother gave him such confidence! Ralph grew into a man with no envy, no jealousy, no wanting what the next guy has."

He would always remember his mother's advice, which he would later pass on to his own children, and to some of his employees: Follow your dream. Seek out work that makes you happy and gives you a feeling of accomplishment.

Sara was beautiful, elegant, charming, intelligent, and popular, the managing partner of a highly functional family. As Ralph remembers it, she never scolded or punished her children, which was unusual for that era. Their classmates were routinely sent to their rooms without supper, or spanked for more serious infractions, but Sara responded to misbehavior by informing her children, gently but directly, that certain words or actions were simply unacceptable. "My parents weren't interested in discipline," says Ralph, "and it didn't seem necessary. My sister was shy, my brother was smarter than anyone, and I was just there to enjoy it all."

The combination of affluence and leniency isn't always a recipe for successful parenting, but Ralph and his siblings grew up without feeling entitled. "If we wanted something," says Ralph, "it was there. We should have come out terribly spoiled, but that didn't happen."

It helped that their parents had a strong marriage, good values, and plenty of friends. Sara loved to entertain, and she and her husband gave wonderful parties. Ralph can still picture his mother standing by the piano and singing. She had a fine sense of humor, and liked to alter the lyrics of popular songs for the amusement of her guests.

With Broadway less than an hour away, Ralph's parents often attended plays and musicals. Sara loved the theater, and so did her son, who later married an actress and eventually endowed a Philadelphia theater in Suzanne's name. Ralph's parents had a subscription to the Metropolitan Opera, and according to family legend, on at least one occasion his father paid for a third seat, which was occupied by Sara's mink coat.

Sara was especially close to Ida Bobrow, her sister in Philadelphia, and there were frequent visits back and forth. Sometimes Ralph took the train by himself to visit his four cousins—two boys, and two girls who were so pretty that a local car dealer arranged for them to drive one of his convertibles around town.

Bob Roberts was a restless businessman. In addition to his drugstores, he acquired a company called T. C. Morgan that made medicinal products, including the mouthwash Rubrol and Morgan's Sabalol Spray for sore throats, which was endorsed by a renowned opera star of that era, Madame Ernestine Schumann-Heink. But most of his energy went into his retail shops, especially his flagship store in the upscale Biltmore Hotel, a landmark building best known for the big bronze clock in the lobby that served as a popular meeting place for young couples, including, years later, Holden Caulfield and his date in *The Catcher in the Rye*. The Biltmore lobby was a social center for politicians, judges, actors, and other prominent people, and Bob Roberts knew them all.

Because the hotel stood next to Grand Central Station, his commute from New Rochelle wasn't too bad. The store included a soda fountain and a prescription counter, but what distinguished it, aside from the unbeatable location, was that Doc Roberts also sold boutique items such as makeup kits, which were not found in many American drugstores at the time. Among his celebrity customers was the movie star Tom Mix, who came in one day and bought a hundred-dollar bottle of perfume; it was amazing, Ralph notes, that his father even carried such an item. But Roberts Pharmacy was a top-of-the-line establishment where a cup of coffee sold for fifteen cents—expensive even for Manhattan.

Bob Roberts was tall, bald, blue eyed, a good dresser, and a great dancer. He was also a hard worker who took an early train to the city and came home late. Sara would often wait for him so they could enjoy a late supper together after the kids were in bed, and Ralph sometimes overheard his parents talking, and occasionally disagreeing. "They resolved everything by discussing it calmly," he says, "and I noticed that my mother was genuinely interested in my father's work."

On weekends, Ralph's father sometimes packed the family into his big Buick and drove to Playland, an Art Deco amusement park in nearby Rye, where Ralph was fond of a ride called the Scenic Railway. But he was just as happy to visit his father's store. At the soda fountain his feet didn't reach the floor, and on his earliest visits he suffered through an anxious moment or two until he figured out how to climb off the stool. He especially loved to sit behind the cash register and hit the keys, and by the time he was ten, the boss allowed him to ring up the occasional sale.

The family spent several summers in the Catskills, where they rented a house on a lake. In one of Ralph's earliest memories, he was standing on a dock, holding a box of Chiclets, when he somehow fell in. "When they fished me out of the water," he recalls, "I still had the Chiclets. I think that was indicative of me not letting go. I'm persistent."

He was also ambitious. As Ralph remembers it, all he ever wanted to be was a businessman. And as he grew older, he was determined to find an enterprise that could provide him with both financial security and the additional security that came from knowing that he was the one calling the shots.

His very first entrepreneurial venture, however, was not a success. When he was seven, Ralph dug up his mother's marigolds and started selling them, door-to-door, to the neighbors, until one of them called his mother. Ralph was surprised to learn he had done anything wrong. "She had plenty of flowers," he remembers thinking, "so why not make a couple of bucks?" It was the first time he was ever in business for himself, and although the entire episode lasted only an hour or two, he never forgot that wonderful feeling.

On the morning of February 18, 1933, Ralph's world fell apart. It was a Saturday, and Sara came into the bedroom that Ralph and Joe shared. "Daddy died this morning," she said softly. Ralph went into his parents' bedroom and approached the lifeless body, lifting his father's eyelids so he could see those blue eyes one more time. He was struck by how calm his mother seemed that day: despite how she must have been feeling, she didn't want to alarm her children.

There was no warning. The night before, the whole family had gone to see *The Mummy*, a new movie starring Boris Karloff. But the real horror came the next day. Early Saturday morning, believing that the discomfort he was feeling was mere indigestion, Doc Roberts went down to his basement lab to mix a potion that might help. He returned to bed and died of a heart attack. Sara called the police, who tried to resuscitate him, but it was too late. Bob Roberts was forty-two. Sara was thirty-eight. Ralph was twelve.

It was several years into the Great Depression, and Ralph's father was one of its victims. He had owned a good amount of Manhattan real estate at a time when investors in both securities and property could buy in with very little equity, which left them exposed and vulnerable to a sudden downturn. Like so many of his highly leveraged contemporaries, he lost almost everything, although his children wouldn't know of the family's financial difficulties for another couple of years. "Parents didn't talk to kids about money in those days," Ralph notes, although he was certainly aware of the general economic situation, and had grown used to seeing unemployed men selling apples on the streets of New York. Shortly after Ralph's father died, his interest in the drugstores was sold to a partner. Fortunately, Doc Roberts had owned a life insurance policy.

As the funeral ended, the officiating rabbi took Ralph aside and said, "Someday you'll be the one taking care of the whole family." It was a strange message to give a twelve-year-old boy with a high-achieving older brother, but the comment was prescient.

Ralph was impressed by his mother's resilience after his father's death. "She stood strong," he says, "and she kept us strong, too. She didn't fall apart and bemoan her fate. She told us we could survive, and that we shouldn't feel sorry for ourselves. And she paid more attention to us than ever." One of Sara's friends suggested that she sell life insurance to make ends meet, and she tried that for a year. She also explained to her children that they had to live more frugally. A year or so later, they moved to a small apartment in a more modest neighborhood.

Ralph was now in high school, and the family's new residence provided the opportunity for what he calls his first business that didn't involve stolen property. Several times a day a private bus shuttled residents from their apartment complex to the center of town, and Ralph wondered why there was no printed timetable. Seeing a need, the boy who used to draw up his own radio schedules decided to fill it. He visited a number of local businesses and signed up half a dozen retailers who agreed to advertise on his schedule. But before he went ahead, he checked with a printer to make sure his expenses would be less than the anticipated revenue. "Somehow," he says, "I just knew how to do things like that."

Although Ralph was trying to help his mother, he was also acting on the entrepreneurial drive that already burned within him: "I was always thinking, How could I earn a little money by doing something nobody else has done?" It was a stressful time for the family, but Ralph is philosophical about it: "Those years make me appreciate what I have now."

In 1936 they moved again—to the Germantown section of Philadelphia so Sara could tend to her sister, Ida, who was dying of cancer. There may have been another reason, too. Ralph had a girlfriend in New Rochelle, whom he describes as "gorgeous, and the best dancer in our school." One night, when he came home much later than usual, he found his mother sitting in a chair, waiting for him. "She gave me holy hell," he says, which didn't happen very often. Suzanne Roberts wonders whether the move to Philadelphia was, at least in part, a way for Sara to separate Ralph from the girl, whom she apparently didn't care for.

Ralph's brother, Joe, remained in New York as a student at Columbia, where he played on the water polo team and was editor of the school paper. Ralph was a fine student, but Joe was a tough act to follow. "He was always a leader," says Ralph, "and he didn't do anything halfway. Although he had a good sense of humor, he was intense, whereas I was more of a happy-go-lucky type."

Sometimes Sara would ask Joe to help his younger brother with his homework. When his English teacher, Phyllis McGinley, who later won a Pulitzer Prize for Poetry, asked Ralph to read his Christmas essay to the class, she stopped him after an especially ornate line: "As the moon hung high, Santa raced in his sleigh across the counterpane-like snow."

"I'm going to give Mr. Roberts a B," she said, "but I'll give his brother an A." She had taught Joe three years earlier, and she recognized his style.

Ralph spent his senior year at Germantown High School. Although he was a little more sophisticated and academically advanced than his classmates, he made friends easily. Encouraged by his English teacher, he tried out for the senior production of Shakespeare's *Twelfth Night* and got the part of Malvolio, the sullen chief steward with big dreams who speaks the famous line, "Some are born great, some achieve greatness, and some have greatness thrust upon them."

Following high school he enrolled at the Wharton School at the University of Pennsylvania; Penn was an easy commute and he wanted to study business. But he took his brother's advice to sign up for as many liberal arts courses as possible. "If you don't get some culture in you," said Joe, an English major who hoped to become a writer, "you'll really be missing something." Ralph welcomed the suggestion. Joe was critical in giving him an appreciation for the arts and a literary sensibility, "but without deterring me from my basic drive to succeed in the way our father did."

Many years later, Ralph is still proud of his brother's success at Columbia, where, among other achievements, Joe tutored football player Sid Luckman, who went on to become the star quarterback for the Chicago Bears in the 1940s. When Joe went to conduct interviews in dangerous neighborhoods for the Columbia *Spectator*, Luckman went along as his bodyguard. Joe's friends were artists and intellectuals, including the poet Robert Lax and the music critic Ralph Gleason, both of whom would become well known. "I liked and admired these older guys," Ralph says, who adds that if his mother hadn't moved the family to Philadelphia, he, too, would have gone to Columbia.

Joe was also friendly with another classmate, Thomas Merton, who became a renowned writer and Catholic theologian. Right after graduation, the two of them shared a house in upstate New York with Gleason and Lax, where they all worked on their writing. In his highly regarded memoir, *The Seven Storey Mountain*, Merton would twice refer to important conversations with his friend Joe Roberts.

At Wharton, Ralph majored in marketing. His professors encouraged the students to start their own businesses, but Ralph didn't need any prodding. Students in those days wrote with fountain pens and used cardboard blotters to absorb the excess ink. Ralph asked a printer what it would cost to produce several thousand blotters with commercial announcements, and went around to solicit local retailers who might want to advertise on them, just as he had done with the bus schedules in New Rochelle. "Your message will sit right on the student's desk," he told the merchants, "and it'll be cheaper than a mailing because you won't have to pay for postage." He hired students to slip the blotters under the door of every dorm room and fraternity house on campus.

Sara put her children through college with the help of the life insurance proceeds, and Ralph did what he could to ease the strain. When he learned how much fraternity houses were paying for eggs, he started driving Sara's Studebaker to New Jersey, where he bought eggs in bulk from a farmer. After checking the daily retail price in the newspaper, he always offered a discount. These eggs, he assured his customers, were not only a bargain but also exceedingly fresh, because "they just popped out of the chicken." It was a winning combination—a product people needed at a good price, with a little marketing and salesmanship to grease the wheels.

At the suggestion of his marketing professor Herbert William Hess, Ralph took a part-time job with a local dairy, which had him knocking on doors near the university to persuade home delivery customers to pay a premium—or, as he described it, "just a wee bit more"—for a new product, homogenized milk. He offered two arguments: homogenized milk helped with digestion, and customers who switched no longer had to shake the bottle to mix in the cream that had risen to the top. Working on commission, Ralph put his salesmanship to good use: he estimates that 80 percent of the households he visited took the upgrade. (Years later, Ralph and his associates would do something similar when they visited cable subscribers, one family at a time, to encourage them to sign up for HBO.)

Although he lived at home, Ralph had a college life. He joined a Jewish fraternity, Phi Epsilon Pi, because the others were open only to Christians. "That was how the world worked," he says, "and nobody dreamed of changing it." When he considered running for vice president of the student body, a college official advised against it because he didn't live on campus, but Ralph believes the real reason was his religion.

Always sociable but with a sensitive stomach, Ralph would line his stomach with cod liver oil before the whiskey bottle was passed around. He played a little cricket and joined the fencing team. "Our instructor was from Europe," he recalls, "and he came to the United States after killing a man in a duel. At least that's what he told us to keep us on our toes."

But Ralph preferred table games like craps and poker, and he has always had a fondness for gambling. He joined the choral society, which performed Mozart's *Requiem* and recorded it with Eugene

Ormandy and the Philadelphia Orchestra. His student days were happy, at least for a while.

But now there were problems at home. Sara's sister had died shortly after the move to Philadelphia, and a couple of years later, Sara married her widowed brother-in-law, Harry Bobrow, a cigar maker. Harry had money, and Sara presumably married for security. "We didn't care for him," Ralph says of his uncle, "and he didn't seem to care for us." Ralph and Shirley found him difficult, but they recognized that Harry was crazy about their mother.

Then Sara developed uterine cancer. She died quickly, and Ralph was devastated. At her funeral he overheard somebody say, "Poor Ralph. He's so upset that he's not even crying." It was true. "I had learned from her example after my father's death," he says, "but I'm sure I cried privately. Everyone knew how close we were. I thought it was the end of the world."

Right after Sara died in 1939, Joe, who had graduated from Columbia a year earlier, married his girlfriend, Betty, whose full name was Elizabeth Grant Van Allen; she was a descendant of Ulysses S. Grant. The newlyweds moved to Philadelphia to be with Ralph and Shirley, who were both students at Penn, and the four of them shared a rented house in Germantown, which was a great comfort to Shirley and Ralph. Betty cooked and provided a maternal presence, Ralph and Shirley continued their studies, and Joe, who had given up on becoming a writer but shared Ralph's gift for product promotion, became the marketing manager for Ranger Joe, the first presweetened breakfast cereal.

In the fall of 1940, Ralph began his senior year at Penn. With the expectation that America would soon become involved in the war raging in Europe, the Wharton School announced an officer recruitment program, with the understanding that students who participated would be rewarded with a commission in the navy. Ralph didn't hesitate: "There was a maniac in Europe, and how the hell could we stay out of it? Besides, the navy guys had nice uniforms." When he graduated in the spring of 1941, the program assigned him to a

Westinghouse plant in nearby Essington, where he was taught how to weld and learned all about construction.

When Pearl Harbor was attacked a few months later, Ralph went to Washington to request a combat assignment. But he was turned down because his business skills were thought to be more useful on the home front. He spent the war years as a matériel superintendent in the Philadelphia Navy Yard, a huge and busy place where, over the next few years, hundreds of ships were repaired and dozens of new ones built—including the USS *New Jersey*, which was constructed right outside his office. Like everyone else at the yard, he spent occasional nights as a duty officer, carrying a pistol and guarding against spies and saboteurs.

Although Ralph had badly wanted to serve on a ship, he came to accept and even appreciate his job, an administrative assignment that included making sure that damaged ships were promptly repaired and got out on time. Later, he became a liaison officer between the Philadelphia Navy Yard and its counterparts in Norfolk and New York, and made regular trips to the Bureau of Ships in Washington.

Although the position wasn't exciting, he performed well and liked the people he worked with. "I've never had an unpleasant working experience," he says. "Every place I've ever worked, I fit in and seemed to be appreciated. And I like to get things organized."

Despite learning how ships were built and having a firsthand view of the enormous manufacturing effort that helped the Allies win the war, he was somewhat embarrassed to spend those years at home while his brother and some of his friends were chasing enemy submarines in the Pacific. But Ralph and his fellow shipyard workers made an important contribution to the war effort. And the results unfolded right in front of them, which offered some compensation for having to spend those years tethered to what the officers called an LMD—a large mahogany desk.

When Ralph is asked about his biggest regret, he answers immediately: not getting married sooner.

He met Suzanne in the spring of 1937, when he was seventeen

and she was a year younger. They were at a dance at Congregation Rodeph Shalom on North Broad Street to honor a confirmation class that included Ralph's sister, Shirley, as well as Suzanne Fleisher, whose family had belonged to Philadelphia's oldest temple for generations. Because they were new in town, Ralph was there as Shirley's escort, and Suzanne was struck by how kind and chivalrous he was. "He treated her like a princess," she recalls. "In no way did he let her feel like a sister." What Ralph noticed was that Suzanne was a terrific dancer.

"Was it love at first sight?" an interviewer once asked him.

"I wouldn't risk any other answer," Ralph replied.

They dated for several years, slowly and cautiously. When Ralph finally kissed her, during Suzanne's spring break, she sent telegrams to her college friends, announcing the news. That summer, Ralph was a counselor at a camp for underprivileged boys, and Suzanne worked in a theater. Instead of communicating directly, Ralph arranged for the boys in his care to write her love letters, with each one signed "Ralph." She enjoyed the prank.

But when Ralph proposed, she turned him down. "I wasn't ready to get married," she says. "I didn't think he was, either, so soon after losing his mother. And I enjoyed having lots of dates." Her refusal must have hurt him deeply, because he responded so sharply: "If I can get over the death of my mother," he told her, "I can get over you."

Another time they were out on a lake. "If you don't say yes," he told her, "I'm going to tip this canoe." But she didn't, and he didn't, either.

Late in 1941, when they were no longer seeing each other, they met up at a dance that they were both attending with other people. "When he saw me," Suzanne says, "he put his arm around the girl he had brought, and I got jealous. I grabbed a guy who was friendly with both of us, and we started dancing. I asked him to switch partners with Ralph, and he did. I grabbed Ralph and took him out on the golf course, and I said, 'I want to marry you.'"

Forgoing a more romantic response, Ralph replied with a single word: "When?"

"Anytime you say."

"She was jealous," Ralph says. "She didn't like me fawning over another girl. She thought I was doing it deliberately."

And he was. "He scared me into it," Suzanne says. "I was afraid of losing him. He was smart enough to know that if he played up to another girl, I would respond."

And so the former marketing major closed the biggest deal of his life. He had waited for her, and had never stopped loving her.

They had much in common. Suzanne's father, Alfred Fleisher, a real estate investor and philanthropist, had died when she was seven. He was a business partner of Jules E. Mastbaum, a prominent figure in town, and was involved with Mastbaum in building Philadelphia's famous Rodin Museum, which opened to the public in 1929. (Suzanne's family still owns two Rodins.) Like Ralph, Suzanne had been chauffeured to school, which she found so embarrassing that she would crouch down on the floor of the car so nobody could see her.

A few years after she was widowed, Selma Fleisher married Leon Sunstein, the husband of her deceased sister. Ralph's mother had entered into a similar marriage—at least on the surface. But unlike Ralph's stepfather, Suzanne's was warm, rosy, and optimistic—much like his name, Sunstein. After opening a luggage store, he became a successful stockbroker. (The firm, Gerstley Sunstein, which Leon started with his brother-in-law, was later sold to Burnham & Co., which soon became known as Drexel Burnham.) Suzanne adored her stepfather and enjoyed introducing him as "Uncle Leon, my father." Her mother, however, had always been depressed, critical, and unsupportive. When Suzanne became interested in acting, Selma told her she would never succeed because she was too tall and not pretty enough.

It was not a happy household. Suzanne's brothers were significantly older than she, and the nanny who raised her was mean and denigrating. Suzanne was the epitome of the poor little rich girl. "I grew up with the best of everything," she says, "except the most important things."

But she did have her late father's example to inspire her. His passionate cause was prison reform, an interest that began when his secretary told him about her nephew, who had been involved in a murder. Moved by the story, he began visiting the young man every Sunday in Philadelphia's Eastern State Penitentiary, where Alfred Fleisher was appalled by the conditions he found. Ironically, Eastern State had once been regarded as a model prison, with no corporal punishment, and over the years both Al Capone and bank robber Willie Sutton were incarcerated there. But like all American penitentiaries, the institution had a harsh tradition of solitary confinement; originally, inmates were expected to sit by themselves all day to reflect on their crimes. It's unclear how much conditions had improved by the time Fleisher started visiting, but he worked to ameliorate life for the prisoners with training programs, boxing matches, and a recreational yard. He later prevailed on the governor to close down the place entirely and build a new facility, known as Graterford, about thirty miles west of the city, with ample room for farming and vocational classes.

Alfred Fleisher died of cancer on Christmas Day, 1928, at the age of fifty. And on December 25, for years to come, Suzanne would imagine that her father returned to ask, "What have you done to help other people?"

His legacy lives on. In the fall of 2008, eighty years after Alfred Fleisher's death, one of Suzanne and Ralph's grandchildren had his bar mitzvah at the newly renovated Alfred Fleisher Memorial Synagogue—the tiny Jewish chapel at Eastern State Penitentiary. (The inmates had named it long before in appreciation of their benefactor, who had served as president of the prison's board of trustees.) The prison had been closed in 1971, and a recent excavation had uncovered the long-abandoned chapel. Although Suzanne had been well aware of her father's involvement, and even remembered driving to the prison with him in his Duesenberg, she hadn't known about the forty-seat chapel, or that Alfred had often attended services there with the prisoners.

The bar mitzvah service was conducted by Rabbi Martin Rubenstein, who had served the Jewish inmates in that very chapel until the building was closed. "We were the only religious group that met without a guard," he recalls. "That was the practice when I arrived; the men policed it themselves. I saw them not as prisoners, but as congregants."

Recalling the bar mitzvah, Rabbi Rubenstein says, "I had been in that room on many occasions, but this was the first time I ever saw a full house."

"It was a very moving experience," says Ralph, "a real family connection in this room that none of us had even known about."

During the war, when Suzanne was acting in plays, Ralph, in his naval uniform, was a regular stage-door Johnny who would go to the theater where she was performing and wait for her after the show. Before the young couple set a wedding date, Ralph approached her stepfather to ask his permission. The two of them got along well, and Leon Sunstein was fast becoming a father figure for Ralph. "He always had time to sit with me and talk—about the war, my work in the navy, or the economic situation," Ralph says. "He wasn't a business mentor, but an older man I could talk to."

Like Suzanne's biological father, her stepfather, too, was a philanthropist and a community activist, and for several years he served as head of the local Federation of Jewish Charities. Ralph befriended his son, Leon Junior, who admired Ralph so much that in 1974 he was one of the very few investors who bought shares of Comcast at their all-time low, when they were selling for under a dollar. Ralph also became friendly with Howard and Bob Fleisher, Suzanne's older brothers. Bob became a partner in some of Ralph's businesses, and Suzanne says that Ralph came to know him better than she ever did.

Ralph and Suzanne were married in the summer of '42 in a small ceremony in the garden of her mother's house in Elkins Park. As newlyweds they lived in Ralph's apartment at 1612 Pine Street in downtown Philadelphia, a third-floor walk-up that rented for forty-five dollars a month. They later found a bigger place in the same building before moving to a house in suburban Wyncote in 1950, when Suzanne was pregnant with their first child.

For the remainder of the war, while Ralph reported to the Navy Yard, Suzanne was part of theater groups that promoted blood drives and war bonds. Ralph continued to show up at the theater almost every night, even when she begged him to stay home. Whenever she prepared for a new show, he would spend hours with her, going over her lines.

"He felt a vicarious enjoyment from my performing," she says. "It's funny, but Ralph seems to get a bigger kick out of the things I do than the things he does." In the years ahead, a good many people in Ralph's orbit, including not only his five children but Comcast employees, too, would notice the very same thing.

3

The Marketer

Ralph Roberts and Bob Hope

When the war ended in 1945, Ralph had to face the same question as hundreds of thousands of other newly released military men. What now?

A Navy Yard engineer named Carroll Stover came up with a plan for both of them. Stover, who owned a small machine shop, realized that as the nation's factories shifted from the war effort back to consumer needs, some of them would be looking for new items to produce. If he and Ralph came up with a few prototypes, Stover could build them and Ralph, with his gift for selling, could take them around to manufacturers. They called their company Altair, after one of the brightest stars in the sky, and advertised in the newspaper for inventions and new gadgets. "We weren't in the manufacturing business," Ralph says. "We were in the idea business."

Their first product was a device for lifting a cluster of soda bottles onto an assembly line, which they sold, not surprisingly, to a bottling plant. Their plan to sell scented ink for love letters went nowhere, but a cleaning compound for offices looked promising until the French promoter who brought it to them and called himself "zee famous chemist from Paris" suddenly vanished. The partners had some modest success with, of all things, a bacon straightener. Was there really a market for such an item? To Ralph, with his designer's eye, the need was obvious: "Flat strips of bacon would frame your eggs very nicely."

Then Carroll Stover came up with his best idea. As a golfer, he knew that no clubs had been manufactured during the war, and he believed that the one club a golfer might be willing to buy outside of his regular set was a putter. Stover designed and produced a distinctive-looking model whose shaft came down just behind the middle of the club's head, rather than the end. Ralph named it the Centric Putter.

To demonstrate the product, Ralph designed a miniature putting green for indoor use: when you sank a putt, the ball rolled right back to you. Then the salesman hit the road. He drove from Philadelphia to Miami, stopping at golf courses along the way and meeting a great many golfers, including two of the game's biggest names, Sam Snead and Porky Oliver. (Years later, he would do business with Arnold Palmer.) At each pro shop, Ralph offered the Centric Putters—"these are not sold in stores!"—for six dollars to the golf pro, who could sell them for a suggested retail price of ten dollars. And they sold! As fast as Stover could produce them, Ralph was able to move the merchandise.

Sometimes the golf pro was busy and would say, "I can't see you now, kid. Go out to the putting green and I'll meet you there in half an hour." With so many opportunities to practice, Ralph became an excellent putter with the funny-looking club he was there to sell. When the pro arrived and saw him sinking putt after putt, Ralph would hand him the Centric Putter and say, "Here, try it yourself and see how much control you have." Looking back on it more than sixty years later, Ralph says, "Control was the whole point." With Ralph, it always was.

When Bob Hope performed at a Philadelphia theater, Ralph saw a special opportunity. With the help of a newspaper photographer, he managed to get backstage with the putter. "Mr. Hope," he told the entertainer, who was already well known both for visiting the troops and for loving golf, "I'm a veteran, and I wonder if we could take a picture of you with my new putter."

"Sure, kid." (In Ralph's stories, everyone called him "kid" until he was forty.)

With the photographer clicking away, Bob Hope posed with the Centric Putter—admiring it, demonstrating it, and doing everything short of kissing it. So, did Ralph give it to him when the photo session ended?

"No, I was too cheap."

And did he ask permission to use Bob Hope's picture or his name?

No again. "He obviously knew what I wanted," says Ralph. And there was no objection from Hope, who was happy to help Ralph with a different product a few years later.

When golf pros around the country received a brochure in the mail for the Bob Hope Centric Putter, the orders poured in. But the partners' success didn't last long. Ralph was demonstrating the putter one day when, as he describes it, the shaft bent around like a pretzel. In a panic, he called Stover back in Philadelphia, who realized that at least one batch of shafts hadn't been sent out for heat treatment. "They're *all* going to bend," he told Ralph.

The party was over. "I didn't wait for the complaints," Ralph says. "We changed our address and took to the hills. I didn't know how far the problem went, and bigger companies were starting to manufacture golf clubs again. But to steal somebody's name and to run away from the people we cheated . . . it wasn't my finest moment." Ralph doesn't say so, but perhaps his regret over the way he and Stover ended their business was an important lesson for the man who, for the rest of his career, would be known above all for his integrity.

• • •

It was time, Ralph decided, to put his entrepreneurial dreams on hold and look for a real job that would pay the rent. He put together a résumé, opened the Yellow Pages to Advertising Agencies, and hit the pavement. His total lack of experience in advertising didn't dissuade him; he was good at both marketing and selling and had plenty of confidence.

"What brings you here?" asked Doc Kynett, the skeptical co-owner of the Aitkin-Kynett Agency. "Are you impressed by our client list, or is it because our name starts with A?"

"It's both," Ralph told him, "but if you don't want me, I'll move on to the Bs." He got the job and started in the research department. Soon he was promoted to account executive, where he began with a tiny campaign for a lozenge called Frog in Your Throat—an echo, perhaps, of his father's medicinal spray. Then came El Producto, for which Ralph came up with a print ad of a man saying, "I smoke ten cigars a day, and each one is better than the last." Doc Kynett was not amused. "Nobody smokes ten cigars a day," he told his young employee. "It's hard to smoke more than three."

Ralph had more success with Publicker Industries, whose liquor business the agency was hoping to land. He advised them to advertise on billboards near liquor stores, and although that seems obvious today, apparently nobody had done this. The results were impressive, and Publicker wanted to work with him, but by then the young account executive was moving in a different direction.

He had been at the ad agency for two years when the Muzak Corporation, whose Philadelphia franchise was one of Ralph's clients, offered him a position at their Manhattan headquarters after Ralph, with Suzanne's help, came up with a way to add dramatized safety messages for factory workers to the mix of music. Although most factories were too noisy for the technique to be effective, Muzak executives were impressed with Ralph's initiative and creativity. When he informed Doc Kynett about his move to Muzak, the boss wished him well and told him not to worry about Publicker, because the agency was sure to land the account. But when Ralph left, the potential client made other plans.

It was 1950 and Ralph was thirty when he accepted the offer from Muzak. Not knowing how long he would be there, and with their first baby at home and the hope of more children to follow, he and Suzanne decided that for the time being, they would stay in Philadelphia and Ralph would commute to New York by train.

Muzak was owned by William Benton, a very prominent businessman and political figure who had founded the famous advertising agency of Benton and Bowles. He had acquired Muzak in 1941 after several previous owners had failed to make it profitable. Ralph found him intimidating, and no wonder: while Ralph was trying to sell bacon straighteners, Benton, an assistant secretary of state, had been involved in organizing the United Nations. Earlier, he had pioneered the use of cue cards (Laugh! Applaud!) for audiences attending radio broadcasts. To promote Colgate toothpaste, Benton decided that in addition to cleaning your teeth, the product "freshened" your mouth. He also owned Encyclopedia Britannica, Inc., and was the publisher of the Great Books of the Western World. In 1950, shortly after Ralph started working for him, Benton won a Senate seat as a two-year replacement by defeating the Republican candidate, Prescott Bush, the father and grandfather of two future presidents, for the right to represent Connecticut.

Ralph, who was quickly brought into Benton's circle of advisors, found it hard to believe the sudden change in his status. He was soon asked to work on the boss's reelection campaign, but the senator didn't care for Ralph's suggestion that he reserve air time in advance to respond to inevitable attacks from his opponent. "He almost killed me for saying that," says Ralph, whose caution turned out to be justified when Benton was defeated.

But mostly Ralph worked with Benton's business deputy, Harry E. Houghton. Houghton, whom Ralph calls the nattiest dresser he has ever known, came to work in finely tailored suits and elegant ties. He lived like a king on Park Avenue, with his own table at 21, the legendary Manhattan restaurant, where Ralph often joined him for dinner. Near the table was a potted plant, and when Houghton wasn't looking, Ralph would empty his drink into it—the only way he could keep up with his host's fondness for Canadian Club. Houghton, who had hired Ralph and put him in charge of Muzak's advertising and promotion, influenced the younger man "to do everything at the highest level I could," Ralph says. Twenty years later, Ralph showed his appreciation by inviting Houghton to join Comcast's first board of directors.

Ralph spent most of his time trying to help Muzak franchise operators around the country sell more recorded music. (Most of the franchises were independently owned, with the corporation receiving 10 percent of their gross revenues.) One of his most successful tools was a campaign to solicit letters from satisfied customers, so when a Muzak salesman met with a car dealer, for example, he could bring along testimonials from other car dealers.

It helped that Ralph really believed in Muzak, which had been shown to improve both the morale and the productivity of workers, especially by piping in livelier tunes during predictable periods of low energy during the workday. Muzak was also used, and still is, to encourage shoppers to slow down and buy more, and to help mitigate feelings of aloneness in hotel lobbies, airline terminals, and other public places. It worked, and Ralph didn't care that it was commonly disparaged as elevator music, or worse. "I worry," Lily Tomlin would say later, "that the person who thought up Muzak may be thinking up something else."

Ralph liked it as a *business*. True, Muzak required an initial capital investment to bring it into a factory, office, bank, or even the White House during the Eisenhower years; and there were other expenses, including royalties for composers and fees for arrangers and musicians. But once the sound system was in place, the same recordings could be used for years. What Ralph loved most about Muzak was that it provided *recurring monthly income*. That phrase, which always brings a smile to his face, would come up again in his career. And again. And yet again.

But he never felt comfortable working for Benton, who once admonished Anna Rosenberg, a member of FDR's cabinet and a woman of notable achievement, by angrily telling her, in Ralph's presence,

"All you do is articulate the obvious!" And he grew concerned when Benton asked him for a quotable line he could use the next day in his 1952 Senate campaign. Ralph came up with one, but he wasn't sure he could do that repeatedly. He was also thinking that the time had come to resume his entrepreneurial ambition, or at least to travel a road that might lead in that direction.

That road came into view when a recruiter told him that the Pioneer Suspender Company, a well-established manufacturer of men's belts, wallets, and other accessories, was looking for a high-level assistant to the president. Pioneer was based in Darby, a Philadelphia suburb, which sounded pretty good to the tired commuter.

But the real appeal of Pioneer was the hope that he could someday own the company. Its president, Leo Heimerdinger, Jr., who had taken over the business from his aging father, suffered from diabetes, which was affecting his ability to work. His father, the healthier Heimerdinger, was looking for someone who could help run the company and take over if the younger man had to be hospitalized. "I saw a potential opportunity," Ralph says. "I didn't have the money to buy the company, but I have always been an optimist who believes that tomorrow will be better than today, and I thought that at some point I might be able to."

Ralph said he would take the job if Mr. Heimerdinger gave him a letter promising that if he ever sold the company, Ralph had the right to match the best offer. "He knew I didn't have any money," says Ralph, "so what did he have to lose?" Ralph got the promise, and Pioneer got Ralph.

Why did the Heimerdingers hire someone with no experience in the accessories business? They knew Suzanne's family, and Ralph was known as a bright and affable young man who worked for the illustrious William Benton.

When Ralph joined the company in the early 1950s, Pioneer was the nation's second-largest maker of men's belts; the only bigger one was the Hickok Manufacturing Company in Rochester, New York. The two competitors had a fierce rivalry and completely different approaches. The Heimerdingers thought their rivals spent too much on marketing and promotion, and told the world that Pioneer spent *its* money on the finest leather and the best designs. In reality, says Ralph, both companies' products were equally good, and Hickok was more successful because of its willingness to invest in marketing and promotion. When department store buyers came to New York to see the new lines, and each company took a hotel suite to display the new merchandise, the differences became obvious. Hickok decorated its showroom with flowers, hired attractive young women to show the goods, and gave away gifts, including ringside tickets to boxing matches. Pioneer took the opposite approach—all steak, no sizzle—by providing only a bare-bones display and letting the merchandise speak for itself.

Although the Heimerdingers were disdainful of Hickok's promotional efforts, Ralph persuaded them to think more expansively. With Pioneer's products available in some fifteen thousand stores, he brought in a designer to improve the company's retail displays and showed his bosses that more aggressive marketing led to higher sales. Whether it was homogenized milk, eggs, Muzak, or men's accessories, he has always known that products don't sell themselves. "I promoted the hell out of Pioneer," he says.

He had a hundred ideas and was able to execute a number of them. He started a line of colorful elastic belts and announced Pioneer's new "peacock colors." He dreamed up advertising campaigns: "Dad is worth his weight in gold," one ad read, accompanied by a picture of a man in a balance scale with a pile of gold coins in the other pan. He commissioned a series of vintage car designs on tie bars and cuff links, and a line of cuff links with the words "I love you" in several languages, including Gregg Shorthand, the most popular form of stenography in those years. (Ralph may have been the first person to produce cuff links with messages.) Not every campaign was a hit, but the successful ones gave Pioneer's product line a new vitality and flair. "I had some talent for creating visual displays," he says, "and a sense of romance about our line."

In one of his promotions, Ralph ran ads in *Look* magazine with the slogan "Give a Party for Pop." If you bought a Pioneer belt, you would be given various party items—little hats, special napkins, and so on. The pop in the picture looked awfully familiar: Ralph had stayed in touch with Bob Hope, who was happy to pose for a photo.

In 1954, when the Heimerdingers decided to sell the company, Ralph reminded them that he had the right to match the best offer. Mr. Heimerdinger had just made a verbal agreement to sell Pioneer to Swank, the nation's largest maker of men's jewelry, but if Ralph wanted to buy the company, that was fine with him. "Where are you going to get the money?" he asked.

Ralph wasn't sure. The only banker he knew was Jack McDowell, a loan officer at the Philadelphia National Bank. Every fall, Ralph would meet with him to arrange a short-term loan for Pioneer's Christmas line, so McDowell knew the company. More important, he knew Ralph.

Still, arranging a sufficiently large loan took some persuading. "If Swank buys Pioneer," Ralph told McDowell, "you'll not only lose our business, but three hundred employees in Philadelphia will be out of work, and some of them are your customers." McDowell, an old-fashioned banker who was fond of Ralph and used to call him "Ralphie," lent him almost enough to buy the company, with the final $35,000 coming from Bob Fleisher, Suzanne's brother. As things turned out, Jack McDowell's loan would mark the beginning of a beautiful friendship.

Nobody seems to recall how much Ralph paid for the thinly traded public company that was mostly owned by the Heimerdingers. But whatever it was, the relatively high price was his own fault. His marketing and design efforts had made Pioneer more profitable—and therefore more expensive.

The first thing Ralph did was change the company's name from Pioneer Suspender to Pioneer Industries, because the original name "didn't sound very romantic." Not surprisingly, the new owner was no longer satisfied merely to match his competitor's marketing efforts. To attract the attention of buyers and merchandising managers, he started putting on musical shows during Fashion Week in New York. Drawing partly on his contacts from his years at Muzak, he hired musicians and actors, who always included Suzanne and some of her friends from the Philadelphia theater world, to perform songs with titles like "Braces Are a Man's Best Friend," which featured a pair of dancing suspenders in black light.

The shows began at the Pierre Hotel, and as they grew in popularity, they expanded to bigger venues. At one point Pioneer's annual musicals were so popular that buyers traveled from Manhattan to the Atlantic City Convention Center to see them. As the company's new owner, Ralph started visiting department stores all over the country, and because of these shows, the buyers always knew him. He was approached more than once about producing entertainment for companies in other industries.

Ralph and Suzanne remember these productions with pride and pleasure. In one scene, a young saleswoman behind the counter (played by Suzanne) described her fondness for another employee, a handsome young man, and hoped aloud that he liked her, too. When the scene ended and she stepped out from behind the counter, you could see she was pregnant—a surprise ending, somewhat daring for the 1950s, that brought the house down. In another show, the cast included a cute little piglet who came along to promote a line of pigskin wallets. To keep the animal quiet backstage, Suzanne fed it milk from a baby bottle.

"It felt as if Ralph and I were in business together," Suzanne says. "I knew how to find the acting talent, and he knew how to use it." The shows, which ran about an hour, were a blend of comedy, jazzy songs, clever lyrics, and creative sets. Each year's production played only once, and was followed by displays of Pioneer's newest products for buyers, store managers, and fashion writers.

Not everyone in Ralph's orbit thought that putting on musicals was the best use of his talent and energy. "You really should get someone else to do that," Joe Roberts told his brother, "because these shows take so much time." Ralph just smiled; Joe couldn't understand how much he loved putting on shows. "I was never in any job or business that I didn't enjoy," Ralph says. "Somehow or other I found the fun parts." Years later, when Ralph was in his eighties, a young man in a Comcast training program asked what he would have done if he hadn't gone into the cable business. "I might have become a Broadway producer," Ralph replied. Everybody laughed, but Ralph wasn't kidding.

He had also long been interested in the cosmetics industry, where packaging and promotion were especially important. When he noticed that some of the perfume companies were starting to develop products for men, he developed a line of men's shaving lotions and colognes that department stores could put right on the counter in men's departments. Ralph was involved in choosing the scents, which were produced by a fragrance company, and Suzanne ran surveys among potential buyers and promoted the colognes on radio shows.

As Ralph had hoped, the new line provided new marketing opportunities. He came out with a cologne called Inferno, which sported a red cap and the slogan "Brings Out the Devil in You." A perfume called Entrée for Women was displayed in men's departments, where it would attract gift buyers. And a fragrance advertised as the champagne of after-shower colognes sat in a little metal frame and resembled a miniature bottle of champagne.

His boldest idea was for a cologne he named Mark II, whose slogan was "The Mark of a Man." He commissioned a jeweler to create a large, solid-gold bottle of Mark II with a shiny black cap, which he set in a fancy rosewood case with a gold funnel. He arranged to display it at Saks Fifth Avenue in New York, where shoppers were informed that anyone who bought the gold bottle, which sold for $2,500, would receive a lifetime supply of the cologne. In an inspired move, he hired a Pinkerton guard to stand next to the display. The presentation at Saks was strictly a promotion; the product itself sold nicely at $3.50, with a more elaborate bottle that looked just like the gold one going for $7.50.

Not everyone understood what Ralph was up to. A front-page story in the *Wall Street Journal* carried this cumbersome headline: "The Lifetime Supply: Some Persons Receive Recurring Yule Gifts. Magazines, Jewelry and Fruit Sell, but Nobody Longs For a Lifetime Jug of Cologne." The article began, tongue in cheek:

Last Christmas you gave him a seat on the New York Stock Exchange. The year before it was a Lear Jet. Before that, it was his and hers ski chalets in Aspen, a pair of tiger cubs and a yacht. But the stock market fell and he lost a bundle, he broke his leg skiing and the tigers have messed up the yacht and the jet.

So now it's Christmastime again and you want to buy the man-who-has-everything something that will last.

Consider the lifetime gift.

For $2,500, for instance, you can buy a lifetime supply of Mark II cologne, handsomely packaged in a 14-karat gold container. It comes with a funnel to be used in refilling the container with the "woodsy, musky" fragrance.

So far, no one has bought a lifetime bottle of the "uncopyable blend of rare oils and essences, entirely masculine in fragrance," although "we almost had a buyer once," according to Robert Cohen, advertising manager of the Mark II division. . . . But the company is serious about the product: It has promoted it in a full-page ad in the *New Yorker*.

Of course Ralph hadn't planned to sell any gold bottles of cologne. He produced a prototype to get attention for the brand, and it worked: you can't do much better than the front page of the *Wall Street Journal*. Ralph's name didn't appear in the article; the man who dreamed up the promotion preferred to remain in the background. Where had the idea come from? Perhaps he was influenced by the Manhattan pharmacist in the Biltmore Hotel who had once sold a hundred-dollar bottle of perfume to a famous actor.

Ralph has always told a good story to explain his business decisions. It's not that these tales aren't true, but the full explanation, as he readily admits, is often more complicated. To explain why he left the men's accessories business, Ralph has often described seeing a newspaper ad in 1959 for the patented Sansabelt waistband—beltless slacks that threatened to make Pioneer's chief product obsolete. But he was also aware of a larger trend: American men were becoming less interested in suspenders, cuff links, and tie bars, which may have reflected the imminent cultural shift from the Eisenhower era to the age of JFK. His principal investor, Bob Fleisher, had never really liked the accessories business and was urging his brother-in-law to sell the company. And as the men's clothing industry was moving away from the old, established brand names with recognizable logos and packaging, even Ralph was beginning to have doubts.

"I got scared," he says. "The business could be going down the drain, and I still owed Jack McDowell a lot of money. Nobody was forcing me to sell, but people were encouraging me, and I wondered if they were right, even though I loved the merchandising, the displays, and the musical shows." As with every business he has ever sold, Ralph still regrets letting Pioneer go, although in view of what lay ahead, it's hard to argue with his decision. At the time, however, it was painful, and he hated to lay off so many employees. Their welfare, after all, had been one of his strongest arguments to secure the bank loan that allowed him to buy the company a few years earlier.

But he received a good price for Pioneer, which was acquired by its rival, Hickok. "I was suddenly rich," says Ralph, although he doesn't recall how much he received for the company. Whatever the number, it was enough to allow him to donate a good sum to the International Ladies' Garment Workers' Union to distribute as severance pay to his employees. Although he sold Pioneer, he kept his line of men's colognes and shaving lotions, which was too much fun to give up.

In 1961, bankrolled by the proceeds from Pioneer, Ralph set up shop in a modest office building at One Belmont Avenue in the Philadelphia suburb of Bala Cynwyd. The site, known as the Barclay Building, would later be called the GSB Building because the Germantown Savings Bank had its headquarters there. He planned to call his new enterprise Equity Corporation, but when he learned that this name was already taken, he settled on International Equity. "I liked the word *equity*," he says. "It sounded important, and *international* made it sound even more important."

As head of International Equity Corporation, which had many more syllables than employees, Ralph was a small-time venture capitalist who started investing in a handful of modest businesses while exploring some bigger opportunities that didn't work out. Al Greenbaum, an accountant who worked closely with Ralph in those years, tried to interest him in a mattress company, but Ralph thought that business would be boring. A few years later he decided to buy a 7-Up bottling company in Flint, Michigan, but the deal fell through when the seller changed his mind at the last moment.

In 1971 he was about to acquire Snelling and Snelling, a family-owned employment agency in nearby Paoli, but here, too, the sellers reneged at the closing. This deal was brought to him by Drew Lewis, who became Snelling's CEO shortly thereafter. Lewis later served as secretary of transportation in the Reagan Administration before becoming CEO of Warner-Amex Cable Communications.

Also in 1971 Ralph took a long, hard look at Frances Denney, a family-run cosmetics company in Philadelphia whose products were sold in the finest department stores. A broker had identified two potential buyers, both of whom were eager to make the acquisition: a coal company called Berwind, which was starting to diversify and was willing to pay cash, and Ralph Roberts of International Equity, who intended to borrow the money. Berwind planned to hire new management, but Ralph preferred to keep Bob Denney running the business. Although Denney wanted to stay, he feared that Ralph, whom he didn't know, wouldn't be able to raise the money, and that his beloved company would soon fall apart.

It did anyway. Denney sold the company to Berwind, but the new owners couldn't keep it alive. "I went with the wrong guys," Denney says, and he wasn't the only one who felt that way. In 2007, when Ralph and Suzanne were guests on C. Graham Berwind's yacht in the Caribbean, Ralph finally met the man who had acquired Denney thirty-six years earlier. The company, he told Ralph, had been one of his biggest failures. "I wish you had bought it," he said.

Losing Denney was a major disappointment. "Ralph would have loved the cosmetics business," says Suzanne. "It was a chance to put his creativity to work, and he would have so enjoyed a business that had some romance."

That's certainly true, but it all worked out for the best. For if Ralph Roberts had acquired Frances Denney, there wouldn't have been a Comcast.

4

The Survivor

Dan Aaron

In 2001, when Dan Aaron published his autobiography, a lawyer who had worked for Comcast ran into Ralph at a meeting. "I've known Dan for a long time," he said, "but until I read his book, I never knew about his early life."

"Neither did I," said Ralph, who had worked closely with Aaron for almost forty years. "He just never discusses these things."

It wasn't only his early life that Dan Aaron kept hidden. David Long, his friend and collaborator on the memoir, had known that Dan worked at Comcast, but he wasn't aware that he had served as vice chairman, or that he joined the company even before it had a name. Erika, Dan's oldest daughter, recalls that when her father died in 2003, many of her friends were unaware that he had been involved in the founding of Comcast until they read his obituary.

Like Ralph, he preferred to focus on other people's accomplishments. And his aversion to talking about his childhood until the final years of his life may have been a necessary part of his success, and perhaps even his survival.

He was born in Germany in 1926, the son of a prominent lawyer. His most vivid childhood memory was the day Hitler's motorcade visited their small town. Spotting a young, blonde girl in the adoring crowd, Hitler stopped the car and lifted her up as the spectators roared their delight and called out, "Heil Hitler!" Dan, who was seven, found the scene frightening, and he was relieved when his father quickly led him away. Albert Aaron was upset, too, his son recalled, "not knowing when such outbursts could turn hostile toward Jews."

It didn't take long. Within a year or two, young men in Nazi uniforms were standing in front of the Aarons' house, chanting in loud and graphic detail about the violence that awaited the family and their brethren. Lilli, Dan's mother, insisted that it was time to emigrate, but what seems so clear and dangerous in retrospect was impossible to imagine at the time. Like so many other educated Germans, Albert Aaron was certain that this madness would pass. But in 1937 Albert, a prominent attorney, was imprisoned for two crimes: belonging to the opposition party and being a Jew.

He had a sister in Philadelphia who agreed to sponsor the family to come to America—assuming that Albert would be released from prison and that the authorities would allow them to leave. In 1938, when Daniel and his brother, Frank, were twelve and eight, and time was running out, the family boarded a ship with little more than the clothes they were wearing.

They settled in the Queens section of New York City, where the boys adapted quickly to their new home. But in the summer of 1939, when they were enjoying life at a YMCA camp, making friends and learning American songs, they were awakened in the middle of the night and told that their mother had killed herself. They came home for the funeral and then returned to camp. Three weeks later came another late-night call: their father, unable to find work and despondent over the loss of his wife, had followed her to the grave.

"These tragic events," Dan wrote in his memoir, "left me with a personal emotional scar. I had to learn to control my emotions, and it became difficult for me to let others know how I felt." That perception wasn't entirely accurate. In the years ahead, his wife, his children, and many Comcast employees would know exactly how Dan Aaron felt—at least about *them*. He may not have expressed his love and caring in words, but his feelings were clear from the questions he asked and the kindness he showed, especially to those who were in any kind of distress.

The boys' aunt brought them to Philadelphia, where they passed through a series of foster homes. In normal times they would have ended up in the Foster Home for Hebrew Orphans, whose president was Leo Heimerdinger, but with so many refugees from Hitler, the orphanage was full. In 1940 Dan and Frank Aaron were taken in by a rabbi and his wife in Williamsport, Pennsylvania. Dan recalled later that they were "totally committed to turning us into Americans, and, if at all possible, into joyous Americans."

They succeeded. Despite everything he had been through, and although he was still struggling to master English, Dan flourished in his new home. He won an essay contest on "What It Means to Be an American." He joined the high school tennis and gym teams. He became a debater, started reading the *New York Times*, and in a community of staunch Republicans, boldly declared himself a Democrat.

When the rabbi was called into military service, the boys moved to a foster home in Philadelphia. Shortly before he graduated from high school, Dan applied to the Army Specialist Training Program, which provided a free college education, but he was turned away at the induction center because he wasn't yet an American citizen. He joined the staff of a community center where, around that time, a boy named Julian Brodsky was playing basketball, and a young woman named Suzanne Fleisher was starting to appear in plays.

During his freshman year at Temple University, Dan was drafted into the army, instantly becoming a citizen. He joined the Eighth Armored Division, which was pushing through Belgium toward the German border. Although his infantry unit saw plenty of action, he escaped injury. Later, because he knew German, he was transferred to Military Intelligence.

Back home in 1946, the GI Bill helped him return to college, where, despite his shyness, his accent, and his poverty, he met a girl and fell in love. If Dan was sober and studious, Geraldine Stone was his antithesis: the life of the party. "Gerri restored my self-respect," Dan wrote, "which had been shattered by the catastrophes of the Holocaust."

Gerri's father, like Dan's, was a successful lawyer, although initially he wasn't thrilled when his beautiful and popular daughter took up with a penniless refugee, a college student who was working weekends as a waiter. They were married in 1948, when Dan was twenty-two, and before long Gerri's parents felt like parents to him, too. In time, he and Gerri would themselves become the parents of five children.

When Dan graduated from college, he was unable to find a job. He never forgot the pain of this demeaning experience, and years later, at Comcast, he would maintain an open-door policy for job applicants. He considered law school, but he knew that a young Jewish lawyer without connections would have trouble finding work. Instead, he enrolled at Penn as a graduate student in finance, with a concentration in economics and journalism. When one of his professors asked if he might be interested in working for a syndicated columnist at the Philadelphia *Evening Bulletin*, he jumped at the chance. Two years later he was writing his own articles about local companies.

In 1955 the young reporter read that the Jerrold Electronics Corporation had been awarded a franchise for a community antenna television system in Dubuque, Iowa. Dan had never heard of Jerrold, so now he had another company to write about. He had also never heard of community antenna television.

Jerrold's president, a dynamic businessman named Milton Jerrold Shapp, showed him a piece of coaxial cable and predicted that it would soon make TV reception in small towns as clear as it was in large cities. Dan liked Shapp's enthusiasm and his operation, and he was especially impressed that one of Jerrold's executives was a woman with a physical disability, which was unusual at the time. In writing about the company, he explained to his readers what Jerrold had been up to in Iowa:

> Dubuque, cradled among seven hills, was cut off from television waves. Even towering rooftop antennas costing nearly $300 each picked up only a faint picture. The solution was a community antenna system. An antenna tower atop the highest mountain would pick up signals and amplify them. Then a coaxial cable would bring the picture down the mountain into town. Subscribers' sets would be hooked onto the cable.

When the article appeared, Shapp called Dan to thank him for getting it right. Dan, who was growing restless at the *Bulletin*, asked Shapp to keep him in mind if the company ever needed a writer. Nine months later, Shapp called to say that Jerrold, which was now a publicly held corporation, was looking for a writer for its annual report. Shapp also needed a PR person, and before long, Dan was doing that job, too.

He quickly made himself knowledgeable about the industry, and accompanied Shapp to the first congressional hearings on what would later be known as cable TV. By the late 1950s, when Jerrold had acquired an interest in so many systems that it needed someone to head up its CATV division, Dan was the man. One of his first assignments was to rebuild the system in Tupelo, Mississippi, a city known both for its honey and as the birthplace of a popular young singer named Elvis Presley. The tiny CATV system was owned jointly by Jerrold and Pete Musser, a Philadelphia entrepreneur.

In 1961, when Shapp decided to run for governor of Pennsylvania, he offered Dan Aaron the top job on his campaign. But although he loved Shapp, Dan decided it was time to strike out on his own. He would become a CATV broker, because an industrious person who knew the business could do very well by bringing together buyers and sellers of cable systems and helping them negotiate a deal.

But the work was harder than he anticipated, and involved more unreimbursed travel than he could afford. Moreover, his serious, intellectual style wasn't right for a job that required a salesman's optimism and a gregarious personality. The only client he signed up was Pete Musser, who had decided to sell his interest in the Tupelo system to raise money for other investments. But it wasn't easy to find a buyer, in part because Mississippi was in turmoil as the flash point of the civil rights movement.

As Dan always told the story, on a fall afternoon in 1962, he and Musser were walking down Chestnut Street in downtown Philadelphia when Musser spotted a familiar face coming toward them. He recognized the man in the Brooks Brothers raincoat as Ralph Roberts, whom he knew from the Young Presidents' Organization, a networking group that was founded, as it happens, by Ray Hickok, who had bought Pioneer from Ralph.

"Here comes our fish," Musser told Dan. "This fellow sold his menswear business a couple of years ago, and he's got some cash." (There is some zoological confusion in this story. When Dan's book came out, Musser objected to the term *fish*. "I might have said *pigeon*," he says, "but I think I said *prospect*." And Gerri Aaron recalls hearing that Musser had said, "Here's our goat.")

Almost half a century later, neither Ralph nor Musser could remember much about that conversation. Musser isn't even sure how, exactly, he knew Ralph, because in 1963 he hadn't yet joined the Young Presidents' Organization. But they agree that this impromptu encounter led to Ralph's purchase of the Tupelo cable system, which was the first step in the enterprise that became Comcast.

Dan probably thought that Ralph was helping him begin his career as a cable broker, but he was actually ending it. When Ralph decided to buy the Tupelo system, he said he would make the acquisition only if Dan came along as part of the deal. He wasn't about to enter a new business without an expert, and Dan knew as much about CATV as anyone in the country. He didn't have to think very long about Ralph's proposal. He liked this man, and he believed in the future of cable.

Ralph may have known about CATV from a talk by Milton Shapp at the Young Presidents' Organization, and Julian says that Ralph had previously turned down a couple of other cable opportunities, including a system in Houma, Louisiana. In any case, although the initial capital investment to build a cable plant presented a real difficulty in getting started, Ralph believed he could overcome that obstacle. But what he especially liked about CATV was that it reminded him of Muzak, with its recurring monthly income. "You put up a tower and some equipment," he says, "and they paid you every month. It looked to me like the greatest business in the world."

Even so, he took his time deciding. Gerri Aaron remembers that Ralph and his brother-in-law, Bob Fleisher, came to their house at least twice to talk with Dan. Ralph also called a few cable owners to solicit their views about the business, and arranged to visit a couple of systems. Even after he was convinced that CATV was a good investment, he wondered if it was right for him. "Cable looked like the dullest business in the world for a man of my temperament," he says, by which he presumably meant a creative type who was used to having fun at work. But although Ralph intended to own the system in Tupelo, someone else would operate it. And he recognized that this was an industry with tremendous potential for growth.

"Are you going to live down there?" asked Jack McDowell from the Philadelphia National Bank when Ralph went to see him about borrowing the money to buy the system.

No, Ralph explained, they had a local man in place, although he and Dan would be there as often as necessary. McDowell, who had almost certainly never made a cable loan before, agreed to lend Ralph half the purchase price, and Ralph raised the rest from four or five partners. Ralph was one of them, and he earned a second share for putting the deal together.

After all these years, nobody seems to know what Ralph paid for the Tupelo system when he bought it on November 13, 1963, about a year after the encounter on Chestnut Street and just nine days before the assassination of President Kennedy. Pete Musser recalls that the purchase price was $600,000, but he isn't sure. Ralph thinks it was

$500,000. An unpublished history of Comcast from 1996, which was approved by Julian Brodsky, puts the total investment at $1 million—half of it to buy the facilities, and the rest for operations. According to that account, International Equity put in $250,000; Ralph recruited five partners to invest $50,000 each; and he borrowed the rest from the Philadelphia National Bank.

One of the original partners of the Tupelo franchise was Ralph's friend Alvin "Vene" Gutman, who recalled that Ralph bought the system for $750,000. Of that amount, he says, $650,000 was financed by the sellers, leaving Ralph to come up with the rest. "Ralph said he was putting up $50,000," Gutman said, "with $25,000 coming from his brother, $9,000 from Bob Fleisher, and another $9,000 from his lawyer, Ray Pearlstine." (Pearlstine's son Norman, who served for ten years as editor-in-chief of *Time*, confirms that his father was an investor.) Gutman said that he "rolled the dice for $2,000." When asked in 2008 how certain he was of these figures, he replied, "I have a good memory." But even he couldn't account for the final $5,000, which may have come from Charles Sunstein, Suzanne's stepbrother.

There is also some uncertainty about the number of CATV subscribers in Tupelo when Ralph bought the system. Dan wrote that when he rebuilt Tupelo for Jerrold, there were 1,700 customers, and that when Ralph bought it, the number had grown to 2,300. That figure appears in Comcast's first annual report, but was later revised downward. (According to the 1988 Annual Report, there were 1,800 subscribers when Ralph bought the system. Ralph often gives the number as 1,200, but sometimes he'll say there were 1,700. Julian remembers 1,800.) Whatever the actual number, everybody agrees that Tupelo was a small system, and that it came with unbuilt franchises in two other communities—West Point and Laurel, which had the dubious honor of serving as the headquarters of the Ku Klux Klan.

Unlike many towns with community antenna television, Tupelo wasn't mountainous. But it was a hundred miles from Memphis, the nearest broadcast center, which made good reception impossible with a conventional rooftop antenna. Although there was no franchise fee in Tupelo, some municipal governments were starting to charge cable operators 1 or 2 percent of gross revenues, which would increase over the years to as much as 5 percent—or even more. Cable franchises were not exclusive, but the systems were so expensive to build that it was rare for a second operator to compete with a company that was already up and running—a practice known as overbuilding. Later on, when satellite and then phone companies entered the mix, there would be competition everywhere.

Dan spent considerably more time in Tupelo than he expected, and much of it was focused on the system manager. The man who had the job when Ralph bought the franchise was said to be difficult to work with. After hearing from a taxi driver that he was also known as a bigot, Dan, who was on his way to the airport, had the driver turn around and go back to the office, where he fired the manager on the spot. To take his place, he hired the former chairman of the local bank, who was active in the community and knew everyone in town.

It was Dan who determined that the system manager would be critically important, that he—and in those days it was always a man— was the face of the company in that town. Dan believed the manager should treat the business as if it were his own, and with Ralph's approval, he established incentives to encourage local managers to maximize earnings.

Back in Philadelphia, Ralph was still operating out of the GSB Building in Bala Cynwyd when Dan Aaron became the fifth employee of International Equity. The others included a bookkeeper and two secretaries, one of whom was Ralph's executive assistant, Ann Gardner, who had worked for him at Pioneer and was now spending much of her time on his cologne business. The office consisted of one large room, which was divided by metal file cabinets. There was barely enough space for the five of them when a sixth person showed up—a man who would play a major role in the history of Comcast.

5

The Auditor

Julian Brodsky

Of the three men who ran Comcast early on, only Julian Brodsky was a native of Philadelphia. The youngest member of the trio was born in 1933, the same year as the novelist Philip Roth, whose depictions of hardworking, upwardly mobile, East Coast Jewish families during the 1940s and 1950s ring vividly true to Julian. The Brodskys, too, loved their country, valued education, and practically worshipped FDR.

The grandson of Russian immigrants who ended up in Philadelphia "because that's where they got off the boat," Julian is the older of two brothers, just as Dan was. His father, David, was a struggling wholesaler of fruit and vegetables who labored long hours to provide for his family. "We weren't well off," Julian recalls. "We weren't even comfortable."

At the age of eight, he had a job in the city's Italian Market, and he continued working through high school and college. At the Wharton School he retained his working-class perspective; he was probably the only student there who considered himself a socialist, and was certainly the only one with a beard. Like Ralph a few years earlier, he took many of his courses at Penn's liberal arts college, where he studied history, anthropology, and American literature while serving as the poetry editor of the literary magazine. For the first two years he made the dean's list, but when his parents moved to Florida, he started skipping classes. "I was lazy," he says, which is difficult to believe for anyone who has known Julian or seen him in action.

His thesis at Wharton was on food and beverage cost control, and he planned to pursue a career in hotel and restaurant management. After college he took a job at a Florida hotel, but he missed the Northeast and his girlfriend, Lois Green, so much that he quit before the first day of work and returned to Philadelphia, where they became engaged.

Even before college, he had received a fine education. Although Julian's father hadn't finished high school, he was a math whiz who tutored his children, as well as his nieces and nephews, in algebra, geometry, and calculus. He was equally familiar with art and literature, and seemed to have read everything. When Julian was thirteen, father and son joined a Great Books discussion group, which met at the library on Friday nights. "I went more or less willingly," Julian says, adding that he wasn't inclined to argue with his dad, a big man who had won a couple of boxing titles in the army.

The Brodsky household was a stimulating place. David was an amateur musician, and Julian describes his mother, Esther, whom everyone called Pat, as the smartest person he has ever known. There were books everywhere, and Julian would add to the pile each week with another armful from the library. His academic learning, though, included some obstacles: the family lived in Philadelphia's multiethnic downtown, where Julian had to fight one set of kids on his way to public school in the morning, and another group as he walked to Hebrew school in the afternoon.

Shortly after college he moved to New York City and worked as an internal auditor for the International Ladies' Garment Workers' Union. (He had other labor connections as well: his godfather was a union official who would soon represent the employees of Pioneer Industries in their negotiations with the company's owner, Ralph Roberts.) He was drafted into the army, and because he could type, he was sent to a course in administration in South Carolina. On his third day there, he was assigned to the faculty: he taught typing on machines with blank keys and lectured on the history of the army.

After finishing first in his class, he was sent to Huntsville, Alabama, the home of the Army Ballistic Missile Program, which included mathematicians, physicists, and a handful of former Nazi scientists, among them the famous rocket designer Wernher von Braun. "We had a barracks full of PhDs," says Julian, who served as a noncommissioned officer in charge of personnel records. "With only a college degree, I was among the less educated." It was an unusual post, where uniforms were optional and the mess hall was always open.

In late 1956 he took a brief leave to marry Lois. A few months later, after Lois graduated from Temple University's College of Education, she traveled to Alabama to spend the summer with her husband. When Julian's parents sent him ten dollars on his birthday, the newlyweds looked at each other and yelled, "Meat!" That evening, as they grilled a couple of steaks, some of their neighbors—like Julian, the men were all draftees earning less than $100 a month—gathered at the screen door. One of them asked, "Do you mind if we linger a little while to enjoy the smell?"

Julian had helped his fellow servicemen prepare their tax returns, and back home in 1958, he opened a seasonal tax business. But it was time to get serious about making a living, and for a man of his abilities, the fastest way to do that was to become an accountant. He briefly considered applying for a job with the Internal Revenue Service, but the budding capitalist in him saw more opportunity in the private sector.

In those days, accounting students had to serve a two-year apprenticeship before taking the CPA exam, and Julian found a job with

William E. Howe & Co. "It was an all-Catholic firm," he recalls, "but they hired me anyway." The pay was low, and he and Lois were living in a basement apartment in Media, twelve miles from Philadelphia. Lois walked to her teaching job and Julian drove off each morning to visit clients.

As it happened, the firm's clients included half a dozen early CATV companies, including Service Electric, whose owner, John Walson, is known as the man who invented cable TV. Walson owned an appliance store in Mahanoy City, Pennsylvania, and when the first television sets arrived in 1947, the many hills in the area blocked reception of the Philadelphia stations. Walson solved the problem by erecting a seventy-foot antenna on a nearby mountain, amplifying the signal, and running a wire all the way to his store—and to the homes of a few customers along the way. Without intending to, he had just created a new industry.

Accountants aren't known for showing emotion, but Julian still remembers returning to the staff room at William E. Howe after visiting his first CATV client. "Guys," he announced, "I just found the greatest business!" It was a feeling he would never lose.

He had taken his time choosing a career, but having found his calling, he moved quickly. To broaden his experience, he decided to change jobs after only a year. Like Ralph at Aitkin-Kynett, Julian claims to have chosen his second employer, the accounting firm of Adler, Faunce & Leonard, because they were listed first in the phone book.

He decided to become an auditor—an accountant who reviews the work of other accountants. He especially liked what is now known as forensic accounting, which means investigating suspected fraud; it is essentially detective work, using numbers instead of words. Auditing was intellectually demanding and morally compelling, a good choice for a man who loved to be challenged and cared deeply about uncovering the truth.

One of the firm's clients was Pioneer Industries, and when Ralph Roberts was preparing to sell the company, Julian was sent to Darby to help him out. "To know Ralph was to love him," he says, and to love Ralph was to want to work for him. When the sale was completed, Julian was happy to continue serving the modest account of International Equity. Every three months he drove to Bala Cynwyd to prepare the quarterly taxes for Ralph's cologne business and other investments, and when the work was done, he enjoyed chatting with his client.

When Ralph decided to buy the CATV system in Tupelo, Julian took notice. His favorite client was going into his favorite business? Here was a once-in-a-lifetime opportunity. "You're not doing this without me," he told Ralph. "I just resigned from Adler, Faunce & Leonard."

Ralph wasn't sure how to respond. Why would a tiny outfit like International Equity need an in-house accountant? But he listened as Julian made the case in dollars and cents. "You're paying our firm $25,000 a year," he explained. "I can cut that down to $8,000, because I'll do most of the work myself. If you pay me $12,000, you'll come out ahead."

"But look around," Ralph said. "This is a small office, and you're a big man. I don't even have furniture for you."

Julian wasn't about to be deterred by the lack of a desk, and if there wasn't room for another employee, okay, so they'd be a little cramped. A few days later, he showed up to work with a folding chair and a card table. That was fine with Ralph, although Lois was not amused when her husband, a CPA at an established firm, informed her that he was moving to a little company that nobody had ever heard of, or that he was bringing their card table to work because his new employer couldn't even give him a desk.

Julian would eventually have more than enough to do, but when the energetic auditor first arrived, the little office was overstaffed. In Dan Aaron's version of events, Julian, with too much time on his hands, chose to focus most of his talent and vigor on auditing Dan's expense account. "After days of Julian's torture about a luncheon at the local restaurant," Dan recalled, "I finally turned to Ralph for help, only to have him show me the back of his hand to sample still another whiff of the newest and most calming scent of the toiletry business."

All three men made regular trips to Tupelo, flying on separate planes to protect the business in the event of an accident. Usually they flew to Memphis, rented a car, and drove two hours to Tupelo before going on to Laurel and then New Orleans, where they caught a flight back to Philadelphia.

Laurel, Mississippi, was the site of their second system, the first one they built themselves. Ralph had decided that when he entered a new community, he would immediately hire a prominent and trustworthy attorney, the kind of man who, in a small town, used to serve as a father figure. In Laurel that person was Carroll Gartin, a former (and future) lieutenant governor, and an unsuccessful candidate for governor in 1959 after being tagged as a "moderate"—which was not meant as a compliment.

Charles Pickering, Gartin's junior partner, remembers Ralph as a dapper fellow who used to bring perfume for the secretaries. When Ralph suggested that the lawyers take part of their fee in stock because his company was short on cash, Pickering and his two colleagues were so impressed with their client that they borrowed money to buy additional shares, which were later converted to equity in Comcast. "Periodically I would sell some of it," says Pickering, "and within a few months my holdings would be worth as much as before. That stock helped educate my children."

One of those children was Charles Pickering, Jr., known as Chip—a future congressman who was just a baby when Ralph met his father. Until Pickering left Congress in 2008, Ralph would often stop in to see him on visits to Capitol Hill. "I grew up in a world of southern gentlemen," Pickering says. "Ralph showed me there was also such a thing as a northern gentleman."

Ralph liked powerful lawyers as long as they had integrity, and Gartin and Pickering certainly did. Years later, around 1983, when Comcast employee Glenn Colvin was trying to get a Mississippi franchise renewed, he and the system manager went to see a prominent local official to get a sense of what the city might be asking for. (A municipality might insist on a higher share of the revenue, for example, or request that the local schools be given free cable.) "You know," the man told Colvin, "the telephone company lets us use their hunting lodge, and the power company lets us use their fishing lodge. We're getting a lot of complaints about dirty movies on HBO and Cinemax. Do you reckon you could bring me a cable box so I could monitor that stuff?"

When Colvin told Comcast's attorney what the official had asked for, Pickering said, "Don't ever go for a private meeting. Anything we do, we'll go before the council and discuss publicly." Ralph was undoubtedly pleased by that response. "He made sure the local attorneys understood his approach," says Colvin. "There weren't going to be any winks, special understandings, or trading favors. There was a lot of that going on in the cable industry, and Ralph wanted no part of it."

When the Laurel system was up and running, subscribers noticed that whenever it rained, the picture quality began to deteriorate. The problem got so bad that the mayor called Dan in Philadelphia and told him to either repair the system or sell it to another operator. Dan flew right down with a mysterious package from a friend at Jerrold. When he opened it with the Laurel employees, they found a dozen broomstick handles with instructions that read, "Beat the hell out of every inch of the cable." It worked. The cable, which was designed to keep water out, had in fact kept it in, which decimated the picture. The service trucks started carrying broomsticks until a new and waterproof coaxial cable became available.

When Ralph bought the Tupelo system, all three of its channels came from stations in Memphis, and the signals were carried by microwave. A year or two later, when a new station opened in Columbus, about fifty miles away, Tupelo was able to add a fourth channel, and the technology provided enough room for a fifth channel as well. To fill it, Dan turned to TeleMation, a small electronics company that showed an Associated Press news ticker through a TV camera on a motorized post. As the camera revolved, it swept past a clock, a thermometer that showed the temperature outside, a barometer, and wind and rain gauges. There was also a removable placard with a brief commercial message, such as "Eat at Joe's." It wasn't much by today's standards, but in addition to serving as a primitive precursor to both CNN and The Weather Channel, Tupelo's fifth channel was part of the birth of cable advertising, a business with revenues that would eventually be measured in the billions.

In the early years of Comcast, it was sometimes said that Ralph had won the Meridian, Mississippi, franchise in a craps game. When asked who might conceivably have come up with this charming cable fable, he just smiles. The most he is willing to admit is that he hasn't always denied the story. "There was a craps table," he concedes, "but that's the extent of it."

The real story of Meridian is one of his favorites. In 1964 Mississippi was still a dry state, so anyone who wanted a drink in the company of others would visit a private club, known as a roadhouse, which offered not only alcohol, but food and gambling as well. On a day when Ralph was planning to drive from Tupelo to Laurel, the Tupelo manager urged him to visit a certain roadhouse in Meridian, which was on his way. Ralph, who has always enjoyed gambling, was happy to drop in.

While shooting dice at the Queen of Hearts, he got into a conversation with one of the locals. When Ralph mentioned that he was in the CATV business, the other man said, "Now, that's interesting. We just had an election to see if the franchise here would go to Mr. Goodling, who's in the trucking business, or Mr. Royal, who owns the movie theater. Mr. Royal will be unhappy, because he thinks he won. But Mr. Goodling received more votes."

"How do you know so much about it?" asked Ralph.

"I'm the city auditor, so I counted the votes. You might want to come to the council meeting tomorrow morning. Mr. Goodling doesn't know anything about this business, and he may be willing to sell it."

Even then, Ralph was thinking about expanding. After the council meeting, he followed the winner back to his office. "Mr. Goodling," he began, "I'm in the CATV business, and I wonder if you'd be willing to sell your franchise."

"Why not?" Goodling said. "Everything I have is for sale." Then, pointing to a photograph of his wife and two daughters, he added, "Including them."

Ralph no longer remembers how much he paid for the franchise, "but I must have offered too much, because he grabbed it right away."

Buying the franchise was the easy part. Before the Meridian city council agreed to the sale, they asked Ralph to put up a performance bond of $100,000—a surprisingly large sum. They also stipulated that unless the company connected 90 percent of the customers who asked for service within a year, they would forfeit the bond. The city officials were so confident that Ralph would fail that they appropriated the money from the inevitable forfeiture and earmarked it for new voting machines.

Julian arranged for a bond, but a local insurance broker happened to be friendly with the man who had failed to get the franchise. When the broker informed the bonding company that American Cable Systems, as Ralph's Mississippi operation was known, was unlikely to fulfill the terms of the deal, the bond was canceled.

By this time Ralph had found his local lawyer, an attorney named Mr. Snow, who had flowing white hair and the manner of a cinematic southern senator. In Ralph's presence, he picked up the phone and called the bonding company. "My name is Snow," he said in a slow southern drawl, "and I want you to take a little time to find out exactly who I am, because I have a message for you. If that bond isn't reinstated within twenty-four hours, your company will never do business in this state again. Do you hear me?"

When the bond was restored, the city council went even further by insisting on a second bond of $125,000 to guarantee the first one, with the money due the next day. Fred Wolf, of the Philadelphia law firm of Wolf, Block, Schorr and Solis-Cohen, which had been doing business with Ralph for years, came to his rescue by borrowing the money from the firm's pension and bonus fund. It was a huge favor, and Ralph would never forget it. (Wolf Block, which had a long-standing connection to Suzanne's family and represented Comcast for many years, went out of business in 2009.)

Normally, a cable company building a new system would advertise by taking ads in the newspaper and signing up customers with as much fanfare as possible. But in Meridian, with its stringent demand that the company had to connect at least 90 percent of the customers who wanted to subscribe, Dan Aaron came up with a completely different approach. This system, he decided, would be built discreetly, almost secretly. He rented office space in a downtown building, but put no sign on the door. Construction equipment was hidden out of sight. The trucks were unmarked, and most of the work was done at night.

Starting with the most densely populated neighborhoods, workmen began laying cable. Just before each segment was finished, a mock newspaper was delivered to houses on those streets, informing residents that "the nice kids" would be stopping by soon to meet them. The following week, clean-cut college students in khaki pants and blue shirts started knocking on doors to describe the new technology and sign up customers. This approach had never been tried for cable television, but it worked. "Dan sat back and solved the problem," says Julian, "and he kept solving problems throughout his career."

Before the year was up, although only certain sections of Meridian were wired, just about everyone who had asked for cable had received it. Dan and his team had made sure that the only people who were aware of this new service were the ones they were ready to connect. "The others never even knew we were there," says Ralph.

American Cable Systems received a glowing letter of commendation from the same city council that had previously been so difficult. And the door-to-door approach worked so well in Meridian that Dan would use it again and again. Although one-to-one marketing is both time-consuming and expensive, in the early days of cable it was often more effective to explain the service to one household at a time than to advertise on the radio or through the mail.

Because they were starting from scratch, Dan had the luxury of putting in a twelve-channel, state-of-the-art cable system. Now an entire channel could be devoted to weather instruments, and another to the news ticker. Meridian subscribers could also watch what was known as the Meditation Channel, which showed a goldfish swimming in a bowl with soothing music (probably Muzak) in the background. In another marketing effort, schoolchildren were taken to visit the system's headend, where their sweet faces were videotaped and shown on television that same evening—an incentive for parents and other relatives to tune in, assuming they had cable.

On another channel, Meridian's new system started showing a bingo game every day at noon. Bingo cards were inserted into the daily newspaper, whose publisher was happy to participate because some readers were now motivated to buy a second paper. Prizes were donated by local merchants, who were thanked by name. In the system's tiny offices, the camera showed only the bingo numbers, while off-screen Glenn Colvin would imitate the voice of a little old lady in the imaginary front row, exclaiming, "Oh goody, I won again!"

To further spur sales in Meridian, Ralph bought a truckload of leftover shoeshine kits from his friends at Hickok and used them as an inducement to sign up new customers. "It's hard to believe, but it worked," he says. "I think we gave away more shoeshine kits than people had shoes."

Glenn Colvin recalls that Ralph bought ten thousand kits, which were in the shape of little golden boots with brown polish on one side, black on the other, and a rag and a brush in the middle. In those days, says Colvin, people from northern states thought of Mississippi as a primitive place where everyone walked around barefoot. "Not only did Ralph believe that some day people in Meridian would have shoes," Colvin says, "but he expected that we'd all have two pairs, one in each color."

Ralph, a tireless marketer, has always loved to give away premiums. Many years later, the leaders of Comcast were discussing a possible deal with executives from the National Football League that would have given the NFL an equity interest in Versus, a Comcast sports channel. "Isn't there something we could give them?" Ralph asked. "Dad," Brian said, "we're already offering them a network!"

There were plenty of willing recipients for Ralph's next giveaway, inexpensive transistor radios. It was unorthodox, to say the least, to use a free radio to promote pay television, but Ralph knew that people almost never turn down a gift. Every promotion helped a little more, and it didn't take long before the Meridian system was profitable.

Ralph, however, was looking in a new direction. Although he still believed in cable, he was thinking of adding another business to the mix. This one, too, was about distribution, but it had nothing to do with television.

6

Branching Out

Joe Roberts

Ever since he was a boy, sharing a bedroom with his older brother in New Rochelle, Ralph had thought of Joe as his best friend. Joe and his wife, Betty, had moved to Connecticut, but the brothers were as close as ever. And although Joe's gifts were more literary and Ralph's more visual, they had surprisingly similar abilities and inclinations. During Ralph's tenure at Pioneer, when he took such delight in marketing, presentation, and design, Joe was vice president of marketing and advertising at Revlon, the cosmetics giant—a job Ralph would have loved if he hadn't been so determined to work for himself. And as if to emphasize their shared talents, a couple of years after Ralph left Muzak to work for Pioneer, Harry Houghton hired Joe Roberts as Muzak's executive vice president.

Joe was still there in 1965 when he called Ralph with a proposal.

Muzak's biggest client was Storecast, a marketing firm that helped food companies track and improve the placement of their products in supermarkets. Storecast was for sale, and Joe, who knew the company well, had recommended it as an acquisition for Muzak. When Muzak's owner decided not to buy the company, Joe urged Ralph to step in.

Ralph was swayed by Joe's enthusiasm, and by the Muzak connection, but above all it was the irresistible appeal of being in business with his brother. For just as he had refused to buy the Tupelo system unless Dan Aaron came along to oversee it, he agreed to buy Storecast only if Joe left Muzak to run this costly acquisition. That was fine with Joe, who was happy to work for International Equity out of Storecast's Manhattan offices.

Storecast was like no other business. Every day it sent teams of monitors to participating stores to ensure that its clients' products were in stock, easy to find, attractively displayed, and, if possible, at eye level on the shelves. In return, Storecast provided these stores with a sound system that could be used for announcements and for Muzak, which had been shown to increase the amount of money a customer was likely to spend.

Because Storecast was an unusual operation, the due diligence work before the deal closed presented a special challenge. "These guys weren't buying something substantial, like a desk or an automobile," says accountant Al Greenbaum. "It was more like a cloud or a concept." Years later, an intern in Comcast's tax department who was reviewing Storecast's expenses came across a phrase that doesn't normally appear on a budget sheet: "Balloons and helium." He paused for a moment and wondered if this was intended as a joke, or perhaps a metaphor.

Storecast was a major acquisition for Ralph's small company, and for the next few years both its size and its profits dwarfed those of his early cable operations. Julian, despite his friendship with, and admiration for, Joe Roberts, wasn't a fan of the company, finding it "strange around the edges." It was profitable, he concedes, "but not worthy of our talents."

But Storecast provided the diversification Ralph yearned for, as well as a link to his beloved Muzak and a working relationship with Joe. It remained part of International Equity, and then Comcast, until the late 1980s, when it was sold to the father and son who were then running it.

Ralph's first bank loan, which he had arranged when he bought the Tupelo system, ran for seven years—the longest financing that Jack McDowell of the Philadelphia National Bank was able to offer. That sounded fine to Ralph, who had been assured by "experts" that a cable system should be able to repay its loans within five years. But nobody had mentioned certain inconvenient details, such as rebuilds, line extensions, and the need to keep growing. The first long-term projection that Julian worked on after joining the company made clear that the loan could not be paid off on time.

Ralph told McDowell that he had miscalculated, and what the Tupelo system really needed was a *twelve*-year loan. McDowell took the news well, as Ralph was the first borrower who had ever disclosed a problem so long before the loan was due.

Ralph was grateful that the bank was lending him money at all. Many other cable operators were borrowing from a company called Economy Finance, and considered themselves fortunate to secure a three- or four-year loan at rates that sometimes reached 10 percent or higher, which was more than twice what Ralph was paying. When they couldn't pay off these debts—and cable owners often knew this would happen—they would sell their systems to other operators, including Ralph. "They couldn't borrow at good rates," he says, "because they were engineers more than businessmen."

Ralph likes to compare McDowell's support of Comcast to the practices of A. P. Giannini, who founded the Bank of America and became the chief lender to the early movie studios; without him, the American film industry might never have developed. "Jack never turned me down for a loan," Ralph says, "and through his questions, he taught me how to make better presentations to other bankers. Without Jack McDowell, there wouldn't have been a Comcast."

When Ralph explained that he needed a longer loan, McDowell offered to help find an insurance company that might be willing to offer one. But it was Joe Roberts who somehow learned that a company called Home Life might be receptive. As Julian remembers it, when he and Ralph visited Home Life's Manhattan office to meet with the loan officer, an executive listened to their pitch and promptly threw them out. But they left him with a detailed plan that outlined all the financial facts of their Mississippi operation, and a few days later he invited them back to continue the conversation.

The result was a reasonably priced twelve-year arrangement that may have been the first long-term insurance loan in the history of cable. It began with two years of interest only, which Julian calls "the kind of thing you dream about." But there was a catch: Home Life insisted on warrants that amounted to 10 percent of Ralph's cable operation. "We probably gave up too much equity," says Julian, "but we were naïve in those days, and the terms they provided were unheard of in our business." This was just the beginning: well into the 1970s, when cable loans were especially hard to get, Comcast continued to borrow short-term from the Philadelphia National Bank and long-term from Home Life.

Bob Guibord, Home Life's loan officer, was ahead of his time in thinking of cable as a reliable utility, and he shared Ralph's trust in the promise of recurring monthly income. "Comcast was a quality company even then," says John Fabian, who worked for Guibord, "and because things went so well with them, we ended up specializing in cable loans."

Ralph, for whom all business is personal, had strong relationships with the company's early lenders. He and Guibord were on a ski trip together in Vail, Colorado, when Guibord went to the infirmary with a pain in his stomach. Following an X-ray, a despondent Guibord told Ralph that the pictures showed a big tumor that might be inoperable. That night, the two men sat together on a bench, wrapped up in their coats, and looked up at the stars in the clear Colorado sky as they discussed the meaning of life and the possibility of an afterlife. "It was the kind of conversation you don't often share with another man," says Ralph, who did his best to console his friend. When Guibord returned to New York, his doctor discovered that the X-rays had belonged to another patient: his death sentence was a false alarm.

Ralph's decision to buy Storecast didn't mean he had lost interest in cable. On the contrary: "My objective was to get as many systems as possible," he says. "I was determined to take a small business and turn it into a big one."

In 1966 he acquired a system in Sarasota, on Florida's Gulf Coast. Dan had been there on vacation and was taken with the area's natural beauty; years later, he and Gerri would retire there. He and Ralph both viewed Florida as a good place to expand because its population was certain to grow as retirees moved down from colder climates.

The modest Sarasota cable system had been owned by a TV repairman with a wooden leg; unable to climb poles, he had buried the wires underground. There were only a handful of subscribers, and potential buyers had to wonder whether that was because most televisions in town could receive NBC and CBS with a basic rooftop antenna; even ABC, which came in from Tampa, was sometimes available. Was there really a market for a service that gave customers better reception, but only half an additional network?

Because Ralph believed in the future of both Florida and cable, he was willing to take the risk. When he flew down to see the city, there were so many trees that he hired a plane to get a better view. "It was perfect for cable," he recalls. "The closer together the houses were, the happier I was."

At Jack McDowell's suggestion, Ralph had formed a partnership with the *Evening Bulletin*; its owner, Major McLean, had become interested in both Muzak and cable. The *Bulletin* put up the money and guaranteed the debt, and Ralph's company provided the management. After rebuilding the Sarasota system, the partners picked up franchises in Longboat Key and also in Venice, where the phone company, GTE, which had tried and failed to secure the franchise, refused to allow the newcomers to attach their cable wires to its poles.

Dan Aaron explained in his memoir that he was determined to

find an alternative to suing GTE, because "as a businessman, I was convinced that nothing good happens when one goes to court." Like several of Dan's early decisions, this one became a guiding principle for the company, which has always viewed litigation as a last resort. "Dan was terrified of the uncontrollable aspects of litigation," says Julian. "Entire years went by with virtually none, which was unusual, given the kinds of complex transactions we did." Instead of bringing a lawsuit, Dan solved the problem by burying the wires, which made Venice, Florida, the nation's first totally underground cable system.

But partnerships can lead to problems. In 1969 the owner of the *Bulletin* suddenly decided he no longer wanted to be in the cable business. "I still like Muzak," he told Ralph, "but I don't think cable is going anywhere." Ralph would have loved to buy him out, and his agreement with the *Bulletin* gave him the right of first refusal, but that posed an ethical dilemma, and he and Julian took the high road. "For our partners to get the highest possible price," Julian explains, "we had to make clear that we weren't a potential buyer, which would have had a chilling effect on the process. We hated to do that, but they had entrusted us to make the sale."

So Ralph reluctantly sold Sarasota and its sister properties to Storer Broadcasting. In the years to come, whenever Comcast applied for new franchises and its founder was asked by local officials if he had ever sold a cable system, a pained expression would cross his face as he mentioned Sarasota.

The sale was also difficult for Dan and Julian, although Julian was left with a compensating memory: on the weekend of the closing, Dan treated him to his first tennis lesson. Dan and Ralph were already avid players, and ever since the sale of Sarasota, Julian has been, too.

At the closing, after the papers were signed, Ralph asked George Storer, the eighty-year-old buyer, if he was aware that it would take ten years to earn back his investment. Ralph never forgot Storer's reply: "When my daddy started me in the communications business, he was looking out for the future. Although I won't see a return in my lifetime, I'm thinking years ahead for my own sons."

On his way out, Ralph said, "Mr. Storer, some day we'll be here again to buy back this system."

George Storer put his arm around Ralph and said, "I have never sold a property in my life, and the company that bears my name never will."

It was Ralph's prediction that came true. Twenty years later he repurchased the Sarasota system, along with many other Storer properties. But he didn't buy them from the family, because the company was no longer in their hands.

It was only a matter of time before the man who loved Muzak would invest in it. In 1968 Ralph acquired a Muzak franchise in Orlando, and over the next few years he would add many more. Orlando was Joe's idea, but it probably didn't take him long to persuade Ralph. As the brothers liked to remind each other in those more innocent days, when nobody found this sort of expression troubling, "These franchises are a license to steal."

Denver was next. Jerry Purcell, the manager, had started in the business by allowing his uncle to use his dorm-room phone number as the local Muzak contact; when Comcast bought the franchise, Purcell became, as he likes to say, the cat that came with the barn. He later moved to Bala Cynwyd to become president of Comcast's Muzak division, which was known as Comcast Sound Communications.

Other franchises followed: Dallas, Fort Worth, San Diego, Detroit, and many more. In some cities Comcast also acquired Muzak's competitors. Ralph and Julian bought dozens of systems, each of them producing recurring monthly income, and most of them with the help of Jack McDowell and his successors at the Philadelphia National Bank. As Ralph describes it, all he had to do was pick up the phone and say, "I've got one in Houston," and McDowell would reply, "Okay, I'll send you the papers." It was almost automatic: "We would draw up a ten-year projection, and thanks to Julian, years later we would be within two or three percent of our estimate." Ralph was especially interested in franchises that were undercapitalized or hadn't been run efficiently. Within a few years, Comcast, as a franchisee, was the country's second-largest owner of Muzak operations. Only the Muzak Corporation, the franchisor, owned more.

During the 1970s Muzak was an important contributor to Comcast's bottom line. But by the mid-1980s, cable operations had grown so dramatically that Storecast and Muzak, while not irrelevant, were, in the opinion of some executives, taking up more time and attention than they were worth. And yet as late as 1986, Ralph tried to buy the Muzak Corporation from Westinghouse, which had purchased it in 1981 as part of its acquisition of TelePrompTer, an important early cable operator. According to one account, some of the Westinghouse executives hadn't even realized that Muzak was included in the deal.

It would take a strong-minded newcomer to get Ralph to sell the Muzak franchises, and it took him years. "I'm the reason there's no Muzak," says Larry Smith, who came to Comcast in 1988 as a senior financial officer. Julian needed no convincing, but Ralph, who still maintains important friendships from his various Muzak connections, hated to sell the division.

Although the younger executives found Muzak embarrassing, and didn't believe it had a promising future, Ralph saw it as a reliable, income-producing business that helped other businesses be more productive. His reluctance to part with it may also have been influenced by the memory of Joe, who died of cancer in 1972 at the age of fifty-three. But when Brian agreed with Larry Smith that it was time to let it go, Ralph allowed himself to be persuaded. "I sold Muzak because Brian didn't like it," he says, calling the sale a regret, but not a mistake. And he certainly didn't act hastily: it took until 1994 before Comcast's Muzak holdings were sold to the Muzak Corporation for $35 million.

The sale of Muzak was one of the very few business disagreements that Ralph and Brian have ever had. Years later, Ralph was recalling the sale when Brian walked into the room. Unsure of the chronology, he turned to his son and asked, "When did we sell Muzak?"

"Not soon enough," said Brian.

• • •

In 1970 Ralph acquired Multiview Cable, in and around Harford County, Maryland, which included four unbuilt franchises. "Several companies were interested in us, and they were all pretty much in the same ballpark," says Virginia Pate, one of the owners. "But Dan Aaron was such a fine person, with the loveliest smile and the nicest manner—and we hadn't even met Ralph yet!"

This was a common response, and Ralph is proud of his personal relationships with other cable entrepreneurs: "They would tell me that if they ever sold the company, they would rather do business with me, because we were friends." On a number of occasions, cable owners made good on those promises.

A year later he made a much bigger acquisition: Westmoreland Cable near Pittsburgh, which included half a dozen systems and the right to build in nine other communities. (Although Pittsburgh was just fifteen miles away, the hilly terrain made it difficult to pick up two of its three stations.) Westmoreland's founder, Bud Wechsler, a CPA and part owner of a local radio station, became interested in cable because he believed that Americans who lived outside major cities should have access to the same broadcast entertainment as everyone else. Although his banker warned that he was risking his accounting practice by doing so, Wechsler invited his clients to invest in cable with him. "I thought I was doing them a favor," he says. He was right.

Rick Ricchuito, a longtime Comcast employee, grew up near Westmoreland's office on the relatively busy corner of 9th Street and Constitution Boulevard in New Kensington, Pennsylvania. In the front window were twelve cubes, each one housing a black-and-white television that was tuned to a different channel. "It was a living channel card," Ricchuito says, "and even without sound, there were always people standing there and watching." Channel 3 was devoted to local programming, including high school basketball, spelling bees, Chamber of Commerce events, and a sports call-in show that was hosted by the same two men for thirty years. Even today, in an era of advanced technologies that couldn't be imagined when the Westmoreland system began in 1962, part of cable's appeal is its unique ability to provide truly local programming.

When Bud Wechsler decided to sell the company, a cable broker brought in several potential buyers. Sam Buffone, Westmoreland's general manager, remembers the day Ralph, Dan, and Julian came to town to see the system. He drove them around for hours, winding in and out of little mill towns and stopping periodically so the visitors could knock on doors and ask residents how they felt about cable. "They were kicking the tires," says Buffone. "They made a nice impression and got a good feel for our business."

Buffone, in turn, had a good feel for Comcast. Of the companies who came to look at the Westmoreland operation, only the Comcast team followed up their visit with a letter of thanks, which Buffone still has. At the office, the visitors from Philadelphia talked to all the employees, not just the executives, and that, too, impressed Buffone. When Comcast bought the company, he continued as GM until he retired in 1985.

But the negotiations over the sale were long and arduous, and Ralph and Dan became so frustrated that Julian and Joe Roberts stepped in to complete the deal. "I did the financing," says Julian, "and Joe did the schmoozing."

"They were tough," says Bud Wechsler, "and I was skeptical. They weren't offering enough cash, and they wanted me to take their stock. But because they weren't yet a public company, it was hard to put a value on those shares. When I finally got them up to a number I felt was worthwhile, I went to my investors and said, 'If these guys work as hard for us as they've been working on me for the past six months, we should do very well.'"

Wechsler and his investors did extremely well, receiving $2.3 million in cash and 25,000 shares of Comcast. "The shares were a kind of throw-in," says Julian, "but within a few years they were so valuable that the cash became the throw-in." From his modest stake in Comcast, Sam Buffone was able to put seven children through college.

As a condition of the sale, Wechsler insisted on joining Comcast's board of directors for three years to represent his investors. Ralph agreed to one year, but Wechsler, whose sole concern was the shareholders, remained on the board for more than thirty. Later, when

Brian Roberts and Julian's daughter, Debbie Brodsky, came of age, they would start their cable careers in the Westmoreland system.

Westmoreland was significant for several reasons. Except for tiny Multiview, and after the unhappy loss of the Florida systems, this was Comcast's first serious expansion outside of Mississippi. It was also a very large purchase; the cash price alone was greater than Comcast's annual revenues. And Westmoreland was Ralph's first acquisition that wasn't financed by the Philadelphia National Bank. This time the lender was the Pittsburgh National Bank. Robert Todd, a well-dressed loan officer, came to Ralph's office one day and said, "Mr. Roberts, our bank has decided to make loans to cable companies, and we'd like to start with you." Ralph must have wondered whether one of his friends was playing a practical joke, but the offer was real.

Todd was one of the first lenders to appreciate the unique financial structure of the cable business. "Because of the nature of the assets of a CATV company," he wrote in a trade magazine in 1971, "the traditional balance sheet analysis approach produces little insight; instead, the nature of the financing required is more apparent in looking at the revenues and cash flows."

Although Ralph and especially Julian kept making that very point, most lenders just didn't get it. Neither did investors. It took quite a while before Wall Street appreciated how the cable business really worked—and how very profitable it could be.

Ralph, however, had no intention of waiting that long.

7

Going Public

Ralph Roberts, Dan Aaron, Julian Brodsky, and underwriter Keen Butcher

Growth is expensive in the cable business. As Comcast continued to expand, the company required increasingly large amounts of capital to buy existing systems and to build new ones. Ralph had always intended to go public, which would allow him to sell both equity and debt. "We did that as soon as we were big enough," he says. "There really wasn't a case against it."

Becoming a public company looked easy during the bullish years of the 1960s, but the initial public offering planned for the spring of 1969 didn't work out. Despite a valiant effort by the little Philadelphia brokerage house of Suplee Mosley, when stock prices fell, the offering was postponed for lack of interest, and then postponed again. Bill Morehouse, a lawyer at Wolf Block, remembers being at the printer with Ralph and Julian. As they rushed to get all the documents ready for the March 31 filing deadline, another lawyer walked in and said, "Eisenhower died! The SEC is closed tomorrow."

But the extra day made no difference. It would take three more years before Comcast became a publicly held company, on June 30, 1972. This time the lead underwriter was Butcher & Sherrerd, another small local firm—"the only one I could find," says Ralph.

Most of the preparatory work had been done during the first attempt, which included naming the company. In legal documents, a business in the process of going public is typically referred to as NewCo, a temporary designation that stands for "new company." In the early months of 1969, this NewCo consisted of three divisions: Storecast, the largest component, contributed 45 percent of the revenues; Cable Communications accounted for 33 percent; and the final 22 percent came from Sound Communications, which included the early Muzak franchises.

A week or so before the scheduled offering, the underwriter pointed out that the corporation still didn't have a name. Julian had suggested Roberts Communications, but Ralph wouldn't hear of it. He, Julian, and Dan tossed around a number of possibilities that included the word *cable*, but with Storecast and the Muzak franchises accounting for two-thirds of its revenues, this was clearly more than a cable company.

Ralph was looking for an invented word that could be registered as a trademark, like Xerox or Kodak or Muzak, because "a name that isn't an actual word is easier to remember and to advertise." He came up with Comcast as a contraction of *communications* and *broadcasting*. "It wasn't hard," he says. "I wrote a few names on a page and this one looked right to me."

"The three of us sat around in Ralph's office, scribbling and doodling," Julian recalls. "For a while, Ralph was concerned that Comcast might be confused with Comsat, the communications satellite company, but that wasn't a problem."

To Ralph, how the name looked was as important as how it sounded. For years he insisted that the letters be printed in heavy block type, so decision makers at financial institutions would think of Comcast as solid and established. "Ralph always looked to the future," said Dan, who recalled a moment in 1969 when the founder was calmly drawing up an organization chart for the year 2000. "Even when we were just getting started, when we were just a speck on the map, he expected that Comcast would someday be the General Motors of the cable industry," he wrote, "and everything he did was to prepare for that day. He spent untold hours on the name, the logo, and the color of the design."

"When we went public," says Brian, who was thirteen at the time, "part of Ralph's and Julian's genius was to create the view that we intended to be bigger than we were. That was our hook for investors." It may also explain why, only five years after going public, Comcast took a surprising step for a small, capital-intensive company: it started paying shareholders a dividend, a practice that lasted until 1999. (The dividend was reinstated in 2008.)

Even on the second attempt, attracting investors was tougher than anyone expected. Ralph, Dan, and Julian met with potential shareholders in Boston, New York, and Philadelphia, but there was little enthusiasm for, or understanding of, cable television in big cities, where the industry was virtually unknown and where most of the money was. And it certainly didn't help that Irving Kahn of Tele-PrompTer, a well-known cable entrepreneur, had recently gone to jail for bribing civic officials in a Pennsylvania franchise renewal bid, then lying about it. Joe Castle, who later joined the Comcast board, handled the IPO for Butcher & Sherrerd. "The potential growth of cable excited me," he said, "but the offering was a disaster."

The IPO, which consisted of 430,000 shares at $7, ran into problems right away. The company had planned to issue 550,000 shares at $10, but as the deadline approached, these numbers seemed overly optimistic. Ralph recalls that just before the IPO, a negative analysis of the cable industry appeared in *Barron's*, the influential investors' weekly. The article, with the awkward headline, "Everything Isn't Coming Up Rose-Colored for Cable Television," was published in the July 10 issue, and Comcast wasn't even mentioned. The writer pointed out that expanding into big-city markets would be expensive, and that for the industry to succeed, it had to come up with new and different programming. "Cable operators must evolve from their historic function as a signal service," he noted, "if for no other reason than areas that need this service are shrinking." Although he was right on all counts, the industry's entrepreneurs were able to overcome these obstacles.

As soon as Comcast began trading, the share price dropped to $5.50. And in a bear market that grew worse with the 1973 oil crisis, it continued falling for more than two years. By the end of 1974, shares had plunged as low as 75¢, despite the fact that the company's earnings had grown in every successive quarter, and that Comcast had $2 per share in cash—in addition, of course, to other assets and liabilities. Julian likes to say that for a while, he, Dan, and Ralph faced a decision after work every day: Were they better off buying another share of Comcast, or, for the same price, enjoying a beer? In those days, he jokes, "We drank a lot of beer. We should have been buying stock like crazy."

Julian doesn't recall that anyone gave him a hard time about the price of the shares, but Ralph had a different experience—or feared that he might: "I walked around town with my coat up around my face, hoping nobody would see me. But I knew that our business was good, even if the stock market said cable was a dumb idea."

Both men have occasionally been asked why, given their strong belief in the future of cable, they didn't buy a lot of shares, either for themselves or for the company, when sellers were practically giving them away. But Comcast carried a fair amount of long-term debt, and its leaders were far from wealthy. Besides, says Julian, "when prices are falling all around you, it doesn't put you in much of a buying mood."

Vene Gutman, one of the original investors in the Tupelo franchise, remembers getting a call from Ralph in 1974. The underwriters had ten thousand shares available at a dollar; did Gutman want them? Unfortunately, says Gutman, he didn't have ten thousand dollars.

Ralph and his colleagues were also facing a legal restriction. For close to a year, starting in the spring of 1974, Ralph considered buying Vikoa, a cable company in New York whose purchase was being encouraged by its CEO and by John Rigas, a Vikoa director who had started his own cable company, Adelphia. During this period, which coincided with the lowest share prices in Comcast's history, the company's lawyers ruled that Comcast insiders could neither buy nor sell shares until the Vikoa issue was resolved.

In the end, taking Julian's advice, Ralph decided against buying the company. "We wanted it badly," says Julian, "but I had questions about the quality of the numbers, the company's undisclosed liabilities, and an ongoing IRS examination that could have produced a large tax bill." Julian was proved right when Vikoa, a larger operator than Comcast, was taken over by its creditors and broken up.

Ralph made three key decisions around the time of the IPO, and all of them reflected his prudence. Knowing that he would need to borrow large sums of money again and again, his first concern was to protect the mother ship. Instead of having the parent company take out loans, he insisted that each cable system would be self-sufficient, so that if it failed, Comcast's other systems wouldn't be affected. Because the only collateral he could offer was the system itself, which often wasn't even built yet, this type of borrowing, known as project financing, usually meant higher interest rates. But Ralph didn't mind, because the security afforded by this arrangement was priceless— even if, as things turned out, the extra layer of protection proved to be unnecessary. "It wasn't sophisticated," says Julian, who was always more comfortable with risk. "It was a little like putting your money in different envelopes to pay the bills." But Ralph's goal was to sleep at night, and he always did.

Project financing was a strong incentive for financial discipline. It was one thing for Ralph to visit a system and talk to the GM about the need to repay the loan that the company had taken out to build the plant. But when he showed up with the loan officer from the bank, as he occasionally did, their joint appearance was a dramatic reminder that both the interest and the principal for that loan had to come from the system's revenues.

Ralph's second decision, which he later came to regret, was to rely much more on equity than on debt to pay for acquisitions. On several major deals in the years ahead, he would use Comcast shares as currency to avoid taking out additional loans. Cable entrepreneurs who borrowed more than Ralph did—and just about all of them did—generally made more money, although some of them were unable to repay their loans. "I was timid," he says. "As enthusiastic as I was, I wasn't nearly enthusiastic enough."

Julian urged him repeatedly to borrow more, and Ralph describes this as their most serious disagreement. "Julian was right," he says. "If we hadn't given up so much of our stock, we could have paid our debts and still kept the company." As a financial man, Julian was more comfortable with leverage, but what really bothers Ralph is the deeper meaning of their dispute: "He was even more optimistic than I was."

There's an adage that an investor can either eat well or sleep well. Ralph chose to sleep well, and it's not as if he missed any meals. The boy whose family had lost its wealth during the 1930s because his father had relied too heavily on debt wasn't about to risk his company's economic future—or his children's—by making a similar mistake.

Ralph's third and most important decision was his refusal to allow the public offering to jeopardize his control of the company. "I was told this would have a depressing effect on our stock price," he says, "but I knew it was possible and I was determined to do it."

So against the advice of the underwriters but with the support of the lawyers at Wolf Block, Comcast went public with two classes of stock: a common stock, with one vote per share, that would be offered to the public; and a second class of "B" shares, known as super-voting stock, which entitled their owner to three votes per share. The Class B shares have never traded: Ralph kept them and eventually passed them on to Brian. As the years passed and more public shares were issued, the number of votes for each share of Class B stock was increased—first to seven votes, and later to fifteen. With each adjustment, Ralph and Julian had to get permission from the public stockholders, who agreed to the company's requests. "You don't have to vote for this," Julian would tell fund managers, "but we think it will be good for you, good for the company, and good for everybody, as long as you have faith in the Class B shareholder. And if you don't, why are you here?"

After the second increase, Comcast began issuing stock with no voting rights at all, which put the issue to rest. There the matter remained until the 2002 merger with AT&T Broadband. Then, with Brian's encouragement, Ralph reluctantly agreed to an arrangement that gave the family less than 50 percent of the votes. And he made that compromise only because it was clear that if he didn't, the deal might fall apart.

Over time, the B shares have given Comcast a level of flexibility that most publicly held corporations don't have: the company has never been forced to focus on the short term for fear that a bad quarter or two could drive down the stock price and make it vulnerable to a takeover. Shares of Comcast have taken any number of hits over the years, but even in 1974, when they were selling for under a dollar, the company was protected from potential raiders. "Owning a control stock allows you to make the right long-term decisions if you have the stomach for it," says Brian, "and my father always had the stomach."

Because supervoting shares are not the "one share, one vote" model preferred by some who evaluate corporate governance structures, it helped that Comcast had established this two-tiered structure from the very start. A number of media, retail, and technology companies have issued two classes of stock, but only a handful have been organized that way all along. As Julian has often pointed out, nobody ever bought a share of Comcast under any other arrangement. "There's one thing you should keep in your wallet," he once told Brian, "and that's a small photo of a B share certificate. That's your legacy from your father."

The supervoting stock may have ensured Comcast's very survival; virtually every cable company whose founder didn't retain high voting shares was acquired long ago. And the shareholders have done extremely well over the years. Even if they missed the bargain prices of 1974, investors who were prescient or fortunate enough to buy

Comcast shares when they first started trading, and patient enough to hold them for the long term, have realized enormous profits. In 2002 *Money* magazine published a survey of U.S. stocks: out of thousands of American companies that had gone public in the previous thirty years, only four—Southwest Airlines, Wal-Mart, Walgreens, and Intel—had outperformed Comcast. An investor who bought a thousand shares in 1972 at the IPO price of $7 would have made out rather nicely: by the end of 2011, after stock splits and the reinvestment of dividends, that $7,000 investment would have been worth nearly $3.4 million.

In the decades since the IPO, the man with the controlling vote has not only provided tens of thousands of jobs; he has also enriched a great many investors. But what really makes him proud is that gains from Comcast shares have made it possible for many young people to afford a college education. And if most of them have never heard of Ralph Roberts, he doesn't mind at all.

8

Bala Days

Ralph Roberts, Dan Aaron, and Julian Brodsky

After Ralph acquired his first cable system in 1963, the corporate office remained in the same modest location for more than twenty-five years; the only change was a move in 1966 from the crowded eleventh floor down to the second. The GSB Building in Bala Cynwyd still stands at the intersection of Belmont and City Line Avenues, just a few feet beyond the western edge of Philadelphia. The concrete structure is long and narrow, with walls angling outward from the ends toward the middle, which created some awkward spaces internally. Inside, both the walls and the filing cabinets were a mustard yellow, a shade that Tom Nathan remembers as being closer to French's than Gulden's. Most of the furniture had previously belonged to an oil company in the same building.

On the twelfth and highest floor was an upscale restaurant called

Williamson, which everyone called Williamson's. It catered to an older, conservative crowd, offered a nice view of the city, and served snapper soup, a classic Philadelphia delicacy made from turtle meat and topped with sherry. Williamson's was certainly convenient, even if, in Tom Nathan's view, taste had been banned from the menu. Dan had lunch there every day, and it was a popular spot to take guests and a convenient place for holiday parties and other corporate events.

For a New Yorker like Nathan, who was accustomed to a variety of restaurants on every block, the scarcity of eating options in the immediate neighborhood took some getting used to. Williamson's was bland and expensive, and the coffee shop on the ground floor was overpriced, so every day at lunch he would wander over to the shopping center across the street. There had to be *some* place where a person could enjoy a decent meal at a fair price, but if there was, he never found it.

The executives worked in modest offices, and the support staff sat together in open areas, which contributed to the family atmosphere of the early years. The décor was simple and utilitarian. "Tacky is too strong a word," says designer Karen Daroff, but others were less kind. When Rosemarie Teta arrived for her job interview, she thought it was the ugliest place she had ever seen. "It was clear that the company's money was in the bank," she says, "rather than on the walls." Anna Hillman had a similar reaction: "Some people liked the tackiness, but I wasn't one of them. But that didn't stop me from going to work there."

Still, frugality had its limits, at least for Ralph. When Abe Patlove, one of the earliest employees, asked for a work table, Julian told him to pick up a plain one with metal legs. One afternoon, when Ralph stepped into Patlove's office, he said, "Where did you get *that*?" A few days later he replaced the offending item with a walnut credenza.

But that was an exception. When Julian arrived in 1963 with his folding card table, he was, without intending to, establishing a style that inspired a kind of reverse snobbery among employees. Patty Thorell remembers getting to the conference room early for meetings so she could claim a chair whose wheels weren't falling off. "We rather enjoyed bringing bankers and investors to see our Spartan way of life," said Stanley Wang. "We took pride in showing that we were careful with our money." Paul Mejean, an investment banker at Shearson, was among the visitors who got the message: "Linoleum floors, linoleum desks, the whole place was linoleum!"

On Mike Tallent's first visit to Bala in the mid-1980s, he was greeted by a simple goldfish bowl with one lonely inhabitant, and a reception desk that looked like it was acquired at a foreclosure sale. Tallent, a financial man from Storer Communications who had visited many other companies, was immediately impressed: "It was the least ostentatious headquarters I had ever seen. I understood why Comcast was buying Storer, rather than the other way around. These guys knew how to run a business."

"Ralph and his people were tough businessmen," says Ted Turner, who used to visit the various cable operators to ask them to carry his channels, and who once got down on the floor in Ralph's office and bowed to him in a dramatic appeal to get Comcast to carry every Turner channel on each of its systems. Turner didn't find Comcast's offices especially modest. "The whole industry was tough," he says. "Nobody had any money. All we had were dreams."

Although new employees were sometimes dismayed by the appearance of their surroundings, they liked their colleagues and appreciated the culture. John Ruth was struck by the friendliness of the top executives: "They made your work life feel as comfortable as your home life, and treated new people the same as the higher-ups." Rosemarie Teta expected to stay a year, but that year stretched into decades. They may be cheap, she remembers thinking, but they treat us well and the work is never boring.

Employees in the field had similar reactions. Gary Shinn from the Meadowlands office in New Jersey recalls that at corporate managers' meetings, the GMs were always reminded to thank the employees and to check on their well-being. "And after those meetings," he says, "we'd see changes that showed our comments were being heard, that we were a real part of the company. The message from corporate was always the same: people, people, people, people, people! They couldn't stress it enough."

In 1978 Lucille Fital began working as the receptionist. Her desk was next to the ceramic stand that held the goldfish bowl, which was often the first thing a visitor noticed, along with those yellow walls and the multihued, earth-toned, coffee-stained carpet. Fital sat off to the side, facing the other desks, so she could see who was there and whether she should pick up their calls. By then the corporate office housed some two dozen employees, with Muzak on another floor and Storecast in midtown Manhattan.

When the mailman arrived, he'd drop the day's load on Fital's desk for her to sort and deliver. She also helped Ann Gardner, Ralph's longtime assistant, with tasks she could handle from her desk. Her other jobs ranged from setting up meetings and stocking the supply room to typing, filing, and running errands. In 1988 she became Brian's executive assistant, and more than twenty years later, she still is. "In the old days we were all generalists," says Ed Rothong, who arrived in 1984 to join the company's tiny tax department. "Everybody was chief cook and bottle washer."

Fital, who had come to Comcast with no secretarial skills, was trained by Ann Gardner, who was a major force in the company's early years. "Ann held the office together," says Julian. A widow with five children, Mrs. Gardner, as she was known, had started working for Ralph at Pioneer and came with him when he moved to Bala Cynwyd to set up shop as an entrepreneur. Among other jobs, she ran his cologne business after his distribution contract with Hickok expired. But Ralph knew it was time to sell his fragrance line, because to keep it would have required building up a separate sales force. "It broke my heart," he says, "but I got a good price."

Mrs. Gardner was the model of discretion. "She knew everything that went on in the Roberts family," says Joan French, who came to Comcast because of Mrs. Gardner, and would later work for Julian before becoming Ralph's assistant, "but she never said a word to anyone. She was the executive assistant that all of us aspired to be."

Ann Gardner was discreet, but she was also assertive. When

women first started wearing pantsuits, Ralph, who has always favored a conservative dress code, suggested to her in the nicest possible way that her outfit was a little casual for the office. "Unless you're going to pay for my clothes," she told him, "I'll wear what I want." Years later, after the company had moved to 1500 Market Street, where smoking was not allowed, Ralph walked by her desk and said, "Ann, you're not supposed to smoke in the building." To which Mrs. Gardner replied, "When somebody comes by and tells me to stop smoking, I'll stop." After thirty years of working together, the lines of authority had become blurred.

It wasn't only pantsuits that Ralph didn't care for. Although he is tolerant and easygoing about most things, he was vigilant about the corporate dress code. Deeply concerned about the company's image, he hated seeing men in their shirtsleeves; the only thing he liked less were men in vests, who reminded him of pool players. (For his sixty-fifth birthday party, the men all showed up in plastic, candy-striped vests.) "We set a certain tone here," he would say, "and it's symbolized by wearing a jacket and tie." Long after most of corporate America had adopted a more casual attitude, especially on Fridays, Ralph held firm. "This is a business," he would say, "and I'm not going along with any fads. A jacket and tie marks you as a professional." If you wouldn't wear it at IBM, he didn't want to see it at Comcast. Not until 2008, when the company moved to its sparkling new headquarters, did Ralph mellow a little. "I still don't take my jacket off in the office," he says, "but I no longer worry about other people."

Everyone who worked for Comcast in the Bala days remembers a warm and friendly environment. Grace Sapinosa, Stanley Wang's assistant, recalls a time when the corporate workforce was small enough that anyone who celebrated a birthday would be given a cake—usually one that she had baked. Sapinosa also prepared hearty lunches for the quarterly board meetings, which featured Italian dishes like minestrone soup, pasta with meatballs, veal scaloppine, and chicken cacciatore, with homemade biscotti or Italian rum cake for dessert. There was no kitchen at the Bala office; she would cook the meals at home and heat them up later in a microwave. This was part of a cozy feeling in Bala that reminded her of the big Italian family in which she grew up.

Nobody asked Sapinosa to provide these meals. "I just started cooking," she says, "and when people liked it, I kept doing it. They even started requesting certain dishes that I had made for a previous meeting. They shared stories about their families with me, and asked about mine. You can't put a price tag on something like that." These lunches were part of a frugal operation where the chef doubled as the recording secretary. Later, when the company moved downtown and Sapinosa had a fully equipped kitchen to work in, the meals became more elaborate. But even then, she makes clear, they were far less expensive than a catered meal.

"The trick," Ralph once said, "is to make everyone feel involved." But it wasn't a trick. Dan and Julian were so deeply immersed in the company, and Ralph was so comfortable giving them power and visibility, that employees and outsiders alike often thought of the leadership as a three-man team of equals. "I feel secure," Ralph says, "and when you feel secure, you can afford to let other people have the credit."

For as long as anyone can remember, the three of them were known within the company, and sometimes beyond, as The Boys, although not in front of Ralph, who didn't like the phrase. The striking thing was how effectively they worked together. "They weren't fighting for the limelight," says Debbie Brodsky, "and when they came together, their different perspectives made them unbeatable."

As Ralph describes the arrangement in his self-effacing way, "We had one guy who knew the business and how to make it work, another who knew how to raise the money, and a third person who sat in the middle and enjoyed it." It was Dan who compared them to three men working together to drive a car, with Julian pressing the gas pedal to the floor, Dan with his foot on the brake, and a smiling Ralph with his hands on the steering wheel. "Normally, the financial guy is Dr. No," says Julian, "but Dan and I reversed roles."

But not always, and especially not early on. "For years," says

Brian, "on every major opportunity we considered, Julian said no. He was doing what a CFO should do, which is to remain cautious and conservative. That's why we were outbid on any number of deals. He later became more aggressive, but early on, Ralph was the one with his foot on the gas."

Julian wasn't against expanding, but he resisted potential acquisitions unless the price was too good to pass up. It has been said, only partly in jest, that TCI, for years the nation's largest cable company, grew into that position by acquiring all the systems Comcast declined to buy. Julian established an important financial discipline, although Ralph was often willing to pay more, and sometimes overruled him. When Comcast refused to meet the asking price of an attractive franchise or acquisition, Julian would console his colleagues by saying, "Life is long," which meant that this particular system might well be available in the future. And often it was.

Although Dan was cautious by nature, there was a practical reason for his reticence. It was easy enough to buy systems, if not always to finance them, but as operators, Dan and his staff knew what it meant to actually build them and run them. It took time and effort and money, and you also had to explain and justify your business to potential customers who didn't see the point of paying for television. "It was complicated," Dan said. "We had to buy electronic equipment and install it in the same general part of a pole as the electric company and the phone company, and then we had to keep it going. It's a fairly technical business, and it took time to control all those factors."

No matter who was stepping on what pedal, Ralph appreciated and respected his fellow drivers. He was happy to have them feel like co-founders, and to be the face of Comcast on various occasions. Dan and Julian soon became stars in the cable industry, and Ralph was proud of their success.

Ralph made the big decisions and resolved arguments, but at meetings he often held back, listening to other voices and encouraging a lively debate as he doodled the faces of those around the table or drew up organization charts for a distant future that was visible only to him. He did much of his talking at home, after dinner, when he and Brian would chat as Ralph sketched out plans on yellow pads of paper with his silver Cross mechanical pencil.

Sometimes he seemed to have a direct pipeline to the future. Bern Gallagher, the company's treasurer, once tried to imagine what would happen if he somehow came to work with tomorrow's newspaper. Dan would refuse to believe it, Julian would dismiss it as a fantasy, but Ralph would turn to the stock listings and put all his money in the company that had shown the biggest gain. It's not only that he could see the future; it's that he was willing to act on what he saw. Sometimes he could explain his thinking in rational terms, but he often relied on what his colleagues came to call Ralph's golden gut. "I was willing to buy systems for up to ten times cash flow," he says, "but I thought the cable business was so good that sometimes I broke that rule. As I scoured the country looking for properties, I turned down many systems because they were too expensive, or I didn't see enough potential for growth. My only regret is that I bought a lot of franchises for stock, diluting us needlessly against Julian's advice. But I never worried about money, because I knew we could pay our debts."

His long-term vision was invariably a sunny one. Not everyone in the industry agreed that buying more cable systems was *always* the best strategy, especially when money was tight, regulations were restrictive, or prices had soared to unprecedented heights. But by the late 1970s, Ralph had become relentless in his thirst for more growth, and he continued to avoid selling cable properties—or anything else.

In the early years, he and his colleagues moved more slowly. "We were realistic," says Julian. "We didn't kid ourselves or act on hunches." When they worked through a projection, they were confident of hitting their numbers. An acquisition might appear risky, but if they thought it through carefully enough, they could pretty much count on its working out.

"The three of them were a great team," says Glenn Jones, an early cable entrepreneur. "They were a good composite of talents, and because they talked to each other all the time, their knowledge grew like a crystal. They learned from every deal, and the company retained that knowledge because they stayed together so long. It was as if their minds were wired together."

Paul Kagan, a media analyst who has followed cable companies since the early 1970s, met Ralph and his colleagues soon after Comcast went public. "It was clear that all three of them had vision," he says, "but they also had a good grip on their finances." In the mid-1980s, long before most people on Wall Street had even heard of the company, Kagan called Comcast "a little blue chip." Reading that, Ralph was in heaven.

Although each of them had his own field of expertise, they felt free to wander into other areas, including each other's, without any turf battles. Julian remembers being "all over operations," while Dan was fascinated by investment banking and Ralph kept an eye on everything. They operated with virtually no bureaucracy or internal politics. "We didn't plan it that way," says Julian. "It's just how things happened."

From the start, employees were treated like grown-ups. Lawyers, whether inside the company or outside, were invited to see themselves as business partners. System managers were encouraged to act entrepreneurially. Accountants were more than scorekeepers; they were expected to understand the business and to offer suggestions.

For some employees, this empowerment came as a surprise—and not always a welcome one. Frank Hayden, an accountant, had just left an old-time manufacturing company with well-established policies and procedures, and was accustomed to a structured environment with a rule book to fall back on. But even in the mid-1980s, Comcast seemed to be making up the rules as it went along. For the first couple of months, he would come home and ask his wife, "What have I done?" Hayden had been in his previous job for thirteen years. "If I stay here less than a year," he told her, "I'll never get another job. But I need a workplace that's not as nuts as this one." He gradually became used to the pace, and then came to enjoy it. "For an accountant to be in an exciting job," he says, "took some getting used to."

But the beginning was slow. Abe Patlove, who was hired in the early 1970s to help find new franchises and acquire existing systems, was exasperated by the long and sometimes arduous process of reaching a decision. Patlove, the first senior-level employee to arrive after The Boys, was chagrined to find that a three-to-one vote didn't resolve anything. "I made recommendations on acquisitions," he said, "and after we pulled every one of them apart in every conceivable way, they wanted unanimity. They had hired me for something they weren't willing to do." Patlove grew so impatient that he left the company, although he returned five years later. "And during the time I was away," he said, still feeling that old frustration, "they acquired Flint—and that's all!" They also added Paducah, Kentucky, but Patlove was essentially correct.

Many years later, Dan expressed some regrets about his earlier caution. "I think we should have applied for franchises that we might have been able to get," he wrote. "I was more conservative than my brethren." True, but there's another way to see it. In the early 1970s, Comcast was so small and fragile that a single wrong decision might have had disastrous consequences.

There was a fair amount of shouting in the Bala office, especially when Dan and Julian went at it. Most of it came from Julian, whose voice was loud to begin with. The two of them were close, but they clashed regularly. "Dan wanted to spend money," Ralph recalls, "and Julian was tight. In operations, I followed Dan." They were both strong men who wanted what was best for the company, but deciding how to get there was often a struggle. Their conflicts were predictable, because operations and finance are natural enemies, the corporate equivalent of the mongoose and the snake. Bob Fleisher, Ralph's brother-in-law, would come into the office and greet Dan and Julian by saying, "Hello, Wires. Hello, Numbers."

Ralph often said little during their arguments and didn't mind the verbal warfare that swirled around him. "I took the time to listen because I respected their opinions," he says. "I was the referee, but I also had my own views, based on what they thought and what I knew. As long as the answer came out right, I didn't care who ranted and raved."

These frank arguments helped create and maintain one of Comcast's greatest achievements: a corporate culture with little politics or infighting. With everything out on the table, there was no need for whisper campaigns or secret alliances. "It was all very frank," says Tom Baxter, who arrived in 1985 and headed the cable division in the 1990s, "but people could deal with it because it was so open. The only one who held back was Ralph, because he didn't want to stifle debate." Ralph wanted to hear the best arguments, and although it suited his personality to play a more reserved role, it also took patience and restraint.

He often insisted on unanimity, and sometimes the three of them would talk for hours before reaching a consensus. "The marvelous thing about Ralph," says Julian, "is that Dan and I had to agree on strategy and management decisions before he would let them happen." From time to time Ralph would terminate the discussion with an executive decision, but some conversations lasted all day. "They had such different temperaments," Stanley Wang said, "and such different outlooks on life that it was amazing *any* decisions got made. Julian would yell, Dan would get emotional, and Ralph would sit there, cool as a cucumber. He knew how to meld diverse views into a common position they could all accept."

Because the walls were thin and space was tight, everybody in the office was aware of these arguments. But as heated as they sometimes became, they were never personal. More than one new arrival was shocked at the tone and volume of a disagreement, and equally shocked when the meeting ended and Julian turned to Dan and said, "So, where shall we go for lunch?"

They all worked hard and they often worked late—especially Julian, who also arrived early, and who for thirty years was almost never home for dinner. "I loved what I was doing," he says, "but there was a price to pay." The final line of his retirement speech at the company's 2004 management conference brought tears to many eyes. "Lois," he said, "I'm coming home!"

In 1988, when the company was twenty-five years old (if you start counting in 1963, when Ralph bought the Tupelo franchise), he and Suzanne invited Dan and Gerri, and Julian and Lois, to their home for a celebratory dinner. At the end of the evening, Ralph presented each of the wives with a dozen roses and thanked them for allowing their husbands to devote so much time and energy to Comcast.

Bala employees like to reminisce about the spirit of the office in the early years. "It had the feel of a small business," Abe Patlove recalled. "My wife used to yell at me because on a Saturday morning or a Sunday afternoon, I'd run over there for a while." When executives returned to Philadelphia after a business trip, they'd often drop in on their way home, even at night.

But the warm environment did not imply a lack of efficiency. People worked hard and were generally well organized. When you attended a meeting, the agenda was clearly defined. Comcast may have felt like home, but it was a household that ran smoothly.

Sometimes the corporate family included members of the next generation. Alison Aaron worked as an intern for Tom Nathan. Debbie Brodsky, currently a vice president in the cable division, used to come in on Saturdays to help out; so did Abe Patlove's daughters, Debbie and Michelle, and their brother, Mark, who later became an installer in Lower Merion. And so did Brian Roberts, who was sometimes joined by one of his brothers.

In those days, instead of billing customers each month, the company would send out coupon booklets that were similar to those once used by mortgage companies. These were produced on a machine known as the Cummins Perforator, which was so easy to operate that a child could do it, and Comcast kids often did. They'd punch in an amount, insert a coupon book, pull a lever, and the perforator would punch holes in the coupons that told customers how much to pay. The youngsters who prepared these books were compensated, but just barely. "I was Brian's paymaster," Julian recalls, "and I would give him a quarter. After several weeks he began to question the rate. So, as we do with all things, we settled."

There was a feeling around the office that work should be fun, and because cable was still fairly new, there was also room for creativity.

This was a friendlier industry than most, in part because the various cable companies were not generally competitors; they operated in different communities. (Competition from satellite and phone companies was still years away.) Although life at Comcast was not without its pressures, especially when it came to meeting your budget, most people were happy and the corporate office experienced very little turnover. Treasurer Bern Gallagher stayed twelve years and wishes he had stayed for twelve more. "Leaving Comcast was the worst decision of my life," he says. "These were great people to be around—bright, ethical, fearless, smart, caring, and fun."

Important decisions were made in the late afternoon, when The Boys would meet to talk things over. On Fridays some of their colleagues would join them, often in Ralph's office after work, when the conversation might be fortified with fat, greasy cheesesteaks from Mama's, the local pizza shop. Ralph, Julian, and Dan, along with Patlove, Gallagher, and later Brian, and sometimes one or two others, would sit around and discuss the state of the company. What sometimes felt like a social occasion was really a business meeting without a formal agenda. The Friday sessions would end with Julian telling the financial employees, "Okay, I'll see you tomorrow." He worked Saturday mornings and expected his people to join him.

He would show up around nine, wearing his tennis clothes. In this more relaxed setting, he'd spend a little time with each member of his team. He made sure to ask what everyone wanted for lunch, and when noon rolled around he'd hand one of the employees fifty dollars and send him out to pick up the food at Mama's. The group would gather at the surprisingly elegant African rosewood table in the conference room where, before leaving for his weekly tennis game, Julian would do battle with, and invariably prevail over, a mammoth cheesesteak known as the Belly Buster.

He was a legendary and enthusiastic eater. "Everything I've ever learned of value," he once told a colleague, "has been over red wine and red meat." He informed a group of friends who were sitting down to a lobster dinner that their mission was to leave behind "nothing but a pile of fine red dust not fit for soup." He maintained that a meal, or at least a hearty snack or a decent sandwich, could make even the most tedious agenda tolerable.

Debbie Brodsky, who was facing a familiar problem at Comcast, once asked her father how he decided between two meetings that were scheduled at the same time. "That's easy," Julian told her. "I find out what they're serving."

When Steve Backstrom arrived in 1981 to become the company's first full-time tax man, he went to dinner with several Comcasters and sat between Ralph and Julian. He noticed that Ralph, after eating his fill, discreetly pushed his plate over to Julian. When Ralph saw that Backstrom had witnessed the transaction, he said, "Oh, that's part of the deal. I've been feeding him for years."

9

Father Figure

Ralph Roberts

"One of my father's great skills," says Brian, "was to make it all look easy. But this was hard stuff. To build a big public corporation with all those pressures and never make a serious mistake? That's a real achievement."

The first step in making Comcast successful was knowing what business to be in—and to stay in. "I could see from the beginning that Ralph was there for the long term," says Ted Turner. "He loved the business, and he struck me as a solid citizen who would still be there when they played the last song."

The second step was picking the right people, especially Dan and Julian at the very beginning—and giving them plenty of running room. They felt that Comcast was their company, too, and to a considerable extent it was. Ralph gave them equity early on, and while it wasn't a large stake, it ended up being worth millions. Although his empowerment of other people and his gentle, soft-spoken style sometimes gave the impression that he was just another member of the leadership team, he was always in charge, even when others were more visible. "You didn't always see Ralph or hear him," says Dave Breidinger, who arrived in 1980 to run a system in Maryland, "but you knew he was in control."

He didn't view leadership as being all that complicated, and when it was, he made it look easy. He ran Comcast from various places within himself—his head, his heart, his gut, and especially his personality, which was relaxed, collaborative, and generous on the surface, with a tough and more aggressive layer hidden underneath. The opposite of a micromanager, he set the vision and the overall policy, which his top deputies debated, communicated, and put into practice with little or no interference from above.

A benevolent boss, he took no pleasure in conveying bad news, and rarely did; those decisions were usually communicated by others. "Ralph would tell you what you were doing right," recalls Glenn Colvin, "and Dan and Julian would tell you if something was wrong, even when you knew the message was coming from Ralph."

Dan Aaron described Ralph as the ultimate entrepreneur, who mulled over his strategy endlessly until it was time to strike: "Once he goes into action, sparks fly. When he attains his goal, he modestly withdraws and lets others take the credit."

The executives appreciated his light touch. "You'd go to Ralph for the final approval," says Dick McCaffery, "and he always had something positive to add. When I was concluding a deal for the company, he would bring up some point I hadn't thought of in a way that made me feel it was coming from a friend."

Even when Ralph was angry, he never raised his voice. And in the rare cases when he did show anger, it seemed more like disappointment. He once called Bob Pick to his office, where Pick was shocked to see his displeasure. Pick had been diagnosed with a tumor in his chest, and had told Brian and his boss, Larry Smith, that he would be out of the office for a few weeks. But he hadn't told Ralph, who was angry—not because he was out of the loop, but because he had missed an opportunity to be helpful. "Who's taking care of you?" he demanded. "I could have helped you with doctors!" The operation went well, the tumor was benign, and when the phone rang the next morning, the woozy patient picked it up. It was Ralph, calling to check on him. "My parents hadn't even called yet," says Pick, "but Ralph kept trying until I answered the phone."

"He's never going to put you down," says Brian. "He believes everyone is entitled to youthful enthusiasm and occasional mistakes." At the end of a management conference, Tom Baxter previewed several new TV commercials for the attendees, and the silence in the room made clear that they were not well received. "I won't be using them," Baxter told Ralph a few days later. "They were expensive, but although our focus groups liked them, they weren't really *moved* by these spots. I realized over the weekend that great advertising moves people."

"In that case," said Ralph, "it was worth it."

Baxter had been feeling guilty for spending serious money on ads that would never be aired. "I remember that as a great Ralph moment," he says. "Instead of berating me, he helped me get better. At other companies they might have yelled at me, but Ralph knew I would improve, and I don't think I ever brought him another bad commercial."

As Brian puts it, "He nurtures, he mentors, and he coaches, but he never uses any of those words. He just does those things instinctively."

Although Ralph felt no need to be out front, and didn't feel drawn to the podium, the lectern, or the head table, he was always there. Even before Woody Allen's famous quip that 80 percent of success was showing up, Ralph had apparently come to a similar conclusion. Muzak manager John Stoddard recalls that Ralph used to travel all the way to San Diego, where Comcast owned no cable properties, to meet with him about the local Muzak budget.

On a Saturday night in December 1990, the Garden State Cable system held its first annual holiday party in Voorhees, New Jersey. The system was owned by a partnership of three companies, including Comcast, and executives from all three were invited. It was a cold, rainy evening with predictions of freezing roads later that night, and nobody from Philadelphia was expected. Ralph lived more than an hour away, and he was seventy, but he drove there alone and showed up early. "Do you believe Ralph Roberts is here?" people asked one another. It was something they would remember.

Dan and Julian were the same way. In the early days of cable, when a new system was built, it was customary to throw an opening party for local VIPs. When Bill Goetz, who ran the Trenton office, organized parties for three New Jersey systems, Ralph, Dan, and Julian attended each one. "For a young manager like me," Goetz says, "it was a big deal to have the top three executives of the company show up."

When Ralph visited a local Comcast office, he wanted to know what the employees were seeing and thinking, and how they thought the business could be improved. "He was always asking for feedback," says Curt Pendleton, who worked in Baltimore County. "He would say that the only way to compete is to evolve, and that the company needed everyone's best ideas."

His questions were often more personal. "How is your boss treating you?" he would ask employees. "Is everything okay?" He wanted them to love working for Comcast, and many of them did. Throughout the years, Ralph has invited employees to let him know that if they had a problem at work they couldn't solve on their own, they could send him a letter or make an appointment to see him. "We all had a Ralph Roberts chip," says Glenn Colvin. "We never expected to use it, but we knew that if something went seriously wrong, we could always cash it in."

"When Ralph showed up, it was terrific for morale," says Gary Shinn of the Meadowlands system in northern New Jersey. "He mixed with everyone, and he didn't want to be called Mr. Roberts. Some of us felt funny calling him Ralph, but he insisted on it."

He would go behind the scenes, too. At a regional call center he would remind employees to offer the latest package, even while some of them were on the phone with customers. "He was always trying to upsell," recalls Jaye Gamble, "always making sure we were offering people every possible opportunity." Sometimes, in his enthusiasm, Ralph would recommend a package that wasn't yet available in that system.

Jan Thompson, a dispatch supervisor in Flint, Michigan, can still picture Ralph, Dan, and Julian walking through the door. "It never felt like the big shots were visiting from Philadelphia," she says, "and Ralph came often enough that we were comfortable when he sat in on meetings."

In 1976 he had acquired Flint along with several nearby franchises in a deal that was significant for several reasons. First, Ralph and Julian were able to negotiate unbelievably favorable financing with the John Hancock Insurance Company in Boston, which provided a sixteen-year loan of $5.3 million, starting with ten years of interest payments only. And not only was the principal payable over the last six years; half of it wasn't due until the final year of the loan. Nobody in the industry had even heard of terms like that. "We thought we had died and gone to heaven," says Julian.

Flint, with 22,000 customers, was Comcast's largest acquisition to date, and boosted its subscriber base by 50 percent. It was the company's first successful attempt to enter a sizable metropolitan area, and it showed that a trend Ralph had noticed in Mississippi had not been an aberration. When the residents of Laurel suffered through several long strikes at the city's biggest factory, the affected families were willing to cut back on a number of other expenses rather than give up cable.

Flint was in a similar situation, but on a larger scale. American automakers were hurting after the 1973 Arab-Israeli war and the subsequent oil crisis, and when General Motors instituted massive layoffs at the Buick plant, the city's unemployment rate rose to 25 percent. Before making a decision, Ralph and Dan flew in to assess whether, in the face of a terrible economy, there was still any appetite for cable television. Knocking on doors in residential neighborhoods, they noticed that in many homes, the laid-off auto worker was in the living room watching TV. Families had to allocate their resources very carefully, but almost nobody canceled cable. This was a vindication of what Ralph, Dan, and Julian had long been telling potential investors—that in addition to being the best entertainment value around, cable also appeared to be recession-proof, or at least recession-resistant.

As Ralph continued buying systems, he and his associates made time to visit them all. When Mike Doyle, the new GM of the Willow Grove system just outside Philadelphia, sponsored a five-mile race to raise money for the American Heart Association, he invited the company's leaders to join his employees at a post-race barbecue in the parking lot. Although it was a weekend, Ralph showed up and so did Dan. Julian and Brian not only attended the barbecue; they also ran in the race.

During the event, Ralph took Doyle aside and said, "The garden looks terrific. I used to drive by this building, and the condition of the garden broke my heart. Suzanne and I picked out this office and we planted the garden ourselves." Ralph also remarked on the clean floors inside, and the clean trucks outside the building, and Doyle believes he was soon promoted at least partly because of how good the place looked.

Ralph was continually surprising employees who came to Comcast with conventional expectations of what the head of the company would do or say. Not long after Mike Doyle arrived, Ralph called and invited him to lunch. Doyle put on his best suit, but when Ralph picked him up, he drove over to Mama's, where he ordered a pizza and cheesesteaks to go. Then he headed to a nearby cemetery for a picnic. They sat together on a bench, and when lunch was over, Ralph reached into his pocket, pulled out a couple of mini Tootsie Rolls and said, "How about some dessert?"

So many Comcasters have had similar experiences that a writer who was working on a profile of Ralph once found himself asking employees if they had any stories about him that didn't involve low-priced restaurants. But it wasn't only the menu Doyle remembers, or the unusual setting. He noticed that during their time together, Ralph didn't even mention the business. "He focused on what the company could mean to me," Doyle says, "and about his hopes for the future. He used the occasion to put a face on himself, and on Comcast. It was all about getting to know each other."

A few months later, Brian became regional vice president, which made him Doyle's boss. When he invited Doyle to dinner, Doyle once again put on his best gray pin-striped suit, only to be taken to the nearest Howard Johnson's. Some people never learn.

There are bosses who demand respect and loyalty, but Ralph preferred to bestow respect and loyalty on others, who almost invariably responded in kind. Early on, Julian had an important technical disagreement with Touche Ross, which had become the company's accounting firm. "The big-time accountants are against you," said Ralph. "Are you sure you're right?"

Julian was highly confident. "Then I'm with you," said Ralph. Julian *was* right, but Ralph hadn't known that at the time. And you didn't have to be right about everything to earn his trust.

You didn't even have to be a longtime employee. Bern Gallagher was new to the company when Comcast applied for a franchise in Erie, Pennsylvania. Julian had arranged for a tax-free Urban Development Grant, and to qualify, Ralph had to declare that Comcast couldn't proceed without it. At Gallagher's request, Ralph had signed the declaration. But in the franchise application, the company had affirmed that it already had the funds to build the system. At the hearing, a councilman pointed out the discrepancy and invited Ralph to blame it on the new arrival.

Ralph refused. "You want me to criticize Mr. Gallagher," he told the committee, "but I'm not going to do it. The franchise is not as important to me as this young man." Gallagher would never forget the night Ralph lost the Erie franchise rather than disparage him publicly: "In many companies, after a mistake like that, heads would roll. But Ralph knew I was trying to do the right thing."

Al Calhoun remembers Ralph's visits to the Lower Merion

system, which wasn't far from the Bala headquarters. He would begin by checking in with the GM, and would then ask questions of Calhoun, whose youth, blue jeans, and work boots made it clear that he wasn't part of management. After the third or fourth visit, it occurred to Calhoun that Ralph already knew the answers, and that he was asking these questions to make the younger man feel important. Calhoun, who already felt honored by Ralph's attention, was even more pleased when he realized what the boss was doing. He promised himself that if he were ever in a leadership position, he would remember how wonderful it feels when the boss knows who you are. Years later, as vice president of operations for Comcast's Eastern Division, he had the opportunity to apply that lesson.

Shortly after Don Daniels became GM of the Meadowlands system in 1984, he was invited to a management conference in Florida, which made him nervous. He thought of himself as a technician masquerading as an executive, and feared he would be exposed as a fraud. Daniels was on his way to the opening session in the main building when he saw Ralph standing in his path. He had never met the boss, and the prospect made him anxious. What could he possibly say to Ralph Roberts? He considered turning around and pretending he had left something in his room, but he forced himself to keep walking.

"Good morning, Don," Ralph said. Daniels couldn't believe that Ralph knew his name. "Did you forget your name tag?" Ralph asked.

"I should go back and get it," Daniels said, almost relieved that he really had left something behind.

I knew I didn't belong here, Daniels was thinking as he rushed back to his room to retrieve the badge. Returning to the main building, he found Ralph still standing there, waiting for him. When Daniels showed him the name tag, Ralph took it and affixed it to Daniels's jacket. "At that moment," says Daniels, "I felt as if I were his son, on my way to the prom, and he was pinning on my corsage. As he walked with me into the conference, all the fear and intimidation I was feeling just melted away."

Beth Arnholt had been at Comcast only a few days when she was asked to give a presentation at a nearby hotel to a couple of hundred customer-service executives. She was introduced to Ralph in the lobby, and when he heard she was new, he took her by the arm, walked her into the dining room, and introduced her to the people at her table before taking his seat. "He couldn't have been more welcoming," she says. "People said, 'I saw you with Ralph, so I figured you were important.'"

"It's always Ralph the father figure that people seem to like and admire," says Suzanne Roberts. Ellen Rosson, an employee in Huntsville, Alabama, was attending a management conference at a Florida resort. The meeting was held in the summer to save money, but there was so much rain that all outdoor activities were canceled. Two buses pulled up, and somebody announced that Ralph was taking everyone to the movies. As they boarded the buses, there was Ralph, handing out ten-dollar bills so the employees could buy snacks. "He was taking care of us," says Rosson. "The guests at his party were having a bad time, and he wanted to fix it. To see Ralph in his bow tie, handing out those bills like we were all his children—that was priceless."

The corporate employees were especially aware of his modesty. Dick McCaffery remembers being invited to Ralph and Suzanne's house for dinner with a few other vice presidents and their wives. When everyone was seated and the table was full, Ralph calmly pulled up a chair and squeezed between two of his guests. It was no big deal: he didn't need to assert himself by sitting at the head of the table.

Kit Benson was one of the company's earliest employees. Of course everyone has their own definition of when "early" begins, and Benson, who arrived in 1965, is a little extreme on the subject: "As soon as there were more than six people at the company," she says, "it just wasn't the same." In the 1970s, when she was moved to a windowless office so small and claustrophobic that she couldn't even bring herself to enter it, she went to Ralph, who had a big piece cut out of the wall so Benson would have a view.

In some companies you can go a long time without ever seeing the chief executive, but the Bala employees saw a lot of Ralph—not only in the office, but at the coffee shop, the local drugstore, and the lunch counter at Woolworth's. Later, when the company moved to the Centre Square building at 1500 Market Street, new employees were often astonished to see the founder of a major corporation in the nearby Liberty Place food court, waiting alone in line for a fast-food meal. But once they got over their initial surprise, he no longer seemed out of place. "Wherever Ralph is," says Debbie Brodsky, "that's where Ralph is supposed to be."

He somehow finds time to talk with everyone he meets without running late. And when Ralph greets you in the middle of a food court or a crowded convention, he gives you his full attention, without ever looking around to see who else is in the room. "Regardless of who you are," says Maureen Cestari from Naples, Florida, "you're important to him during that conversation, and he really listens to what you're saying. You can see it in his eye contact and in his gestures, and you can tell it comes from his heart."

Louis Toth, the senior managing director of Comcast Interactive Capital, once noticed Ralph and Julian walking the aisles together at a cable show. When Toth went over to say hello, Julian said he was trying to teach Ralph the art of "pump and dump"—of shaking somebody's hand while you continue walking, without stopping to chat. Julian laughingly complained that it was taking forever to walk through the show because Ralph was "all pump, no dump." He had advised Ralph never to square his shoulders to the person he was talking to, and not to stop moving, but Ralph was enjoying the encounters and saw no reason to rush.

You didn't have to be an employee to get his attention. Randy Mossor, a college student, was thinking of leaving school to become a union electrician. His father, Brian, who ran the Executive Leadership Forum at Comcast University, suggested that Randy might want to have a conversation with Al Peddrick, the head of HR, who knew a lot about unions. Peddrick's office was in the east tower of the Centre Square building, and when the conversation was over, Randy took the elevator down and crossed the lobby to visit his dad in the west tower.

"I just met the greatest guy," he said.

"Yeah, Mr. Peddrick is really something."

"No, I mean on the elevator. He asked why I was there, and I told him I was talking to Mr. Peddrick." Randy went on to describe their conversation.

"What are you interested in?" the man on the elevator had asked.

"Maybe becoming an electrician, but I'm not sure yet."

"Are you still in school?"

"Yes."

"At your age, it's okay not to know. But it's a good idea to finish school, and then you can figure out what your passion is."

The elevator stopped at almost every floor, Randy reported, and they continued talking.

"When you're all done with school, do you think you might be interested in coming to Comcast?"

"I don't know. My dad works here."

"That's okay. My son works here. I'm going to the parking garage to get my car. Why don't you come down with me?"

Brian Mossor asked what the man looked like.

"He was kind of old, and he was wearing a bow tie."

"It sounds like you were talking to Mr. Roberts, the founder of the company."

"No, no," said Randy. "He got into an old minivan. It wasn't a limo or anything."

Brian found a picture of Ralph and showed it to his son. "That's him," said Randy.

Comcast employees tend to remember even the most casual or innocuous comments if they were made by Ralph. Kristin Lewandowski once entered the elevator at 1500 Market Street just after Ralph, and as the doors were closing and the elevator across the hall was also about to ascend, Ralph looked at her and said, "Let's race them!" When Bill Goetz first interviewed for a job with Comcast, somebody introduced him to Ralph as he was leaving the office in a heavy coat with two briefcases. Goetz remembers how Ralph put down his bags, removed his gloves, and took the time to shake hands and say something nice to a young job applicant. When Gary

Waterfield, who worked in Hightstown, New Jersey, first met Ralph, he recalls, "He took my hand and looked at me for a few minutes, but it felt a lot longer. He said, 'I'm really glad to have you on board.' That's all, but there was something about the way he said it that made an impact on me. Great leaders put you at ease. They don't want you to be nervous; what good does *that* do?"

The interesting thing about Ralph, says Lucille Fital, is that he is shy and sociable at the same time. When she came to the company, Fital was struck by something else, too. At other places she had worked, there was one set of rules for employees, and another for the top executives. But not here. If there were no cash advances for travel expenses, nobody, not even Dan, Julian, or Ralph himself, could get an exception. "Ralph treated everyone the same," Fital says. "I came here only a week before Christmas, but just like everyone else, I received a bonus and a gift. As soon as you joined, you were part of the family."

Naturally, there is more to the man than kindness. Although his thoughtfulness and compassion are genuine, they mask an inner toughness that has expressed itself openly only on rare occasions. "Julian was the hammer," says Jerry Purcell, "and Ralph was the velvet glove."

Sometimes the glove came in to negotiate the final points of a deal. Ralph was so nice about it, and so calm, that he could ask for almost anything without angering the people on the other side of the table, who sometimes agreed to his terms because they liked how he treated them. "At the end of an encounter with Ralph," says Howard Fischer, whose Philadelphia executive search firm has brought a number of executives to Comcast, "people walk away feeling good, even when they don't get what they want." More than one observer has concluded that Ralph's charming approach makes him all the more effective, because it's so disarming. "When one of the nicest people on the planet is also a very tough businessman," says Mark Coblitz, "that's a rare and effective combination."

Comcast was going through a difficult franchise renewal in Tallahassee when Sheila Willard, the company's first government affairs executive, decided to bring in Ralph. "His charm opened the door to resolving the issues," she says. "His gracious style and his respect for other people are so obvious that he can change the way people think about each other."

Steve Volk, an attorney who advised Comcast on some of its early deals, describes Ralph as a happy warrior. "He was aggressive," says Volk, "and he knew what he wanted, but he always had a smile on his face. He wanted to win very much, but he could tolerate losing, which is the mark of a well-grounded person."

"There's no fooling Ralph," says Julian. "Despite his gentle way, he is very thick skinned. When there are lawsuits, disagreements, or other problems, he doesn't take them personally."

"Although Ralph controlled the whole vote," says Mike Tallent, "he was a great listener who gave dignity and respect to other people. His mere presence at a meeting gave it an air of authority and purpose. He didn't speak much, but when he did, you knew it was important. He was the spark plug who asked the penetrating questions and forced us to justify our arguments and question ourselves in a productive way."

Sometimes Ralph's questions were the only observable indication of his toughness. Barbara Gehrig was in a budget meeting when a colleague gave an unconvincing presentation. Ralph asked a few polite but pointed questions, which the executive was unable to answer. Gehrig had heard about Ralph's toughness, but had never seen it in action. She was struck by his ability to ask the necessary questions without embarrassing the man who was trying, without much success, to answer them.

Perhaps the most striking thing about Ralph's tough side is how rarely it shows itself. "I've certainly heard about his toughness," says Lucille Fital, who has worked within a few feet of him for many years, "but I've never actually seen it." Even Brian is hard-pressed to think of examples, but he points out that toughness often takes the form of persistence and perseverance. "He'll ask me something, I'll answer it, and he'll be back tomorrow with the same question. When he doesn't like the answer, he keeps bringing it up."

He is ferociously determined. "Ralph is a sweet man," says Joan French, who was his longtime assistant, "but when he wants something, he wants it." Ralph agrees. "You have to stick to your guns sometimes," he says, "and they call that tough."

"Being tough," says Bob Pick, head of corporate development, "is the conviction of knowing you're right, and not taking no for an answer." Pick believes the reason it's difficult to find direct examples of Ralph's toughness is that he shows his combative side only in private, to avoid embarrassing anyone.

Just as power doesn't always have to be exercised, toughness doesn't have to be demonstrated. It's enough that people know it's there, and everybody does. Ralph is unfailingly pleasant, but anyone who may have mistaken his affability for weakness has soon learned otherwise.

10

The Conscience and The Cop

Dan Aaron and Julian Brodsky

The Conscience

As the company grew, Dan Aaron began taking on new responsibilities. In addition to overseeing cable operations, he emerged as both a politician and a diplomat. In his public role, he often addressed employees, community groups, and especially city councils who were awarding cable franchises. "Dan could speak off the cuff in complete sentences," says Barbara Lukens, who worked on securing new franchises and watched him explain to skeptical audiences why it was perfectly reasonable to ask people to pay for more access to television. The boy who was forced to learn English when he arrived in New York as a refugee from Nazi Germany had become a master of the spoken language. "He would jot a few words on a paper napkin," says Lois Brodsky, "and you'd think he had worked on that speech forever."

Dan, who was also considered the best-dressed man in the corporate office, became a spokesman not only for the company, but also for the entire industry. He was elected to the board of the National Cable Television Association, the industry's lobbying group in Washington, and became its chairman in 1977, when cable was still relatively new. "We had a lot of adversaries in those days," says Bill Bresnan, a cable entrepreneur and a fellow NCTA board member. "The phone companies didn't want us on their poles, the movie studios were suspicious, and the antenna dealers, the networks, the TV stations, and the FCC were all against us. So we had to stick together. The only ones who liked us were the customers."

There weren't many Americans who knew as much about cable television as Dan Aaron. And he must have been effective in Washington, because the NCTA board offered to change its bylaws so he could continue as chairman for a second year. He declined that honor because there was so much to do back in Bala, but his temporary leadership of the organization gave Comcast the stature and visibility of a much larger company, which pleased Ralph and helped him attract new talent in the years ahead.

Back at work, Dan was becoming known as a tough negotiator. Ed Breen, the CEO of Tyco International who later served on Comcast's board, remembers negotiating over set-top boxes when Breen was at Motorola: "Dan was the closer who came in at the end, after Julian had beaten us up. We knew we probably had the deal, but it was tough because he would ask for the moon." When the other side was finally ready to sign, Dan would typically go after one more concession, which happened so often that vendors learned to withhold that last nickel until Dan made his final attempt to lower the price. But once the terms were set, he was easy to work with.

Operationally, despite his skill and experience, Dan wasn't an innovator and didn't pretend to be, although in special situations, such as his decision to bury the wires underground in Venice, Florida, or the surreptitious building effort in Meridian, Mississippi, he showed his creativity. But mostly he agreed with Julian, who used to say that pioneers were the ones who got arrows in their backs, although Julian was quite the innovator in finding ways to borrow money at favorable rates. Dan was more of a fast follower, replicating the best practices of larger companies, which was Comcast's operating procedure for years. Not until 2002, when Comcast became the nation's largest cable provider, did it really begin to innovate operationally.

He was attentive and patient with customers who had problems or complaints. Sometimes, when Marie Molchen, his assistant, was trying to mollify an unhappy caller, Dan, whose door was always open, would come out and signal for her to hand him the phone. "He didn't just placate these people," Molchen says. "He got involved in the nitty-gritty, and called whomever needed to be called."

The employees loved him. He never walked by Molchen's desk without stopping to say good morning, and every Monday he would ask about her weekend. "It wasn't pretense," she says. "He really cared." When Lucille Fital first came to Comcast, it was Dan who made her feel at home. "It didn't matter that you were just a secretary," says Joan French. "He took the time to talk to everyone. Although I never worked directly for him, he always asked about my children."

He was diligent at thanking people, and sent handwritten notes to acknowledge even the smallest kindness. In the days before faxes or e-mails, he would write a couple of lines that cut to the heart of the issue, or he'd send you a note of appreciation that made you feel terrific. When Brian Roberts made a presentation to a city council in suburban Philadelphia, requesting a monthly rate increase of three dollars, the council members, who had already decided what they wanted to do, granted only half that amount. Brian was devastated by his perceived failure until Dan wrote him a letter, saying, "Do you realize how much money you made for the company with that rate increase? This is a terrific outcome, so don't be discouraged." Brian kept that note, and many other recipients of Dan's letters kept theirs as well. "He made me feel better," says Brian. "He knew I had done my best, and he reminded me that you don't always get what you want."

Like Ralph, Dan was known as a great listener. "When he talked with you," says Sharon Ingram, the company's first head of Human Resources, "he would be thinking about everything you were saying." He was always looking for teaching moments, and he loved to explain how a business problem might connect with some larger issue.

He was a good judge of character who did much of the hiring, and in the days before Comcast had a director of HR, he filled that role, too. "In addition to having a terrific analytical mind," said Abe Patlove, "he was the most gentle, humane person you ever met."

When Comcast was still small, if an employee at the corporate office or in the field had a personal problem, or was facing an illness, Dan would call to ask what the company could do for that person's spouse and children. "He knew my wife and my kids by name," says Dave Breidinger, "and he remembered them. He established a very personal connection with many of us."

He had especially strong relationships with the general managers. When he made Don Daniels GM of the Meadowlands system in northern New Jersey, he said, "Don, I'm entrusting something sacred to you. It's like my family, and it holds a special place in my heart." Daniels understood that Dan was reminding him that the job wasn't just about making money, although that was certainly important. It was also about looking after the people who worked there. "Don't ever try to improve your cash flow at the expense of your employees," Dan would tell the GMs.

Although he was part of management, his heart was with the workers. During a strike at the Westmoreland system, three men with picket signs showed up in the Bala parking lot. It wasn't clear whether they were employees or professional strikers, but Dan didn't care. It was snowing, so he went out to greet them with cups of hot coffee.

He disliked hierarchies and felt at home with even the most junior workers. "Whenever you walked into a cable system with Dan, you lost him," says Sheila Willard. "One moment he was with you, and suddenly he was gone." Willard would eventually find him outside, chatting with the men in the trucks. To learn what was really going on, he went to the techs and the telephone agents. He believed in getting information without filters or administrative spin, and the way to do that was to speak directly with the employees who actually dealt with the customers. It wasn't just Dan; when Ralph and Julian visited the systems, they, too, would talk to the frontline employees.

Dan was known as the conscience of Comcast. During board meetings, before a proposal came to a vote, he might ask, "Is this the right thing to do? Have we considered the effect on our employees?" When he raised these questions—and he didn't raise them casually—the directors would pause to consider whether there was something they might have missed.

Al Peddrick, the head of HR in the 1990s, recalls that even then, when Dan was disabled by the Parkinson's disease that would severely shorten his life, he remained deeply concerned about the welfare of the employees. "Our relationship was strictly about my doing the right thing to help them," Peddrick says. "He was concerned about people he had never even met."

Long after Dan had retired and was confined to a wheelchair, he would visit the Sarasota office near his home in Florida and talk with employees about their jobs and their lives. Every year, he and Gerri would have dinner with several dozen Comcasters. During the evening, Dan would ask the GM to introduce every employee in the room and explain what that person did—not only because he wanted to know, but also because it was good for a manager to appreciate his people in public. Sometimes he came to the office and listened in on customer calls, often with a big smile because, at least for an hour or two, he was back at the work he loved.

Ed Mount, the longtime manager of the Paducah, Kentucky, system, remembers a visit from Dan in 1978. When Mount drove to the Holiday Inn to pick him up for dinner, Dan mentioned that he and Gerri had been taking dancing lessons and that he had just been watching ballroom dancing in his hotel room. Then, to the astonishment of his host, the head of Comcast's cable division said, "I think we'll get a television." He wasn't kidding. Dan's son, Jud, says, "It was funny that my father was in the cable business, because he had as little interest in television and popular culture as anyone I've known."

He preferred real-life encounters, and he connected with just about everybody. When Bob Pick came to Comcast, Dan learned that Pick's parents were both refugees from the Nazis, and that his father, like Dan's, had escaped from Germany very late, which created a bond between them. Barbara Lukens says that after her father, Dan Aaron was the single biggest influence on her life. When Art Block was first invited to join Comcast's in-house legal team, it was Dan who recognized his ambivalence and advised Block not to leave the law firm until he was ready, which took another three years.

Although his speeches at cable association meetings were often quite funny, most employees were not aware of Dan's dry and understated sense of humor; he was such a serious person that his occasional quips would take you by surprise. When a parking lot attendant in Detroit asked what kind of car he was driving, he replied, "It's a Hertz." Once, when he got off a flight, somebody asked what had become of the colleague who had flown with him. "I lost him on the plane," Dan said. He hated flying. He had ear problems, and air travel was often painful.

He could laugh at himself, too. Late in his career, he visited the Meadowlands system on the last day of October. Because of his illness, he was pleased to find a uniformed nurse, and he thanked her for being there. When she told him it was only a Halloween costume, they both had a good laugh.

Dan also had a strict side, but he was no more likely than Ralph or Julian to fire someone. If you weren't right for the job, he would try to find you a more appropriate position. And in the unlikely event that you really *were* fired, he made sure you were treated generously, to the point where people sometimes joked that the best thing that could happen to you at Comcast was to lose your job. Stanley Wang liked to tease Dan by saying, "Fire me—please!" This wasn't just kindness. Dan, Julian, and Ralph were well aware that a company's reputation is formed, in part, by the comments of the people it lets go.

• • •

Dan was famous for his incessant questions, and the former journalist kept asking them until he had all the information he wanted—and he wanted a lot—or until you were stumped. But because he hated to embarrass anyone, you wouldn't always know why his questions had stopped. Even if you told him something ridiculous, he just nodded.

Sometimes he posed the same question to four or five people. Or he'd come back and ask the same question he had asked yesterday, but in a slightly different way. Or he'd quiz you about something that seemed to make no sense, because you were sure he already knew the answer. So why was he asking?

When friends of his kids came to the house, he grilled them, too. "What they didn't realize," says his daughter Alison, "was that my father was genuinely interested in people, and this was his way of learning more about them." But that wasn't always clear, especially to potential boyfriends. After being questioned by Dan, some were reluctant to return; their conversation with Mr. Aaron had felt more like an interrogation.

It wasn't his initial question that people remembered so much as the follow-up, and the question after that. Employees who worked for Dan were always aware of the *next* question. You could try to anticipate what he would ask, but often it was something you hadn't thought of. And he wouldn't let you get away with a glib or shallow answer.

He had a knack for finding the area in which you were weak. In the process of trying to anticipate what he might ask, you would educate yourself by beginning to internalize that next question, which would deepen your grasp of the issue. Talking to Dan was a little like going to law school: it trained you in a more rigorous way of thinking.

Sometimes the right answer wasn't enough, because he would then ask, "How do you know?" The answer he really wanted was, "I have personally checked this with my own eyes and ears." If you provided almost any other response, he would tap his lip with his finger and appear thoughtful, which meant you were failing to provide the level of certainty he was looking for.

His questions might startle you, especially if you weren't used to them. Bob Pick had been at the company about a week when Dan took him to lunch and said, "Tell me why you came here." Why is he asking, Pick wondered. Was coming here a mistake? Is there something I should be aware of? Pick later realized that this was Dan's normal, inquisitive style, and that he genuinely wanted to know why Pick, who had come to Comcast from Bell Atlantic, had decided to join a much smaller company.

If you sat next to Dan at a dinner, by the end of the evening you'd be exhausted. But if you asked him to back off, he quickly relented. Once, when he asked Mike Doyle about the Baltimore County system, and Doyle replied that everything was fine, Dan said, "You may be giving me a load of bull, but your answer makes me feel better. And right now, that's good enough."

The Cop

It is impossible to overstate Julian Brodsky's role in the company's success, or his influence on its culture of hard work, financial discipline, and ethical behavior. In the early years, his outsize personality and creative intelligence helped put Comcast on the map. "His impact was out of proportion to who we were in the business," says Art Block. "One reason we were able to play beyond our size is that Julian was so visible."

All his working energy went into the company, and especially into helping Ralph. "Julian has never put himself first," Ralph says. "He quit his job to work for me. He could have gone out and created his own cable business, but he wanted to be part of what I was doing, and I really appreciated it."

To survive in its early years, when Comcast started building a new system, the company had to find ways to raise or borrow large sums at reasonable rates without going broke during the long wait for revenue. For a small business in a relatively new and little-known industry, that challenge could be insurmountable.

Happily, Ralph already had an excellent relationship with his banker, Jack McDowell, and would soon form productive associations with other lenders at banks, insurance companies, and Wall Street firms. And he was especially fortunate to have Julian, who effectively served not only as chief financial officer, but also as the company's unofficial investment banker, especially during the Bala years, when he was remarkably active and innovative. By the mid-1980s, when the company was on more solid footing, Julian had succeeded in making parts of his job obsolete as Comcast was finally able to secure the funds it needed from major financial institutions and the public bond and equity markets. He handled these transactions, too, but here there was less room, or need, for creativity.

Raising money was only one of his jobs. Julian led many of the company's merger and acquisition activities well into the 1990s, when Larry Smith became more active. And along with Dan, he negotiated major supply contracts with Jerrold Electronics, cable suppliers, and contractors, and programming contracts with content providers like HBO, ESPN, and Turner.

To get the company on solid financial ground, Julian engineered a remarkable array of inventive financings, including partnerships, safe-harbor leases, joint ventures with investors, and several types of bonds—industrial revenue, zero-coupon, and Eurobonds. Comcast also sold a good amount of junk debt, although issuers of high-yield bonds don't care for that term. Julian's fierce linguistic integrity didn't allow for euphemisms, but he was willing to dress them up a little by referring to them, on occasion, as "junque."

"During the years when money was available," says Ralph, "Julian could find it cheaper." When interest rates soared in the early 1980s, Storer Broadcasting, hardly an unknown company, was borrowing long-term at market rates, which ran as high as 18 percent, while little Comcast was paying less than half as much. Both before and well after Comcast went public, Julian looked into every conceivable form of financing to determine, as he puts it, the right horse for the right course. And for every financial instrument the company ended up using, he researched and considered a dozen harebrained schemes— and that's *his* phrase—that he decided not to use. One of them, he likes to say, might have required a skull and crossbones on the cover of the prospectus, with the slogan, "Beware: The money you receive from this investment may be your own."

"He was an exceptionally innovative borrower," says Ralph. "He was also a fine interpreter of different markets, and so inventive—like the time he sold tax benefits that we couldn't use to a major corporation. As a result, we were never short of money to buy something we really wanted. When Julian said he could get the funds, I had complete confidence that he'd make good on that promise—and he always did."

This is Julian's legacy: every single financing he arranged worked out, and nobody ever lost a nickel lending money to Comcast. Even when shares were selling for under a dollar, the corporation was never in serious trouble. Not a single cable system ever failed, and Comcast never missed a loan payment. Despite occasional anxious moments, there were no terrible times, no close calls, and no real missteps—except, you could argue, for errors of omission. "We passed up many acquisitions," says Julian, "and I regret every one of them." Ralph regretted them even more.

One reason for the company's early success was that within Julian were two completely different financial officers who somehow shared one body. The investment banker was imaginative, aggressive, and bold. If a financing was complicated, new, or untested, he liked it all the more. "He was never put off by the fact that other people hadn't done something," says banker Paul Mejean. "Everything he did was clever," says Glenn Jones, "and he operated in a staid world where there wasn't much room for innovation."

On the other side of the ledger was the old-school auditor who made sure the company's accounting was careful, conservative, and clear, which in turn made some of its bolder financings a little easier to execute. From the start, Comcast carried the credibility of a larger corporation because bankers and other lenders had learned that Julian and Ralph were candid and straightforward, and that their fundamental impulse was to disclose information rather than hide it. Julian presented real numbers, without color or exaggeration, and when he offered a prediction, a projection, or a prognosis, you could literally take it to the bank. When it came to disclosing the facts and obeying the law, he tolerated only the plain, unvarnished truth. Even in the years right after the 1972 IPO, when the company's stock was floundering and the broader economy was in a serious recession, Comcast was able to borrow money because its numbers were credible and its statements reliable.

Julian was colorful, conspicuous, complicated, and contradictory. He started out as a socialist who went to business school, and then turned himself into a self-taught and virtuoso capitalist. (His education as a Wharton undergraduate did not cover the many complexities of investment banking.) And unlike other financial wizards, who tend to be single-minded, he has always had serious outside interests, including literature, art, technology, travel, and especially photography, at which he excels.

For all his achievements and his formidable intelligence, employees were struck above all by the paradoxes of his personality: a stern man with a short fuse who is capable of patience and compassion; a demanding and sometimes volatile boss with a terrific sense of humor; a teacher who is both feared and loved, often by the same people; a tough disciplinarian who is also the life of the party; a huge and happy eater who could also run marathons; a wealthy man who enjoys the finer things in life but has never lived ostentatiously and is clearly not motivated by money; and a professional penny-pincher who can be very generous.

He has always had an enormous capacity for work. Until his official retirement in 2004, he routinely stayed at the office until eight o'clock or even later, and he wasn't just putting in time. "Julian worked a twelve-hour day," says Bern Gallagher, "and with his facile mind and his ability to focus, he could accomplish sixteen hours of work in those twelve." Once, during the early stages of a transaction, when he pointed out that the deal had to be completed quickly, an employee had the temerity to mention that the weekend was approaching. Julian quickly set him straight. "I beg your pardon," he said. "Deals *have* no weekends." Bob Johnson, a banker who worked with Comcast in the late 1980s, used to spend the occasional weekend at a country house, where he didn't have an answering machine. Back at the office on a Monday morning, he found a recorded message from Julian: "Either you'll get an answering machine in the country or we'll get another banker."

But as hard as Julian worked, that's how hard he played. Although he was a micromanager who might stand over your typewriter to read what you were writing, he could also go on vacation without ever calling the office. It was his unusual ability to work extremely hard and enjoy life at the same time that people noticed. When Mike Tallent was being interviewed for CFO of the cable division, Julian invited him to Atlantic City for the company's annual accounting meeting, which was held off-season in an inexpensive hotel. (As a financial man, Tallent appreciated that cost-saving move.) After splitting a six-pack in the afternoon, they had dinner together, where Julian consumed most of a bottle of wine. Later that evening, Tallent watched him hold forth informally over several glasses of scotch.

At ten thirty, Tallent called it a night because the next day's meeting ran from 8:00 a.m. until 6:00 p.m. But although Julian stayed up late and consumed more scotch, Tallent was the one who awoke with a hangover. He then watched in amazement as Julian jumped right into a complicated, high-level, early-morning debate about bad-debt reserve, followed by a presentation as insightful as anything Tallent had ever heard. "I thought at some point he was going to collapse," said Tallent, "but he just kept going at full speed." Julian had a saying for those who tried, in vain, to keep up with him: "If you want to stay out with the boys, you have to get up with the men."

He could have a wonderful time without drinking, too. He was a master of celebrating, and in a room full of people, he usually stood out as the one who was having the best time. And he would do his best to see that you were having fun as well.

He ate big, drank big, and talked big. For years he also smoked big—the kind of addict who would light his first cigarette of the day before reaching over to shut off the alarm. By the end of the day, he had gone through up to five packs of Pall Malls, which were strong and unfiltered. Ralph recalls that Julian used to sit at his desk with a whole plate of butts, because a mere ashtray wasn't big enough.

Knowing that his health was at risk, Julian repeatedly tried to quit. (Ralph was concerned, too. His mother once showed him that if you blew cigarette smoke through a handkerchief, it left a residue of tar, and that powerful image stayed with him. Although Ralph was a smoker when he started working at Pioneer, he was able to quit on his own, but he was never the smoker that Julian was.) Ralph came up with various plans to help Julian quit, including offering a bribe to his three young daughters so they would get involved, too. Then, early in 1972, Joe Roberts died of pancreatic cancer at fifty-three, which was a huge blow to Ralph, and to Julian as well. It was Joe's death, Julian believes, that pushed Ralph to try to end Julian's smoking habit once and for all.

Ralph came up with a clever campaign that catered to several of Julian's other inclinations. In the spring of 1972, when the company was required to go through a mandated "quiet period" before the IPO, Ralph invited Julian to go away with him. It would be just the two of them, anywhere in the world Julian wanted to go, where he could eat, drink, play tennis, and gamble as much as he liked. The only thing he couldn't do was smoke. If Julian abstained during the trip, and for thirty days thereafter, Ralph would pay for everything, including Julian's gambling losses.

Julian was touched by Ralph's generosity, his caring, and his creative solution to a difficult problem. If he was going to stop smoking, and he genuinely wanted to, this was the most appealing method he could imagine, an offer he couldn't refuse. He fantasized about France. He pondered Polynesia. He mulled over Macau and mused about Monte Carlo. Then reality set in. If he failed to stop smoking, this trip could cost him a fortune!

They settled on a week in the Bahamas. Lois didn't mind; she was used to her husband's traveling and grateful for what Ralph was trying to accomplish. Suzanne was less enthusiastic. Although this was certainly a good cause, the plan was both time-consuming and expensive, and Ralph, at the time, was far from wealthy.

Before the trip, Julian imagined himself boarding the plane and immediately lighting up. So two days before they left, he threw away his cigarettes. Those first couple of days were agonizing, but he wasn't going to suffer alone. Ralph insisted that they share a room, because he had no intention of letting Julian out of his sight. They stayed busy—eating, drinking, playing tennis, and gambling at night, when they bet such tiny sums that the bored casino dealers started helping them count cards at the blackjack table. Ralph, who tends to be lucky in these matters, actually made money that week.

Julian made out even better. They left Philadelphia on April 25, 1972, a date he remembers because he hasn't had a cigarette since. "That's the genius of Ralph," he says, "to figure out how to get it done in such an enjoyable way. If he hadn't taken me away, I don't think I could have quit."

Emboldened by his success with Julian, Ralph tried to help other employees. He made several bets with Jerry Purcell to encourage the head of Muzak to lose weight, and when Purcell reached his target, he was allowed to take his wife and children to a convention in Mexico. Ralph promised John Stoddard, another Muzak man, a bonus of five thousand dollars if Stoddard lost fifty pounds. Although Stoddard wasn't able to do it, he was moved that Ralph would take such a personal interest in his health.

Although nobody would call Julian a natural teacher, Comcast employees have learned a lot from him—and not only about finance. "He taught me to lead by example," says Brian, "and he showed me that you need to tell the financial people that they're more than accountants, that they carry the integrity of the corporation. Whether we make or break cash flow by a point or two will soon be forgotten, but integrity, or the lack of it, will always be remembered. And while Julian's perfectionism can drive people crazy, it's about establishing the highest of standards. He urges his team to resist the temptation to cut corners. He says, 'The long way is the short way,' and that's true. There's no excuse not to do things right."

Julian believed that no matter how fast the company was growing, it was important to know and recognize as many employees as you possibly could. He had a gift for remembering people in the field, and if he didn't know someone's name, he'd make sure to find out. "A senior executive interacting in a friendly way with lower-level employees is important to our culture," says Art Block, "and I learned to do that from watching Julian."

Knowing names was just the beginning. In the early years, when Julian went out to visit the systems, he'd often bring a case of beer for the installers and the technicians. Like Ralph and Dan, he showed up at events he easily could have skipped. He would surprise employees with spontaneous acts of kindness, such as buying a little gift or taking two or three couples to dinner. He was good at showing his appreciation.

And his disapproval, too. When Art Block made a rookie mistake as a young lawyer, Julian rebuked him strongly. Block felt terrible, but he was also grateful that Julian didn't go straight to Block's law firm to demand that he be taken off the Comcast account. Instead, in subsequent deals and financings, he took the time to educate Block about every issue that came up, and to help him develop both as a lawyer and a businessman. These lessons weren't always pleasant, but they were appreciated.

When Julian spoke with investors, he was exceptionally candid and direct. John Alchin, another of his students, says, "He resisted any temptation to make the situation sound better than it was." According to Alchin, who followed Julian in that job and continued the practice, "He teaches by grabbing you by the scruff of your neck, but he helped me learn so much."

Whether he was addressing Wall Street or working on the company's annual report, he took pains to communicate precisely and to avoid unnecessary adjectives. He believed in letting the numbers speak for themselves. Early on he established a disclosure committee to deal with complicated accounting issues that might be open to more than one interpretation. As a former auditor, he was familiar with the myriad ways that errors or distortions can creep in, and the committee was there to remove judgment calls from the purview of any one person, who might be inclined, even unknowingly, to color or interpret the facts.

Some of Julian's more informal lessons, especially those pertaining to travel, were embodied in what he called The Code of the West. The Code was an amorphous, quasi-mythical list that was never really codified; despite the macho name, it seemed to consist of two or three compassionate reminders, plus whatever Julian decreed at that particular moment. He would proclaim a rule, and when he added the phrase "Code of the West" in his loud and authoritative voice, people paid attention. The first rule was that when you were on the road, you never left a restaurant, a reception, or wherever you happened to be without informing the people you had come with. The second rule was that when you were going out to dinner on the road, you made sure that nobody in the group was left alone—unless by choice. If a few veterans were getting together, the new manager on his first trip was always invited to join them.

He was especially attentive to newcomers. When Payne Brown, who came to Comcast in 2000, attended his first cable trade show, Julian greeted him by saying, "Payne, come walk the floor with me." By then, Julian was so well known in the industry that he couldn't take three steps without somebody calling his name. When people came over to greet him, Julian would say, "Have you met Payne? He's with us." To Brown, those seven words constituted the warmest possible welcome.

And he could always make you laugh. Paul Kagan, the cable analyst, used to hold seminars in New York where industry leaders would speak to investors. Julian was on a panel when a member of the audience said, "We're hearing that telephone companies are eager to form partnerships with cable companies. Will the cable industry be open to this?"

"I can answer that one," said Julian, "because I'm schooled in the Bible." Suddenly the room grew quiet. "Somewhere it is written that the lamb shall lie down with the lion. Let me tell you something: that lamb ain't gonna get much sleep." The line, which owed something to Woody Allen, brought the house down.

When Bern Gallagher left Comcast to take another job, and he announced at his farewell dinner that Julian had taught him everything he knew about cable, Julian got up and said, "I want to drink a toast to Bern's new employer, because it's true: I did teach Bern everything he knows. And I want to offer a second toast to Ralph and to Comcast, because although I taught Bern everything he knows, I didn't teach him everything *I* know."

But it wasn't all laughs with Julian. Whether by instinct or by design, and it may have been both, he assumed the role of the bad cop during the Bala years, and occasionally the very bad cop. When you ask Comcast veterans about him, they describe a combative figure:

"We all fought with Julian. That's what we did."

"It didn't pay to argue with him, because he could chew you up and spit you out."

"When I did something he didn't like, he screamed, 'You do that again and I'll throw you through the [expletive] wall!' It was the first time I saw his temper, and I thought, Maybe that's it, I'm gone. Twenty minutes later, he bought me a beer."

"When he was yelling at someone, people would cower. One secretary was so afraid that when she saw him coming, she would slide under the desk."

Was Julian aware of these reactions? He certainly wasn't oblivious, even if he did tell one employee who complained about an outburst, "I didn't yell at you. That was a *discussion*!" He once joked that his motto was slightly different from Theodore Roosevelt's, that *his* version went, "Speak *loudly* and carry a big stick." He told Kevin O'Connor, back when O'Connor was a student intern, "Don't worry when I yell at you. Worry when I *don't* yell at you." When somebody asked about the then-popular idea of management by objectives, Julian responded, "Around here it's management by violence. You meet your budget, or you get my size 13D shoes on your backside." Once, at a meeting with analysts, somebody described Comcast as "lean and mean." After Ralph spoke, Julian introduced himself by saying, "I'll let you guess who's lean and who's mean."

And he often expressed regret. If he went too far, he might take you out to lunch or dinner, often before you were ready for the apology, which was never expressed in words. Once, after shouting at an employee who was devastated by the outburst, he was openly remorseful. "I shouldn't have done that," he told a colleague. "I should never pick on somebody who can't defend himself." One morning, when he yelled at Ken Mikalauskas, who worked for him, the tirade was so hard to follow that his victim said, "Julian, I have no idea what you're saying." Julian leaned back and said, "Ken, a word of advice. When in doubt, mumble."

Part of it was his high energy level; he told one employee that on his way to work in the morning he listened to rousing marches on the car radio. Another part was his booming voice: even when he wasn't yelling, people thought he was. The first time Al Calhoun came from Lower Merion to the nearby corporate office in Bala to get a purchase order signed, he heard Julian's voice from the reception area and thought, Somebody is getting reamed, and I hope I'm not next. When the receptionist told him to go right in, Calhoun saw that Julian was merely telling a story.

Roger Leonard, who worked at Comcast in the early 1980s, had previously been at a company that manufactured cork products, including cork walls, which are ideal for soundproofing. The first time Leonard went into Julian's office, he noticed that one of the walls was made of cork. When he mentioned this to Ralph, whose office was on the other side of that wall, Ralph smiled and said, "That's for Julian." But it was really for Ralph.

For every employee who complained about Julian's fierce temper, there was somebody—often the same person—who would explain it, defend it, excuse it, or put it into context:

"Everyone was afraid of him, but he was really a pussycat." (Or often, "a teddy bear.")

"He yelled at me, but he loved me."

"He never yelled for no reason. If he hollered at you, you probably deserved it."

"As long as I yelled back, everything was fine."

"He had patience for people who needed patience."

"He would bark, but he never held a grudge."

"His yelling was just a voice. He had a heart of gold."

"He was like a storm cloud that would pass over you, rain, and move on. A moment later the sun would come out."

Among other duties, he served as the company's truant officer. On the afternoon before a holiday, a long weekend, an expected snowstorm, or sometimes just before five o'clock on a regular workday, he would walk the halls in a jovial mood, greeting employees with a hearty, "Hey, team, how are we doing today?" New employees wondered about these sudden bursts of buoyancy until they realized that the chief financial officer was taking attendance.

He controlled the purse strings at the Bala office, and to some extent, early on, at the system level as well. On a visit to one local office, he asked about a line in the budget for "plants." The amount was clearly too small to mean cable plants, and someone explained that it referred to the purchase of plants and flowers to spruce up the building. "Okay," said Julian. "Now be sure to add another line—for plant *removal.*"

He liked to refer to the entire corporate office as "the overhead," a useful and humbling reminder that all of the company's revenues came from operations, and that its headquarters produced no income. And he did everything possible to limit spending. When Al Gencarella, the controller, bought electronic calculators for his staff, Julian was livid. "He was merciless when it came to cost control," says Gencarella, "and that's part of the reason we were successful."

There are many such stories, and people love telling them. When the price of coffee went up, Julian posted a memo explaining that the company was switching to smaller cups. The new ones, one coffee drinker insists, were only slightly larger than the cups used for urine samples in a doctor's office. In 1984, when Comcast had a cash position of $100 million, Julian circulated a memo asking employees to look up numbers in the phone book rather than calling directory assistance.

During the Great Paper-Clip Crackdown, he mandated that nobody could order paper clips because too many were being thrown away. From now on, he decreed, employees should remove the clips from incoming mail and reuse them. They did, and some of them, like Tom Nathan, still do. "When you received a document with a butterfly clip," Nathan recalls, "it was like gold."

Nobody was immune from his auditing. Dan Aaron had been there for a decade or two when he and Julian got into an argument over who should pay for a movie that Dan had watched in his hotel room. Even into the 1980s he personally reviewed every expense report, sometimes with the help of Helen Perlman, who worked in accounting and had a special talent for finding unauthorized or inappropriate entries, which she would circle in red ink. Although employees were often annoyed by these measures, they knew that he was trying to instill a corporate ethic of thriftiness.

For Julian, careful spending and accurate expense reports were not just about saving money; they were also about candor and ethical behavior. At every management meeting he would remind employees, "Nowhere is integrity demonstrated more clearly than in your expense reports."

Sometimes he would end on a lighter note with one of his favorite stories. A salesman returns from a business trip and hands in his expense report, which includes the line "Miscellaneous—$30."

"What's that supposed to mean?" asks the controller.

"I left my hat on the train and I'd like to be reimbursed."

"I'm sorry," says the controller, "but we don't pay for lost clothing. I'm taking this off your charges."

After the salesman's next trip, he says to the controller, "Here's my expense report. The hat is in there. Try to find it!"

After the laughter had died down, Julian would look out at the audience and say, in a voice that left no room for doubt, "Believe me, ladies and gentlemen, *I will find that hat!*"

His retirement has been more symbolic than real, and his influence is still powerful. "Julian bleeds for this company," says Brian. "We wouldn't be where we are today without his achievements and the sheer force of his personality. And people around here still hold themselves accountable to Julian's expectations."

11

Cable Becomes Cool

Ted Turner

Cable began as a strictly rural phenomenon. City dwellers and suburbanites required only a rooftop antenna to watch television, but everyone else needed a cable hookup. The exception was New York City, where tall buildings blocked over-the-air reception to the point where some residents couldn't see much of anything. In the early 1960s, an entrepreneur named Charles Dolan, who went on to become one of the leading cable operators and the founder of Cablevision Systems on Long Island, began to wire the lower half of Manhattan. This was difficult and expensive, and Dolan sold 20 percent of his company to Time Inc., the magazine publisher, which was already in the cable business. Two years later, Time made a second investment in Dolan's company.

In 1971 Dolan had another big idea: What if cable could improve not only reception, but content? What if, for an additional fee, subscribers could watch a premium channel that offered uncut movies, sports, and original programming, all without commercials? And what if this new channel were made available to other cable companies, too, whose customers would help pay for it? Time Inc. agreed to support Dolan's new venture, which was known initially as the Green Channel, and then Home Box Office, and finally, HBO. It was a gamble: never before had consumers been asked to pay extra for the right to watch a single channel.

Dolan's deputy, a bright young lawyer named Gerald Levin, who would later become chairman of Time Warner, arranged for HBO to be distributed through a microwave tower system. On November 8, 1972, the new network went on the air with a New York Rangers hockey game, followed by a movie, *Sometimes a Great Notion*, with Paul Newman and Henry Fonda. HBO began with fewer than four hundred subscribers, all of them in the coal-country town of Wilkes-Barre, Pennsylvania, where cable pioneer John Walson was the first operator to carry its programs.

Two years later, at the end of 1974, Dolan's new channel had fifty thousand subscribers, which wasn't nearly enough to break even. Then Levin, who was now running HBO, learned that it would soon be possible to rent space on a communications satellite. He told the executives at Time Inc., which had become the sole owner of HBO, that the way to save the struggling network was to distribute it to cable systems nationwide on a satellite, something that had never been done before. Although Levin was proposing a huge and expensive solution for a channel that was still distributing some of its shows by sending around videotapes, HBO's corporate owners were willing to make the investment.

In the fall of 1975, at the annual convention of the National Cable Television Association, the young network inaugurated its satellite distribution system with a live broadcast from the Philippines, where Muhammad Ali was defending his heavyweight title against Joe Frazier. It was a brilliant move that made front-page news in the *Wall*

Street Journal. "Ali won the fight," somebody said, "but HBO won the crowd." Three months later the network had close to 300,000 subscribers, a sixfold increase over the previous year.

Although HBO had always been committed to original programming, the prize-winning shows for which it would later become celebrated were still a long way off. Its first original offering, a 1973 broadcast from the Pennsylvania Polka Festival, gave little indication of what lay ahead. A more popular show featured some of the nation's best comedians performing without censorship, starting with Robert Klein and eventually including almost every major comic in the country, often before they became famous. (The late George Carlin held the record with fourteen appearances.) "I thought comedians were more relevant and provocative than politicians," says Michael Fuchs, who came to HBO to develop its original programming. "I wanted us to be more candid and more daring than the broadcast networks. People associated us with nudity and obscene language, and I didn't want that to be our only calling card."

In some parts of the country, that calling card got a lot of attention. During a weekend of free programming to induce cable viewers to subscribe to HBO, the Comcast office in Laurel, Mississippi, received angry calls from area ministers, and then from the mayor's office, asking the company to "turn off that pornography." But before the weekend was over, many residents had ordered the new channel. Soon after that, Ralph went to see the mayor. "Are you sure you want us to remove HBO?" he asked. "People seem to love it."

"We've had some complaints," the mayor replied, "but I guess people want this thing. Just don't tell me about it!"

HBO was just as popular with the cable systems that carried it, and before long, they all did. Ralph was an early fan: "Movies on TV without commercials? That alone was enough to persuade a lot of people to order cable." In addition to directly increasing the operators' revenues, HBO provided another, less visible benefit. Until 1984, when Congress ruled that cable should be mostly unregulated, the monthly fee a system charged its customers was subject to the approval of the local municipality. In some communities, even a tiny increase could lead to a long battle. But the price for premium channels was not subject to local approval.

Viewers were so pleased with HBO that they signed up in droves. For a while, operators in some Comcast systems were greeting callers with, "Comcast HBO. May I help you?"

The new channel changed the entire industry. "Until HBO came in," says Ralph, "we would never have thought of trying to sell cable in urban markets. And even then the cities seemed risky, because building new systems required a tremendous amount of capital with no guarantee of a return. But the risk paid off beyond our wildest dreams."

The test case came in northern New Jersey. When the unbuilt Meadowlands franchise became available in 1977, Ralph had a big decision to make. The area, which included East Rutherford and several other towns along the ridge behind the new Giants Stadium, offered high home density, which was always appealing to a cable operator. But the huge transmitter towers atop the World Trade Center were close enough that some residents could see them from their front porches. These communities already received a dozen or so stations over the air, which was more free TV than anyone else in the country. Why would *they* want cable? The only logical reason was that cable could give them HBO.

To determine whether Meadowlands residents were likely to sign up, Ralph, Dan, and Julian drove to the area and started knocking on doors. But they weren't looking for a simple yes or no. "Nobody *ever* said they'd pay for television," says Julian. "We were trying to determine the degree of their No-ness."

The availability of HBO meant that the decision about both the Meadowlands and all subsequent possible franchise purchases would require a different set of assumptions. Julian worked up numbers showing that because of the high home density in these towns, and the conservative assumption that half the people who ordered cable would also take HBO, Comcast could break even with a 30 percent penetration, rather than the standard 50 percent. In fact, more than half the residents ordered cable, and of those who did, more than

90 percent ordered HBO. "The brilliance of these guys," says Brian, "was in grappling with the reality of a change while it was still happening, and being farsighted enough to make the model show something it hadn't shown before. HBO was too new to count on, and it took courage to plow ahead." Other operators had turned down the Meadowlands, but Ralph and his colleagues were able to see just a little further.

A year after HBO went up on a satellite, an Atlanta entrepreneur named Ted Turner read about the new technology in a trade magazine and saw it as a way to expand the audience for his independent UHF station. "The satellite sounded like a big microwave tower in the sky that could reach the whole continent," he says. "I thought we could use it to leapfrog the rest of the industry."

WTCG, as Atlanta's Channel 17 was known, could not have been more different from HBO. Its hodgepodge programming lineup consisted of old movies, old TV shows such as *Lassie* and *The Flintstones*, and a pair of unglamorous Atlanta sports teams—the Hawks (basketball) and the Braves (baseball). Turner had already pushed the station's audience slightly beyond Atlanta by using very tall microwave towers, but the satellite would make it available wherever people had cable. Turner called his newly enhanced channel a *superstation*, which soon became the generic term for independent local channels that used satellites for national distribution. Two of them, WOR in New York and WGN in Chicago, quickly followed his lead.

Cable systems didn't charge extra for Channel 17, which was renamed WTBS (for Turner Broadcasting System), and subscribers were happy to have it. Although its offerings were unexciting by today's standards, they added substantially to viewers' choices; as Ralph likes to say, people always want more TV. A free channel that carried both NBA and National League baseball games was of real interest to sports fans, especially those who didn't live in major markets. And Turner's station held a special appeal for southern viewers. "If you were in Tupelo or Meridian," says Ralph, "to be able to watch a channel from Atlanta was a big deal."

Next to go up on the satellite was a channel that began with the modest goal of broadcasting sports events in Connecticut. When Bill Rasmussen realized in 1979 that it was cheaper to buy a continuous feed than to lease a few hours of satellite capacity every evening, he expanded his network to twenty-four hours and started showing games and competitions from all over the country. Known as the Entertainment and Sports Programming Network, ESPN would become, for many viewers, the most popular cable channel of them all—quite an achievement for a station whose first televised event was a slow-pitch softball game between the Kentucky Bourbons and the Milwaukee Schlitz.

ESPN was followed by Showtime, C-SPAN, Nickelodeon, Arts and Entertainment (A&E), the Christian Broadcasting Network, and ultimately hundreds more. In 1980, when Ted Turner launched a twenty-four hour news station, CNN was greeted by hoots of derision and mocked as the Chicken Noodle Network. Comcast's John Ridall was working for Continental Cablevision in Ohio when Turner showed up to pitch his Cable News Network. "We were scratching our heads," Ridall says. "How could they possibly find things to talk about twenty-four hours a day?"

To Turner, it was obvious: "All-news radio was doing well in big markets, so you didn't have to be a genius to figure that if it worked on radio, it would probably work on TV. And it seemed like a nice thing for people who came home at different times of the day and couldn't catch the regular evening newscast." Competing with the network news divisions wasn't easy, and it took until the 1991 Gulf War, when it was the only American network with a camera crew and a correspondent in Baghdad, for CNN to be fully accepted. Once again, Ted Turner was ahead of the curve. As he liked to say, "I was cable before cable was cool."

And cable *was* cool, as more networks kept coming—Music Television (MTV), Discovery, Lifetime, CNN Headline News, USA, Bravo, Home Shopping Network, QVC, and many others. Cable operators were quickly persuaded that the appeal of these new channels easily justified the considerable expense of installing satellite dishes in each system. Before long, every cable system in the country would be using this new technology.

With the exception of HBO and Showtime, which as premium channels had their own source of revenue, the new cable networks would soon produce an additional income stream for operators: advertising. From the start, each channel that was part of the "basic" cable package gave operators two minutes per hour to sell local ads. "We were all starting from scratch," recalls Bernie Hayes from the Meadowlands system, who persuaded a local car dealer to advertise on CNN by asking, "Don't you want people to see your family on *Larry King*?" The dealer, a tough customer, refused to pay the asking price of $25 a spot, and said he wouldn't go higher than $2. Desperate for a sale, Hayes accepted the offer. A few days later, the dealer called and said, "Bernie, I'm hearing from all these people who say I look good. But I think I look fat!" From these humble origins, Comcast went on to develop Spotlight, a cable advertising division led by Charlie Thurston, which in 2011 employed thirty-six hundred people and took in $2.1 billion.

Because of these new cable channels, and especially HBO, many new franchise opportunities became available in the late 1970s and well into the 1980s, as cable companies rushed to acquire the right to build systems in the nation's cities and suburbs. "We are optimistic about the coming year," Ralph told the attendees at Comcast's annual shareholders' meeting in 1979, "but we anticipate increased costs in seeking new cable franchises." Suddenly it was no longer enough to have coffee with members of the town council in an effort to bring better reception to television-starved communities. When companies with big budgets began showing up with slick, multimedia campaigns, Comcast's informal, ad hoc approach was ineffective.

So Ralph put together a three-person franchising group. The cable expert on the team was Abe Patlove, who had returned to Comcast five years after leaving in frustration because of the company's sluggish expansion in its early years. The second member was Ed McGuire, who had served with Ralph on a board that oversaw Pennsylvania's state college system. McGuire knew little about cable, but he was a polished public speaker "who could talk for half an hour without saying anything," says Barbara Lukens, who adds, "and I mean that in a good way." Lukens, the third member of the team, was adept at the intricacies of municipal politics, "and because I was a woman, well spoken, with gray hair, people tended to believe me."

As competition grew, cable operators began hiring prominent or well-connected residents to serve as local advocates, a process known cynically as "rent-a-citizen," which was often abused. In one Michigan town, when an official told the Comcast team, "Just give me fifty thousand in cash and I'll take care of everything," they knew it was time to leave. And Michigan was by no means the worst. "We went 0 for 22 in one New England state," says Julian, proudly. "On the other hand, none of our people went to jail."

For the most part, though, misdeeds in the franchise wars didn't rise to the level of blatant corruption. More often, cable companies were making promises they couldn't possibly keep. Sometimes a representative had to go back, after a franchise had been granted, to request that some of its earlier assertions be deleted from the application. In one well-known case, an operator promised to plant ten thousand trees in the city of Sacramento. In a Michigan town, another company pledged to bury all its wires underground, but reneged on that commitment when they couldn't afford to keep it. In yet another community, a cable provider assured local authorities that subscribers would pay no more than two dollars a month—a ridiculous assertion for a company with any intention of staying in business.

"It was an impossible situation," says Lukens. "If you kept your promises, you couldn't possibly make a profit, but if you broke them, you weren't keeping your word." Later on, when Comcast purchased entire groups of cable systems, and sometimes entire companies, Lukens visited city councils across the land and was able to assure them that Comcast always kept its promises and had never once returned to a municipality to request a give-back. Understandably, some local officials found that hard to believe.

In 1983 the franchise team was summoned back to Bala Cynwyd, where Ralph, Dan, and Julian had been discussing the ethical issues that kept coming up in what was now a gold rush. Julian explained that with franchise fees going as high as 20 percent and cable operators making extravagant promises to secure new franchises, it was time to withdraw from the feeding frenzy. "The price of poker got too high," he says.

In the short term, the company paid a price for its integrity, but some of its more aggressive competitors were later forced to sell their systems—often to Comcast—because they couldn't deliver on their promises and still make a profit. One cable executive spent his first two years on the job going from city to city in an attempt to undo commitments that his company had made and was unable to keep. Ralph and his team valued their reputation, and as much as they wanted to grow, they refused to do anything that might compromise their credibility.

There was one prize that Ralph especially wanted to win—the right to build a cable system in Comcast's hometown of Philadelphia. The company had been awarded a franchise for a section of the city back in 1966, but complicated local politics had resulted in Comcast's having to submit four separate applications over the years, during which only a tiny section of the city had been wired for cable.

In the early 1980s, Barbara Lukens took charge of the fourth and final application, a huge undertaking in which each of the twenty applicants had to submit fifty copies of the necessary documents. At eight in the morning of December 22, 1982, after Comcast was the first to deliver its applications to the city's Municipal Services Building, a photographer from the *Philadelphia Inquirer* snapped a photo showing an entire wall of the storage room covered with Comcast material, with the logo clearly visible. It was great publicity, and free—although the company had spent over a million dollars on its various Philadelphia applications.

Two years later, Comcast was granted the cable franchise for Area 4, the northeast quadrant of the city, a neighborhood with very high home density. When the city council made clear that preference would be given to companies in which women and minorities were well represented, Ralph and Julian came up with an inventive solution. Comcast would create a small public company just for the northeast sector, which would be known as Comcast of Philadelphia. With the parent corporation maintaining a majority ownership, 20 percent of Comcast of Philadelphia's shares would be sold to women and minorities in Area 4, some of whom would sit on a special advisory board.

To make the investment more appealing, the shares, which were offered at $7.00 each, came with an unusual degree of protection: for the first two years, Comcast agreed to buy them back at $6.00, giving investors, including people who had never before bought shares in a public company, unlimited upside potential combined with minimal downside risk. An offer like this was hard to resist, which is why, despite the company's good intentions, most of the initial interest in these shares came from lawyers, suburbanites, and other upscale customers. "We worked a little longer," Julian recalls, "and reviewed the sales tickets with the underwriter to make sure the shares were distributed in the way we had intended."

Ten years later Comcast bought out the stockholders, paying them $92.50 per share—quite a nice premium if you had bought those shares at $7.00. Over the next twenty years the company was gradually able to acquire the other three quadrants as well. Today Philadelphia is an all-Comcast cable city.

To gather support for the application for Area 4, Ralph had met with a variety of community groups, telling them, as he describes it, "how wonderful we were and what we were planning to do." One of the people he met was Sister Francesca Onley, the president of Holy Family College (it's now a university) in the northeast section of the city. They developed a good rapport: Sister Francesca agreed to address the city council and recommend Comcast, and she later served on the board of Comcast of Philadelphia. When the company was ready to buy back the stock, Ralph asked her to chair the committee that would decide whether the offer was adequate. "We recommended a higher amount," she says, "and Comcast complied. I was impressed that they took our recommendation seriously."

They stayed in touch after Comcast won the franchise. "I felt

Ralph's gratitude for years," she says. "Whenever I asked to see him, he always made time for me, no matter how busy he was. He gave me advice about fund-raising and introduced me to a number of people who could be helpful to the school." In 1994, in recognition of his assistance to the school, Holy Family College awarded Ralph an honorary degree.

"Once I make up my mind about something," Ralph says, "I like to stay the course." Everyone who has worked closely with him knows how true that is. And those who were working with Ralph in the summer of 1983 will never forget his sudden visit to Timonium, Maryland. The town, which is just north of Baltimore, was the home of Calvert Telecommunications, known as CalTec, which owned a horseshoe-shaped cable system surrounding the city. This was one of the country's largest and most advanced systems, serving 100,000 homes in suburban Baltimore County.

CalTec was for sale and Ralph had submitted a bid, in part because its system was adjacent to Comcast's Harford County operation. There were other bidders, too: Continental Cablevision and Jones Intercable. When Ralph called Leonard Berger, the retired physician who controlled the company, to ask why he hadn't responded to the Comcast offer, Berger replied that the bid had been inadequate, and that CalTec's board was meeting that very day to award the system to Jones.

"Can you wait?" said Ralph. "I can be in your office in an hour and a half."

Berger said it was too late, but if Ralph insisted on coming, he was welcome to try. Ralph rounded up Jay Baer, Comcast's outside counsel, and Art Block, who was still working with Baer at Wolf Block, to tell them to be outside their building in fifteen minutes for a sudden trip to Maryland. Then Ralph and Julian climbed into a van and drove to the law firm. When Baer and Block joined them, Ralph explained that he was trying to buy a big cable system in Baltimore County. This came as a surprise to the lawyers; they had been working on a contract for the deal, but hadn't heard anything for a while.

When the Comcast delegation arrived in Timonium, Berger said the board had halted its meeting, and the Jones people were waiting in their hotel across the street.

Ralph got right to the point: "Len, what do we have to do to pull this out of the fire?"

"I told you, Ralph, it's too late."

"Len, what aren't they giving you that you want? Give me your list."

Berger had a list, but having seen a draft of the contract, he saw no point in going through it. "These are all things you wouldn't do," he said, but Ralph insisted on hearing them. Berger was explaining the first item when Art Block said, "Dr. Berger, that would be a problem for us."

Ralph held up his hand as if to say, "That's enough out of you." Then he turned to Berger and said, "Okay, you've got it. What's next?"

In the middle of the second item, Art Block objected again. And this time Ralph said, "Arthur!"

"I was trying to protect my client," Block says, "but by the third or fourth item, I finally realized that I should keep my mouth shut, that Ralph was running the show." When Berger had enumerated all his concerns, and Ralph had agreed to each one, including a significantly higher purchase price, Berger said, "Okay, it looks like you guys are getting it."

They walked over to the board meeting, where Berger introduced Ralph as the man who had just come in with a better offer. When the board agreed to the terms, Berger turned to Ralph and said, "This won't be fun. Now I have to tell Glenn Jones that he didn't get it."

Jones, who had flown in from Denver, wasn't expecting his trip to end this way. "We got shot out of the saddle at the last minute," he says. "We had the deal done and they swooped in and took it away from us. I was mad for a while, but I've done the same thing. That's how it works. It's just business."

CalTec's original stockholders were delighted: Comcast was paying them fifty times what they had paid when the company began.

Berger was happy, too: "Comcast did everything they promised. They continued building the system, which grew from 100,000 subscribers to around 500,000. Julian and I butted heads a little, but he was a very bright guy who pulled off the financing. I was comfortable with Ralph, and Dan, a real diplomat, defused every issue that came up."

"Ralph seemed more genuine than some of the other owners we met with," says Barbara Dannettel, Berger's executive assistant. There isn't much Ralph brags about other than his dancing skills, but he takes real satisfaction in knowing that sellers so often felt comfortable with him. "People hate to sell their businesses, even when there are good reasons," he says. "I was able to form strong relationships with them. I would assure them that we were there for the long term and would honor any promises they had made to the community."

From that day on, Jay Baer and Art Block started using a new expression: *Timonium Mode*. It meant that when Ralph was determined to acquire a property, the only thing you could do was get out of his way. Stanley Wang once defined Timonium Mode as the point where, after all the financial analysis was complete, you had to trust Ralph's gut about a system's true value. "Part of it is instinct," Wang said, "but another part is his competitive desire not to lose."

The Baltimore County acquisition was a major step forward for Comcast, and it boosted the company's subscribers by about a third. It turned out to be highly profitable as well, not only for Comcast, but also for investors in the gigantic $60 million off-balance-sheet limited partnership that Julian put together to finance the acquisition.

"Did I occasionally overpay?" says Ralph. "Julian would say we shouldn't exceed a certain amount, but sometimes there's only one of something, and you can't wait around forever. I overpaid in Baltimore County, and again in Indianapolis." Ralph was so eager to buy the Indianapolis system that he offered the sellers more than their asking price to make absolutely sure he got it. Even at their high prices, both Indianapolis and CalTec turned out to be excellent acquisitions.

By the mid-1980s, Ralph was no longer trying to hedge his bet on cable. Dan and Julian remained disciplined and cautious, and did their best to restrain Ralph's growing and seemingly irrational exuberance for additional properties. But it had taken twenty years to reach this point, and now there was no stopping him.

Typically, at the closing dinner that marks the end of a deal, participants are given souvenirs, which are often miniature Lucite versions of the "tombstone" ads that appear in the business section of newspapers and spell out basic details of the transaction. Baer and Block prepared a memento for the Baltimore County deal that was a replica of an actual tombstone, with the inscription, *Timonium Mode, R.I.P.* If this was intended as advice, Ralph failed to take it.

By the end of 1983, Comcast had close to half a million subscribers, with annual revenues of $84.4 million. New executives came in to help Dan Aaron manage the rapidly expanding cable business, but in most respects, what was now the country's fourteenth-largest cable operator had not changed much since the acquisition of Tupelo twenty years earlier. The company was still run by the same three men out of the same modest building in Bala Cynwyd, and as the Timonium acquisition made clear, they were still able to respond rapidly to good opportunities.

The cable industry had changed enormously during those twenty years, and much bigger changes lay ahead. This would certainly prove true for Ralph and his company. During the next two decades, Timonium Mode would be more than just an expression. It would pretty much define the Comcast way of life.

12

The Future

Brian Roberts

Many boys dream of becoming firefighters or ballplayers. Brian Roberts just wanted to work with his dad. "My father was in the men's belt business," he says, "and if he hadn't decided to do something else, I would probably be in that business today."

Suzanne and Ralph encouraged their five children to find work they really loved, and the kids followed their hearts. Brian's siblings pursued a variety of interests, ranging from architecture, art, and design to psychology, philanthropy, and law. At the dinner table, their father never discussed his work. Instead, he would ask each of his daughters and sons, "What happened in your life today?"

Brian liked to return the serve: "Dad, what did *you* do?" Ralph would sometimes say that all he had accomplished that day was to move papers from one side of his desk to the other, but Brian wanted to know more. As Ralph describes it, "This kid was interested in the business from the time he could talk."

Suzanne says that Brian was the only one of her children who didn't go through an adolescent rebellion; maybe he just couldn't wait to become an adult and do grown-up work. As a child, he loved coming to the office on Saturdays. When he was in high school, Ralph agreed to bring him along to a negotiation for what was then the biggest loan in the company's history. Three years earlier, just before Comcast went public, he had accompanied his father to a long night at Packard Press, the company's financial printer, where Ralph, Dan, Julian, and two lawyers were examining each page of the prospectus as it came off the press. The proofreading was nearly done when Brian spotted a chart that was printed backward. Even at thirteen, he had something to contribute.

Later, when Comcast was applying for a franchise in Philadelphia, he helped out in a telephone survey about the preferences of potential customers. "We were still in the infancy of a new industry," he says. "I always felt I had been there near the beginning, and that this was a fun place to be with my favorite person."

He was born on June 28, 1959, near the end of the postwar baby boom. Although Comcast veterans still think of him as young, in 1981, when Brian graduated from college, nobody he knew owned a personal computer. "I'm the youngest of the old guys," he once said, "rather than the oldest of the young guys."

He has always been interested in new technologies. At fourteen he took a summer job with Praxa, a computer company just across the river in New Jersey, and lived in Cherry Hill with Julian and Lois Brodsky and their three daughters. Brian worked on programming, but what he remembers most vividly from that summer are his many tennis matches with Julian and the hearty breakfasts that Lois prepared every morning for her husband and their guest.

The following summer he worked for Storecast, the supermarket promotion company that Ralph had recently acquired. Together with a friend who was old enough to drive, Brian would ride around from store to store to ensure that certain products, including L'eggs pantyhose, *People* magazine, and a line of ice cream toppings, were in good supply and easy to find. On their first morning, when the boys were filling out employment forms, one of the executives brought Brian into her office, closed the door, and said sternly, "Listen, I don't care whose son you are. If you're working for me, you're going to *work*!" Brian, caught by surprise, had to fight back tears. What could he possibly have done wrong, he wondered, to deserve this? He hadn't even started yet.

He later decided that this woman had actually done him a favor. She was telling him that he had better get comfortable with being the boss's son, because if the future worked out as he hoped, he would be spending a good chunk of his life in that role, where he would have to work a little harder than the next person just to stay even. In the years that followed, he would sometimes draw on that encounter to motivate himself.

He spent the next summer at the Westmoreland cable system in western Pennsylvania, where he was trained as an installer. It wasn't easy: At six feet tall, but weighing, he recalls, only 125 pounds, he could barely lift the ladder. It must have looked like an old silent comedy, with this rail-thin kid staggering around with a heavy ladder, pulling it up to the pole, and somehow climbing to the top. But he learned how to install cable in homes and handle routine service calls. He also became aware of the job's potential hazards when a fellow worker was almost electrocuted after backing into a downed power wire. It was a scary reminder that a cable tech's work isn't free of danger.

He would call his father every night, and soon after he mentioned the electrical accident, he was transferred to door-to-door selling. As Ralph tells the story, Brian had said, "Dad, it's great out here. After work these guys go into a bar, have a beer, and flirt with the waitresses." To which his father responded, "I think it's time for you to move on."

During high school, when he was reading the *Wall Street Journal*, he became interested in the stock market, and during the spring of his senior year he worked in the Philadelphia office of Drexel Burnham

Lambert, the investment firm. When he noticed that Comcast wasn't listed in the *Standard & Poor's Stock Guide*, he contacted the publisher and made sure the omission was corrected. He was popular at Drexel and stayed on for the summer, preparing reports for clients, assisting the analysts, and developing an interest in investment banking and deal making.

The summer he turned nineteen, he was off to Michigan to work with Abe Patlove, who was lining up new franchises. One afternoon he joined Patlove's team at a city council meeting, where he observed how local officials managed the selection process among competing applicants. That evening, after the group had presented their final application following months of hard work, they went out to celebrate and ended up at a kind of gentlemen's club.

Before long, a young woman came over to dance at their table. She started undoing Brian's tie—one of Ralph's favorites, which Brian had borrowed for the trip. (Ralph wasn't always a bow-tie man.) When her dance was done, she tossed the tie up into the rafters. Looking up, Brian saw hundreds of ties hanging there. His companions were enjoying the moment too much to intervene, but when somebody said he could recover the tie for twenty dollars, he gladly paid up. As they left the club, Brian said, "It's been fun tonight, but let's keep this evening to ourselves, okay?"

"Absolutely."

"Of course, Brian."

"No problem."

Back home a few days later, he came to work and was greeted by Dan's assistant: "I hear you had a pretty wild time in Michigan the other night." Brian forced a smile. "And that," he says, "was when I learned that there were no secrets at Comcast."

Another summer, another Comcast job. Now he was in Dallas, working for the Muzak division. But like Storecast, Muzak didn't really interest him. While Ralph was open to almost any good business, Brian loved cable—and, in time, the exciting new products that cable would lead to.

Throughout these years, Brian talked with his father about every aspect of the company. Evidently, he also thought deeply about its future. In 2005 the widow of a former Comcast executive found a lengthy memo to the company's top leadership that Brian had written twenty-five years earlier, in the summer of 1980, when he was entering his senior year of college.

It is an extraordinary document. Much of the memo addressed the franchise wars, and Brian sided with those, including Ralph and Julian, who thought Comcast should become more aggressive before the best opportunities were gone. Because it took just as much time and effort to apply for a large franchise as a smaller one, he recommended a greater focus on larger communities. He pointed out that earnings might decline for several years if the company was serious about expanding but argued that the trade-off was worth it: "In 1985," he asked, "will we care what our 1981 net income was, or will we care that our total subscriber base is x% higher than it might have otherwise been?"

Like any good debater, he also addressed the most compelling counterargument—that a decline in earnings would hurt the stock price. Cable stocks were doing well, he pointed out, so if Comcast could ever afford weaker earnings, this was the time. Besides, he asked, wasn't management required to act in the best long-term interests of the shareholders? "If, in our opinion, earnings growth should be temporarily sacrificed for possible future growth, then we should act accordingly." It was a prescient point, and the language was revealing. By using the pronouns *our* and *we*, Brian, at twenty-one, seemed to be including himself as part of management.

He also called for hiring new executives to serve one level below Ralph, Dan, and Julian. In a comment that foreshadowed the hiring, years later, of Larry Smith, John Alchin, Dave Watson, and especially Steve Burke, he recommended bringing in businesspeople who could learn about cable, rather than cable executives who could learn about business. His memo touched on several other concerns before he ended with a joke that may have been intended to mollify anyone who took offense at these bold remarks: "Send your comments to: Brian L. Roberts, c/o TelePrompTer, New York, N.Y."

• • •

A year later, shortly before he graduated from Wharton with a degree in finance, Brian was offered interviews with leading investment banks and other financial institutions. He went to one, but his heart wasn't in it. Even with the whole world open to him, he just wanted to work with his father.

But first he was planning to participate in the Maccabiah Games, a quadrennial summer competition in Israel for Jewish athletes from around the world. He had played squash in college, a sport he took up after being cut from his high school basketball team before he had reached his full height. At Penn he played for the legendary squash coach Al Molloy, a former marine whom Brian has called the second most influential person in his life. "He was the complete opposite of my father," he says, "who was nurturing and only wanted me to succeed. With Coach Molloy, if you lost a match he would lecture you for an hour and then demand another hour of running sprints." The coach's motto, written on the board of the locker room, was "No Pain, No Gain." He taught Brian that winning requires not only preparation and practice, but physical and mental toughness. "Go for it," he would say. "Take your shot."

In Israel, Brian was a member of the U.S. squash team, which won the silver medal. He would return to the Maccabiah Games four more times, most recently in 2009, when he won his fourth silver medal to go along with a gold from 2005, when he was captain of the U.S. team in the 45-to-50 age group. (On his two most recent trips he was accompanied by the older, and then the younger, of his squash-playing daughters, who competed in their respective age groups.)

Before he left Philadelphia, father and son had some long and difficult conversations about where Brian would work when he returned. Everybody he knew—professors, advisors, friends, and his father, too—had offered the same advice: "Of course you can work at Comcast, but what's your hurry? You'll be better off going somewhere else for a few years, where you can prove yourself, gain experience, and become your own man. Then, with all that knowledge and confidence, you'll be more valuable to Comcast."

"My father begged him to get experience at other companies," says Brian's sister Lisa. "We even had family discussions about the value of learning how other people do business."

But to Brian, five years anywhere else meant five years down the drain. It wasn't just that he wanted to work at Comcast; he wanted to work with his father, and there was some troubling family history to consider. Ralph had lost both parents by the time he was twenty-one; his brother, Joe, had died at fifty-three; and his sister, Shirley, at fifty-two. He was in his sixties, and although he was healthy, Ralph had never expected to live a long life. Fifteen years earlier, he had bought Suzanne a "widow's house" in the city, just in case. "You're not getting any younger," Brian told his father. "I want to work with you while you're still around."

In a sense, they had been working together for years. During high school and college, Brian had attended industry conventions and other meetings with his father, and they had always shared a room. He had listened to Ralph's hopes and dreams from the day the company was named, and probably even earlier. Now that his formal education was over, he wanted to continue that ongoing conversation with his father.

When Ralph remained unconvinced, Brian blurted out, "I guess you don't want me." (Or, as Ralph remembers it, "Why are you rejecting me?") However he phrased it, his heartfelt appeal turned the key.

Ralph, who had long been thinking of Brian as his likely successor, explained that even if he started at Comcast, they wouldn't actually be working together for quite a while. First, Brian had to continue learning the business, which meant putting in time at several cable systems. They agreed that in the fall of 1981, when Brian returned from Israel and Europe, he would become a trainee at the new Comcast system in Trenton, New Jersey. At some future date, Ralph told him, if he performed well in other jobs, he could come to headquarters to work in finance.

On his first day in Trenton, where the office was housed in a former car dealership, all his hopes could have crashed and burned. A summer job is temporary, but this was the real thing. Trenton, a gritty urban center and New Jersey's notably unglamorous capital, is less than an hour from Philadelphia, but to Brian it seemed like another world. After his mother helped him set up his modest apartment, he reported to work.

The next day, when a truck pulled up to the office with fifty cartons of set-top boxes, the whole staff formed a spontaneous bucket brigade to unload them. In Trenton, as in most cable systems in those days, everybody did everything. Brian, who was prepared to be disappointed by the mundane reality of his first full-time assignment, warmed to the job immediately. "It felt like we were running our own business," he says, "and we all did whatever needed to be done." Tuesday might be devoted to set-top boxes, and Thursday to answering the phone because the late notices had gone out. Friday meant standing at the counter on Payment Day, when customers without checking accounts came in with cash.

Brian was known for his customer-friendly approach. "The service reps said I was undermining our policies," he says, "but I grew up with the idea that our real boss was the customer." He was popular at the office and played third base on the company softball team. Sometimes, when he was running late, you could see his black dress socks under the pants of his uniform.

Because so many customers paid in cash, there was a safe in the office where the money was stored until somebody could take it to the bank. One morning, $20,000 was missing. "One of our employees showed up the next day in a fur coat and resigned," Brian recalls. "We couldn't prove anything, but I was the controller, and I probably should have been fired."

About a year later, Brian and Dan Aaron were driving to a meeting when Dan pulled over and said, "You may not like this, but I'm moving you to Flint, Michigan. It's a bigger operation and we need an assistant manager."

In Flint he was responsible for marketing, customer service, and getting cable into new apartment buildings. At one point he spoke with residents of a building who had to wait months for cable because of all the paperwork. He told Ralph that the local systems needed more flexibility and authority, and years later, when he was in a position to shape corporate policy, he would remember Flint and push for still more local control.

Jan Thompson, a dispatch supervisor when Brian arrived, says, "He was there to learn the business. He would ride out with the techs and sit down with all of us. Although we worked twelve-hour days, six days a week, we were always having fun, and he was part of that. But we could see he was a visionary. He told us that in ten years we would all be carrying around a little phone that didn't need wires, and I remember thinking that this guy could see into the future when some of us couldn't figure out what to wear tomorrow."

A year later, Dan Aaron asked Brian to return to Trenton as the general manager. It was a promotion, but Brian didn't see it that way because Trenton was a smaller system. "Trust me," Dan said, "there's a big difference between being number two in a big system and number one in a smaller one." Brian wasn't buying it, but he went anyway.

These various postings were not part of any master plan. Comcast was growing quickly, executive talent was always in demand, and opportunities were constantly opening up. At the same time, Ralph had high expectations for his son, and Brian had his eye on a much bigger prize: he wanted to run the company when his father no longer did. But they both viewed this outcome as a possibility, not an entitlement. As much as Ralph loved him and hoped he would rise to the top, Brian had to earn his way there.

He soon discovered that Dan was right, that being in charge of a system, even a small one, really *was* different. The company's youngest GM, who was all of twenty-three, now had to deal with entirely new situations, like the news that an employee was pregnant and that the expectant father, an installer in the same office, was married to someone else.

And he didn't have to wait long for his first crisis. Comcast technicians were cutting through pavement in downtown Trenton when they accidentally severed a major telephone line that was critical to both New Jersey Bell and AT&T long distance. On the Friday before Mother's Day, half the city had no phone service; within an hour, twenty-four phone company trucks had arrived at the site. Brian was quickly able to show that the accident occurred because New Jersey Bell had failed to identify the line—a standard precaution that was intended to avoid this very problem. But he worried that Comcast might be blamed for the outage. "Here's the deal," he told his counterpart at the phone company. "In an hour we're going to issue a statement saying that this is your fault, or you can put out your own statement right now taking responsibility." The manager called back and said, "You're right, it's our fault, we admit it."

Although the incident barely registered outside of Trenton, it was the biggest moment thus far in Brian's career. It was also a lesson. "It's part of our culture that the GM should feel like he owns the business," he says. "There's no cookie-cutter way of doing things. We seek out people who are entrepreneurial and can improvise in a crisis."

He was soon transferred again, this time to the corporate office in Bala to become group vice president for the Trenton, Philadelphia, and Lower Merion areas. Although Brian was at headquarters, where he had always wanted to be, the move was a letdown, at least initially. Compared to his time in the field, the corporate office seemed slow, bureaucratic, and far removed from the action. Instead of stepping out of his office to say, "Hey, let's try this," he had to wait for the next meeting, or worse, write a memo. And his new responsibilities included hiring and firing GMs—managing the managers, in other words, which can be awkward when they're all older than you.

Bob Clasen was running the cable division, and Brian was appointed as his deputy. They formed an effective partnership, with Clasen looking at the big picture while Brian concentrated on the details. "He was like my younger brother," Clasen says. "We were a good team, and he was such a quick study. We were also the face of the next generation, and I think we gave the senior guys some comfort."

• • •

In 1985 Brian married Aileen Kennedy, a beautiful banker who had grown up in nearby Wayne, Pennsylvania. They met on her birthday at a fund-raiser for the U.S. Olympic Ski Team. "Haven't I seen you somewhere?" he asked when he passed Aileen on the staircase of the Franklin Institute. "No," she replied. She was there with a date, but Brian had come alone, which pretty much summed up his dating life, he said later. He asked her to dance, and because her date wasn't a dancer, Aileen said yes.

On Monday he called her at work: "Hi, it's Brian."

Brian who? It took her a moment to realize that this was a social call, and that Brian was the tall fellow she had danced with. Although Aileen was seeing someone else, Brian kept calling and asking her out to romantic places—like squash tournaments. "Some of these dates didn't sound all that appealing," she says. "I must have canceled five of them." When she bailed out of a Philadelphia Eagles game because she was genuinely sick, he left chicken soup and flowers with her doorman. Aileen was touched; when she broke their next date, she sent *him* flowers. The way things were going, that was progress.

"Brian was a man on a mission," Aileen says, noting his unwavering determination in the face of her early ambivalence. His perseverance paid off: eventually they went to dinner, and then to the movies. Aileen says that even on their first date there was something about this guy that she hadn't felt before. As for Brian, "Aileen may not have been the first girl he kissed," says a friend, "but she was probably the first girl he kissed twice."

That summer she joined him in Israel, where he was back at the Maccabiah Games. Then they went to Egypt, where he proposed during a boat cruise on the Nile. Aileen had come down with a bad case of food poisoning, and when Brian popped the question, she was holding on to the railing. "I have to sit down," she told him. Then she said yes.

In the weeks leading up to the proposal, he had tried to reduce the odds of being rejected. Like a character in an old logic puzzle, he would ask, in various ways, "If I were to ask you to marry me, how would you respond?"

Aileen refused to answer. All she would say was, "You'll have to ask me first."

In 1987 Brian was named a corporate vice president and began to specialize in programming negotiations with CNN, HBO, ESPN, MTV, and other networks. By this time, some of the larger operators, especially John Malone of TCI, the country's largest cable company, were starting to invest in content. Although Ralph, Dan, and Julian had other priorities, Bob Clasen and Brian made every effort to change their minds.

The issue came to a head in 1986, when Ted Turner bought the MGM film studio and its library of 3,500 movies. Turner, who had spent a fortune on the acquisition, was soon forced to sell parts of MGM back to Kirk Kerkorian, its previous owner. But he still faced financial problems and was in danger of losing control of his company. To prevent that, John Malone convened a meeting of his fellow operators and urged them to help Turner by investing in his company; otherwise, Malone warned, Ted's cable properties could fall into less friendly hands, such as those of a broadcast network.

After considering a much larger investment, which Brian and Clasen were recommending, Ralph and Julian put in only $5 million, a token amount in a $565 million rescue plan. Around the same time, Ralph and Dan decided against taking an equity position in the Discovery Channel. Not investing in Turner and Discovery, says Julian, were "our two worst decisions. Our mind-set was to plow every nickel back into distribution, rather than buying a little of this and a little of that. We didn't see the point of owning 10 percent of Turner. We were operators, rather than investors, but those minority positions came to have enormous value."

These weren't easy calls. Ralph agreed that Comcast should be investing in content. But funds were always limited, and the more urgent priority, he believed, was to continue doing what the company had always done by acquiring more subscribers. Besides, he never liked the idea of owning a fraction of a company that he couldn't control.

Even so, Ted Turner thought enough of Brian to appoint him to his board. Brian and Ralph welcomed the invitation, but Julian wondered if this wasn't a conflict of interest. Weren't programmers and distributors essentially at war?

"He had a case," says Brian, "but Ralph saw this as part of my continuing education." Brian's friend Tim Neher from Continental Cablevision, who also sat on the Turner board, gives credence to Julian's unease: "Brian and I were both concerned about how Turner would price new programming services, but in board meetings we wore our Turner hats and acted in the best interests of the company. Later on, when Ted wanted to add a surcharge for CNN after the Gulf War, we persuaded our fellow directors that this wasn't a good idea."

Brian relished the opportunity to get a good, close look at programing deals that often had no bearing on Comcast. As the youngest board member, he came to know some of the leading cable operators and gained a much wider view of the industry. Most of the meetings were in Atlanta, but the Turner board also traveled to Russia and even to Cuba, where Castro showed up for an extended late-night conversation with Turner as the others listened in.

For Brian, the Turner board was like an elite graduate seminar. Turner, too, was pleased, and calls Brian's appointment "one of the smartest moves I ever made." He may have been thinking of the day in 1993 when the board was evenly divided on whether to allow him to buy two movie companies, New Line Cinema and Castle Rock Entertainment, and Brian cast the deciding vote that made the deal possible.

His education continued in 1988 when TCI's John Malone, aware of Brian's interest in emerging technologies, invited him to serve on the board of the newly created Cable Television Laboratories, the industry's R&D consortium, which soon became known as CableLabs. Malone was friendly with Ralph and liked Brian, and he admired Comcast's scrappy, entrepreneurial style. CableLabs organized research trips, which included a 1991 visit to Japan, where the group saw its first high-definition television set. (The price was $30,000.)

On the long flight over, while the others were sleeping, Brian sat with Malone, who spent the whole night talking with him and answering his many questions. Later, the group would visit leading technology companies in Europe, California, and the Pacific Northwest. As Brian describes it, "We all recognized that we would soon be rebuilding our systems for a digital future, and that we should see the full range of what was possible. Otherwise, we would risk experiencing the technological equivalent of 'I could've had a V8!' just after we had invested in tomato juice."

By the end of the 1980s, there wasn't much at Comcast that Brian wasn't involved in. In early 1989, making good on a commitment that was part of its successful Philadelphia franchise application, the company left its longtime home in Bala Cynwyd and moved downtown. The developer Willard Rouse was building One Liberty Place, which was going to be the newest, nicest, and highest building in town, with retail space on the ground floor. Comcast was planning to occupy the top four or five floors.

During the construction, the owner's representative brought Ralph, Brian, and Julian up in an open-air elevator to see what had been advertised as the best view in Philadelphia. Later, when the windows were in place, Ralph went up to see it again. But because of the glass the builder had used, when Ralph looked out, he mostly saw his own reflection. That, he said, was a deal breaker. One way of compensating employees for the inconvenience of moving, he believed, was to offer them a wonderful view of the city. If he couldn't do that, he would find another space.

Comcast ended up renting four floors two blocks away in a building known as One Meridian Plaza, which faced the south side of City Hall. Brian was in charge of the move, and he and Ralph, together with designer Karen Daroff, spent hours picking out carpets, wood, and desks.

Shortly before the move downtown, Brian called the Chamber of Commerce to ask what other companies had done to compensate employees for lunches, parking, and the city's wage tax. The response was a long silence, followed by, "You know, I can't think of another company that has moved from the suburbs to the city in recent years."

To compensate for the wage tax, the company granted a 5 percent raise to every corporate employee earning under a designated amount. Although Comcast could do nothing about parking, the City Hall neighborhood was easily accessible by both public transportation and commuter trains. Of the 225 employees in Bala Cynwyd, all but two remained with the company when it moved to Center City. And when the interior was completed, with an atrium lobby and a beautiful staircase with a tree in the middle, the new corporate home was a vivid reminder that the Bala days were over.

Shortly after the move, Brian hired consultant Mark Coblitz, who joined the executive team to help think about and plan for the next few years. With the phone companies using a powerful new tool called fiber optics as they prepared to take on the cable companies, the industry would soon be more competitive. "We needed a few specialists who would look at specific aspects of where the world was going," Brian says. "What got us to this point was not going to carry us to the finish line." He had always kept a close eye on the future, which was now rushing toward him at unprecedented speed.

13

Big Deals

Bob Clasen and Ralph Roberts

By the mid-1980s, Ralph had both the muscle and the appetite to hunt for bigger game. Before the decade was over, he would make two sizable acquisitions and a modest but important investment in a brand new business that was made possible by cable. Together, these ventures would put Comcast on the map.

By the end of the 1970s, cable's entrepreneurial era was over. The industry was starting to consolidate, and some veteran operators were allowing their companies to be acquired. But Ralph hadn't started this business with any intention of selling it. For the man who had always seen Comcast as a future industry leader, the way forward was clear: the company had to get bigger.

Just as Brian had recommended in his 1980 memo, Ralph and Julian were willing to accept lower earnings as the price of expansion.

In the 1982 Annual Report, Ralph was candid about their intentions: "Our philosophy is long range," he told the shareholders, "and we will, if necessary, sacrifice short-term profits to ensure long-term growth in earnings and shareholder value."

This was a dramatic change for a company that had experienced one quarter after another of steady earnings growth. From the start, the policy had been to generate earnings and avoid losses. To maintain that practice, Julian had financed some acquisitions off-balance-sheet, using limited partnerships. But when cable values started to rise and the company's financial partners were reaping returns as high as 40 percent, it was clear that too much money was being left on the table.

And so the long-standing practice of maximizing accounting earnings was finally abandoned. Now the emphasis would be on growing cash flow, which savvy investors already recognized as the key to shareholder value. As Julian had been telling lenders and investors from the day he arrived, the true measure of a cable company's financial health wasn't operating income, but EBITDA—Earnings Before Interest, Taxes, Depreciation, and Amortization. As John Malone liked to say, "There's a big difference between reporting income and creating wealth."

It took Wall Street a long time to appreciate this. Back in 1968, four years before Comcast's IPO, a young E. F. Hutton analyst named Paul Kagan had authored a report on five promising cable stocks. But Hutton wouldn't release his recommendations because none of these companies showed a profit. Kagan thought this policy was misguided, and he left Hutton to publish his own cable investment newsletter.

Years later, he calculated that at the bottom of the market in December 1974, the average share price of a cable stock was $2, and that by January 2000, a market peak, it had (unadjusted for splits) soared to $6,095. To put these numbers in perspective, cable stocks during this period outperformed even Berkshire Hathaway, Warren Buffett's legendary holding company, during its first forty years.

• • •

As Ralph was planning to grow the business, Dan Aaron was becoming even more cautious than usual. In the early 1980s, he had started feeling sluggish, off balance, and less alert. "You're working too hard," his doctor said. "Relax, and the symptoms should go away." When Dan developed tremors in his arm and his hand, other doctors, too, told him not to worry. It was a psychiatrist who finally realized that Dan had Parkinson's.

Around this time, he drove to Ralph's house one night for a private conversation. "You're ruining the company," he said.

"What do you mean?"

"You're buying more systems when we don't have enough people to run the ones we already own. We should stand pat for a year."

"We can't afford to," said Ralph, "because other people are out there, looking for properties. But I can see you're being stretched, and I think we should bring in somebody to help run the cable division."

Dan didn't tell Ralph the whole story that night, and it's possible that he hadn't yet been diagnosed, although Ralph had noticed the tremors. Dan had always been in favor of slowing down, but to ask Ralph to stop expanding? This was new.

Dan hired several cable managers until he found the right one. By 1984, when his illness forced him to cut back, his increasing absence, together with Ralph's decision to grow faster, meant that Comcast urgently needed an infusion of professional managerial talent.

In the summer of 1984, Ralph and Dan brought in Bob Clasen, who had run the U.S. division of Rogers Cable, a Canadian company. At first, Ralph hedged his bet by retaining the cable division's existing president, Dan Gold, and making Clasen the chairman. "Ralph was cautious," Clasen says. "Having come from the belt and suspenders business, he wanted to make doubly sure his pants stayed up." When it became clear that Clasen was the right man, Dan Gold moved on.

Clasen was a super-organized type who kept minutes of every meeting and generated a lot of paper. He was punctual, too: if a meeting was scheduled for nine o'clock, he would close the door at 9:01. He distributed elaborate daily planning books and taught senior managers how to use them. "The training for those books took two days," says Dave D'Ottavio, who was vice president of the Northeast Region, "but I still use mine. With so much going on, he wanted us to be as organized as possible."

Clasen's arrival was a culture shock for a company that still felt like a family business. But most veterans agreed that he introduced some essential big-company procedures to a place that needed them. "It wasn't easy," said Stanley Wang, "but he dragged us into organizationville."

Clasen stepped into a growing operation that was still being run like a small company. There was no structure in place for human resources or marketing, so he filled those gaps. To make the cable division more efficient, he installed a team of regional vice presidents, including Tom Baxter, who would follow him as head of the cable division. His biggest challenge was persuading Ralph, and especially Julian, to let the company be more decentralized, and he succeeded. Regional vice presidents were given more autonomy and authority, although Comcast continued to emphasize its long-standing annual budgeting process. Eventually the division presidents, as they would later be known, would evolve into princes of the realm, with the corporate office gradually assuming more of an oversight role.

To control costs, Clasen made sure that a CFO was hired to work closely with each region's operating executives, just as Julian had long worked closely, if not always smoothly, with Dan. Years later, this arrangement is still in place. "We look for one and one to make three," says Rick Palmer, who was senior vice president of finance for the Eastern Division. "The operating talent of one person and the business sense of another are more than the sum of their parts. If the term weren't overused, I'd call it synergy."

These were big changes. Ever since 1963, when Ralph bought Tupelo, The Boys had run the company informally, with little interest in titles or lines of authority. They made decisions by reaching a consensus, even when that process was slow, painful, or loud. Typically, the three of them would gather together in the late afternoon to plan for the short term. Clasen had the good sense not to interfere with this practice, but he did institutionalize it by scheduling a formal meeting every Monday at six. With these administrative reforms in place, Comcast was more prepared for the kind of growth that Ralph was looking for.

Back in 1970, when it acquired the Sarasota system from Comcast, Storer Communications, as it would later be known, wasn't yet a cable powerhouse. But in the early 1980s, Storer's aggressive posture during the franchise wars transformed the company into one of the nation's largest operators, with about a million and a half subscribers in eighteen states. The industry leader was John Malone's TCI (Tele-Communications, Inc.), followed by ATC (American Television and Communications Corporation), the cable arm of Time Inc. In third place was Group W, which was owned by Westinghouse, with Storer in fourth. Depending on who was counting, and on what day, Comcast was in sixteenth or seventeenth place.

But Storer's big spending had led to problems. "One year we were awarded the most franchises," says Buck Dopp, who managed a Storer system in Connecticut before coming to Comcast, "but it was a Pyrrhic victory because it broke the company." In 1985, after a power struggle with a large shareholder group that wanted to liquidate the company, Storer's leadership turned to Kohlberg Kravis Roberts & Co., the prominent leveraged buyout firm, and asked them to acquire the company at a premium over its languishing stock price.

By now Ralph and Julian had developed a close working relationship with Paul Mejean at Shearson, a leading investment bank. When word got out that KKR had agreed to buy Storer for $1.8 billion, Mejean and his colleagues urged Comcast to consider making a competing bid.

Ralph didn't need much encouragement. He called Peter Storer, whose father, George, had bought the Sarasota system from Ralph fifteen years earlier.

"Does this mean your company is for sale?" Ralph asked him.

Storer answered carefully. "If you make a bid," he told Ralph, "we would have to take it to the board." Ralph, of course, took that as a big fat yes.

Shearson came up with a bold plan in which Comcast, which had never borrowed more than $100 million, would make an offer for Storer in the neighborhood of $2 billion. The bid would depend on a loan of $900 million from a consortium of banks, which was fine with Ralph. But when Mejean explained that the entire corporation would be responsible for that loan, that Ralph would have to bet the company to bid for Storer, he refused to consider it. "Although he wanted to buy everything in sight," says Brian, "there were certain risks he wasn't willing to take."

Eager to be part of a big transaction, Shearson came up with a different proposal, whereby the investment bank itself would guarantee the value of the TV stations that were part of the package and then quickly sell them off, leaving Comcast with what it actually wanted — Storer's many cable properties. Under this arrangement, Ralph would no longer have to put the company on the line.

On Wednesday, July 3, 1985, with two weeks left to make an offer, Ralph and Julian were at the Manhattan law offices of Shearman & Sterling, which was representing Comcast in its bid for Storer. They had already met with a diverse group of bankers, who were seeking approval for various loans. Now they were waiting for the official go-ahead from Shearson, whose credit committee was meeting to approve the deal. Mejean had assured them that this was just a formality, but as the hours passed with no word, they began to wonder. Then, at the last moment, Shearson demanded significant changes in the terms, including considerably more money for the risk it had to assume. "The deal they presented to us was so different that we didn't even recognize it," says Julian.

He was angry, but not at Mejean. "I felt sorry for Paul, who was double-crossed by his own team." Mejean remembers this as one of the most difficult moments of his career. "They backed out at the last minute," he says, "and I had the unhappy task of informing Ralph and Julian after telling them repeatedly not to worry." Although Mejean knew he might never again do business with Comcast, he traveled to Philadelphia to offer a personal apology to his clients. "Paul was heartbroken when we dropped Shearson," says Ralph, "but we knew it wasn't his fault." Nineteen years later, Mejean was especially pleased to be invited to Julian's retirement dinner.

When they heard the news from Shearson, Ralph and Julian left the law firm in shock. Out on the street on a hot summer day, they stood on the sidewalk in stunned silence. Their deal lawyer, Steve Volk, who was working with them for the first time, said what they were all feeling—that Shearson's new terms were unacceptable. But Volk wasn't giving up: "This deal might be perfect for Merrill Lynch," he said. "Maybe they'll see us."

With the Fourth of July weekend about to start, that seemed like wishful thinking. But with nothing to lose, Volk went to the nearest pay phone and called Ken Miller, the head of Merrill Lynch's Mergers and Acquisitions department. "Come right over," Miller said. "We're just a couple of blocks away."

Sometimes when one door closes, another one opens. For Merrill, the opportunity to jump into a big, highly leveraged transaction was exactly what they were looking for. For the past couple of years, both KKR and Michael Milken's team at Drexel Burnham in Los Angeles, which was backing KKR's bid for Storer with its trademark junk bonds, had been taking business from the bigger, older investment banks. In the hot, new financial world of the 1980s, Merrill Lynch was increasingly viewed as a lumbering and irrelevant dinosaur. Then, without any warning, says Julian, "these little guys from Philadelphia, who had just been jilted by Shearson, walk in with just the right need at the right time."

Merrill quickly committed $1.2 billion of its own money to the Comcast bid—a huge sum in those days, and the first time a Wall Street firm had formally agreed to use its own capital in this way. This bridge loan, a temporary financing until a longer-term package could be arranged, was contingent on Comcast's ability to secure the $900 million loan from the consortium of commercial banks that was already in the works. "They were getting people in over the holiday weekend," Julian recalls, "and we were telling them what Merrill was going to do. They said, 'Merrill? What happened to Shearson?'"

"That was last week," Julian told them. "Things have changed."

Nobody at KKR had expected a competing bid for Storer, and certainly not from a company as small as Comcast. Julian received a call from KKR's Henry Kravis, who pretty much told him not to bother, because KKR and Storer already had an agreement. Kravis offered a consolation prize: Comcast could buy Wometco, an over-the-air pay-television service that was part of the Storer empire. Julian said no thanks, because he and Ralph were going after the whole package.

"If that's the case," said Kravis, "let your actions be guided by how you feel about Comcast." In other words, if we can buy Storer, we can easily buy you.

"Mr. Kravis," Julian replied, "we always welcome new shareholders." A year or so later, when they finally met, Kravis said to Julian, "Obviously, I didn't know about the voting stock."

Now that Comcast was playing with the big boys, the company's name started appearing in the business press. A *New York Times* article about the Storer auction in the summer of 1985 reported that the little-known cable operator "is considered among the best-run companies in the industry. Its management style and its consistent profitability explain why several industry observers have compared its bid for Storer to Capital Cities Communications, Inc.'s pending purchase of ABC." This flattering analogy would gain some additional resonance in the years ahead.

At the end of July, when both suitors had made their final offers, which involved complicated mixes of cash, equity, and other considerations, the Storer board chose KKR. It was a curious decision: one of the Storer directors told the *Times* that the Comcast offer appeared to be four dollars a share higher, but that KKR's bid included certain tax advantages.

Ralph's candor may have played a part. Although he offered Peter Storer the chance to continue running the company, the proposal made clear that Comcast would be selling off the TV stations, an issue that KKR might have danced around. A few weeks after the deal closed, KKR sold the stations and Peter Storer either quit or was forced out. "We lost this one on Ralph's integrity," says Brian. "He didn't try to sugarcoat what was happening."

"When it was over," says Julian, "Ralph, Dan, and I had a serious conversation. Did we lose because of our Boy Scout behavior? Maybe, but that's who we were, and every now and then we might lose a deal. But it's also true that KKR had the inside track because Storer's management had invited them in as the white knight."

It was a tough defeat, because Ralph had been willing to raise his offer substantially, but Merrill Lynch wouldn't go any higher. "The bidding stopped at $92," says Julian, "but we were prepared to go to $110 and maybe more. But Comcast ran out of money and Merrill ran out of courage."

Henry Kravis was said to be furious with Ralph and Julian for making the acquisition so expensive. When KKR first started selling off Storer's cable systems, Comcast wasn't even allowed to make an offer.

Sometimes a disappointment leads to a positive outcome, even if it's not the one you were hoping for. Storer wasn't the only cable operation that had grown too quickly in the early 1980s; something similar had happened at Westinghouse. After acquiring TelePrompTer in 1981 and putting its cable systems into its own broadcasting division, Group W, Westinghouse continued buying franchises. Three years later, the company decided to sell its cable holdings.

A few weeks after KKR acquired Storer, Ralph heard from Nick Nicholas, the head of Time Inc., who asked whether Comcast would like to team up with his company's cable division in a joint bid for the cable systems of Group W, which were expected to be available soon. Ralph said he'd love to. Then TCI's John Malone called with a similar invitation. "I just got through telling Nick Nicholas that we would do this with them," Ralph said. "But if he doesn't mind, three ways is okay, too."

"I couldn't believe they both called," says Ralph, who was delighted by these invitations from the industry leaders, which were a direct result of the Comcast bid for Storer. That same week, Julian was sharing a taxi with Stewart Blair, his counterpart at TCI, when the conversation turned to Group W. "Why don't we do this together?" asked Blair.

"Why us?" Julian asked.

"After what you guys did with Storer, you're the last people we'd want to meet coming down the alley the other way on this one."

In December 1985 a consortium of the three companies, plus two much smaller ones, agreed to pay $1.73 billion for the Group W systems and to assume certain tax and other liabilities, making this the cable industry's largest transaction to date. (KKR's purchase of Storer was more expensive, but the price had included several TV stations.) "Group W was a fantastic deal for the consortium," says Bill Bresnan, who served as a consultant for the buyers. "Westinghouse didn't really understand the value of their assets. They just wanted to get rid of them."

Each of the three major partners ended up, more or less, with the systems it wanted. Comcast took a 25.7 percent interest in Group W, and acquired systems in California, Alabama, Connecticut, and Florida, which Ralph especially valued because he believed, correctly, that the Sunshine State would continue its dramatic growth. "All this was because of Storer," Brian says. "Suddenly we were partnering with the big boys, which catapulted us into one of the top cable companies. You have to take a swing every now and then, and even if you miss, as we did with Storer, something good might come out of it."

To pay for Comcast's share of the acquisition, Julian arranged a triple-header financing in August 1986 by having the company issue $110 million in high-yield bonds, $95 million in convertible bonds, and two million shares of common stock—all in a single day. He had wanted to finance the entire amount with high-yield bonds: "The junk bond market was the rocket booster that made everything happen," he says, "and the easy money environment of the 1980s was a great time to expand." But Felix Rohatyn, the well-regarded financier whom Ralph had hired as an advisor, argued that with the Dow at 1,500, an all-time high, companies should sell all the equity they could. It was sensible, prudent advice, and Ralph took it, but he should have listened to Julian. "My father is wildly enthusiastic at the start of a deal," Brian says, "but as soon as it's done, he starts to worry. What if the worst happens? Ralph was more aggressive about bidding, and Julian was more aggressive about borrowing." And they were both right.

Jim Francisco was the technical operations manager of the Group W system in Danbury, Connecticut. When the division was sold, he and his colleagues were hoping they'd become part of the Time Inc. empire, rather than TCI, which they knew little about, or Comcast, which they had never heard of. But when Ralph showed up, Francisco felt differently. "Just meeting him made us more comfortable," he recalls. "He had that fatherly image, and when he put his hand on your shoulder, you knew you could trust him. He came to Connecticut for just two systems, Danbury and Middletown, and that also impressed us."

Francisco soon noticed the differences between Comcast and his previous employer. "Westinghouse was more formal," he says, "whereas Ralph, Julian, Dan, and Brian were known by their first names. And the Comcast people understood that as newcomers, we had some concerns and fears." At Group W, local managers had little involvement in the budget process; their budgets were issued from on high. At Comcast, managers were asked to grow cash flow by 10 percent a year, but how they achieved that growth was up to them. "Suddenly," Francisco says, "we were intimately involved with our own budgets, down to the price of gas for the trucks. That taught us the business. There was a P&L meeting every month, and we learned how the finances worked. Soon after we joined Comcast, I felt that Danbury was my system, and I wasn't even the GM."

Between the acquisition and the closing, Group W held a series of meetings in New York, where Comcast executives learned just how centralized that company had been. "It was like McDonald's," says

Brian, "with the same formula in every system. At first we were impressed, because it looked like they had everything figured out. But they were bloated and their margins were small."

Brian was asked to integrate the new systems, which was his first major assignment. Because Comcast ran a leaner operation, he had to dismiss some three hundred Group W executives. He did this fast and early, in part so he could reassure those employees who were moving to Comcast that the cuts were over and their jobs were safe. Over the next few months, he visited every Group W system that Comcast acquired, and the 1986 Annual Report showed a photo of Brian with his suitcase on an airport tarmac.

Early on, he and Bob Clasen ran a retreat for the Group W regional managers who were asked to stay on. Clasen had called them at home as soon as the deal was announced, two days before Christmas, to assure them that their jobs were secure. At the retreat, the new arrivals were pleasantly surprised that Ralph and Julian showed up and mingled with them. They were accustomed to the corporate culture at Westinghouse, where the top executives would leave in the evenings and go out together.

Two years earlier, in 1986, KKR had bought the Storer systems with the intention of improving and then selling them. Now, leaner and more profitable, they were back on the market. Here, too, TCI, ATC, and Comcast joined together to make a bid, although ATC dropped out at the last minute with no explanation. (It later became clear that Time Inc. had been busy preparing for its merger with Warner Communications.)

Brian was assigned to head up the consortium's due diligence efforts, and he and his team concluded that the former Storer properties carried liabilities the bidders hadn't known about. Prices for cable systems had risen considerably in the past two years, but even so, the cost of the Storer systems seemed unreasonably high. As Ralph remembers it, he and John Malone went to see Henry Kravis at his palatial office overlooking Central Park to negotiate a better price. "Julian and I joked about how long they would be in there," Brian recalls. "We figured an hour or two, but they lasted about six minutes." That was all it took for Kravis to tell his visitors that if they didn't like the price, they were free to walk away.

Soon after that meeting, during a conversation with a reporter from the *Wall Street Journal*, Malone compared the consortium's examination of the Storer properties to "buying the last buildable lot on the Florida Gold Coast and then finding out it had been a toxic-waste dump." Henry Kravis was understandably furious.

Although Comcast and TCI were still eager to make this deal, some time had to pass until tempers died down. Steve Rattner, a Morgan Stanley banker who was working with KKR, suggested in the spring of 1988 that the time had come to resume negotiations. Cable values had continued to rise, which made TCI and Comcast more willing to meet KKR's asking price.

The buyers ended up paying around $2,000 per subscriber, twice what they had paid in the Group W deal less than two years earlier. This was Comcast's largest acquisition to date, and it marked the third time during the 1980s that the company had doubled in size. Comcast was now the country's fourth-largest cable operator, with no intention of stopping there.

At their first meeting with the Storer managers, Ralph and Dan welcomed them with a soft-shoe song-and-dance routine about the two companies coming together. "Storer was a buttoned-down place with little informal contact between senior officers and the other employees," Julian says, "so you can imagine the shock of the new employees when the meeting opened this way." Sanford Ames, a Storer accountant, liked what he saw: "Storer had the family name, but it didn't feel like a family business. Comcast did." Visiting the Comcast headquarters in Bala Cynwyd, he noticed that most employees ate lunch at the local coffee shop. At Storer, the executives had been served in the corporate dining room, with white tablecloths, a huge chandelier, and a chef.

In 1989 Ames experienced another surprise. When Hurricane Hugo came to shore near Charleston, South Carolina, the site of one of the former Storer systems, somebody at the Comcast corporate office asked Ames to help the employees. When word reached Philadelphia that the local supermarket shelves were empty after the storm, the company bought a huge load of food from a distributor, loaded it on a tractor trailer, and had it driven to Charleston. "I got there as soon as it was safe to visit the Comcast office," Ames recalls. "I thought I was early, but the man holding the door when I arrived was Dan Aaron, who somehow found his way there even before I did."

Over the next few years, Ralph visited many of the former Storer systems. In 1993 he came to Chesterfield County, Virginia, where Buck Dopp was the GM. "After he spoke," Dopp recalls, "he stayed around and talked with employees. They couldn't believe how approachable he was, or that he arrived alone, with no entourage."

Ralph was especially pleased with the Storer acquisition, because it included the Sarasota cable system. He had told a skeptical George Storer in 1970 that some day he would return and buy it back. Eighteen years later, that day had finally arrived.

14

Ralph Plays a Hunch

Joe Segel

In the spring of 1986, after what he describes as his seventeenth or eighteenth retirement, Joe Segel was feeling restless again. The serial entrepreneur and marketing master was thinking of starting a mini-conglomerate that would serve as an incubator for new businesses. It would be run by alumni of the Franklin Mint, the enormously successful direct-response company Segel had started in 1964.

He had another idea, too. He had recently heard about Home Shopping Network, a new cable channel that was unlike anything else on television. Instead of programs punctuated by commercials, Home Shopping Network showed nothing *but* commercials. And instead of airing advertising for companies that paid the station to promote their products, HSN featured products that the network itself was selling.

Segel lived in suburban Philadelphia, but the network wasn't available there. He called friends around the country until he found someone who could record a couple of hours so he could see this new channel for himself.

His first reaction was, This is awful! The high-pressure sales tactics reminded him of a boardwalk hawker in Atlantic City. But he admired the concept, and he was certain that a more dignified approach would yield even better results.

Segel decided to start his own shopping channel that would be called QVC—for Quality, Value, and Convenience. When he learned what it would take to launch a TV shopping network, he realized he would need the active support of cable operators. What good was a new channel if nobody could watch it?

He went to see his friend Pete Musser, who had built the Tupelo cable system years earlier. Musser was so taken with the home shopping idea that he urged Segel to go and see Ralph Roberts at Comcast.

He had picked the right man. From Ralph's early days in advertising, he knew that whenever a product could be demonstrated—in a store, at an airport, or even on the street—people responded. Ralph had actually learned this lesson even earlier, when he was the pitchman who demonstrated the Centric Putter to golf pros. As Brian once put it, the idea of QVC hit Ralph's sweet spot.

"Are you the Joe Segel from the Franklin Mint?" Ralph asked when Segel came to see him. He already knew the answer, and he had long admired the company and its ubiquitous print ads. "Mr. Segel," he said, "I'm prepared to make a major investment in your idea. And I can guarantee you a million subscribers within twelve months."

Whoever coined the phrase "Ralph's golden gut" was aware that not everyone at Comcast could see what Ralph saw. Tom Nathan, who attended one of the early meetings with Joe Segel, went home and told his wife, "You know those late-night commercials where they say, 'Call now, operators are standing by'? A guy came in today who wants to do that twenty-four hours a day on his own channel! Can you believe it?" Recalling that comment years later, Nathan says, "I guess that's why I'm a lawyer and Ralph is Ralph."

Knowing how expensive this endeavor would be, Ralph urged

Segel to take QVC public as soon as possible. He then called every cable operator he knew—and he knew most of them—to tell them about QVC and encourage them to carry it. If they did, Ralph explained, in addition to earning a 5 percent commission on every sale to one of their subscribers, they could acquire shares in the new company for a fraction of the issuing price. The more subscribers they delivered, the more equity they could buy.

The equity sweetener was Ralph's idea, and the cable owners, who were, of course, well aware of HSN's success, responded with enthusiasm. The only exception was Charles Dolan from Cablevision, who later told Ralph more than once that not investing in QVC was the biggest mistake he ever made.

QVC was Ralph's first investment in programming and Comcast's first diversification since Storecast and Muzak. Ralph agreed to put $560,000 in Segel's new venture, which entitled Comcast to a 14 percent equity stake. Brian was given a seat on the board.

With little more than a business plan and good timing, QVC went public in September 1986. On the first day of trading, its share price more than doubled, which had also happened with Home Shopping Network.

Joe Segel was already hard at work—buying buildings, creating call centers, establishing warehouse and shipping procedures, hiring staff and on-air talent, and developing and implementing telephone and computer systems. He had planned to rent space on a communications satellite so QVC's signal could be sent to cable systems around the country. Because all the available satellites were full, Segel's only option was to make a deal with Pat Robertson's Christian Broadcasting Network, which was transmitting the same program on three different transponders in case one or two of them failed.

On the evening of November 24, 1986, just two months after the IPO, QVC went on the air from its studio in West Chester, Pennsylvania, and began selling waterproof "shower radios" for $11.49. Initially, the network was on the air weekday evenings and all day on weekends. On the first day of 1987, it began broadcasting around the clock, with Joe Segel making several appearances to sell cameras and bread machines. In its first year of business, QVC rang up more than $100 million in sales—an amazing achievement for a new company.

Segel, who had already ruled out high-pressure tactics, soon decided that shipping and handling charges for each item ought to be displayed on the screen. Other shopping networks omitted these awkward details, but Segel disagreed. "If we discourage sales by being honest," he said, "that's the price we'll pay. I think customers will appreciate our policy." After QVC started posting these charges, its competitors eventually followed suit.

Two years later, QVC acquired CVN, a competitor that was twice its size. To help finance the deal, Comcast invested $30 million, which was more than fifty times its original commitment.

The network continued to grow. On a single day in late 1991, QVC sold $80 million in merchandise—mostly to customers who ordered a Dell personal computer. Dell's big day helped dispel the myth that shopping networks appealed mostly to lower-income or uneducated viewers. In reality, their customers have always had above-average incomes, but that downscale image has never entirely disappeared. "I was a QVC watcher," says Brian, "and people were shocked by that. Partly it was because we were involved in the business, but I bought some terrific products as well."

By early 1992 Joe Segel was feeling restless again. QVC was doing a billion dollars a year in sales and could be seen in close to fifty million homes, but Segel, who was never one to linger, wanted to try something else.

On the other side of the country, Barry Diller was also feeling restless. He had started his storied Hollywood career in the mailroom of the William Morris Agency, and had served for ten years as CEO of Paramount at a time when the studio produced several hit TV shows (*Laverne & Shirley, Taxi, Cheers*) and such films as *Saturday Night Fever, Grease, Raiders of the Lost Ark, Terms of Endearment,* and *Beverly Hills Cop.* During one amazingly successful run in the late 1970s, Paramount released twenty consecutive profitable movies.

In 1984 Diller went over to Fox, where he launched the first successful new TV broadcast network in forty years and greenlighted a new animated show called *The Simpsons*. Early in 1992 he announced that he was leaving Fox to go out on his own.

Diller sent faxes announcing his decision to a number of people, including Brian Roberts, although they had met only once. For Brian, the timing seemed fortuitous. He was determined to move the company deeper into programming when he learned that the most talented programmer in the country was out of a job. With nothing to lose, he called Diller to suggest some kind of association with Comcast. "Now that I'm unemployed," Diller said, "I'm going to rent a red convertible and drive across the country. When I get to Philadelphia, we should get together."

It sounded like a brush-off, but over the next few months Brian pursued him. They had several long telephone conversations, especially about the new Apple PowerBook that both men had fallen in love with. Brian told his new phone pal how the digital future was going to open up a range of new possibilities. The hardware was coming, he said, but what Comcast really needed was software, or programming. Diller promised to visit when he came to Philadelphia.

That summer, unbeknownst to Brian, Diller accompanied his future wife, designer Diane von Furstenberg, to QVC, where she sold some of her merchandise on the air. Diller was amazed to find a huge and efficient retail operation that was brilliantly run and enormously profitable. Most of all, he says, "I saw televisions, telephones, and computers working together, converging in a way I had never seen before."

In late September Diller met with Brian and Ralph in Philadelphia. They discussed several scenarios, including the possibility that Comcast might buy Paramount and that Diller would run it again. When Diller described his visit to QVC, Ralph told him that Joe Segel was thinking of retiring as the company's CEO. Might Diller want to step in and buy Segel's share of the company? Ralph knew that was unlikely, but he also knew that Brian would do anything to land Diller, so why not try? Diller loved the idea.

In a deal worked out with John Malone, whose company, TCI,

owned a significant stake in the network, Diller invested $25 million in QVC and became its CEO. When the news broke, nobody could believe it. Barry Diller, who could have done anything in the entertainment industry, was running a *shopping* network? It made no sense!

Although Diller was serious about coming to QVC, he was equally serious about using the company, with its $200 million of cash flow and no debt, as a base for whatever came next. In the fall of 1993, Sumner Redstone's Viacom, which owned Showtime, MTV, and other content companies, made an agreement to acquire Paramount. Brian and Diller, who had been led to believe that Paramount wasn't for sale, decided, together with John Malone, to make a higher offer, using QVC shares as their currency. Over the next few months, the battle for Paramount was front-page news.

In the midst of it all, Malone called Brian at home one night and said, "Are you sitting down? I'm selling TCI to Bell Atlantic." Although that deal never closed, the announcement set off a boom in cable stocks. Every major cable company, including Comcast, was approached by at least one telephone company to discuss a possible merger. Malone, too busy with Bell Atlantic to focus on anything else, dropped out of the Paramount bid, leaving Diller and Brian to find other partners.

In the end, Paramount went to Viacom when Diller concluded it had become too expensive. More than a decade later, he appeared at a Comcast management conference, where somebody asked him to name his biggest mistake.

"Not bidding more for Paramount," he replied, "even though Ralph told me to."

When he allowed Viacom to have Paramount, Diller issued a five-word statement: "They won. We lost. Next." Brian, who had worked closely with him in their joint pursuit of the studio, paid close attention to how Diller dealt with the news media. "I've seen so many hours wasted on press releases that nobody ever reads," he says, "but when Barry issues a statement the media always use it, because his comments are short, unexpected, and to the point. He taught me that the key to being heard is being brief."

When Diller said "Next" after letting Paramount go, he meant it. A few months later, when the Tisch family decided to sell its controlling stake in CBS, Diller wanted to bid for the network, which was in dire need of his talents. Initially Brian liked the idea of buying CBS with QVC stock. CBS, after all, was a major content company—at least it would be under Diller, while QVC was not Comcast's core business. But Ralph didn't want to be pushed out of QVC, which was still hugely successful, and he had little interest in owning less than 10 percent of CBS, which would have been the result if the merger went through. At that time, cable operators could not own broadcast stations, so Comcast would have ended up with nonvoting shares in the new company, which to Ralph was unacceptable.

On June 30, 1994, Diller and CBS agreed that CBS would acquire QVC for $1.9 billion, and that Diller would run the merged company. Ralph and Brian were disappointed, but what could they do? Brian ruminated for several days, until a solution came to him in the shower. With no debt, QVC was not impossibly expensive. What if Comcast came in with a higher bid? Was CBS likely to raise their offer when what they really wanted from QVC was Diller? Probably not. And because Comcast already owned 15.6 percent of QVC, it wouldn't have to finance the entire deal.

Ralph loved the plan, but he and Brian needed to answer two big questions. First, what was the likely growth potential of QVC? And second, what did investment banker Felix Rohatyn think of this idea?

Larry Smith, the company's co-CFO, said that a higher bid made sense if the network could add 200,000 new customers a year. "That shouldn't be hard," said Joe Segel. "Lately they've been averaging 300,000." But in 1994, was it realistic to expect that QVC could continue growing by 15 percent a year? Segel was certain of it, which was all Ralph needed to hear. And Felix Rohatyn gave the bid his blessing because the price was reasonable.

Although bidding for QVC had been Brian's idea, he wasn't entirely convinced. But Ralph was. "Of course QVC will continue to grow," he said. "It's shopping, and it's TV. This operation is still in its infancy." That was vintage Ralph: who else would use *infancy* to describe a seven-year-old company whose annual sales were already measured in the billions?

Brian tried to remain objective. "Are we doing this because we can," he asked his colleagues, "or is this really a good idea?"

They decided to push ahead. With the boards of both CBS and QVC meeting to approve the merger in just a couple of days, they had to move fast. But before they announced that Comcast was bidding for QVC, Ralph and Brian believed they should tell Diller what they were planning. "This was a very aggressive move on our part," says Ralph, "and we wanted to give him fair warning."

Diller was flying to New York on a private plane for a dinner with the CBS board before its meeting the next day. With time running out, Ralph and Brian chartered a helicopter to Teterboro Airport in New Jersey so they could speak with Diller when he landed.

When the plane touched down, Ralph went up to Diller and said, "Barry, we have to talk. I was there at the creation of QVC, and I don't want to sell it. You were right when you said that maybe we should bid for it ourselves."

Ralph was referring to an earlier conversation in which he had expressed his uneasiness about the merger. "If you don't like my plan," Diller had said, "why don't you outbid me?" But they both knew that Diller hadn't really meant it.

When Ralph dropped his bomb, Diller replied calmly, "Ralph, you do what you have to, just as I will."

Diller has a different recollection of these events. "I did not anticipate that Comcast would do this," he says, "because Ralph gave his word that they would not."

Ralph has no memory of that. There was an agreement that most decisions could be made by any two members of the trio—Malone, Diller, and Comcast—but would that cover something as important as the sale of the company?

Despite the awkwardness of their airport meeting, Diller rode into Manhattan with Ralph and Brian. Years later, a writer who was astonished to learn this detail asked Diller, "Weren't you angry at them?"

"I was actually so angry that I did not react. I dealt with it politely and did not speak about it anymore that day. But I felt that Ralph had broken his word."

"That's not the sort of thing Ralph is known for," said the writer.

"True. And I like Ralph very much. I respect Ralph in every area but this one incident."

Soon after they returned to the city, Brian learned of a stunning development. As soon as he heard about the Comcast offer, CBS chairman Larry Tisch had withdrawn his bid for QVC.

Brian was ecstatic. Never in his wildest dreams did he think that CBS would fold immediately.

That night, Ralph and Brian went to see Diller again, this time at his apartment at the Waldorf Astoria, where they told him they were sorry it had ended this way. "It felt like a condolence call," says Brian. "We were probably the last people he wanted to see, but we felt we should go because we had wooed him to QVC. It was a horrible moment." Before they left, they told Diller that if he wanted to go after CBS without involving QVC, they would be happy to partner with him again, just as they had on the Paramount bid.

There were some difficult moments the next day, too. When Julian and co-CFO John Alchin spoke with investors and fund managers who had big equity positions in Comcast, they heard a lot of anger. "You're a cable company," investors said. "Why would you spend $2 billion that you don't even have to buy a shopping channel?" Shares of Comcast finished the day down 9 percent.

To Brian's relief, John Malone, who had been part of Diller's bid for CBS, responded well to the news and asked to be part of Comcast's all-cash offer. In the end QVC was sold to Comcast and Liberty Media, TCI's sister company, with Comcast owning 57.5 percent of the shopping network. At certain designated intervals, both partners had the right to end the partnership by triggering a buy/sell deal for QVC. If Comcast or Liberty named a price, the other one would have the choice of either buying their partner's stake in the network or being bought out.

Although Comcast had won the battle, neither Ralph nor Brian was happy with the way things had ended with Diller. They knew how angry he had been, and Ralph, who had led the opposition to Diller's plan, worried that he would blame Brian. A couple of years later, when Diller was visiting Comcast, Ralph said, "Barry, I don't want you to hate Brian. You can hate me, because I'm the one who didn't want to sell QVC. I was involved in starting it, and I didn't want to lose it."

"I'm glad you told me that," said Diller.

Gradually, the relationship was repaired. When Diller agreed to speak at Comcast's 2004 management conference, Brian took it as a sign that they were back on track.

Diller, who has certainly known his share of tough operators, calls Ralph the toughest executive he has ever known: "His appearance notwithstanding, I think Ralph has more steel in him and more guts than anyone, and I've really thought about that. If you look at what Comcast has done from its beginning until now, it's remarkable that Ralph was able to prevail in every instance, with a combination of optimism, willfulness, and toughness. The bow tie is nice, and he's a kind and pleasant gentleman, but the substance of Ralph is remarkable."

In 2003 John Malone chose to exercise the buy-sell mechanism, which led to a difficult decision for Comcast. Ralph couldn't bear to part with his baby, and nobody at Comcast was eager to sell QVC. But at the right price, the company had to consider selling—especially now, when Comcast was burdened with enormous debt after acquiring AT&T's cable properties.

In a series of meetings before Malone named the price, Comcast's top executives wrote down their estimates of QVC's total worth. The numbers ranged from $10 billion at the low end to Ralph's valuation of $12 billion. "We got Ralph to agree to be a seller if the number was high enough," says Larry Smith.

When Liberty Media valued QVC at more than $14 billion, the Comcast team was astonished. The only way they could explain it was that Malone had deliberately overvalued the company in the belief that Ralph, who hated to sell anything, would be a buyer at any price. It was a reasonable assumption, but every now and then Ralph has allowed himself to be outvoted, as he did here.

The sale of QVC still bothers him. "It was a mistake," he says, "but only in retrospect. It was a heartbreak to sell a company that was throwing off so much cash, but QVC wasn't a cable company and AT&T Broadband was, and this was a chance to pay down a lot of debt."

Father and son had worked together nicely. When it came to buying QVC, Brian had needed a push from Ralph. And when the time came to sell, Ralph needed a push from Brian.

The company's total investment in QVC came to something like $500 million. When Comcast sold its share to Liberty Media, the price was $7.9 billion. Whatever his regrets about the sale, and they are understandable, Ralph's decision to back Joe Segel had turned into one of the most profitable investments in Comcast's history.

15

The Transition

Brian Roberts and Ralph Roberts

"There is something about wanting to pass things on," Ralph says. "It's a little like giving birth, or producing another generation." But although it may seem inevitable in retrospect, Brian's ascent was neither preordained nor inevitable. Had he not been right for the job, Ralph would have made a different choice. From years of paying close attention to the complicated issue of succession in family companies, he knew that sons and daughters often enter the business expecting special treatment. He decided early on that this would not happen at Comcast.

Generational transition has long been part of the landscape in Europe, but America has not been kind to the heir who goes to work for his father. In novels, movies, and in real life, too, he is often seen as pampered and undeserving. To succeed, he must overcome these stereotypes and prove himself again and again.

Although Ralph didn't know where Brian would end up, there was no question where he would start: climbing poles, working as a trainee, and learning about cable from the ground floor. The rest would depend on Brian and his abilities. His passion for the business was clear from the start, but passion isn't the same as ability, leadership, or judgment. Those would have to be learned and demonstrated.

As Brian moved up the ladder, he and Ralph remained as close as ever. This father and son had a special bond; they genuinely loved working together and complemented each other's strengths. There was no hint of the intergenerational conflicts or tensions that often seem unavoidable in a family business of any size.

"It's an astounding relationship," Dan Aaron observed. "It's what everyone would like with their own son. They truly are friends. They are not competitive. The father doesn't try to dominate the son, and the son doesn't resent his father." Their relationship has been so widely admired that more than one businessman has come to Philadelphia to ask Ralph how he managed it. But it wasn't about managing. It was about character, chemistry, and some inexplicable alignment of the stars.

Although Ralph and Brian hold similar beliefs, they feel no need to agree on everything. When they differ, they discuss their views openly and candidly, as the company's senior executives have always done.

To most observers, including the Comcast board, the only surprise was that the transition from Ralph to Brian began so early, with Brian becoming president of the corporation in 1990, at the age of thirty. To Ralph, on the eve of his seventieth birthday, it was his own age rather than Brian's that concerned him: "I thought that if I were knocked off, people would say, 'Ralph died, so Brian got the job.' I realized that it ought to happen while I was still here. Brian was young, but I would be standing there with him."

And he did. "Ralph was Brian's principal counselor," says Julian, "and it was a beautiful thing to watch the love between them actually grow."

The early transition was a risk, but a calculated one. "There was no way that Brian, at thirty, was ready for that job," says Steve Burke. "But at forty, he had more experience at the top than anyone his age in corporate America. And Ralph knew all that experience would pay off."

On February 7, 1990, the board of directors named Brian Roberts president of Comcast. (Ralph retained his title of chairman of the board, and the company continued to operate with nobody holding the title of CEO.) A few days later, Julian brought the new president into the lunchroom for a surprise party to celebrate his promotion. Aileen Roberts was there with Sarah, their three-year-old daughter. Aileen has made a practice of showing up, unannounced, at key moments in her husband's life. Years later, when Aileen was undergoing treatment for breast cancer, she told Brian that her radiation treatments would prevent her from being in Denver when he was inducted into the Cable Hall of Fame. That night, as he mingled with some of the guests, his cell phone rang. "You're wearing your tux," Aileen said, "and you're talking to three men." Brian looked up and there she was: she had flown in to surprise him, and returned to Philadelphia the next morning for another treatment.

Suzanne Roberts was in the lunchroom, too, along with Ralph, Dan, and other employees who had known the new president since he was a boy. Brian made a brief, impromptu speech about wanting to expand the company in the years ahead while preserving, as much as possible, the feeling of a small, family-owned business. He said he wasn't a fan of big corporations, and that what mattered most at Comcast, however large it became, was the way the company made decisions and how it treated its employees. The words were Brian's, and they were sincere, but it could have been Ralph speaking.

Not many corporations have been able to manage a successful generational transition while the founder was still active. Usually the old guard has to depart before the younger team can fully assert itself, but at Comcast the process was more gradual. This was partly because Dan Aaron's worsening illness had forced him to step back, and also because Larry Smith and John Alchin, the charter members of Brian's leadership team, were already in place. And Ralph wasn't going anywhere. He and Brian had long had adjacent offices, and Brian was accustomed to coming in and asking Ralph for his opinion.

Ralph and Julian began a long, slow retreat, serving increasingly as advisors—a safety net, as Ralph liked to say. They and their colleagues took on a role that Stanley Wang compared to tribal elders, who sit by the campfire while the young braves run around and make war, secure in the knowledge that the older generation is watching over them and standing by to provide wisdom and counsel. "Most companies wouldn't tolerate that arrangement," said Wang. "The young people would shoot the elders. Our message was, 'We'll give you our best advice, but we won't be angry if you don't take it.'"

Ralph set the tone for these changes, and his new role seemed to flow naturally from his personality. Unlike most CEOs, he would just as soon be the coach as the guy with the ball. What he really enjoys is seeing other people reach their potential.

Brian was eager to have the ball in his hands. A company video from 1993 showed him driving to the Comcast office in Willow Grove, where there was a basketball hoop behind the building. As he got out of the car in his suit and overcoat, somebody passed him a ball; he then sank a shot from half-court, hitting nothing but net. "We didn't script it for him to get a basket," says Steve Brookstein, a marketing executive. "He was just supposed to take a shot. And you wouldn't know from the video that he made it on the first and only take. That was a metaphor for me, that Brian was the real deal."

Ralph, who had previously called himself president whenever a title was necessary, soon made clear what he had in mind. When executives came to him for a decision, he would say, "Why don't you check with Brian?" Or, "Don't do that until you get Brian's okay." As Ralph tells it, "It sank in that Brian would be the guy, and people thought it was nice of me to get out of the way." More likely, they had never known a leader who cheerfully surrendered a lot of his power.

And it *was* hard to believe that Ralph, for whom control had always been paramount, was willing to relinquish so much of it. "I don't blame them for being skeptical," he says, "because I'm usually tenacious."

When Amy Banse arrived in 1991, only a year after Brian became president, Ralph seemed to her to be more of a father figure than the head of the company. Like many of her colleagues, she marveled at his willingness to step back while still playing a major role. It wasn't hard to think of other companies, and especially media companies, where the patriarch seemed determined to retain all his authority until the final nail was in the coffin. Ralph, by contrast, was loosening his grip while he was still healthy and vigorous, because he thought it was best for the company—and for Brian. "A move like that takes strength of character," says John Alchin. "And giving up the reins before you have to sends a powerful message of confidence to the next generation of leaders."

Ralph recognized that there were certain areas, particularly those involving new technologies, where his son had long been on the cutting edge, and that Brian knew considerably more about the details of cable operations than he did. And even in areas where Ralph was more experienced, he wasn't the type to say, "Son, I'm older than you are, I've been through it all before, and this is what we're going to do." He was supportive without being patronizing.

"What do you think we should do about this?" he might ask Brian. If Ralph agreed with the answer, he would say, "That sounds pretty good." If not, he would say, "You might want to think that through a little more," or, "That's an interesting idea, but have you considered doing it this way?"

Brian likes to say that as far as his father was concerned, he hadn't had a bad idea in years. And by the time the two of them had finished discussing a proposal of Brian's that needed anything from a minor tweak to an extensive revision, Brian was left with the feeling that the new, improved version had been his all along: "My father doesn't take credit for ideas, even when they're his own. He doesn't put you down or steal your thunder. He doesn't even say, 'We just don't do that around here,' which is common in corporate life."

Although Ralph remained involved in making decisions, Brian could, and sometimes did, override him. "If he absolutely wanted to do something," says Ralph, "we would do it."

In 2002, when the Sarbanes-Oxley Act became law, the Securities and Exchange Commission asked the company to identify its CEO. At first, nobody knew how to respond. There was no clear demarcation point between Ralph and Brian, no solid line delineating where one man's authority ended and the other's began. Brian would have answered by saying, "Ralph is the boss," and Ralph would have said, "I guess I have the last word, but I don't intend to use it." Although these blurry boundaries were fine for a collegial company where nobody paid attention to organization charts, the SEC operates in more definitive terms. When somebody had to be the CEO of Comcast, that somebody was Brian.

By then, Brian had been leading meetings for years. Ralph would offer his comments, but with no suggestion that they carried any special weight because they came from Ralph Roberts.

Back in 1990, there was some discussion about how to explain the transition to the financial community. Comcast was a growing and public corporation, and if its leadership was shifting to a younger generation, that was a material event that had to be communicated with care to a world where even the smallest change carries financial ramifications. The PR professionals stressed the need for clarity and recommended that now that Brian was president, he alone should be the public face of Comcast.

Ralph overruled the advisors and insisted on candor. Brian's appointment was the beginning of a process, rather than a full and completed change. The message from Comcast was, Brian is our new president, but Ralph isn't leaving, which gave the company the best of both worlds—the experience and wisdom of Ralph, Julian, and the other senior executives, together with the youthful energy and creativity of Brian and his team. As the controlling shareholder, Ralph still had the last word, should it ever come to that. But as early as 1990, when Comcast reported its numbers for the previous year, the comments in the press release were attributed to Brian.

Cable industry leaders, who knew Brian from conventions, committees, CableLabs, and other events, welcomed him into their ranks. They were pleased that a well-spoken and knowledgeable young man was on track to become one of the industry's most visible spokesmen.

Although the transition was successful, it wasn't quite as seamless as it appeared. Julian, thirteen years younger than Ralph and still at the top of his game, was neither as ready nor as eager to step aside as Ralph was. Ralph was happy to become a coach, but Julian was a dynamic, spirited player who was still in his fifties. For all his experience and financial brilliance, he wasn't cut out to be a behind-the-scenes mentor. And because there was no executive in place with his particular skill set, there was no immediate need for Julian to pull back.

Ralph had known that the transition wouldn't be easy for Julian. For a year or two before Brian became president, the three of them had a number of dinners together to discuss how the new alignment would work. Julian said he couldn't see himself working for Brian, whom he had known since Brian was a child. But neither Brian nor Ralph wanted Julian to leave. Brian valued his experience and his advice, and Ralph knew that Julian would be protective—not only of Brian, but of the company Julian had done so much to build.

The first few years of the transition were sometimes difficult for all three of them. Who, exactly, should be attending this meeting, that conference, or next week's lunch with Rupert Murdoch? For a while they operated as a three-man team, and then a two-man team (Brian and Ralph), and then a three-man team again (Brian, Ralph, and Larry Smith), and finally a two-man team (Brian and Smith).

Some executives in his situation might have left, but Julian had a better idea. For the next few years he continued to chair the finance committee while making deals and representing the company in many public situations. In the mid-1990s he reinvented himself and led Comcast into the Internet era. He founded Comcast Interactive Capital (now known as Comcast Ventures), a highly profitable in-house private equity fund that invested in high-tech companies. And through the spring of 2011, Julian continued to serve as one of the corporation's directors.

The transition at Comcast was more than generational. For all their closeness and shared values, Ralph and Brian have different styles and strengths. Ralph, while certainly thoughtful, operates primarily by instinct, whereas Brian is more analytical. Ralph is a marketer, a sales-man, and a merchant; Brian is a deal maker, intense and cerebral. He doesn't pursue wild-eyed long shots, and what may seem like an un-likely idea tends to be one he has studied carefully. Ralph, despite his laid-back style, is more of a gambler. Although Brian loves to make deals, he often has last-minute doubts: Do we really need this acquisi-tion? Might it hurt the company or damage our reputation? Ralph's anxieties come into play *after* he pulls the trigger, although he is adept at hiding them. "He rises above the fray," says Brian, "and remains wonderfully calm in the middle of the storm."

Although Ralph came from New York, he has long had a Phila-delphia perspective, while Brian, who has spent his life in Philadel-phia, has always been drawn to the investment banking world of New York. One of his first decisions as president was that Comcast had outgrown Wolf Block, the Philadelphia law firm that had served Ralph and the company for as long as anyone could remember. To represent Comcast in major transactions, Brian hired a New York firm, Davis Polk & Wardwell, and later teamed up with one of its principal lawyers, Dennis Hersch, a mergers and acquisitions special-ist. Ralph likely would have stayed with Wolf Block, but when Brian made the change, he supported the move.

In situations where Ralph seems to operate intuitively, Brian collects information and opinions that inform his decisions. Over the years, he has educated himself by drawing on the wisdom and experience of others, including Ralph, Julian, Dan, Ted Turner, and John Malone. He thinks nothing of asking half a dozen colleagues for information and advice. "His leadership style is amazingly inclusive," says David Cohen, the corporation's executive vice president, "not only because he wants to hear every idea, but also because if everyone has their say, they will all feel part of the decision." And if they disagree? "If Brian wants to do something," says Bob Pick, "and his colleagues don't agree, he'll often back off. He's a consensus builder."

He consults regularly with board members, who find him a terrific listener. "These are not check-the-box conversations," says board member Mike Cook. "And when there is disagreement within the leadership, he makes no attempt to hide it. Like Ralph, he appreciates a culture of openness."

Joe Waz, a former public policy executive who wrote speeches for both men, says that Ralph likes to tell stories, and resists anything that hints at pontificating. He has no interest in giving a "what I've learned" kind of speech and prefers to talk about the ways in which Comcast is like a family.

Brian would rather focus on business and technology. He has what Waz calls "a constructive form of attention deficit disorder that allows him to make surprising connections and to come at you from several different directions." Both men worry about their speeches, but while Ralph may change two or three words a day as he reviews the text, usually with Suzanne, Brian will solicit comments from his colleagues.

Ralph is known for his patience, whereas Brian is more hurried. Where Ralph used to read every word of a contract, Brian will ask for a summary. Conversations with Brian tend to be shorter. "He gets it immediately," says Fred Shabel, vice chairman of Comcast Spectacor, "so I learned to get to the conclusion pretty fast." But Brian will often challenge that conclusion. "Why do you say that?" he'll ask. "Are you sure?"

Although both men have hired strong and talented executives and they hate to fire anyone, Brian finds it easier to replace an employee who may have ended up in the wrong job. They have both been committed to growing the company, but Ralph tends to be opportunistic and Brian more strategic. While Ralph could be satisfied, at least temporarily, with a single new franchise, Brian tries to hit home runs. Although he will ask detailed questions about even the most modest deal, he has a special fondness for dramatic, transformative transactions.

They also have much in common. They are both skilled at getting along with a wide variety of people, including, when necessary, individuals whom others may find difficult. They like to laugh, and neither one takes himself too seriously or puts on airs. Ralph is famous for his modesty, and Brian is unpretentious. "There is nothing imperious about him," says Amy Banse. "He and Aileen work hard to create normal lives for their family in a city where everyone knows who they are." A colleague who happened to know that Brian was attending an evening event at the White House noticed that he returned home the same night and took his kids to school in the morning without ever mentioning the visit.

Like his father, he has always been approachable. "When you have a fancy title," says Scott Westerman, an area vice president in the Southwest, "people treat you differently. But Brian doesn't behave differently back. He is empathetic and responsive."

Neither man is threatened by colleagues who disagree or who may be more knowledgeable in a particular area. They both have a gentle touch, even when they are displeased. They are comfortable with delegating responsibility and sharing the spotlight—Ralph with Julian and Dan, and Brian with Steve Burke. They avoid limousines and usually take the train to meetings in New York, which pleases employees who run into them en route.

And they are both devoted to family—both the family of Comcast and their own families. More than most CEOs, Brian seems to have struck an effective balance between work and family, and comes home for dinner whenever he can. As with so many other lessons, he learned that one, too, from watching his father.

16

Money Men

Larry Smith and John Alchin; Michael Angelakis

The Farmer

In 1987, when Larry Smith first met with Ralph and Julian to discuss a possible job at Comcast, there was something he wanted to know: Was the company's recent acquisition of Group W an isolated event, or, as he hoped, a harbinger of bigger things to come? Smith, an accomplished tax consultant, wasn't looking for a new position. But he loved making deals, and if Comcast was planning on further growth, he wanted to hear more.

He grew up on a farm outside Philadelphia, where his parents and grandparents raised goats and had once operated a goat dairy. As a young man, he bought a farm of his own, a 25-acre fixer-upper,

213

and for years he and his dad spent every weekend restoring it. Like his father, who was head of manufacturing at a chemical and paint company, Larry was a country boy with a city job; for all his skill at finance, he was, at heart, a farmer. Had he not shown a gift for accounting, he might have become a large-animal veterinarian.

Every morning, before leaving the farm at six to drive to the city, he would strap a pair of overalls over his suit and go out to the barn to check on the animals. If a ewe was giving birth, he would put on gloves, deliver the lamb, and make sure its mother's milk was flowing properly. On weekends he did farm chores, including digging graves, because a sheep might die during the week, when Smith was always pressed for time. Although he wore overalls to protect his work clothes, when he got to the office nobody was fooled by the man who sometimes arrived with flecks of manure on his dress shoes.

He had majored in accounting at Ithaca College, where he hoped to play baseball and become a major league catcher, and where he learned that not all dreams come true. But he was an excellent student. Graduating with a 4.0 average and his pick of jobs, he chose the Philadelphia office of Arthur Andersen, the legendary accounting firm. He joined the tax department and made partner at the unusually young age of thirty-one.

Although he was happy at Andersen, he left when the firm wanted him to take on more administrative tasks, which would have left him less time for the deal work he loved. He joined Advanta, a Philadelphia financial services company, but although he became the CFO, there weren't enough transactions to satisfy him. When he told Sheldon Bonovitz, a local tax attorney, that his job wasn't much fun, Bonovitz, a Comcast board member, mentioned that Ralph Roberts and Julian Brodsky were looking for a chief accounting officer. Although Smith had never heard of their company, he was happy to meet them.

The hiring process took a while. Smith wasn't in a hurry, and Comcast's leaders have never liked to rush into what they hope will be a long-term relationship. But Ralph told him that Brian would become Comcast's president in a couple of years, and that just as Ralph had relied on Julian to handle the company's financial concerns, Brian would need a Julian of his own.

Smith liked their entrepreneurial spirit. At Andersen he had seen any number of CEOs who, when presented with exciting opportunities, always found a reason to say no. But he had the feeling that if someone at Comcast came up with a good money-making idea, even if it was outside the company's core business, it would be taken seriously. Ralph and Julian would consider the likely reaction on Wall Street but they wouldn't let it stop them from making an attractive acquisition.

He also liked the company's self-effacing culture. He was used to executives who insisted on a power breakfast at the Four Seasons, and he was pleased when Brian arranged to meet him at a Friendly's restaurant in a modest part of town. He noticed that the executives he met with cared deeply about integrity, and he had worked with enough companies not to take that for granted.

But although he knew what he liked about Comcast, he wasn't sure what Comcast liked about him. After all, he knew nothing about cable, or about cellular phone service, the company's newest venture. As far as Smith was concerned, Comcast could be selling coffee or making radios. What he enjoyed was business, making deals, and helping good companies grow.

And that's why he was hired, because he loved business and was awfully good at it. And because Julian, Ralph, and Brian were impressed by his intelligence, honesty, and judgment.

In his 1980 memo, Brian had urged his elders to bring in executives who knew about business, rather than cable, and Smith was the first of several new arrivals who fit the bill. He was also hired because he was terrifically smart without being full of himself.

On his first day of work, the Storer acquisition was announced. The timing couldn't have been better. This was a huge and complicated transaction, and Smith was the ideal person to unravel the convoluted tax situation at the heart of it.

He turned out to be ideal in other ways, too. After the Storer systems were integrated, Comcast had some administrative shoring up to do. The company had grown enormously in recent years, but its informality and lack of bureaucracy were starting to undermine its efficiency. The corporation's systems and procedures needed upgrading—assorted mundane details ranging from how and when paychecks should go out to the best way to buy officers' and directors' liability insurance.

Although Smith had been hired for very different reasons, and although he had left Andersen because he disliked administrative tasks, he was willing to do them at Comcast. "Larry moved us from being a small entrepreneurial company to a successfully managed one," says Brian. "He took some arrows by setting limits and saying no to people, but he was comfortable making tough decisions." Because he didn't care about getting credit, his administrative accomplishments were the least-known part of his work. But now there was a top executive who was willing to fire people and to make other unpopular but necessary moves. He made sure the company ran smoothly as it expanded, and he brought another level of discipline to its inner workings.

Not much escaped his attention. When Don Harris, the president of the cellular division, was interviewed on CNBC, the host suddenly asked him about Barry Diller's attempt to merge QVC and CBS. Smith, who was watching in his office, didn't think Harris should answer that question. Some people would have yelled in frustration at the TV set, but Smith dialed Harris's cell phone, which rang on the air, causing Harris to lift it out of his pocket and shut it off. That's all it took; the ringing phone reminded the host that Harris was there to discuss the cellular industry. But Smith had imagined that Harris might actually answer the call, whereupon he would have told him, in a classic Larry Smith moment that never actually happened, "Stop talking about QVC!"

His quiet toughness, combined with a frugality that felt familiar, led some employees to call him "Julian with a smile." But unlike Julian, he rarely got worked up. As Smith once put it, "Julian's gruff, but not tough. I'm tough, but not gruff."

But like Julian, he was willing to give up popularity for the sake of productivity. When he arrived, the support staff worked from nine until five, with an hour for lunch; he moved the daily starting time to eight thirty. When he was in charge of determining whether to close the office on heavy snow days, it always stayed open. No matter how hard it was snowing, he would assure employees that by the time they left, the commute would be easier because the roads would be empty. "He always had a reason for us to work harder," says Lucille Fital, who adds that Smith worked harder than anyone. But he also enjoyed a rich family life and encouraged his people to do the same.

He was equally tough with the company's top executives. He considered it outrageous that several of them, himself included, were driving company cars. What did that accomplish, he asked, other than setting a few people apart from everyone else? There wasn't even a tax advantage—the one thing that might have changed his mind. The cars were soon gone.

Muzak went, too. It took years, and Brian's active help, but Ralph gradually gave in after Smith persuaded him that the longer Comcast retained its Muzak division, the less it would be worth.

Sentiment played no part in his decisions. At one point he planned to trade away the Tupelo franchise as part of a swap with another cable company. Tupelo! "Ralph wouldn't let me," says Smith, who seemed surprised that the founder, who hated to sell anything, might not be eager to surrender the system on which the company was founded. "To me," Smith says, "franchises were like pork bellies, but not to Ralph." No, not to Ralph.

One example of Smith's pragmatism quickly entered the company's folklore. He had been there about a year when Comcast moved downtown, and here, too, he offered to take care of the administrative arrangements nobody else wanted to work on. As the movers were clearing out the Bala offices, he noticed four large men standing around the reception area, discussing how, exactly, they were going to transport the goldfish who were swimming peacefully in their bowl. "Let me take that," said Smith, who carried the container into the men's room and emptied it into a porcelain receptacle normally used for other purposes. The story spread quickly and added considerably to his tough-guy reputation: a man who could flush away Ralph's goldfish wasn't someone to be trifled with. Smith confirms the story: "I wasn't paying these guys fifteen bucks an hour to worry about fish."

He stood firmly in the Julian Brodsky tradition of cost cutting, and as with Julian, employees loved to cite examples of Larry Smith's frugality. When the company moved downtown, he couldn't bring himself to throw away the outdated corporate stationery; twenty years later, he was still using Bala envelopes for his personal correspondence. During the move he retrieved dozens of bottles of cologne left over from Ralph's old business and used them for gifts and stocking stuffers. His thrift was more than a corporate pose: a friend remembers running into him at the New Jersey shore, where Smith was beaming after he found a nice pair of used shoes at a flea market. Back at the office, the company's head deal man didn't even subscribe to the *Wall Street Journal*; he read Brian's copy every morning. As with Julian, people smiled and shook their heads. But they also got the message.

His value to Brian can't be overstated. Among other things, he served as the new president's executive filter: "Nothing happened at Comcast that I should have known about that Larry didn't tell me," says Brian. "But hundreds of small things happened that Larry quietly made go away, without bothering me or taking any credit."

"He had his hands in just about everything," says Denise Daniele, his longtime assistant. That's not to say that Smith enjoyed his administrative duties; he was delighted when David Cohen arrived in 2002 and took over many of them. "I didn't care about that stuff," he says. "I saw some vacuums and I filled them." Is there a better definition of a team player?

"Larry made us able to handle the scale we were thrust into," says Brian, who believes it was no accident that just about all the senior executives who arrived after Smith turned out to be good hires. After all, Larry had interviewed and recommended every one of them.

He and Brian were in sync from the start. For years, on his way to work, Brian called him every day at seven thirty, when Smith was already at his desk. At Smith's retirement dinner in 2007, Brian stood up and said, only partly in jest, "Larry, it's not too late to change your mind!"

Brian compares their nineteen-year work relationship to a long, happy, and honest marriage, with echoes of the earlier partnership between Ralph and Julian, which had been everyone's hope when Smith was hired. Corporate executives are often reluctant to tell the boss that his latest idea is misguided, but Smith was always candid. A dispassionate, independent-minded truth teller is critically important in a family-run business. "This place could have developed a 'Sun King' syndrome," says Steve Burke, "where nobody ever tells Brian he's wrong. But that could never happen when Larry was around. He could say blunt things in a tactful way." He could also say them in a blunt way if the other person could take it, and Brian could.

"He didn't survey the room before he gave his opinion," says Peter Luukko of Comcast Spectacor. "And he was probably one of the last guys at a big company with whom you could make an agreement on the back of an envelope. When you made a deal with Larry, it got done."

He had no interest in small talk and wasn't the type to ask about your weekend. He may have been the least political executive at the company's corporate headquarters. Once, when Brian asked a few colleagues to contribute to a certain charity, Smith said, "I'm not doing that," and the conversation was over.

He didn't tell stories, although he had a good sense of humor, and he never spoke for the sake of hearing himself. But if you wanted to discuss plans or complicated scenarios, he was always interested. The conversation at Comcast is idea-driven, and Smith was a big part of those discussions, even in meetings where he didn't say much.

He was entirely without pretense. He rarely talked about himself, preferring to speak in terms of "we" or "Comcast." He listened attentively—to everybody. "He looked for the best idea, no matter who came up with it," says Josh Steiner, an advisor to the company. That's true of Comcast in general, but it was especially true of Larry Smith.

For a man who appeared to be unemotional, he had a real passion for being at work. When his doctors ordered him to stay home for two months after a quadruple bypass operation, he found it enormously difficult. His wife, Christine, set up an effective system with Denise Daniele: anyone who wanted to talk to Larry had to go through Denise, who then called Christine. Nobody, not even Brian, could call him directly.

Another time, when he returned to work just two days after heart catheterization, Abe Patlove said, "You're a living legend, Larry. You had a heart procedure on Tuesday, you're back on Thursday, and I didn't even know you *had* a heart." Smith loved that joke. He wasn't warm and fuzzy, and didn't pretend to be. His son, Chris, heard him say more than once that the world would be a wonderful place if there just weren't any people involved. And yet, almost despite himself, Larry Smith was loved.

But it's deal making where he made his mark. "Larry is the greatest moneymaker I've ever seen," says Brian, "and he's as excited by a small deal as a large one." He and Ralph liked to discuss private investment opportunities that came their way, and Ralph had a simple rule: if Larry was committing some of his own money, he did, too.

Like Julian, the more complex the transaction, the more he enjoyed it. "Larry can make you think he's a good old boy from the farm," says investment banker Fehmi Zeko, "but he's wickedly bright at complicated thinking." He had no interest in confusing people, and he had a knack for explaining sophisticated transactions, especially to the board. "He didn't do complicated things for their own sake," says Julian. "He did them when nobody could figure out how to get something done in a simple way, and his skill at doing them gave us a competitive edge." Some of Smith's deals were elaborate because he took pains to protect the company's exposure, which couldn't always be done easily.

He was a terrific negotiator. "He thought of everything," says Ralph, "and the people on the other side of the table didn't hate him when the deal was over." Like all great negotiators, he was steadfast and persistent. "He was a bulldog," says Bob Pick. "If he got a thought in his head, he wouldn't let go until he ran it all the way down."

He enjoyed a good argument and didn't take disagreements personally. "You couldn't hurt his feelings," says Ralph, who recalls that Smith sometimes started out as a minority of one before persuading his colleagues to change their minds by offering compelling reasons, rather than trying to dominate the other people in the room.

Although he had joined Comcast to make deals, his strong financial discipline wouldn't allow him to pursue an acquisition beyond what he saw as its fair value; what made sense to him at $40 million might not be worth doing at $41 million. "He was totally analytical," says Julian. "Only the dollars and cents counted." But when he was overruled by Ralph or Brian, who were sometimes willing to pay more for an asset than Smith considered prudent, or when it came time to act for any other reason, he didn't hesitate to pull the trigger.

He had a gift for spotting opportunities. It was Smith who told Brian in 1992 about a pair of entrepreneurs who were cobbling together two-way radio frequencies used by taxi dispatchers and delivery companies. He and Brian wrote a contract on the spot that allowed Comcast to buy an option for 30 percent of the company, which owned licenses to frequencies that would later prove useful to the cell phone industry. Comcast ultimately invested $50 million in FleetCall, which changed its name to Nextel and was later acquired by Sprint.

Smith was the prime mover in the acquisition of Teleport Communications Group, which provided a way for companies to reach long-distance providers that was less expensive than going through the local phone company. Teleport, which was once owned by Merrill Lynch, was acquired in 1994 by a consortium of cable companies, TCI and the three Cs—Cox, Continental, and Comcast. Comcast had earlier bought Eastern TeleLogic, a Philadelphia-based version of Teleport, which Teleport later acquired. In 1998, when Teleport was acquired by AT&T, Comcast's stake was valued at more than $2 billion—many times its original investment. Comcast ended up with a considerable amount of AT&T stock, which it would later use in other deals.

A couple of years later, under Smith's direction, Comcast joined with Sprint, TCI, and Cox to create a new national wireless phone company. Later, Sprint took the company public, which facilitated the consortium's sale of its shares. The cable companies had invested $680 million, and their share of the proceeds came to $3.4 billion.

His greatest business success was the company's investment in At Home (also known as @Home), an early high-speed cable Internet service provider in which TCI (the control shareholder), Comcast, and Cox had ownership stakes. When TCI took the company public in 1997, the stock soared. Two years later, At Home acquired Excite, a popular Internet portal and search engine, to create a kind of AOL on steroids.

Excite@Home, as the merged company was known, experienced rapid growth, but suffered from technical problems, in part because it was the first company to offer high-speed Internet service. Its share price, which had reached $128 in early 1999, began a long, slow decline; two and a half years later, it had dropped all the way to a dollar.

In 1999 AT&T acquired TCI and ended up with control of At Home. After its engineers were able to improve its service, AT&T wanted to own the company outright. So Larry Smith and Dave Woodrow, his counterpart at Cox, went to New York to meet with Dan Somers, the head of AT&T's cable division. At the time, At Home was selling for $18 a share. Somers began by offering a modest premium, and then raised his bid to $27 a share.

"If that's all you think it's worth," Smith told him, "we'll be happy to take it off your hands."

Somers dismissed that idea, which was just as well because Smith and Woodrow were bluffing. And now they knew for certain what they had already suspected—that Somers was willing to go higher.

With Brian's encouragement, they went back and told Somers the price would be $54 a share, which was twice what he had offered. A few hours later they settled on $48.

AT&T paid Comcast and Cox in stock, which turned out well for the sellers. AT&T was so certain that its share price was rising that it didn't ask for protection in case that price fell by the time the deal closed—and it did, substantially. At the closing, AT&T had to pay Comcast and Cox, which had each invested only $8 million in At Home, more than $3 billion in stock for their equity in the company, although it was now worth very little. A year later, At Home filed for bankruptcy.

But nobody's perfect. A horse named Artistic Fella, who was born on Smith's farm, went on to become a harness-racing star who earned $3 million. Smith, however, was on the losing end of that deal, having sold the horse as a yearling for $9,000 in a transaction that *USA Today* called the best buy in racing history. "Fortunately," he jokes, "they didn't say who the seller was."

Larry Smith had come to Comcast hoping to make deals. He ended up accomplishing far more than that, and both his hopes and the company's were fully realized. In his nineteen years at Comcast, he was one of the most successful executives the cable industry has ever seen.

The Gentleman

John Alchin was sure he had missed the boat. In September 1989 he read in the *Wall Street Journal* that Bern Gallagher, Comcast's treasurer and Julian's top deputy, was leaving the company. Too bad, Alchin thought, because if that job had opened up three or four years ago, Julian might have called him. Alchin had long admired the company, and a few months earlier he had seen another article in the *Journal*, this one on the front page, where a fund manager called Comcast "the best operator in the business"; another described it as "the Tiffany of cable companies."

Alchin had headed TD Bank's media group when it was the cable industry's largest source of capital. But he was now at another division of the bank and no longer attended cable meetings. Out of sight, out of mind, he thought. But Julian called the very next day.

Alchin grew up in Australia, where his father worked for a company that owned a string of department stores and moved his family from one small town to another. When John was in high school, he had a part-time job at a bank, and as soon as he graduated, he was selected to work at its headquarters in Brisbane. One taste of city life and the young man was hooked.

Like so many young Australians, he was eager to see the world. He ended up in Toronto, where he took a job with the Toronto Dominion Bank, as TD Bank was then known. With the bank's support, he became a full-time student, earning both his undergraduate degree and his MBA at the University of Toronto.

Although he had planned to go into investment banking, he returned to TD Bank in the spring of 1980. To encourage Alchin to join its new U.S. division, based in New York, the company offered him any specialty he wanted. He picked cable loans because the bank was well established in that area.

During the 1970s TD Bank had become the leading lender to Canadian communications and media companies, with a special interest in cable providers. Virtually every major Canadian city is near the U.S. border, which made it easy for cable operators to pick up broadcasts from places such as Buffalo, Cleveland, Detroit, and Seattle, and to offer programming that wasn't available in Canada without static and interference. By the early 1970s, well before HBO and other new channels brought cable into American urban areas, Canadian cities were already wired.

But south of the border, only a handful of banks were lending to cable companies. Most financial institutions showed little interest in a business they didn't really understand, which was why Julian had come up with inventive solutions during Comcast's early years.

When Alchin moved to New York, he had what he jokingly calls the world's easiest job. Compared to what U.S. banks were offering, TD's terms were irresistible. Cable loans were highly profitable, especially in cases where the bank received warrants that entitled it to

5 or even 10 percent of the borrowing company. And the loans were wonderfully safe: to the best of Alchin's knowledge, every dollar the bank ever lent to the industry had been repaid. Three years after Alchin moved to New York, he made that point in a presentation to the board to explain why the bank's cable loan portfolio was larger than that of any American lender.

From their early start in Canada, TD bankers had discovered what Ralph, Julian, and the rest of the industry had long maintained—that cable was a highly predictable business. You could calculate how much a new system would cost, how many customers were likely to sign up, and how much your customer base would grow over time. You could even anticipate how much your customers would be willing to pay you every month. At a time when American lenders still saw cable loans as risky, TD Bank understood that the money was going to a kind of utility whose cash-flow stream was both reliable and predictable. The bank was responding to the same three words that had attracted Ralph Roberts to cable: recurring monthly income.

Julian liked Alchin and respected him, although they had never done business together. Alchin knew the business and understood capital markets, and Julian was confident that his engaging personal style would go over well with both loan officers and investors. And unlike anyone at Comcast, Alchin understood cable loans from the lender's perspective, which would be enormously helpful when it came to negotiating financings and managing the company's extensive loan portfolio. (Because Comcast was still arranging separate financings for each of its systems, that portfolio was unusually complicated.)

Although Alchin had spent his whole career at the bank, he was ready for a change. He was aware that Comcast was changing, too, and was no longer the quiet little company it used to be. He knew Ralph and Julian and interviewed with them, but he didn't know Brian until they met in a hotel coffee shop across from New York's Penn Station.

"In walks this kid who looked like he had only recently started shaving," Alchin recalls. "He was thirty, and I thought, He'll be my boss?" Instead of conducting a conventional job interview, Brian simply started talking, and for a long time, Alchin just listened. He liked what he heard, and decided he would be happy to work for this young man. Whether or not Brian had the managerial skills to run a company, he certainly knew the cable business. And he spoke with a degree of experience and wisdom that made him seem older. Alchin couldn't miss Brian's determination to make Comcast larger. Like Larry Smith a year or two earlier, he wanted to join a company that was headed for bigger things.

When he and Julian finally agreed on the terms of his new job, they were sitting in a conference room at Merrill Lynch in New York. Just down the hall, Brian was in another meeting, working on QVC's attempt to acquire Paramount. Although Alchin was already on board, the symmetry of the two meetings pleased him, and made it clear that Brian's bold plans were more than just talk.

But his first day of work wasn't quite what he had imagined. During a financial meeting, Ralph turned to him and asked, "John, what do you make of this HLT problem?"

HLT stood for highly leveraged transaction. In response to some of the problems of the 1980s—especially the meltdown of junk bonds and the savings and loan disaster—federal banking authorities had imposed strict limits on highly leveraged buyouts. Like so many well-intended government solutions, this one went too far. Cable companies had always been highly leveraged, but now it was almost impossible for them to secure bank loans.

Alchin assured Ralph that the issue would soon be resolved, but he still winces when he recalls that moment: "I couldn't have been more wrong if I tried." Because he had been working for a Canadian bank, he had been shielded from the problem, which was far more serious than he knew.

In the months ahead, he would spend a great deal of time, much of it with his counterparts from other cable companies, working on the HLT issue. In meetings with bankers and regulators, the cable executives maintained that the government had spread too wide a net, that not all highly leveraged transactions were alike, and that, as John Malone put it, the regulators had gone fishing for tuna and were catching porpoises. Alchin could speak with authority about the historically high performance of cable loans, and how the unique economics of cable justified financings that might indeed be risky in other industries. Securing bank loans was an urgent issue for both TCI and Comcast; having recently acquired the Storer properties from KKR, they needed to borrow $1.2 billion to pay for them. Alchin's work paid off: he and Barney Schotters, his counterpart at TCI, were given an award by the cable industry for their work in making bank loans available again.

In the formative years of Comcast, nobody cared about titles. In the early 1980s, the board made Julian chief financial officer when Bern Gallagher became treasurer, which had been Julian's title. When Larry Smith arrived in 1988, he wanted to be the CFO someday. And when John Alchin showed up in early 1990, he did, too.

From 1992 until the Sarbanes-Oxley Act of 2002, Comcast had no chief financial officer. But the new law required the company to have one, if only to sign off on certain financial documents. "We codified reality and made them co-CFOs," says Julian. "They worked well together, without politics or turf battles, just like the old days."

This new arrangement didn't change anything: "We just formalized what we had already been doing for over a decade," says Smith, who immediately accepted the idea. So did Alchin. Like so many elements of the company's collegial culture, this one, too, goes back to Ralph and his willingness to share power, first with Dan and Julian, and later with Brian.

The cooperation between Smith and Alchin went well beyond their joint title, and the company's lack of bureaucracy made it easy for them to cross over formal reporting lines to work with each other's teams. For years, the geography of the executive floor at 1500 Market Street gave concrete evidence of their partnership, with Alchin in one corner office, Smith in another, and most of their top people along the corridor between them.

It helped, certainly, that they had different interests and talents.

"John raises the money," Smith would tell visitors, "and I spend it." As Alchin describes it, "Larry would invest weeks and months on a deal, and then he'd hand it over to me to explain to Wall Street and everyone else. He could have done that himself, but he was more interested in working on the next transaction."

This arrangement allowed each man to focus on what he most enjoyed: in Smith's case it was deals, accounting, and tax issues; for Alchin, it was capital formation (raising both debt and equity) and talking to investors. A partnership like this can't work if the participants are territorial or egotistical, or if either one is angling to get what the other has. Not surprisingly, high-level job sharing is virtually unknown in corporate America.

Brian once described the two of them as well-matched bookends: Alchin was the genial host who provided confidence, never lost his temper, and was a marvelous ambassador for the company. Smith was the brilliant analyst and strategist who preferred to operate behind the scenes.

Although it worked out beautifully, neither man enjoyed a smooth entry to Comcast. For years Julian had been telling the company's story to Wall Street, and it couldn't have been easy to relinquish that role to the man he had trained to succeed him. (Before coming to Comcast, Alchin had never put together a financing from the borrower's side, addressed investors, or prepared an annual report.) "It was hard for Julian to let go," says Brian, "but eventually he became a mentor to John, and John was willing to take it—up to a point." Although Alchin seemed to be patient with Julian's tendency to micromanage, there were times during his first year when he thought he had made a big mistake in coming to Comcast, and Smith experienced similar misgivings. But Alchin followed in Julian's footsteps, and when he finally became the company's chief financial spokesman, he didn't seem to mind that Julian was often in the room, talking with some of the same fund managers and analysts he had known since the company began. What made it easier was that John Alchin and Julian Brodsky had become great friends.

For all his talent and experience, it was Alchin's warm and

generous personality, and his natural ease and kindness, that his colleagues and other employees responded to. Even as a boss, he was relaxed and congenial. "Without acting tough," says Lucille Fital, who has observed quite a few high-level executives, "John got as much out of his people as anyone ever did." At Alchin's retirement dinner, Julian quoted baseball manager Leo Durocher, who famously said that nice guys finish last. To which Julian added, "He obviously didn't know John Alchin."

His affability blended nicely with his gift for communicating. "He's a great speaker," says Mike Tallent. "People with Australian or British accents always sound smart, but John really is." Greg Hecker, who manages the company's in-house TV studio, says he could listen to Alchin talk about anything—"even wallpaper." In meetings or phone calls with investors and other groups, Alchin would describe the company's situation in a clear and winning way, and he was known for answering questions, including hostile ones, with patience and grace. Dealing with Wall Street can be demanding, and investors are often faddish and short-term oriented. But when disappointed fund managers expressed their frustrations, he was prepared for their reactions and never lost his cool. Once, when Alchin was walking toward him, Ralph whispered to a visitor, "Now here comes class."

Although Alchin mingled easily with the wealthy and the privileged, he was also attentive to the company's younger employees. "You could stop by John's office with a question," says Jennifer Khoury in corporate communications, "and get something more substantial in five minutes than in half an hour with some other people."

They were an odd couple, Smith and Alchin, but they had the talent, the character, and the temperament to carve up the financial territory and work together smoothly and effectively. Had Comcast been a private company, Larry Smith might have done the job alone. But in the increasingly challenging world of public corporations, John Alchin was a godsend.

For more than ten years, Alchin had not disclosed an important part of his life to most of his colleagues. That began to change in 2002, when, as chairman of Equality Forum, a national gay rights organization, he was contacted by a similar organization in Canada. The Canadians had received letters of support from a number of banks and corporations, and they were requesting one from Alchin as the co-CFO of Comcast. He was happy to sign, but because he would be doing so as an officer of the corporation, he checked with David Cohen, the company's executive vice president. Then he went to see Brian, who looked up at Alchin with a big smile and said, "I always wondered when we'd have this conversation." Alchin had never told Brian he was gay, but Brian had figured it out. "That took a burden off my shoulders," Alchin says. "It wasn't a secret, but it also wasn't something I had talked about very much."

The first person in Philadelphia Alchin had told was Lois Brodsky. Soon after he came to Comcast, he was at a wedding with the Brodskys when Lois, who noticed that Alchin had come to the event alone, said to him, "John, who is the most important person in your life?"

"That would be Hal Marryatt," he replied. "He's the man I left Australia with twenty years ago." Marryatt, a physician, was still living in Toronto. They had met in 1969 and remained in a committed relationship even through Alchin's years in New York, when they saw each other two weekends a month.

When the Comcast job became available, Alchin had been in New York for ten years. Hal had been counting on John's return, and they were both looking forward to resuming their life together in the same city. But after the two of them spent a long weekend in Philadelphia, Marryatt conceded that the distance between Toronto and Philadelphia wasn't meaningfully different than between Toronto and New York.

A few years later, when Marryatt retired, they ran into an unexpected roadblock. Because he didn't fall into the legal category of "spouse," he couldn't immigrate to the United States. When Larry Smith retired, Alchin agreed to stay on as co-CFO for one more year, but then he, too, retired—partly because he wasn't eager to continue without Smith, but mostly to spend more time with Hal in both

Toronto and Philadelphia. In 2009 Hal finally received his green card and was able to join Alchin in the United States.

Coming out at Comcast was a slow process for Alchin. He had told a few colleagues, who had probably told a few others, but it wasn't until the spring of 2006, when he agreed to be mentioned and to have his photo appear as part of a *Philadelphia Inquirer* story about Equality Forum, that his private life became a matter of public record. Just after seven that morning he received an e-mail from Brian that read, "Congratulations on your courage. You make the company proud." It was a powerful and supportive comment, but John Alchin had been making the company proud for a long time.

Three years later, in a Comcast "Lunch and Learn" series of programs on diversity, Alchin was part of a panel on the concerns of gay, lesbian, transgender, and bisexual employees. He ended his remarks by describing the e-mail from Brian that had meant so much to him. Then Ralph, who was sitting in the front row, took the microphone and said, "Of course Brian would say that. I taught him everything he knows."

The Protector

When Michael Angelakis, Comcast's fourth CFO, arrived early in 2007, the skies looked pretty clear. Nobody in corporate America suspected that a bone-crushing recession was just around the corner, but Angelakis, who is cautious by nature, had a feeling the economy would turn ugly. He moved Comcast to a more defensive position by making sure the company wasn't overly reliant on the major banks, and he reduced its exposure to weak financial partners, including Lehman Brothers. Although some investors were urging the company to borrow more money to continue buying back stock, Angelakis refused to take that risk.

His prudence was soon appreciated. "Mike was the right man for that awful moment," says Brian, whose hiring of Angelakis after Smith and Alchin retired marked his first generational transfer of leadership. "Ralph always wanted us to be protected, and even in a terrible economy our financial strength remained solid. Mike combined Ralph's caution with Julian's attention to detail. Even in 2008 we had a strong balance sheet, and we went to bed at night knowing our money was locked down. We came through the recession in pretty good shape."

After a year of sharing the job with John Alchin, Angelakis became sole CFO in 2008. By then, everything he worried about had happened. "He stepped in during as tumultuous a time as I can remember," says Dave Watson, "and he provided absolute steadiness. He gave a talk to explain to our employees how we were a solid company and all set for money in the near term. He reacted to the crisis quickly and effectively." Julian agrees: "He had a tremendous calming effect on our employees when the economy was falling apart."

Because Angelakis came from the world of private equity, most people assumed he was coming to Comcast to do deals. He likes deal making and is obviously good at it, but if that's what he wanted to do, he would have remained at Providence Equity, where he could have worked on deals all day. He came to Comcast to find some long-term stability, and to manage a set of assets and get involved in operations. But he never lost his interest in deals. "Some CFOs are deal killers, because that's the safest path," says Peter Luukko. "But as long as your projections are well thought out, Mike wants to support you in whatever you're hoping to do."

Having been there and done that, Angelakis had no *need* to do deals. When conditions weren't right for acquisitions or other transactions, there were plenty of other items on his plate.

A few things became clear even before Angelakis had been at the company very long. His modesty alone made him a good fit. "People from the private equity world, especially with the success he's had, often have an inflated view of themselves," says Alchin, "but Mike is understated and genuine." He is also balanced and composed, and never seems to be too up or too down.

He's a prodigious worker—"a work machine," Brian says—who assumed the responsibilities of two outstanding predecessors. Colleagues say he combines John Alchin's credibility with Larry Smith's financial abilities. He has a huge appetite for information and encourages his colleagues to show him as much relevant material as they can, rather than filter it down into a brief summary. If you give him a fifty-page presentation, he'll plow through it and may surprise you with a provocative or insightful comment on page 47. He's interested in everything, including internal reports from the cable division—the kind of detail most corporate CFOs wouldn't ask to see. "Mike doesn't want a story," says Ashton White, a financial-planning executive. "He just wants the facts, all of them, good and bad, with no sugarcoating." Bill Stemper, the head of business services, says Angelakis is so objective and unemotional in processing information that he's a little like Mr. Spock on *Star Trek*.

Much as Alchin brought a banker's outlook to the job, Angelakis brings the perspective of a private equity executive who spent years examining media companies through the eyes of an investor. He is fiscally conservative—even for Comcast. "He understands where every penny is," says Brian. "He knows where our money comes from and exactly how we're spending it, and he's able to show Wall Street that we are disciplined and focused." He is personally conservative as well. Although Angelakis is personable and easy to work with, he is serious and sober.

Having once been a cable operator, he understands the business and is genuinely interested in it, and he worked with Steve Burke—and now Neil Smit—in the cable division as closely as he did with Brian. Early in his tenure at Comcast, the company missed an earnings projection, which spurred him even further into operations. "I saw him become a more activist CFO with a huge interest in the products we offer and the pace of our innovation," says Sam Schwartz, who has headed up many innovative projects at Comcast. Angelakis looks ahead, too. One of his first moves was to hire Bob Victor from the Boston Consulting Group to head up his strategic and financial team.

Although Angelakis had never worked in a large public corporation, he adapted quickly to his new environment. "As a guardian of both our exposure and our corporate reputation," says Art Block, "he's especially sensitive to the legal requirements that govern public corporations, which he had to learn on the job."

Above all, colleagues speak of his discipline, whether in controlling spending or putting in place more sophisticated tools of analysis. He gives special attention to his favorite phrase—return on investment, or ROI. "He's taking us to the next level in terms of financial sophistication," says treasurer Bill Dordelman.

"He's great at listening to people and giving feedback," says chief accounting officer Larry Salva. "I don't think I've ever been in a meeting where he hasn't thanked people for their effort and complimented them for what they have accomplished." At the same time, he has tightened up the ship and made sure the company is run with a little more structure and restraint. Although he didn't come to Comcast for this reason, Angelakis served as a kind of fiscal umbrella for the rainy day that Ralph, especially, had always known was coming. The sun would come out again, and when it did, he, too, would begin to shine.

17

The Teacher

Mike Tallent

Six days after Mike Tallent came to Comcast, the whole building went up in flames. On the night of Saturday, February 23, 1991, Suzanne Roberts was watching the news on television when she woke up her sleeping husband: "Ralph, there's a fire in your building!"

"What floor?"

"I think they said the twenty-second."

"That's okay," said Ralph, who knew that Comcast's offices, which began on the thirtieth floor, were equipped with sprinklers. The optimist closed his eyes and went back to sleep.

An hour or two later, when Suzanne woke him again, Comcast's corporate home was engulfed in the worst office-building fire in the nation's history. Before it was over, three firefighters were killed and fourteen injured. The Comcast sprinklers ultimately extinguished the flames, but the devastation at One Meridian Plaza was so great that the building was never used again and was ultimately demolished.

The company was flooded with offers of help. Some employees moved to an empty floor at Comcast's law firm, Wolf Block, while the rest found temporary space in several nearby buildings. Fortunately, no vital information was lost, and customer records had never been stored at the corporate office.

Ralph quickly convened a company-wide meeting at a downtown hotel, where he assured the corporate employees that although their offices were inaccessible, their jobs were safe. He, Brian, and Stanley Wang immediately started looking for new space. The fire was still smoldering when they found several available floors nearby, at 1234 Market Street, which would serve as the company's corporate headquarters for the next three years.

Just six days after the fire, Comcast was able to meet its next payroll. Ten days later, all 250 displaced employees moved into the company's new home. Larry Smith had found a stockpile of used furniture, and soon it was more or less business as usual, with everyone pitching in to help.

Almost everything at Meridian Plaza was lost: furniture, computers, files, photographs, and other memorabilia. Rolodexes had to be reconstructed, which took forever. But these were mere possessions. Firefighters had been injured and killed, but there was relief and gratitude that the blaze hadn't erupted during working hours, when all thirty-eight floors were occupied. It could have been so much worse.

Because toxic chemicals had settled everywhere, nobody was allowed into the building. "They took Ralph and me over to the basement of the building next door," recalled Ann Gardner, "and we watched on a television screen as men dressed in space suits pulled out files and we told them what was worth saving." Those pages were copied through a rudimentary and inefficient scanning technology that didn't really help. Comcast's historical records were lost, including documentation of its earliest transactions.

• • •

Mike Tallent, who had just moved to Philadelphia, lost some personal items in the fire that he had shipped up from Miami, but he told himself it didn't matter. He was making a new start in a new city, without his family, and that might be easier without those reminders of home.

A few weeks earlier, when cable division president Tom Baxter tried to hire Tallent as his CFO, Tallent had turned him down, in part because he had the impression that Brian wasn't eager to bring him in. He had spent seven years at Storer Communications, most of them as controller of its cable properties. Even after Comcast and TCI acquired those systems, Storer remained alive as a company for tax reasons. The new owners needed someone to run it, and although Tallent had not been Storer's most senior executive, both Julian and Larry Smith, who were on the Storer board, were impressed with him. "We pushed like crazy for Mike," says Julian, "and we talked TCI into making him president." Now that Storer was finally closing, Tallent planned to stay in Miami. His family was there, and Tallent, a dedicated and excellent golfer, enjoyed being able to play all year long.

Because Julian and Tom Baxter thought so highly of Tallent's abilities, Brian called to see if he might change his mind. When Tallent realized that Brian really wanted him, he agreed to become CFO of the cable division.

Mike Tallent loves to tell stories, and his favorite one at Comcast, which he told at every opportunity, was about the importance of controlling costs. Soon after he arrived, the company's senior executives went out in pairs to visit the former Storer systems and meet with employees. Tallent accompanied Ralph to Florida and Alabama, a trip that had them leaving Philadelphia on a 7:00 a.m. flight and flying coach. When they landed in Palm Beach, they took a taxi to the Comcast office, where Ralph insisted on staying until he had answered every question that any employee wanted to ask. Then they drove to Miami to meet with the Storer computer group, which was now part of Comcast. They repeated the entire exercise, including the part where Ralph wouldn't leave until every question was answered. Then they took two flights to reach their next destination.

It was midnight when they finally arrived at their modest hotel in Mobile, and both men had been up since five in the morning. The desk clerk told them that rooms were $45 a night.

Fine, thought Tallent. Just give me the key and let me go to sleep.

"Do you offer a corporate rate?" Ralph asked.

It took the clerk a few minutes to check, and Tallent was annoyed. After three flights, two presentations, and an hour-long car ride, who cared about the room rate? Besides, Ralph was seventy. Wasn't he tired? The man was worth millions, and he wanted a corporate discount?

When the desk clerk returned and offered a $3 reduction, Ralph was pleased to accept it. Tallent was incredulous. Storer's previous owners, the executives at KKR, stayed in the best hotels, with limousines to ferry them to the finest restaurants. That night, as he was falling asleep, he realized that for Ralph, the $3 discount represented an investment in the company. "This business will always spill off cash," he would tell employees after he described his first trip with Ralph. "If you let a dollar get away, it's a dollar compounded at ten or twelve percent a year."

Knowing that the natural tendency of employees is to spend more of the company's money each year, he did everything he could to get them to spend less. That took discipline and vigilance, and it sometimes meant turning down marketing initiatives. He was skeptical of introductory specials, because customers who took advantage of these offers often left within the year. As a result, he would remind the GMs, the company ended up running two trucks when it shouldn't have been running any.

There is no single type of person at Comcast, but even so, Mike Tallent was one of a kind. Tall, with a paunch, a comb-over, and a light southern drawl, he came to work in a white shirt and striped tie, carrying a beat-up briefcase that looked as if it had been through a war. He grew up in Maytown, a small community in eastern Kentucky where his mother's family had lived since settling the area in the late

1700s. Tallent was a basketball star at George Washington University and led the Southern Conference in scoring during his junior year. He graduated with a degree in zoology, of all things, before becoming an accountant.

At the Washington office of Coopers & Lybrand, and then in Miami, he helped corporate clients with auditing and accounting. In 1984 he was hired by one of those clients, Storer Communications, which made him vice president and controller of its cable division. In his new job, Tallent learned pretty much everything there was to know about the economics of the business.

It wasn't just his background and his accent that made him stand out at Comcast. He was also a serious smoker. Whenever the subject came up, he would remind you of his Kentucky roots, as if to suggest that he was merely carrying out his patriotic duty. Or he'd say, "This is the best cigarette I've ever had, so don't talk to me about smoking." Sometimes, if you wanted to talk to him, he'd bring you along to the smoking room at 1500 Market Street, and you'd go home with the smell of cigarettes on your clothes. (He might also tell you that visiting the smoking room helped him be more effective, because it allowed him to get to know a different group of employees.) At least once, in order to enjoy a cigarette, he conducted a job interview outside the building on a windy afternoon. Although he conceded that smoking might shorten his life by a couple of years, he liked to point out that those years would come from the end of his life, when he would be older and not having as much fun.

He was good at so many things. He was an outstanding golfer and a terrific poker player who taught his team the finer points of the game as they flew to meetings. They used Chiclets as chips and he'd take their money, but his students had to pay him only thirty cents on the dollar. He was also a history buff with a special interest in English coins from the early seventeenth century, when metal currency was still made by hand. History was always on his mind: he was surely the only executive who compared AT&T's last-minute bid for Media-One's cable properties to Winston Churchill's 1915 naval bombardment of the Dardanelle Straits.

Once, when employees complained of being overworked and underappreciated, he told them how much worse the German soldiers must have felt during the Battle of Stalingrad. Another time, during a budget meeting where a GM was reluctant to make a necessary move, Steve Burke leaned over to Tallent and said, "McClellan." He knew his colleague would appreciate the cryptic reference to the overly cautious Civil War general who could never pull the trigger.

Tallent was also a wine connoisseur, thanks to his final years at Storer, when executives from KKR took him to expensive restaurants and ordered the best bottles. Some of his wine-loving colleagues at Comcast were impressed by how much he knew about certain French vintages—a remarkable amount, really, for a man who had never been to France and had no interest in going there. "What's there to see?" he would say. "It's just agriculture."

He thought about wine like he thought about history. "You're like a good bottle," he told Fred Graffam in an attempt to get him to become CFO of the West Division. "When I brought you up here a year ago, you were just a little immature, so I put you back in the case. But now it's a year later, you're my bottle, and it's my daughter's wedding." Graffam took the job.

Mike Tallent was the first senior financial executive who came to Comcast with real cable experience, and when he spoke, people listened. "If Mike said something was going to happen," says Brian, "it always did." He loved the "plumbing" of the business—the mundane, technical details of running a cable system. He was so well informed that although he reported to cable division president Tom Baxter, people often treated Tallent as if he and Baxter shared that title.

Baxter had come to Comcast to run the Midwest Region and was promoted to vice president of operations for the cable division before becoming its president. He was a demanding, effective, no-nonsense boss. "He knew what the company expected," says GM Ed Mount, "and he knew how to get there. He also knew how to crack the whip." An aggressive budgeter, Baxter was known for asking tough and testy questions that made some GMs think of him as a prosecutor. He also had a temper that would flare up periodically for reasons that were not always apparent to the objects of his wrath.

But he built a good team and knew how to motivate people, and he was loyal. "Many executives will fight for their own compensation," says Mike Tallent, "but they'll sacrifice other people's if they get what they want. Tom wouldn't do that."

Baxter was especially good at keeping the corporate leadership informed and up-to-date about cable operations. He was an early champion of C-SPAN, and well before Comcast became a powerhouse, he made sure the company's voice was heard and listened to at HBO and CNN. His predecessor, Bob Clasen, had been focused more on process, and Baxter represented a return to the hands-on, less bureaucratic management style of Dan Aaron. "Under Tom's leadership, we never missed a budget," says Brian. "He delivered," says Julian. "Whatever it took to hit the numbers, Tom did it."

It was Baxter who came up with creative ways to minimize the damage in the early 1990s, when the cable industry was once again regulated by Congress. His solution was to offer customers a package with more channels at a higher rate, which satisfied everybody— subscribers, the corporate leadership, and even the FCC. This move allowed Comcast to weather that storm with less damage than other cable companies. Baxter and Tallent were an effective team, with Baxter focused on the big picture while Tallent drilled down into the details.

Although Mike Tallent seemed to be juggling a hundred different balls, if you came to him with a question, he always had time for you—sometimes more time than you asked for, or even wanted. He loved to hold court, and once he started, he couldn't always stop. If you showed up in the late afternoon, when the teacher was at his best, you could count on being late for dinner.

But unlike most people who love to hold forth, he wasn't impressed with himself. And he was a little like the Wizard of Oz—if the Wizard of Oz had been honest. He'd remind you that he didn't really produce anything or create value; he just sat there, talking to people and dispensing advice. But the man behind the curtain was a source of both knowledge and wisdom, which is why people kept coming back. "Going to see Mike," says Filemon Lopez, "was like getting your MBA an hour at a time."

Employees with an agenda learned not to go to him without thinking through their proposals. "He always listened to what I had to say," says John Ridall, "but if any part of it didn't make sense, he'd let me know." Not everyone believed that Tallent was open to persuasion. "You could argue with Mike until your teeth fell out," says Rick Germano, the head of Customer Care, "but he wouldn't change his mind."

He was great at explaining things. Sometimes he answered questions by drawing a chart on a big sheet of paper on the easel next to his desk, and more than one visitor left Tallent's office with pages in hand. When another cable company was indicted for manipulating its subscriber numbers, and David Cohen asked Tallent to explain exactly how Comcast's subscribers were counted so Cohen could then brief the board, he left the tutorial with five pages of charts.

Tallent liked to help executives become better educators, which he considered a vital element of leadership. "Make your message clear," he would say. "Make sure it's right, and repeat it often." He took his own advice, to the point where talking with him sometimes felt like going to Mass: week after week, he would repeat the rules of the game. Repetition, he liked to say, is the best teacher.

"Mike has the highest cable IQ of anyone in the business," says Steve Burke. But it wasn't just cable. He knew so much about so many things that people sometimes wondered if he was bluffing. You'd listen to him and scratch your head; how on earth could he possibly know *that*? In one meeting, Tallent mentioned a fact so obscure that Burke discreetly sent a text message to his assistant, Susan Arnholt, asking her to verify the statement, which she quickly did. When Tallent was in the room, you didn't need Google.

He carried his learning lightly. Like Dan Aaron, he often engaged you through a series of questions. When he thought it might be helpful, he would reframe your answer in slightly different words, so you'd hear your own argument in a fresh way and see the flaw in your logic. If there was a weakness in your plan, he would help you uncover it; he liked to analyze mistakes and failures, and he could do that without making you feel bad. "More than anything else," says Brad Dusto, "he taught me how to teach by getting people to the point where they could answer their own questions." Ernie Pighini, a fellow student at Mike Tallent University, says, "He would show you how to make good decisions. He knew you wouldn't learn anything from a simple yes or no."

What he taught, above all, was *business*, and he could distill almost any issue to dollars and cents. If you came to him with a personnel problem, he'd help you think about it in a way that might suggest an economic solution. Addressing employees in local systems, he would say, "You may work in HR, engineering, or government affairs, but if you work for Comcast, you're also in business." More than one job applicant was surprised when Tallent asked what the prime rate was, or where the Dow had closed the day before. The message was clear: never forget that we are part of a much larger economy.

He had a compassionate side as well. When the company, for valid reasons, terminated a single mother with two children, Tallent got her job back, telling Al Peddrick in HR, "Look at all the money we make, and look what she makes." He gave lavish tips to cab drivers and twenty-dollar bills to the shoe-shine man. "Be generous," Tallent would say, "but with your own money, not the corporation's." He made an exception on the road, where he took employees to dinner and ordered good bottles of wine. This, too, was a teaching moment. When the check arrived, he'd evaluate it in familiar terms, telling his guests, "That was a two-sub meal."

His office was a mess, with papers everywhere, but it didn't matter because the facts and figures he needed were in his head. "He knew the numbers," says Ralph, "and he always seemed to be right. If you wanted information in a hurry, you'd call Mike." His colleagues knew that there wasn't a cable market in the country that he didn't know something about. "When we bought this system from Scripps," he would say, "they had ninety-five thousand subscribers. But then, near the end of the third year..." Tallent says he remembered the numbers because it was his job to know the details and the history of many, many systems. As often happens with gifted people, he couldn't see what the fuss was about.

He was at his best during the extended and often intense budget meetings that have long been at the heart of Comcast's culture. To Tallent these sessions were a living classroom where he could explain how the business really worked, and where new employees could learn the Comcast way of life. During the 2003 integration of the former AT&T systems, he and Steve Burke conducted a traveling Socratic dialogue to show the managers how Comcast was able to achieve much higher margins than their previous employer. "He didn't want there to be any mystery to the numbers," says Ron Hartz, who worked with him. "He wanted everyone to understand the P&L statement. He'd tell us that if we made the process too complicated, we weren't doing our jobs."

A big part of the cable business consists of keeping your hands on all the dials, especially the Four Ps—pricing, promotion, packaging, and plant. If you adjust them all just right, you can achieve profit margins of 40 percent or even higher; if not, you can end up at 20 percent or even lower. Mike Tallent was a master at working the dials.

Again and again, he reminded employees that the business was really very simple, that it boiled down to buying programming wholesale and selling it retail. "Don't make it so complicated!" he would say, adding that success depended on doing dozens of little things well: answering the phones, giving good service, booking the installations, keeping gas in the trucks, stocking the right equipment, and not fixing what isn't broken, because even a small adjustment in one of the dials can affect all the others.

He loved the Comcast culture and took delight in its "intellectually pure" approach, by which he meant that ideas were taken seriously and argued about. He took a special pleasure in locking horns with Julian. "When the two of us started talking," he says, "we were like a pair of cardiologists with years of knowledge and experience."

For his part, Julian enjoyed having someone around who really understood the economics of cable.

When Tom Baxter resigned in 1998 after two of his brothers died, Tallent was named interim president of the cable division. "You're the heart and soul of this company," Brian told him, "but I'm going to begin a wide search to replace Tom because we don't get an opportunity like this very often."

When Brian hired Steve Burke, whose background was in retailing, theme parks, and broadcasting, Tallent was mystified: "Tell me again why you're bringing in someone who doesn't know anything about cable to be my boss," he said to Brian. But he promised to make the partnership work, and it did. "I didn't know what to expect," says Brian. "It could have been a disaster."

Burke and Tallent turned their very different perspectives into a creative conflict that reminded Brian of the early battles between Dan and Julian. Tallent represented the old way of doing things. His goal was improving cash flow, and he was reluctant to do anything that might put that at risk. And he was right, especially about the present. Steve Burke believed that in an era of increased competition and new products, the old ways were no longer effective. He was right, too, especially about the future.

Burke was a big-idea man who wanted to transform the business and had the skill to do it. Tallent wanted to run the current business as efficiently as possible. For years they were able to work together, with Burke pushing the company into the future while Tallent applied the brakes. Burke hated to slow down, but as he once told Brian, "Mike is right. It drives me crazy that we can't do everything at once, but he's got a point."

When Burke was new at Comcast and new to cable, Tallent served as both his teacher and a source of continuity for the cable division. "Steve knew he could rely on Mike to keep the train on the tracks, which gave him time to learn the business," says Art Block. "He didn't have to rush into decisions he wasn't ready for. But it wasn't easy for Mike to see the company moving in new directions."

The partnership lasted longer than anyone expected, but nobody was surprised when it ended. As the business completed its evolution from a single product to the varied offerings of the digital age, Comcast was facing a new and more competitive world where marketing was critical and corporate frugality gave way to product development. In 2005 Tallent decided it was time to retire: the AT&T integration was complete, and his wife and their children, who had spent a few years in Philadelphia, had been back in Florida since 2002. He loved his job, but he was tired of eating dinner alone.

He had a knack for providing the appropriate story or insight, and his many students still recite his most quotable lines. He generally dispensed them as the occasion warranted, although there were some that he mentioned almost daily. Had he woven together his essential teachings and favorite sayings, they might have gone something like this:

- *It's about the money.* When I was a boy, my mom would say money wasn't important. But when I watched my parents draw up the family budget, money clearly *was* important. She meant that in a family, money isn't the most important thing. What matters is love.

  Money isn't the goal in politics, either—or in science, academics, law, religion, sports, or almost anything else. But in business, money *is* the point. That's why we're here. Never forget that we are operating a commercial enterprise.

- *A million dollars is a million one-dollar bills.* Our business consists of countless small and seemingly immaterial transactions. We're not like a jewelry store, because even if a customer comes in and buys everything we offer, that doesn't change anything. We depend on volume and repetition, and even the tiniest expense or the most inconsequential-looking revenue source can have big implications. So don't ever think that what you're doing here doesn't matter.

- *Raising prices is the second worst thing we can do.* The only thing worse is going broke. Cable is a revenue-driven business, and once customers are hooked up, our costs are predictable. In a revenue-driven business, you want as many customers as you can get, because that last customer is the most profitable.

Raising rates is an easy fix, but for the customer, it's death by a thousand cuts. Raising rates should be a last resort after you've exhausted every other solution.

- *It's not personal. It's just business.* People take things too personally. If you criticize their decision, they think you're criticizing *them*. When I hear an idea, I don't care whose mouth it came from, because now it's floating out there as an idea. Sometimes I ask difficult questions to make sure I understand what you're saying, or to help you make a more effective argument. When I think I'm being perceived as critical, I say, "This isn't personal." I try to make that clear so people will be intellectually honest. Cable, at least the way we do it here, is a giant, ongoing conversation.

- *Whenever possible, leave yourself the wide side of the field.* Unexpected things happen, so don't get ahead of yourself. You may still have time to consider your options, so don't lock yourself in or make decisions before you have to.

- *Cable is a simple business.* It comes down to four words: Buy wholesale, sell retail. Look at the facts and pay attention to the numbers, which should tell you what you need to know. This isn't rocket science.

- *And above all, remember this: take your business seriously, but take yourself lightly.*

The professor has left the building, but his lessons are still being repeated—not only by his students, but by some of their students as well. Can a teacher enjoy any better legacy?

18

The Big Boys Club

Dave Watson

There are two versions of how Comcast entered the cellular telephone business in the late 1980s, and they're both true. In one account, Ralph wanted to diversify. "I didn't like having all our eggs in one basket," he explains. "The broadcast networks were pushing to regulate us, the phone companies were spending like crazy to compete with us, and cellular seemed like a nice new business with recurring monthly income." The new industry reminded Ralph of the good old days of cable: "You put up a tower, you put up some money, and it's the same business in a different form."

A few years earlier, he and Julian had agreed to buy Beep, a New York paging company that owned the cellular rights to New York City—an extremely valuable asset, although nobody realized it at the time. "At the last minute," Julian recalls, "the owners demanded an extra $250,000. That felt like extortion, so we let it go." Wireless would have to wait.

In the second version, opportunity knocked and Ralph jumped up to open the door. "It was a fluke that we even looked at cellular," says Brian. "When we discussed it earlier, Ralph wondered why anyone would want to compete with the phone company if they didn't have to." (When cellular service began, the local phone company in each community was awarded a license as a kind of birthright, with a second franchise going to the highest bidder.)

When Amcell, a cell phone operator in New Jersey, found itself under attack from a unwelcomed bidder in early 1988, the CEO called Ralph to see if Comcast might be interested in being the white knight by making a better offer. Amcell's treasurer, Al Gencarella, who used to work for Julian, called his old boss with the same idea. For Comcast the timing was perfect. Talks with KKR about Storer had been suspended, leaving the company with enough cash for an acquisition that fulfilled Ralph's desire to diversify.

Brian remembers surprising Julian with the news that Ralph wanted to bid for Amcell immediately. "He's got that twinkle in his eye," Brian said, "and it looks a lot like Timonium Mode." It was. Four days after Ralph learned that it might be available, Amcell accepted Comcast's offer of $240 million. "I thought cellular was a marvelous business," Ralph says. "To walk around with a phone in your pocket? I figured everybody would want one."

Three years later, in 1991, Comcast expanded its cellular holdings by buying Metromedia's operations in greater Philadelphia and parts of New Jersey from media mogul John Kluge. The company agreed to pay half of the $1.1 billion purchase price in cash and the other half in equity, for which Julian had designed a custom-made financial instrument. But when Ralph, Kluge, and their teams met with the bankers at Lazard Frères to sign a deal that both parties had agreed to, Kluge raised a last-minute objection about the equity arrangement: "Hold on! If I take this paper, where will I get the cash to pay the taxes on the interest?" Whereupon one of the country's wealthiest men walked out of the room. Ralph followed him down the hall and into the men's room, where Kluge asked for, and Ralph agreed to, an additional $25 million. "You don't often see someone take Comcast to the hoop," says Brian. "Kluge was playing tough, but it wasn't unfair."

Comcast Cellular, as the new division was known, flourished under the leadership of Dave Watson, who came over from Metrophone. The cellular business had considerably more pizzazz than cable and spent far more on advertising, and this first foray into an industry that was competitive from the start was a learning experience for a company that had never faced such immediate pressures. "Comcast Cellular was a wonderful place," says Sam Chernak, who arrived in 1995 as director of operations. "If you came up with a new idea, you could make it happen within a week. We were a lean, entrepreneurial business that moved remarkably fast from idea to execution."

Despite its success, Brian and Larry Smith reluctantly decided to sell the cellular division in 1998. Larger companies were building national networks that allowed their customers to avoid roaming and long-distance fees, and regional providers just couldn't compete. Brian hated to give up wireless, but the only alternative was to make Comcast Cellular into a national business, and there was no realistic way to do that. "We had to sell," he says, "because there was nobody we could buy." Even Ralph agreed that selling was the only strategy that made sense.

The cellular properties went to Southwestern Bell, which later became Cingular, and, eventually, AT&T. "There's just one thing," Brian told Larry Smith, who was negotiating the sale. "I want to keep Dave Watson and his team." Brian had been impressed with the division's advertising and marketing, which had helped it outperform Bell Atlantic in Philadelphia, the phone company's hometown. Over the years he had seen Comcast hire several marketing executives without finding the right one, and Watson was an effective leader who knew how to compete. Brian also wanted to retain four of Watson's key people: Dave Juliano, Greg Butz, and the two Rays—Dombroski and Celona.

"Are you kidding?" said Smith. "If they're buying the division, I can't tell them that Watson and his team are off-limits."

"Of course you can," said Brian. "Make sure it's in the agreement."

"You can thank Brian for your job," Smith told Watson later. "I would have thrown you to the wolves."

Watson appreciated the support. Well before the deal closed, Southwestern Bell had tried to hire him, but he was hoping to stay at Comcast. Brian thought Watson would do well as the head of the cable division's marketing efforts, but he felt awkward bringing this up to Steve Burke, who had recently joined the company to run the division. He had already asked Burke to work with Mike Tallent, rather than inviting him to bring in his own CFO. And Burke came from Disney, which had plenty of marketing talent.

Brian was equally concerned about Watson's reaction: How would he feel about having a boss after *being* a boss? A breakfast meeting at the Rittenhouse Hotel was all it took for Burke and Watson to give it a try. Burke didn't mind that Watson had run his own operation. "To me that was an advantage," he says. "The more senior people you have with experience in running a business, the better off you are."

In 2005 Steve Burke was promoted to chief operating officer of the corporation while remaining president of the cable division. Dave Watson, who is known for his patience and his problem solving, was named executive vice president of operations (and later, chief operating officer) of Comcast Cable. In addition to heading up marketing and customer service, he was in charge of what were then the company's five cable divisions. (They were later consolidated into four divisions, and eventually into three.)

Although the 1990s were a great period for Comcast, the decade did not begin well. First came the government's restraints on highly leveraged transactions, which made bank loans almost impossible to secure. Then, in 1992, the cable industry was hit with a second government-sponsored obstacle. Congress regulated the whole industry, which led to the FCC's requiring cable operators to roll back their rates and follow complex and restrictive guidelines that would limit future price increases. The low point came in 1994, the only year in Comcast's history when revenue and cash flow actually declined.

But the company continued to expand, mostly from the kinds of big acquisitions that had fueled its growth in the 1980s. In June 1994, after a heated auction, Comcast won the right to buy the U.S. cable systems of Maclean-Hunter, which were then owned by Rogers, a Canadian company, for $1.27 billion. (Ted Rogers, who liked Ralph and preferred to sell to him, had called to say that he merely had to match the highest offer.) The acquisition made Comcast the third-largest cable operator, with 3.5 million subscribers, although it still lagged well behind TCI (with 10.4 million) and Time Warner (7.3 million), and was only slightly larger than Continental and Cox.

In previous acquisitions, Comcast had gone to great lengths to line up financing early, but this time the company agreed to buy the systems before it had the money. "We knew we'd find a way," says Brian, but it wasn't as easy as he had expected. With its near-simultaneous acquisitions of Maclean-Hunter and QVC, and with cable stocks faring poorly in the wake of re-regulation, Comcast needed another source of cash to supplement its large bank loans. Brian, Alchin, and Bill Dordelman, Alchin's deputy, met with two or three private equity firms to discuss a possible partnership for the Maclean-Hunter systems, but they all insisted on more generous terms than Comcast was willing to provide. And other than private equity funds, which were then known as LBO firms, there weren't many options.

Sometimes you get lucky. A former colleague at TD Bank told John Alchin that the California Public Employees' Retirement System, the huge pension fund known as CalPERS, was now interested in direct investment deals. Their first such venture had gone well, and they were happy to meet with Comcast to discuss another one.

The basic terms were set early on. "They would invest on the same basis we did," says Julian, "and they gave us a generous management fee." But getting approval for the partnership was an arduous process. The board of a public pension fund includes members with little or no financial expertise, and companies seeking loans or investments from CalPERS often felt as if they were being investigated by a congressional committee. "You have to jump through a lot of hoops," says Dordelman. "It's not a conversation. You answer their questions and leave without knowing their decision." Alchin still cringes at the memory of those excruciating meetings in Sacramento. He and Dordelman were a long way from Wall Street.

But all their discomfort paid off when CalPERS agreed to become an equity partner in the Maclean-Hunter acquisition. At the time, the fund's investment of $250 million was one of the largest private equity deals ever done with a single investor. It was a significant deal at a time when Comcast had no good backup plan.

The CalPERS investment worked out well for both sides. Five years later, Comcast bought out the fund's equity position for $750 million—three times what CalPERS had paid, but still a bargain after cable values had soared. The investment served as a valuable third-party endorsement of both the industry in general and Comcast in particular.

In 1996, using stock, Comcast bought the cable systems of the E. W. Scripps Company, which had 800,000 subscribers. Because Comcast was still carrying a lot of debt and the Scripps properties came with no outstanding loans, the acquisition deleveraged the company and strengthened its balance sheet. "It was a huge stock payment for us," Brian explains, "but it put us in a better position to make other acquisitions."

By now Comcast was trying to acquire properties in contiguous areas, with a special emphasis on the mid-Atlantic states. This was also a favorite hunting ground of cable veteran Glenn Jones, who had started out in 1967 by borrowing against his Volkswagen to buy a tiny system in Georgetown, Colorado, with a hundred subscribers. By 1998 Jones Intercable had grown to 1.4 million subscribers in seventeen states, with a heavy presence in the area surrounding Washington, D.C. It was Glenn Jones who had been about to acquire the large system near Baltimore when Ralph swooped in with his last-minute offer in Timonium.

In 1994 Jones sold 30 percent of his company to Bell Canada in a deal that gave the buyers an option to acquire the control shares of Intercable. In 1998, having heard that Bell Canada might be willing to sell its interest in Jones, Alan Mnuchin, an investment banker at Lehman Brothers, told Ralph he had figured out a way for Comcast to acquire not only the equity position but also the "path to control"—the option to acquire a majority interest. This would require some complicated legal work, but it seemed possible. "A lot of this deal was about not taking no for an answer," says Peter Ezersky, a Lazard banker who worked on the Jones acquisition. "Anyone could have done it if they had figured out how, but only Comcast did."

It was an aggressive move, and nobody imagined that Glenn Jones would be pleased. Although he knew that Bell Canada wanted to sell its stake, he never imagined that the rest of his company might be sold along with it—or that it might be acquired by Comcast. In recent months, Jones had been talking with Cox, a friendly rival of Comcast, about a possible sale of his company.

On the Friday of Memorial Day weekend, Comcast quietly signed an agreement with Bell Canada. Glenn Jones would have to be informed, and Comcast's leaders thought it was only right to tell him in person, before he heard the news from anyone else. "One reason Comcast has been successful," says Ezersky, "is that it never occurred to them not to send somebody to see Glenn Jones."

Everyone agreed that the only appropriate emissary for this awkward assignment was Ralph, who had known Jones for many years. Jones was spending the holiday weekend at a conference in Jackson Hole, Wyoming, when Ralph called and asked if they could have breakfast the following morning. Jones assumed that Ralph was also attending the meeting; he didn't realize that the founder of Comcast, who was now in his late seventies, was flying to Wyoming just to see him.

When they sat down together, Ralph said, "Glenn, we just bought Bell Canada's option, and we're going to exercise it. We'd like to merge your company into ours."

As everyone expected, Jones was shocked and angry to learn that the deal had been made without his knowledge or consent. He believed, and still does, that Bell Canada had no right to sell their option without his written permission. "I could have fought it," he says, "and if the buyer had been anyone but Ralph, I might have."

But having already decided to leave the business, he soon came to accept, and even embrace, the new plan. "I didn't want to be a mid-size company in an elephant dance," he says. "We were highly leveraged, and when I threw the chicken bones on the table, it was time to sell. I thought Comcast would be a good home for my people, and I was right. They treated our employees fairly, and a lot of them are still there. In the end, Comcast did us a favor."

Jones, who received what he calls "an excellent price," was understandably proud of his systems, which were well constructed and located in good markets. He is equally proud of his dealings with Comcast, and calls the transaction "probably the smoothest large-scale cable deal ever done." When issues came up, he and Ralph were able to resolve them quickly on the phone. "We were such good friends," he says, "that we didn't let anything get in the way."

A number of the Jones systems were more technologically advanced than Comcast's, which led to problems in their integration. "In some ways we were taking them back to the Stone Age," says Fred Graffam, who was asked to head up finances for the newly acquired systems. "Although we may have been better operators, their purchasing software and other tools were far ahead of ours. Now they were forced to start doing things on paper that they had already been doing electronically. It was a mess for a few months, but we worked it out."

The human side of the transition went more smoothly. "Comcast was good to us," says Mike Molinaro, who had just arrived at Jones when Comcast came along. "They went out of their way to make us feel part of the family, and it was clear they had done this sort of thing before."

In a decade when Comcast was acquiring cable systems in bulk, Las Vegas was a special case. The city was served by a single system with more than 300,000 residential customers. It was jointly owned by Prime Cable and the Greenspun family, whose patriarch, Hank Greenspun, the colorful owner and publisher of the *Las Vegas Sun*, had died in 1989. In 1998, when the Greenspuns invited several companies to make an offer, Ralph and Brian flew in to have dinner with the family, which had decided to retain a minority interest in the business. When Brian Greenspun, the founder's son, outlined his idea for a cable channel that would draw upon the city's many entertainment offerings, Ralph loved the concept. "Of everyone we spoke to," says Greenspun, "he's the only one who really got it."

The Greenspuns were fond of Ralph, and they liked the idea of selling their system to another cable family. "It would always be ours, at least in our minds," says Greenspun, "and we wanted it to go to the right people. I told Ralph and Brian that all they had to do was come close to the highest offer."

But an auction has its own momentum, and the bids soon rose to unprecedented levels. At Comcast, everyone but Ralph believed that the price was far too high. "The system was selling for seventeen times cash flow at a time when ten was normal," says John Alchin. "Larry and I agreed that it was seriously overpriced." It boiled down to around $4,000 per subscriber, which was roughly twice the going rate. "Even when we factored in all the expected growth in Las Vegas, it still seemed too expensive," says Brian.

Although Ralph could have insisted, he backed off after a 10-1 vote against making a higher bid. "I thought my responsibility was to keep the group together," he says. "And I didn't want to overrule Brian."

For the acquisition to be profitable, Las Vegas would have to grow by 7 or 8 percent a year for many years. "And guess what?" says Mike Tallent. "It did! But that was unimaginable at the time, except to Ralph."

Brian had another concern. He was hoping to acquire MediaOne, which had millions of subscribers, and Comcast investors often reacted negatively to highly priced acquisitions. Paying an outrageous price for Las Vegas would result in a serious hit to the company's stock, which would make it harder to buy MediaOne.

Ralph still regrets that he couldn't persuade his colleagues to make a higher bid. "I don't believe we *ever* overpaid for an acquisition," he says. "I could have insisted, but this place is not a dictatorship. In the case of Las Vegas, I bowed to the mob—only it was our mob."

MediaOne, a short-lived company that was larger than Comcast, was created by a 1995 merger between US West and Continental Cablevision. With close to six million subscribers and many systems that were geographically close to Comcast's systems, it was an attractive target, but a very ambitious one. In the spring of 1999, Brian started calling CEO Chuck Lillis to discuss a possible merger. Lillis kept saying no, but Brian kept calling. Finally, at a conference in Arizona, he met with Lillis and laid out the case for a merger, and before long they agreed on terms. If the deal went through, the largest acquisition in Comcast's history would give the company a total of 11 million subscribers, putting it on a par with the two largest operators—Time Warner Cable, and the newly created cable division of AT&T, which had recently acquired TCI.

Knowing that an offer for MediaOne might encourage another bidder to step in, Comcast pushed for, and received, an unusually large breakup fee of $1.5 billion. Larry Smith thought that was still too low, but his colleagues believed that a higher fee might be blocked by the courts.

Just before the Comcast offer was announced, Brian placed a courtesy call to Mike Armstrong, the new chairman of AT&T, to let him know about the bid. Armstrong called back the next day and said, "Welcome to the Big Boys Club. We thought about bidding, but decided not to." A few weeks later, Brian was hosting a reunion of college squash players when his cell phone rang with bad news: AT&T was about to announce a substantially higher bid for MediaOne—all of it in cash (Comcast planned to pay with stock). Although Brian & Co. were aware that something like this could happen, nobody saw it coming.

Comcast had a limited amount of time to raise its bid, and Ralph and Brian were determined to try. It would take another $20 billion to top AT&T's offer, and Brian worked every angle he could think of. When he realized he couldn't go any higher, he and his deal team continued to give the impression that something could happen. "We recognized that another bid was impossible, and maybe not even prudent," he says, "but we wanted to put up a good front to get the best possible terms."

The bluff worked, and Armstrong called Ralph with a tempting offer: If Comcast dropped out of the auction, AT&T would sell it two million subscribers.

"That's an interesting idea," Ralph said. "Why don't we leave the details to Brian and Leo?" Leo was Leo Hindery, Jr., the CEO of AT&T Broadband, the company's cable division.

Although Brian was heartsick to lose MediaOne, Armstrong's proposal was the best available option. And it looked even better when he said Comcast could pay for the new subscribers in a tax-free transaction, using the AT&T shares the company had received from its earlier sales of Teleport and At Home. For its part, Comcast had to agree to offer its customers local phone service from AT&T—but only if other cable companies made a similar agreement, which Brian thought was unlikely. (He was right. Before long, cable companies would be selling their own digital phone service.) Comcast also received the agreed-upon breakup fee of $1.5 billion.

What felt at the time like a necessary compromise turned out to be a stroke of luck, as AT&T's purchase of the MediaOne properties set the stage for the biggest cable acquisition ever a couple of years later. Although nobody knew it at the time, the MediaOne deal marked the all-time high price for new subscribers; in the months ahead, AT&T's stock fell by 40 percent, in part because the company had paid so much for MediaOne. Comcast actually won by losing, which is why Julian calls the episode "the sweet smell of failure."

Among the properties Comcast acquired from AT&T were the systems belonging to Suburban Cable in Philadelphia, which had well over a million subscribers. Suburban's founder, H. F. (Gerry) Lenfest, had once worked for the publisher and media mogul Walter Annenberg, and in 1974, when Annenberg decided to sell off some of his

Pennsylvania systems, Lenfest had bought them. He continued buying cable systems and made a fortune by using as much debt as possible, rather than giving up equity. Lenfest, in other words, did what Ralph wished he had done.

Ralph had long wanted to buy those systems, and Hindery promised they would be part of the package. But AT&T Broadband owned only a 50 percent stake in Lenfest, and Hindery had to do some fast bluffing to acquire the rest. Lenfest said he would agree to a buyout by AT&T as long as Hindery didn't turn around and sell Suburban Cable to Comcast, which would probably end up firing most of his top executives; if that happened, he told Hindery, AT&T would owe him an additional $300 million. "I picked that number out of the air," says Lenfest, "but I neglected to get it in writing." Big mistake! As soon as AT&T bought the rest of Suburban Cable, a reporter told Lenfest that Hindery was already in the process of selling his systems to Comcast.

Lenfest was furious, but like Glenn Jones a few months earlier, he made out extremely well. Comcast was planning to pay for the Lenfest systems with AT&T stock, but Larry Smith had a better idea. He told Brian the transaction would be more tax efficient if Comcast bought those systems directly from Lenfest, using its own shares.

"You can talk to Gerry," said Brian, "but he'll never take our stock because he's bitter about the deal."

Smith, who had nothing to lose, and who hated to pay more taxes than necessary, met with Lenfest and showed him the financial advantage of accepting shares of Comcast. Lenfest was persuaded, and he would be grateful when Comcast shares turned out to be far more valuable than those of AT&T.

As the twentieth century drew to a close, Comcast had morphed into a much larger company. Its cell phone division had come and gone. With new properties from Maclean-Hunter, Scripps, Jones Intercable, Lenfest, and some from AT&T, along with the many Group W and Storer systems it had picked up in the 1980s, the sleepy little company from Bala Cynwyd had become a major player.

Although Brian, Ralph, and their colleagues were pleased with how things had turned out, they remained ambitious, even if it wasn't clear what form that ambition would take. Later, they would realize that AT&T's acquisition of MediaOne had set the stage for the kind of expansion that nobody at Comcast had dared to dream about. Not even Ralph.

19

The Fast Lane

Brian Roberts and Bill Gates

Karen Nathan was just about the last person you would have expected to test Comcast's high-speed Internet service. In the spring of 1994, she was an at-home mother with two small children in the Philadelphia suburb of Wynnewood. She didn't own a computer and had never even used one.

But her husband, Tom, had been with Comcast for ten years, and their house was in a perfect spot for hooking up a cable modem. And if cable companies had any hope of succeeding with high-speed Internet, which Brian and his colleagues saw as the Next Big Thing, they would have to engage millions of Karen Nathans, who were nowhere near the cutting edge of technology. To the astonishment of some observers, cable industry executives across the country were betting that cable modems would soon unleash a mass market high-tech revolution.

Nathan was willing to test the new device because she had some free time and enjoyed learning new things. One morning a Comcast technician brought over a personal computer and set it up in the children's playroom in the family's finished basement, which seemed appropriate for a machine she wasn't expecting to use very often. He showed her how to turn it on and how to use the mouse, and he gave her a tutorial in Windows 3.1. After activating a five-pound modem that was roughly the size of a shoebox, he showed her how to use Prodigy, an early online service provider, and Mosaic, the first popular Web browser.

She was a quick learner, and she enjoyed accessing the Internet— or what there was of it. In 1994 the World Wide Web was still under construction, and such future household names as Google, Yahoo!, Amazon, and eBay had not yet appeared. Some people, including Vice President Al Gore, were already talking about the information superhighway, but when Karen Nathan first sat at the keyboard, it was more like an unpaved country road.

Another driver on that road was Julian Brodsky, although when it came to computers, he and Karen Nathan couldn't have been more different. An early adopter of new technologies, Julian had been using a home computer well before Windows and even before MS-DOS— back when the operating system for microcomputers (other than those made by Apple) was known as CP/M. In the days before Visi-Calc, the first electronic spreadsheet, a program called MicroPlan allowed Julian and his team to prepare "electronic worksheets," which helped the company analyze potential acquisitions and other financial issues.

In 1993, when Julian first heard about the Internet, he asked his brother, a physicist at IBM's Watson Research Center, to explain what it was. Soon, at Marc Brodsky's lab, he got to see it for himself. The Internet looked like a fine tool for scholars and scientists, but it seemed so crude and clumsy that Julian couldn't envision any commercial applications.

He changed his mind two years later when he tried Mosaic in a

Box, an improved version of the early Web browser. Using a telephone modem, the only tool available, to access Prodigy and America Online, he was amazed at what he found. "I didn't know the first thing about the Internet," he recalls, "but I could see it would be gigantic."

Because he thought Comcast should be participating in this exciting new world, he started attending conferences and meetings to learn more about it. He enlisted his colleague Mark Coblitz to join him in making a series of small, early investments in start-up companies. On a visit to Silicon Valley, they put $2 million into the first company they saw, which provided domain names and digital certification to other Internet companies. Five years later, Comcast sold its stake in VeriSign for a hundred times its investment.

In 1996 Philadelphia entrepreneur Pete Musser came to see Ralph and Julian. Musser was the man who had sold Ralph his cable TV operation in Tupelo and who later introduced him to QVC's Joe Segel. This time he described a combined venture capital fund, incubator, and operating company that would specialize in business-to-business Internet activity. He was hoping Comcast would be one of his investors.

"We'd love to participate," Julian told him, "but we see this as more than an investment. We want to learn about the Internet, and we'd like the right to invest side by side with you if we see an opportunity." Musser had no objection, and Comcast ended up making two such investments, both of which worked out extremely well.

One of them, LinkShare, which was started by Stephen Messer and his sister, Heidi, invented the technology to follow a purchase from an online ad all the way through to a sale, which allowed marketers and promoters to be paid when their efforts were successful. When the Messers starting raising money, the computer era was still so young that their first ten slides explained what the Internet was, and the next few explained why consumers would soon be buying goods online. Often, Heidi Messer recalls, they didn't get to explain what the company actually did because the investors they were meeting with were convinced that the Internet was just a fad.

After a strong start, LinkShare ran into trouble when Internet stocks crashed in 2000. Skeptical about its prospects, Julian offered the Messers a bridge loan if they agreed to sell, but they refused the offer and were able to turn around the company. "Julian was more of a fan after we proved him wrong," says Heidi. "He wanted us to succeed more than he wanted to be right, and our relationship flourished. He's tough on entrepreneurs. He doesn't give you any sweet talk, which makes him a valuable friend." Comcast had invested $1.7 million in LinkShare. A couple of years later, when the company was sold, Comcast's share came to $42.5 million.

Initially Comcast had invested only a couple of million dollars in the company Musser had described, but it added more later, for a total investment of $23 million. Internet Capital Group, as the venture was known, went public in 1999, and was a screaming success; within months, its market cap exceeded that of General Motors. In early 2000, when Comcast was allowed to sell 10 percent of its stake in ICG, the company received $460 million for an investment of $2.3 million. But when it finally liquidated its stake, shares of ICG had fallen to $1.32. And yet even at that price, Comcast made money.

In 1998 Julian decided it was time that his colleagues were better informed about the Internet. He organized a two-day conference, held at the company's old headquarters in Bala Cynwyd, for about two dozen of the company's top executives. He brought in outside experts who described the high-tech world and identified the major players. On the second day, every participant was asked to open an e-mail account and to make a purchase on Amazon.com.

A few months later, he asked the Comcast board for $100 million to start a high-tech venture capital fund inside the company to continue the investments that he and Coblitz had been making, but in a bigger and more professional way. Comcast Interactive Capital, or CIC, was born in 1999 with the corporation as the sole limited partner, which meant that Comcast would participate in the profits of the fund, but not in its management. The first person Julian hired was Sam Schwartz, a former software engineer turned venture capitalist. Schwartz would later become president of the fund and would move on to take a leading role in developing new forms of technology for Comcast.

One of CIC's earliest investments was an Internet business dreamed up by a young man named Josh Kopelman, who had recently graduated from Wharton. Kopelman wanted to create an online marketplace that combined the best features of Amazon—big selection, ease of use, and fixed prices, with the best parts of eBay, which maintained no inventory and served, back then, as a marketplace for previously owned products, which were often available at steep discounts. "If you're choosing between a new CD for fifteen dollars and a used one for five," Kopelman likes to say, "that's not a decision. That's an IQ test."

Half.com, as the company was called, was an online marketplace for books, CDs, DVDs, and video games, in which sellers would deal directly with buyers for items that sold for no more than half their original retail price.

Kopelman's group was able to line up plenty of sellers, but how could they tell potential buyers about Half.com without an expensive ad campaign? "We had a daylong brainstorming session to come up with something that would put us on the map," Kopelman says. After a few hours of frustration, somebody said, "If we really want to be on the map, why don't we buy a town?"

Before long, and for a modest fee, Kopelman persuaded the citizens of the tiny community of Halfway, Oregon, to change the name of their town for one year to Half.com. The enormous publicity included a *Today* show interview with Kopelman and the town's mayor. Then, at a Chinese restaurant, Kopelman noticed that the back of his fortune cookie message was blank, so he arranged with a large cookie manufacturer to print coupons for half.com on the other side of its fortunes. And when he saw that plastic urinal screens in public bathrooms had no writing on them, he ordered a few hundred that read, "Don't Piss Away Your Money. Head to Half.com," and hired young men to place them in men's rooms at airports and train stations around the Northeast. Some of those screens remained in place for years.

In September 1999 Comcast Interactive Capital invested $500,000 in Half.com. In December the fund invested an additional $3.5 million. Seven months later, when eBay bought the company, CIC received almost $35 million in eBay stock, giving it more than an eightfold return in less than a year. It wasn't one of the fund's biggest gains, but it was certainly one of the fastest.

Comcast Interactive Capital, which is now Comcast Ventures, has been strikingly successful; when Julian retired as an executive in 2004, its annual rate of return was over 60 percent during a period that included the bursting of the Internet bubble. But the fund was never just about profits: it has also served Comcast as an important source of intelligence and R&D about the Internet and other new technologies.

Back in 1994 Karen Nathan was learning about the Internet more or less on her own. She would have loved to use e-mail, but nobody she knew had it yet. She started buying computer magazines to read about websites that might interest her. When she found one she liked, she was able to get there much faster than almost anyone else in the country, although, having never used a dial-up modem, she didn't realize how fortunate she was. But she knew that while other users were experiencing painfully slow connections and frequent interruptions, her high-speed cable modem was providing nearly instantaneous connections—at least when it worked.

Much of the time, though, it didn't. Comcast engineers had anticipated a host of problems during the initial months of their new cable modem, which was why they enlisted an employee's family to try it out. When Nathan called to report a malfunction, a technician drove over to fix it. She soon got to know these men, especially early on, when only two or three technicians had enough training to fix the problems.

In 1995, after a technician installed Windows 95 on Karen Nathan's computer, Comcast expanded its modem test to include a few dozen other households in her neighborhood. Now she and her friend Shari Rosenbloom could correspond on e-mail through

America Online. Previously Nathan could e-mail only the Comcast technicians, which wasn't very practical because the main reason she needed to reach them was to tell them her modem wasn't working.

Before long Mosaic evolved into Netscape and many more websites started to appear, along with the first search engines, including Archie, Veronica, Gopher, WebCrawler, and Infoseek. In the Nathans' basement, seven-year-old Sarah spent hours on her mother's lap playing Mind Maze and other games that Karen had found on Prodigy.

A few months into the test, high-speed Internet was still so new that a story about Karen Nathan's experiment appeared in the *Philadelphia Inquirer*. It began with a passage that read like a paid advertisement for Comcast's next product:

> Frustrated by delays when traveling the Internet?
> Tired of waiting for that irritating hourglass symbol while on American Online?
> Relief is at hand. Electronic life is about to get much faster.

The article reported that Comcast was preparing "a new PC Connect service" at speeds between fifty and several hundred times faster than telephone modems, and that this was another sign of sharpening competition between cable and the phone companies. A few months later, in its 1995 Annual Report, the company confidently announced that a major new product was about to be unveiled for navigating the information superhighway:

> A Ferrari is meant to do more than be driven up and down the driveway. We have the solution. . . . When consumers use our service, as they have been doing over the last year in our test market, they can't imagine going back to the much slower telephone technology. We plan a rollout of cable modem service later in 1996 in a number of communities.

It's impossible to pinpoint the precise moment when somebody, somewhere, first realized that cable wires could be used for something other than television, and perhaps the same basic idea had occurred to several people. Mark Coblitz, who had been hired to think about the future, was working on cable modems back in 1992, when the entire World Wide Web consisted of no more than about thirty reliable sites. During a chance meeting with Avram Miller, a vice president at Intel, Coblitz learned that Miller had been wondering about transmitting data over cable lines. Comcast and Intel ran some trials to see how such a service might work, and Intel developed a working modem. But when it became clear that Intel was going to stick to its core business of computer chips, Coblitz started looking elsewhere.

He and Frank Ragone, Comcast's vice president of engineering, went to Schaumburg, Illinois, where Motorola was already making equipment for Comcast's cable and cellular divisions. When they asked if Motorola might be interested in working on cable modem technology, it marked the start of a relationship that is still going strong. A couple of years later, Coblitz and Steve Craddock helped run Comcast's first trials for Motorola cable modems in Lower Merion, which is where Karen Nathan enters the story.

Other cable companies were moving in the same direction. Working through CableLabs, the industry's R&D consortium, Coblitz and Brad Dusto started collaborating with their counterparts at TCI, Cox, and Time Warner, where Jim Chiddix was already on the case. In 1996, hoping to avoid the high-tech equivalent of the Betamax/VHS divide that plagued videocassette recorders in the early 1980s, the group decided to develop a common technical standard for cable modems. They came up with a platform they called DOCSIS, which stood for Data Over Cable Service Interface Specifications. "We called it that," says Coblitz, "because it was named by engineers, rather than marketing people."

When cable modems first appeared, they had to be explained and marketed. Although potential customers understood that these new devices were much faster than dial-up, they were reluctant to pay for equipment that didn't seem necessary. "Customers liked the

Internet," says Mitch Bowling, whose job at Comcast was to launch new markets for cable modems, "but most of them didn't grasp the benefit of getting there faster. They reminded me of people a hundred years ago who rode a horse and must have wondered why anyone would need a car."

The early cable modem installations didn't always go smoothly. Sometimes, technicians would arrive at a customer's house only to find that the family that ordered a high-speed modem didn't even own a computer. Consumers had heard about the Internet, but they didn't always understand what it was, or that they needed a computer to access it. Generally, when the installers came to a customer's house—and at first they always worked in pairs—one tech's job was to find the coaxial cable coming into the house for the television and branch it off into the room with the computer. (No household in those days had more than one computer.) The other tech worked on the customer's machine, which had to be either an Apple or a PC with Windows 95. Because computers did not yet include Ethernet jacks, the second technician opened the machine, installed an expensive Ethernet card, and tried to establish an Internet connection. It didn't always work, and sometimes the installers would damage the customer's computer, and the company would have to replace it.

Although the early years were slow going, with stability issues and other problems, cable companies became increasingly confident that they were uniquely positioned to connect customers to the Internet. At Comcast, Dusto and Coblitz developed a business plan that assumed 8 percent of cable customers would sign up for a high-speed connection—which sounded pretty bold at a time when only 20 percent of Americans were familiar with the Internet, and virtually everyone who went online was using a dial-up modem. Computers were expensive, but once you paid for one, you owned it. Would consumers be willing to shell out a hefty monthly fee for a faster connection?

They said they wouldn't, but when they tried a cable modem at a friend's house, or saw one being demonstrated, they were amazed by the difference. Local Comcast systems would set up side-by-side demonstrations in a school, with one computer connected to a telephone modem and the other to a cable modem. The company created a website that showed a simple drawing of a cannon in the act of shooting. Typically, the cannon would fire half a dozen times on the high-speed connection before the telephone-linked computer had finished downloading the image.

"We ran countless demonstrations," says Jim Gordon, who used to show cable modems in an affluent Baltimore suburb. "We even set up living rooms in our building, so you could see how a high-speed connection would look in your home. We'd bring the media through on tours. We were offering a great product, but it had to be seen to be believed."

If consumers were fortunate enough to live in a city or a suburb where cable companies had begun to offer Internet service, they signed up in large numbers. Others had to wait for their neighborhood systems to be upgraded, which could take anywhere from a couple of months to several years.

Although Comcast employees would tell potential customers that the three best things about cable modems were "speed, speed, and speed," there were other advantages as well. The connection was always on, and interruptions were infrequent. Cable modems didn't tie up your phone or force you to order an extra line. And before long, routers would make it possible for a household to have several computers with high-speed connections from a single hookup. As the Internet began providing more sophisticated content, including music, graphics, and streaming video, cable modems (or their equivalents) became essential.

Many industries tried to capitalize on the Internet, but cable was one of the few that succeeded early on. Part of it was the sheer good luck of being in the right place at the right time—and with the right wires. By the mid-1990s Comcast and most other cable companies had started upgrading their systems with fiber optics, a huge investment to facilitate the transition to digital technology, which would lead to additional channels and new products, including On Demand, digital video recorders, and high-definition television. The rebuild, as the upgrade was known, also made it possible for cable operators to offer faster connections to both their video customers and other consumers who might want to order this service on its own.

From time to time, CableLabs would organize research trips for a dozen or so CEOs. There were trips to Korea, Japan, and Europe, and, in the spring of 1997, a visit to three high-tech companies on the West Coast—Oracle, Intel, and Microsoft, who were all hoping to have their codes and software included in the operating system for the next generation of set-top boxes.

Brian organized the trip, whose participants included John Malone of TCI, Jim Robbins of Cox, and Ted Rogers of Rogers Communications. Although Comcast and most of the others were well along in their rebuilds, Malone had recently interrupted TCI's effort because he wasn't certain that upgrading the company's infrastructure was really worth the expense.

After visiting Oracle and Intel in California, the group flew to Seattle to spend a day at Microsoft in Redmond, Washington. About halfway through the meeting, Bill Gates entered the room. Brian had met him before, but nobody in the delegation knew him well.

In a remarkable act of restraint, the CableLabs group had brought only a single slide, a chart showing that almost two-thirds of the rebuild they were all working on had already been completed. Gates hadn't realized this. Turning to Malone, he said, "John, when you announced that you were no longer rebuilding, I thought that was true for everybody."

"We don't have a single strategy," said Brian. "This is the real number, and it includes TCI."

That evening, Gates gave a dinner for the group at a private club overlooking Lake Washington. There were several round tables but no assigned chairs, and Brian and Cox's Jim Robbins took seats on either side of their host. As Pacific salmon was being served, Gates turned to Brian and said, "I'm excited about that slide, and I like what you're doing. How can I help?"

"Why don't you buy ten percent of everybody in this room?"

Brian replied. His comment was greeted with laughter around the table.

Jim Robbins, who may have been embarrassed by Brian's bold suggestion, quickly changed the subject: "Bill, we've been reading about your travels. Where are you going next?"

"Tomorrow," said Gates, "Paul Allen is taking Melinda and me to the Amazon to see some rare chimpanzees. We'll stay on Paul's yacht and a helicopter will fly us into the trees, because those chimps don't come down very often. The poor chimpanzees! Can you imagine, these rotors are right in your face as these guys are staring at you?"

He turned back to Brian: "How much do you think that would cost?" he asked. "We have ten billion in cash."

"I'm not sure," said Brian, who wondered whether Gates was teasing him. "Maybe five billion?"

Gates turned to Robbins to say more about his trip. Then he toggled back to the Brian window: "Would there be any regulatory implications?"

"Gee," said Brian, who hadn't had a moment to think this through. "I wouldn't think so." Wow, he thought, Gates actually seems to be considering this.

Back at the hotel, Brian called his father. "I may have humiliated myself tonight," he began, "but let me tell you what happened. . . ."

"Good for you," said Ralph. "I think it's a great idea."

At the group's concluding breakfast the next morning, John Malone and a couple of the other CEOs gave Brian a hard time. "That was painful," said Malone, "watching you on bended knee, begging Bill to help us out." Brian didn't bother defending himself because he was thinking the same thing.

A day later, back in Philadelphia, he heard from Greg Maffei, the CFO of Microsoft, who said that Gates had e-mailed him from the Amazon to follow up on Brian's idea.

"Which one?" said Brian, who didn't want to make any assumptions.

"That we should invest in cable companies."

"Right," said Brian. "Why don't you start with Comcast? I'm not asking you to be monogamous, but if the other guys want your money, they can bug you separately."

"That might work," said Maffei. "How large an investment were you thinking of?"

It was time to stop improvising. "Let me think about that and get back to you."

Meeting with his financial team, Brian said he was going to ask Microsoft to invest half a billion dollars.

"That's too little," said Bob Pick. "You should ask for a billion, and they should give us a big premium because our stock is so low."

Brian was willing to try. "He thought it was crazy," says Pick, "but he agreed there was no harm in asking."

And Gates said yes.

Bill Gates had not yet become a philanthropist, and his interest in helping the cable industry was no act of charity. As the head of a company with an enormous stake in seeing the Internet succeed, he was eager to speed up the completion of the rebuild.

But why had Gates chosen Comcast when there were several bigger companies? First, perhaps, because Brian had made the suggestion, and second, because the two men had apparently established their own high-speed connection during the CableLabs visit, which led to the start of a real friendship between Brian and Aileen Roberts, and Bill and Melinda Gates. In a video tribute that was shown at Brian's fortieth birthday party, Gates joked about the time Brian had called him to ask for a loan of $20 billion so Comcast could outbid AT&T for MediaOne. "Now that's real friendship," he said, referring to the request. But friendship has limits: Gates had turned him down.

In his conversation with Maffei, Brian said he couldn't promise that Comcast would do business only with Microsoft, which didn't offer a product just then that filled any of the company's needs. He offered to come to Redmond to discuss the terms, and when Gates returned from the Amazon, Brian and investment banker Steve Rattner went to see him. Before the trip, Greg Maffei sent Brian a term sheet, which Brian forwarded to Dennis Hersch, Comcast's lead outside lawyer.

"When are you showing this to Microsoft?" Hersch asked.

"No," said Brian, "this is *from* Microsoft."

"Really?" said Hersch. "It's fantastic."

Brian had decided not to ask Gates to buy a billion dollars' worth of Comcast stock, because the current share price was too low. Instead, the two companies worked out an agreement whereby Microsoft's billion-dollar investment would be divided into two parts: half in common stock, and the other half in convertible preferred shares, which would be issued specifically for this transaction. This part of the investment was handled by Julian.

Just before the deal was announced, Comcast's shares closed at $18.44. The two sides had agreed on a 10 percent premium for Microsoft's purchase, because the share price would likely rise by at least that much when the deal was announced, and also to compensate for the dilution when the new shares were issued. Microsoft ended up buying 24.6 million shares at $20.29 per share, which gave it approximately 11 percent of Comcast's equity.

Brian had tried for a higher price. "Let's round it up to $20.50," he told Gates.

"No, it's $20.29."

"Can we call it $20.30? It should sound like a round number."

"Brian," Gates said, "I don't know why we're paying you a premium at all. It's $20.29, and you're lucky to get that."

The Microsoft infusion allowed Comcast to increase its investment in high-speed Internet without taking on additional debt. It also served as a public announcement from the biggest name in the business—in *any* business, actually—that the cable industry offered the best way of accessing the Internet, and that Comcast was a major player in that industry. Before long, Gates and Microsoft made other cable investments as well.

Brian hoped that Microsoft would hold a press conference to announce its largest outside investment to date. Gates opted instead for a photo opportunity with Ralph and Brian, and a press call on June 9, 1997. Brian and Greg Maffei did several interviews, including one with the *Financial Times*, whose reporter asked why Microsoft was making this investment.

"A few years ago," Maffei explained, "when we moved from DOS to Windows, people needed to use a mouse. When the companies that produced the mouse didn't provide the functionality we were looking for, we started making them ourselves. We didn't want any piece of the equation to slow down our software, and the mouse was the weak link. We believe there's going to be a lot of data coming in and out of people's homes, so we want to encourage the building of bigger pipes. Our investment in Comcast is to send a message to the cable industry—go ahead and build!"

The Microsoft investment was front-page news in the *New York Times*, although the reporter wrote, incorrectly, that the investment would give Microsoft "a crucial foothold in controlling and distributing television programming." The article ended by describing Brian Roberts as "an unwavering champion of the cable industry's future as a distributor of entertainment and information, and particularly of cable modem technologies." He got that part right.

The announcement had an immediate effect. "It put us on a far bigger corporate map," says Brian, who recalls that some 650 securities analysts—three times the usual number—joined the conference call after the announcement. Comcast shares jumped 17 percent that week, and shares of other cable companies rose sharply as well.

Comcast wasn't the only winner in this transaction. Five years later, Microsoft's investment in the company was up 400 percent.

20

The Change Agent

Steve Burke

When Tom Baxter resigned as president of the cable division in 1998, Brian made a bold decision. After talking it over with his father, he concluded that Baxter's successor didn't have to come from the cable industry. Because the business was changing so quickly, with an array of new products and services on the horizon, it might be better to hire someone from the media business who had sophisticated marketing experience and could design and implement competitive strategies. This was a more complicated search than any in the company's history, and Brian found it difficult to describe the ideal candidate. "Don't worry," said Larry Smith. "We'll know him when we meet him."

Steve Burke was born to the breed, although it was a more corporate breed than people at Comcast were accustomed to. His father,

Dan, had spent most of his career at Capital Cities Communications, which began with a single TV station in Albany, New York; by 1986 Capital Cities was large enough to acquire the American Broadcasting Company, which was four times its size. Dan Burke, the company's longtime president, worked closely with Tom Murphy, the CEO. They shared the conviction that the company's managers should be empowered and entrepreneurial, and their guiding principles were outlined in a statement that appeared on the first page of every annual report:

> Decentralization is the cornerstone of our management philosophy. Our goal is to hire the best people we can find and give them the responsibility and authority they need to perform their jobs. Decisions are made at the local level, consistent with the basic responsibilities of corporate management. Budgets, which are set yearly and reviewed quarterly, originate with the operating units that are responsible for them.
>
> We expect a great deal from our managers. We expect them to be forever cost-conscious and to recognize and exploit sales potential. But above all, we expect them to manage their operations as good citizens and use their facilities to further the community welfare.

If you didn't know where these lines came from, you might think they were written for Comcast.

Steve, the oldest of Dan and Bunny Burke's four children, grew up in Rye, New York, not far from New Rochelle, where Ralph Roberts had grown up a generation earlier. The family's dinner conversation was often about television—not just the programs, but the size and demographics of their audience. Burke, a journalist once wrote, was perhaps the only teenager in town who knew the difference between ratings and share before he learned how to drive. "We weren't being groomed to follow our dad," says Bill Burke, Steve's youngest sibling, who, among other things, has been CEO of The Weather Channel, "but we all gravitated to media because we thought it was interesting and fun."

Unlike many firstborns, Steve was not an early achiever. He had a knack for getting into trouble, and his teachers, while aware of his abilities, did not expect much from him. When he applied to Colgate University in upstate New York, the college agreed to take him only if he improved his grades by the end of the school year. He did, but it was a close call. Four years later, when Burke graduated with honors, Colgate's dean of admissions told him that he had been the very last student accepted to the class of 1980.

During Burke's freshman year, his uncle invited him on a family ski trip to Sun Valley. James Burke was the CEO of Johnson & Johnson, and he brought along a couple of friends—William E. Simon, a prominent businessman who later became secretary of the Treasury, and Peter McCullough, the CEO of Xerox. Steve enjoyed the skiing, but what really excited him was all the talk about business. He decided that he, too, wanted to be in corporate life, like his father, his uncle, and his aunt, Phyllis Burke Davis, a vice president at Avon Products. "We had wonderful role models," he says. "We grew up among people you could be proud of," says Bill Burke, "people with ethical and family values."

Those values became more visible in 1982, after seven people in the Chicago area died from ingesting capsules of extra-strength Tylenol that had been laced with cyanide. (The killer was never found.) As chief executive of Johnson & Johnson, James Burke handled the crisis quickly and decisively. He pulled thirty-one million bottles off the shelves, and instead of hiding from the press, as corporate leaders normally did when disaster struck, Burke went public. Appearing on the CBS show *60 Minutes*, he acknowledged the problem, accepted responsibility, and announced that Tylenol would soon be available in tamper-proof packaging.

When Steve Burke graduated from Harvard Business School—he had also applied to Harvard's Divinity School, but decided against it—most of his classmates were looking for jobs in investment banking or consulting. Burke preferred to run something. He was hired by General Foods in White Plains, New York, where he became assistant product manager for Grape-Nuts. (His father, who had graduated from the same business school in 1955, had also begun his career at General Foods, as brand manager for Jell-O.) Early on, when Burke was asked to come up with fifty uses for Grape-Nuts, one of his recommendations was that the cereal could provide traction for tires on icy days.

When his wife, Gretchen, was in her final year at Harvard Business School, Burke read an article in *New York* magazine about the bright young men who were running Paramount—Barry Diller, Jeffrey Katzenberg, and Michael Eisner. His reaction was immediate: he wanted to join the entertainment industry.

Late in 1984 he flew to Los Angeles to interview with several media companies. That Sunday he picked up the *New York Times*, whose magazine featured another show business trio: the new Walt Disney team of Michael Eisner, CEO, who had come over from Paramount; Frank Wells, president; and Mickey Mouse, icon. Disney had been drifting since the death of its founder, but when Burke read about its dynamic new leadership, he knew where he wanted to be.

He already had an interview scheduled at Disney, where one conversation led to another until he was introduced to Frank Wells, who offered him a job on the spot. "With your MBA and your background in marketing," Wells told him, "we'd like you to work in consumer products."

Burke was both flattered and disappointed. Consumer products? He could have done that at General Foods. But he liked Wells and wanted to work at Disney, so he accepted the offer and lived a bicoastal life until Gretchen finished her MBA and joined him in Los Angeles.

Burke quickly saw that Disney was full of talented people who, under the previous regime, had been reluctant to try anything new. So he announced a contest: the employee who submitted the best proposal for a new business initiative would win a dinner for two at any restaurant in the world. But you had to get there on your own, because transportation was not included.

Burke picked the best ideas and invited their creators, who ranged from secretaries to top executives, to pitch them at a meeting with Frank Wells. Wells brought along CEO Michael Eisner, whom Burke had never met. When the meeting ended, Eisner turned to Burke and said, "That was terrific. Let's do them all!" Eisner's favorite was a store selling Disney products that wasn't attached to a theme park. Burke, who knew nothing about retail, was charged with making it happen.

The first stand-alone Disney store opened in a Southern California shopping mall in the spring of 1987. It was so successful that the day it opened, Eisner and Wells pulled Burke into a nearby coffee shop, where Eisner asked, "How fast can you build a hundred of these?" By the year 2000, there were 742 Disney stores around the world.

Five years later, when Eisner asked Burke what he wanted to do next, he replied that his dream job was to run Disneyland. "That's what I thought you'd say," said Eisner, "and that's what we will soon be asking you to do."

Burke was overjoyed. That weekend he visited Disneyland with his oldest child and took notes on the changes he wanted to make. He had been there before, of course, starting with the company's executive training program, where the trainees, dressed as Disney characters, wandered through the park greeting visitors. Burke had gone out as Friar Tuck, and had enjoyed meeting children on Main Street who were excited to see, and maybe even talk to, one of Robin Hood's Merry Men. And now, all he could think about was how wonderful it would be to run Disneyland.

He never got the chance. Instead of Disneyland, Frank Wells asked him to help run Euro Disney, the company's new theme park in France. Steve and Gretchen dutifully moved their growing family to Paris, where Burke discovered that Euro Disney, which everyone knew was having problems, was in fact a disaster. Burke was devastated, but little by little, he and the park's CEO were able to turn the place around. Four years later, when the Burkes returned to America, Euro Disney was showing a profit.

His next assignment came shortly after Disney acquired his father's old company, Capital Cities/ABC, when Burke was sent to New York to help integrate the television network into the rest of Disney. (On the way to his office each morning, he walked by a portrait of his father.) Soon he was overseeing the network-owned TV and radio stations under Bob Iger, who ran Capital Cities/ABC after Dan Burke retired.

Burke's new job landed him at the center of Disney's internal politics, which was very different from serving in a distant outpost overseas. The contrast was accentuated by the death of Frank Wells in a helicopter crash while Burke was in France. Burke loved him and considered him a mentor, and he would never forget how Wells used to call him on Thanksgiving, when he knew Burke would be homesick, to thank him for moving his family to France. With Wells gone, there was no buffer between the top Disney executives and the sometimes volatile Eisner, who wanted Burke to help him move ABC to California.

Burke thought that was a mistake. "Why not move just the entertainment division?" he asked. But Eisner insisted on moving the whole network.

The more Burke thought about it, the less he liked the idea. He had a personal reaction, too: he and Gretchen now had four children, with a fifth on the way. They were living in Westchester County, and they preferred not to bring up their children in Los Angeles because, as Burke puts it, "things happen too fast there."

Eisner changed his mind about moving the whole network, but Burke wasn't sure he wanted to stay at Disney. Although he was slated to succeed Iger as the next president of ABC, he wondered how much freedom he would actually have under Eisner. In 1998 when a headhunter asked if he would consider running Hasbro, the toy company, he agreed to an interview. He also heard from Howard Fischer, the Philadelphia-based recruiter, who told Burke that Brian Roberts from Comcast wanted to speak with him.

"What's the position?" Burke asked.

"President of the cable division."

"I'm about to become president of ABC," Burke said. "That's a much better job." But he went to Philadelphia anyway.

Burke had instant chemistry with Brian and good meetings with the company's other leaders. He saw that at Comcast, just like at his father's old company, executives had a lot of running room. He also believed that Comcast would soon be expanding. At ABC he had seen the consolidation of the radio business, and Burke thought cable companies would follow a similar path—that only a handful would survive, and Comcast would be one of them. It was the future Comcast that he wanted to be part of, which reminded him of a comment attributed to hockey great Wayne Gretsky: "I don't go where the puck is. I go where it's going to be."

Ralph, who has always seemed to know where the puck will be, had an especially good feeling about Burke. "I evaluate people pretty quickly," he says. "When I met Steve, he struck me as the kind of person Brian should have as a friend."

As a friend? This was a job interview, but Ralph was onto something: the two younger men, who were both around forty, had a lot in common. Brian was a biker and a golfer; Steve ran marathons. "We're not twins," says Brian, "but we complement each other."

Brian took longer to make up his mind. "He had a few concerns," jokes Ralph. "Steve was better looking and had a lot more hair. He also had natural leadership gifts."

Although Brian had decided that a cable background wasn't necessary for the job, it was still hard to imagine that the head of Comcast Cable could be effective without one. When Brian hesitated, Ralph gave him a push. "Don't even think about it," he said. "Do it."

Burke had his own doubts about moving to a small company in Philadelphia. He told his brother, Bill, that he had to decide between staying in a job that other people coveted, but where he might be miserable, or moving to a less visible and less glamorous company where he could accomplish a great deal and have a wonderful time doing it. When he put it that way, he realized, the question answered itself.

People who knew Burke were shocked when he moved to Comcast in the summer of 1998. Running the cable division of a little-known company seemed too inconsequential for a rising star at Disney who was already being mentioned as a possible successor to Eisner. Even Dan Burke believed his son was making a mistake. "People thought Steve was nuts," says Bill Burke, who was familiar with Comcast and supported his brother's decision. Most observers thought Burke was being foolish on three counts: for moving from New York to Philadelphia, for shifting from broadcast to cable, and for joining a family business where he would probably never have a shot at the top job.

Some Comcast employees had reservations as well. Burke's talents were obvious, but with his Harvard MBA, his family connections, his ease in front of large groups, and his comfort with the razzle-dazzle, celebrity-infused worlds of Disney and ABC, how would he fit in at a much smaller, warmer, more modest company?

And Burke *was* different. In a company where terminations were rare, he didn't hesitate to fire executives who weren't succeeding. "Steve ruffled some feathers," says Amy Banse. "He sees what needs to be done and who needs to do it, and if somebody isn't doing their job, he lets them go."

He was often impatient, which made some people nervous. "He likes fast meetings," they told one another, "so prepare well and give him information in as few words as possible." He was decisive, and he acted quickly to implement his decisions. And his dapper appearance and sophistication stood out in the folksy and more intimate corporate culture he was now part of.

Yet none of this seemed to matter. Or maybe it mattered a great deal, but in a good way. Steve Burke came to Comcast to help make the company bigger, more professional, and more competitive, and he succeeded on all counts.

Brian advised him to start slowly, to take six months to learn about the company and the cable business: "Mike Tallent knows what he's doing," he told Burke, "and we're not in a crisis mode. We don't need you to fix anything that's not broken. I hired you because I have a dream of where we want to go, and you have the experience and talent to help us get there."

Brian had urged other new executives to start slowly, but Burke was the first one who took the advice. "It seemed like months before he spoke at meetings," says Larry Smith. Burke's other colleagues noticed his early restraint, and the respect he showed them. "He didn't come in and blow his own horn," says John Alchin. They also noticed that he didn't rush to bring in his own management team. "Only after he had been here a while did an organization take shape that reflected his concerns," says Alchin.

"It didn't take a genius to see we were going to get bigger," says Burke, who was thinking about what a bigger Comcast would require. The most pressing need, he concluded, was more executive talent: the company had 4.5 million subscribers, but if that number were to grow to 10 million—and Burke believed that would happen—Comcast would need twice as many good managers.

"Is there someone I can talk to," he asked Brian, "who is not in the industry at the moment and could serve as a sounding board for recruiting new executives?" Brian recommended Bill Schleyer, who had spent most of his career at Continental Cablevision, until it was acquired by US West. Burke flew to Boston to meet with Schleyer, who recommended five managers who could each handle a million subscribers, and five more who could handle half a million. The list included John Ridall, Bill Connors, and Steve Reimer, all of whom Burke hired before he needed them. "It was a buyer's market for talent," Ridall says, "and we could see that Comcast had momentum for the long term."

Burke was impressed by the quality of the existing Comcast management teams, both at headquarters and in the field. He saw nothing that seemed to require urgent action—unlike, say, at Euro Disney, where he and his colleague "had to fire five thousand people in the first forty-five minutes," as Burke once described it.

Once he had settled in, he moved quickly on several fronts. Believing that much of the company's future leadership had to come from within, Burke began a program called Comcast University. In addition to preparing executives for bigger jobs and providing technical training in the field, the university offered a way of acculturating the many managers who had recently come to Comcast, or would soon be arriving from other companies. "If I'm running a call center a thousand miles from Philadelphia," he told Brian, "and I've been with this company for three years, I'd really want to meet the senior management." Borrowing the idea from Disney, Burke planned to bring executives from around the country to a special facility that would occupy part of a floor at 1500 Market Street. Both Brian and Larry Smith resisted the idea, but Burke refused to give up.

Comcast University's first series of programs, known as Spirit of Comcast, brought managers from across the country to Philadelphia, where they heard from the company's leaders about its history, its values, and its immediate priorities. As the groups came in, senior executives—including Ralph, Brian, Julian, John Alchin, Larry Smith, and Mike Tallent—met with them in small sessions, with plenty of time for questions. After three days at headquarters, the managers returned home with a deeper and more personal connection to the company and the people who ran it.

It wasn't just his Disney experience that inspired Burke to start Spirit of Comcast. In his first year at General Foods, he never once met the head of the division he worked in, although it had only fifty employees. One day a new division head arrived and called everyone into the conference room. Standing in his shirtsleeves, he explained who he was, where he came from, and what he wanted to accomplish. His appearance made a huge impact on Burke, who still remembers what the man wore and what he said. Burke was so impressed that he decided to stay on for another year.

Comcast University would soon establish two leadership development programs: Fundamentals of Leadership, and a more advanced seminar, Executive Leadership Forum. "We had no bench," explains Burke, who is fond of baseball metaphors, and who brought in Filemon Lopez from ad sales to run Comcast University by telling him, "Now I'm going to throw you a curve." Burke's ongoing nightmare, he told colleagues, was that Brian would make a big acquisition that the company wouldn't be prepared for. He started telling managers that if their teams weren't ready for ten million subscribers, they should get them ready. Even Brian thought that was a tall order for a company with four and a half million customers. "Ten million? Steve, that's a lot of pressure. What if we never get there?"

But Burke saw no real downside to planning for a bigger future. Even if the company didn't grow as dramatically as he expected, a central training and acculturation facility was overdue. In the old days, he liked to say, Ralph could shake every employee's hand, but over the years that had become increasingly difficult. Now it was impossible.

He kept moving. Although Comcast was a communications company, it wasn't taking advantage of its own technology to communicate with employees. As a boy, Burke had watched his father and Tom Murphy conduct video meetings with ABC employees around the country, and now, drawing on that model, he set up two company-wide video programs, *Comcast Live* and *Leadership Link*. Skeptics doubted that employees would actually tune in, but the broadcasts were effective from the start. "We always say we're a family company," says Burke. "This is how you remain a family company with tens of thousand of employees. This is how you run a decentralized company without being chaotic, by repeating over and over what you're trying to do." Employees in the field appreciated the clear, unambiguous messages emanating from Philadelphia after Burke came in. "With Steve," says Maria Carriere from the Meadowlands system, "if you don't know what's going on, you're not paying attention."

The change agent kept moving, and made significant upgrades to the management conferences. To save money, these events had previously been held at second-tier Florida resorts in June, when it was often too hot or too rainy to go outdoors. Burke started holding more ambitious, quadrennial meetings at the grand Arizona Biltmore resort in Phoenix and brought in top-level guests: business leaders like Starbucks CEO Howard Schultz, Yahoo!'s Jerry Yang, and JPMorgan Chase's Jamie Dimon; celebrities including General Colin

Powell, Ted Turner, and Oprah Winfrey; and entertainers such as The Beach Boys, Bon Jovi, Jay Leno, Dennis Miller, Penn & Teller, and Bill Maher. These events are not cheap, but Burke sees them both as an investment in employee morale and an added incentive for managers around the country to remain with Comcast in the face of other offers.

One of his early initiatives, the Credo, was considerably less popular. A statement of purpose wasn't part of the Comcast style, although Bob Clasen had put together a vision statement in 1991. Aware of the resistance to what seemed like the needless trappings of some other company's culture, Burke explained his thinking: "When you get to a certain size, physical contact goes down. How does a manager make a decision if he can't reach someone in authority? How do you get employees to understand what the company is all about? Do you realize," he asked Brian in 1999, "that two out of every three employees did not work at Comcast two years ago?"

To develop the Credo, Burke enlisted Dave Watson, who had recently become head of marketing, although Watson, like many others, didn't really see the point. The Credo wasn't going to directly impact the numbers, so why spend all this time and money to put into words what most people already knew? To draft the document, Watson, with both Burke and Ralph in attendance, brought together ninety employees from all over the country to discuss the company's main operating principles. Over two days at a downtown hotel, they identified three main ideas: First, that Comcast was committed to rolling out new products and services. Second, that it was essential to continue the company's excellent financial performance, because new products are irrelevant if you can't meet your numbers. And third, that Comcast had to improve customer service. "Creating the Credo wasn't fun," says Cindy Cade, GM of the system in Tuscaloosa, Alabama, "but it turned out to be very helpful in communicating who we are."

In the end, the Credo emerged as a single sentence: "We will be the company to look to first for the communications products and services that connect people to what's important in their lives." It was distributed to employees in several forms, including a small version in a Lucite cube, which sat on many desks and took only a moment to memorize.

When the Credo was launched, Ralph, Brian, and Burke traveled around the country to promote it. This was an announcement that the business was going to get tougher and more competitive, and it served notice to employees who still didn't believe the company was changing that it was time to get on board. In 2009 the Credo was revised, again under Dave Watson's leadership, to reflect the increasing importance of the customer experience—an area in which the company had long been weak: "Comcast will deliver a superior experience to our customers every day. Our products will be the best and we will offer the most customer-friendly and reliable service in the market."

Although the rebuild and the upgrade to digital had already begun when Burke arrived, he speeded them up. If this is how we're going to compete with satellite companies, he asked, why aren't we moving faster? Comcast had traditionally shied away from new technologies, letting bigger companies take the lead, but things were different now. "Steve knew we had to become a technology leader," says Art Block. "He didn't know we'd become the biggest cable company, but he acted like we would."

The rebuild had started as an industry-wide defensive strategy, but Burke saw it differently. "He thought we should use the rebuild as an offensive tool," says Julian, "to create new and better products. We were a little aghast, and Wall Street didn't like our increased capital expenditures, but he saw that the satellite companies were offering a better product, and he was right to push us ahead."

Even Brian wondered about the speed at which Burke was moving. Did it really make sense to provide customers with early digital set-top boxes that would cost the company $300 but would soon have to be replaced with more advanced boxes at $500? Burke gave him a business answer: "The boxes we can put in now bring in revenue right away," he said, "and if we wait for the perfect box, we'll wait forever. As soon as we put one of these in a customer's house, they'll get more channels and have a better experience. Satellite is breathing down our neck, so we have to step on the gas."

He hated to stand still. Once, when a colleague suggested delaying an initiative to get it right, Burke said, "Yes, but part of getting it right is getting it going." Brian had wanted a leader who understood what it meant to compete. He had certainly found him.

For all his impatience, Burke knew there were limits to what the local systems could handle, which is why he decided, with Mike Tallent's active encouragement, that the company should concentrate on only one new product or major initiative a year. In 1999 it was digital boxes, followed by a push, a year later, into high-speed Internet. Being first is exciting, Burke would explain, but it's not always essential. Unless employees are truly ready to move on to the next product or service, it's often better to wait. Comcast was among the last cable companies to introduce digital telephone service, but that didn't prevent it from growing to become the nation's third-largest residential telephone provider in 2009.

"I've never seen anyone take charge of an organization as effectively as Steve did," says Brian. "He comes to work not just to put out fires, but to start something new that day." People who work for Burke describe him as a consensus builder and a calming influence, and they admire the way he stays positive: "He never seems to be having a bad day," says Peter Luukko. "He can motivate all kinds of people," says Ashton White, "and he's effective with groups of any size."

"He's the most dynamic leader I've ever seen," says Al Peddrick, "and it's not just talk. There were programs we tried to put in place for years, and when Steve came in, they started happening."

One reason he has been effective is that Brian has given him an unprecedented degree of authority and latitude. In 2004 Burke took on a second title when he became the corporation's chief operating officer. Not every CEO could accept such a high-profile partner, but during all those years of watching his father, Brian had learned the art of sharing power.

From the start, the two of them forged such a strong partnership that they sometimes seem like co-CEOs. "There's a yin and a yang," says David Cohen. "Steve has a Hollywood flair, and Brian has steadiness and a wide-reaching vision." Like Larry Smith, Burke doesn't hesitate to argue with the boss. "If Steve doesn't agree, he'll say so," says Brian, "but whatever gets decided, he's the ultimate team player."

Just as Ralph had hoped, Brian and Steve together formed a complete leadership package. "What Steve provides," says Amy Banse, "is decisiveness and a propensity for action. Brian is so democratic and collaborative that he sometimes finds it hard to reach a decision. Steve helps him do that."

Burke liberated Brian from parts of his job that Brian didn't especially enjoy. "Each of us knows what the other is good at and what we like to do," says Burke, who has a sufficiently long attention span to sit patiently (or so it appears) through a five-hour budget meeting in the field. "How do you do that?" Brian once asked him. "Don't you want to duck out and do something else?" But when they're visiting Microsoft, and Brian goes over to chat with Bill Gates, Burke tends to hang back. "Brian likes high-stakes deals," he says, "but that's not my strength."

His strength is communication. "He could fall out of bed and give as good a presentation as I've ever seen," says Charlie Thurston, president of Comcast Spotlight. When Burke addresses employees, he lets them know where the company is going and exactly what he expects. He speaks plainly, without hidden agendas. And often without notes.

It helps, too, that Burke looks the part—or, according to some employees, like a network news anchor. Like many effective leaders, he is a relentless optimist who inspires loyalty and makes people feel they are part of something bigger and more important than themselves. "He drives you to perform at the top of your game," says Bob Victor.

He has a light touch. He enjoys teasing his colleagues, including Brian, and likes to poke fun at his associates, especially about their clothing. ("If a guy walks into a meeting in a brown shirt and an orange tie," he says, "somebody has to *say* something.") It works both ways: Burke's colleagues and subordinates enjoy teasing him, often about his hair, which sometimes looks too good to be true. But his charisma is impossible to miss. "When you get into an elevator with Steve," says an employee, "you can feel the energy radiating off him."

As befits a former Disney executive, his public self includes a dollop of drama. "Steve doesn't just let things happen," says Brian. "He knows how to frame the moment." After the AT&T deal closed, when Ralph, Brian, and Burke traveled the country to visit the many systems that were moving over to Comcast, Burke would introduce Ralph to the audience. "I used to work for the Walt Disney Company," he would say, "and I would have given anything to have heard Walt Disney himself. But you are fortunate enough to meet the founder of Comcast, who will tell you who he is and what he stands for." Although Brian had heard Burke say those same words yesterday, and knew he would hear them again tomorrow, every time Steve introduced Ralph, Brian would tear up. And he wasn't the only one.

For all the glamour he generates, Burke has always been a family man; everyone at headquarters seems to know that he drives his children to school in the morning. And when he addresses groups from the field at Comcast University, he often makes a point of thanking them for leaving their families for a few days to come to Philadelphia.

A few years ago, he was invited to give the commencement address at Colgate University, his alma mater, where he spoke about his values, and, without saying so explicitly, about the values of Comcast. "Your job should not be the most important thing in your life," he told the graduates. "The key to a successful and happy life is balance. Your job is part of that balance, but only a part. Make time for your family and friends—and for yourself."

After advising the students to look for work opportunities they genuinely enjoyed, and not to shy away from tough assignments, he touched on something corporate leaders don't often mention: the limits of materialism. "If your life is all about accumulating things," he said, "you will be disappointed. If you stop and think about it, things are more fun to pursue than they are to have. Things wear out. Things break down. After all, things cannot make you truly happy."

Then he paused and said, "Only people can do that."

If Ralph had been in the audience, he would have been smiling—and nodding his head in agreement.

21

The Prize

Michael Armstrong, Ralph Roberts, and Brian Roberts

In the late 1990s, the American telecommunications industry was suddenly turned upside down. AT&T, which had shown no previous interest in cable, acquired John Malone's TCI and its sister company, Liberty Media, for $48 billion. Less than a year later, AT&T paid an even higher price for the MediaOne properties. What Americans had long thought of as the phone company was now the nation's largest cable provider.

Fittingly, it was the telephone business that prompted these moves. When the government ruled that long-distance companies could also offer local phone service, Michael Armstrong, the company's new CEO, decided to jump in.

But AT&T lacked the infrastructure to provide local service. After the company was broken up in 1984, it no longer owned the "last mile"—the wires that fan out from national and regional networks and connect into homes and offices. Those lines now belonged to the Baby Bells, the regional Bell operating companies, which had once been part of AT&T.

Armstrong intended to offer consumers a bundle of services—cable, Internet, and telephone—a combination that cable companies were also planning to provide. To achieve that goal, he would need a broadband pipe into the home, and there were three ways to accomplish that. He could continue leasing lines from the Baby Bells, but their copper wires might not be able to support the newer services. He could build a whole new network from scratch, but that would be enormously expensive and would take years. Or he could try to partner with—or acquire—one or more large cable companies, and make use of the robust coaxial lines that were already connected to a growing number of homes.

This last option was his best choice, but AT&T ran into unexpected problems. Its long-distance business was suffering huge losses, in part because WorldCom, a major competitor, was charging less with no apparent effect on their earnings. These earnings later proved fraudulent, but at the time, AT&T was forced to lower its rates to unprofitable levels. On the cable front, Armstrong had paid dearly for TCI, whose plants had not been well maintained. He had invested in cable to be able to move quickly, but his executives hadn't realized the extent to which TCI was lagging behind other cable companies in its digital rebuild.

AT&T's new cable division, known as AT&T Broadband, was a top-down, heavily staffed, centralized bureaucracy. That model was fine for a national telephone company that had been a monopoly for most of its history, but cable began as a local phenomenon, and every community is slightly different. Profit margins at AT&T Broadband systems were running around 18 to 20 percent, compared to 40 percent or even higher at systems owned by other operators.

At Comcast, Brian and his colleagues were confident that if they could acquire the Broadband properties, those margins could be doubled. There was just one problem: Broadband wasn't for sale.

Why, then, was Comcast so interested in buying it?

Broadband owned great markets, including Chicago, San Francisco, Dallas, Seattle, and Boston. And Comcast's management team had plenty of experience in integrating other cable companies. Although Broadband was large, with many more customers than Comcast, the combination of Steve Burke's leadership skills and Mike Tallent's operational and financial expertise had persuaded Brian that no cable company was too big to absorb.

To compete with satellite operators, Comcast would be better off with a national profile and many more subscribers than the eight million or so it had in 2001. Economies of scale would lead to better programming deals and would help the company acquire and sell new products more efficiently.

AT&T's financial situation was getting worse. When Chuck Noski was hired as CFO in late 1999, he was shocked to discover that when the MediaOne deal closed, the company's debt would rise to $65 billion—half of it in short-term obligations. The long-distance losses were old news, but the extent of AT&T's other woes caught Noski by surprise. His position was similar to Steve Burke's a few years earlier at Euro Disney, when Burke was forced to disclose, and then expected to solve, problems that had developed before he arrived.

At a board meeting, Noski laid out the facts. Then he and Armstrong proposed the unthinkable: the company should slash its dividend, spin off its wireless division, and create a tracking stock for Broadband. The directors agreed. By the end of 2000, when AT&T announced a major dividend cut, its shares, which had traded as high as $64 only a year earlier, were as low as $17. This was an unprecedented plunge for a company whose stock had long been considered the ideal safe investment for widows and orphans.

The impending breakup of AT&T, described by the company as Project Grand Slam, had major implications for Comcast: if and when Broadband became a separate company, anyone could acquire it. But maybe a potential buyer wouldn't have to wait that long.

"With our investment bankers and legal advisors," Ralph says, "we figured out that we could offer more for Broadband than AT&T could raise in a public offering, because it was worth more to us. This was our chance to acquire all the systems collected by both Malone and MediaOne, a one-time opportunity to become the country's largest cable company."

Rob Kindler at J.P. Morgan had already talked with Brian about going after Broadband. He pointed out that before AT&T issued a tracking stock for its cable division, the company would need the approval of its shareholders. Kindler believed that if Comcast came in with an attractive offer, that vote would never be held. Dennis Hersch, the head M&A lawyer at Davis Polk and a longtime Comcast advisor, called Brian with the same basic idea.

But nobody imagined that acquiring Broadband would be easy. Even if Comcast put forth a plan that would benefit both sides, that didn't mean that AT&T, an old and proud company, would agree to sell off one of its divisions.

It might actually be easier for Comcast to go after *all* of AT&T. Uninvited attempts to buy public corporations are routine events, with established rules and procedures, and AT&T's shares were so low that this option had to be considered. But it was hard to make a compelling case for a company whose huge long-distance business was still sinking. Over the next few months, Ralph, who has always believed that no dream is impossible, would repeatedly bring up the possibility of buying AT&T, and there were times when Brian wanted to explore the idea. "Forget it," the bankers would say. "These are not businesses you want to own."

"But maybe at the right price?"

"There is no price at which you should buy AT&T," said Paul Taubman at Morgan Stanley.

There was nothing to prevent Comcast from making an unsolicited offer for a single division of a publicly owned company. But such transactions, known as subsidiary bear hugs, are so rare that most of the bankers working with Comcast could not recall when such a thing had even been attempted, let alone completed. There was no precedent, no road map, no established procedure for the plan they were discussing, whose prospects seemed to lie somewhere between unlikely and impossible. "It was worth trying," says Art Block, "but nobody expected that we would succeed."

Over at AT&T, however, Chuck Noski remembered that in 1995, WorldCom went after WilTel, a subsidiary of Williams, an oil and gas company that owned fiber-optic lines. WilTel's management didn't want to sell, but the stockholders had forced the issue. Noski thought Comcast was bold enough to try something similar.

Unless, of course, there was an easier route. Sometimes you can get what you want just by asking for it, and if you don't succeed, at least you have started the process in an amicable way. The Comcast deal team agreed that Brian should request a meeting with Mike Armstrong. They made a date for December, but when the *New York Post* reported that the two men were planning to discuss a possible merger, Armstrong canceled the meeting.

In early 2001 Brian met with Armstrong and Noski at an investor conference in California, and left with the feeling that the men from AT&T had little interest in making a deal. Armstrong asked for time to consider the proposal, but a couple of weeks later, he told Brian that the lawyers had instructed him to suspend the dialogue because AT&T had already begun the process of spinning off its wireless division. The Comcast team saw this as a stall tactic, but Noski says a delay was essential because any conversation between the two companies would now have to be disclosed. "We couldn't even agree to meet in the spring," Noski says, "because we would have had to disclose *that*. But we re-engaged with Comcast as soon as we could."

It took until May for AT&T to complete its SEC filings for the wireless spin-off. In June Brian and Noski met for dinner at the St. Regis Hotel in New York. The setting was a ballroom off the lobby with a single table under a crystal chandelier, which both men found strange. But they had a good and extensive discussion about the potential benefits and drawbacks of combining Comcast with AT&T's cable division.

Brian was also making contingency plans in the likely event that

AT&T's leadership, or its directors, did not respond well to what was being called a merger. (Others saw it as an acquisition.) To help engineer an unsolicited bid for Broadband, Comcast quietly hired two investment banks, Morgan Stanley and J.P. Morgan, and Quadrangle, an advisory firm founded a year earlier by Steve Rattner. Later on, Merrill Lynch would also join the team.

Noski and Brian soon met again for dinner, this time at the Four Seasons Hotel in Philadelphia. By now they were comfortable with each other and the conversation was more specific, although it was still hypothetical. What would the new corporate entity be called? Noski proposed AT&T Comcast, which was fine with Brian. Where would the headquarters be? Brian said Philadelphia, but Mike Armstrong, who lived in Connecticut, preferred New York. Who would run the merged company? Armstrong saw himself as the CEO, which wasn't what Brian had in mind, so that topic was deferred.

Noski raised the delicate issue of voting control. Brian owned shares that represented 87 percent of the votes, which would have to be pared down considerably in the event of a merger. Although he knew an adjustment would be necessary, he wasn't looking forward to having that particular conversation with his father.

After the Philadelphia dinner, Armstrong and Noski agreed it was time to brief their board on Noski's informal talks with Brian. Reaction was mixed, and the AT&T directors instructed Noski to convey two messages to Brian. First, in the event of a merger, the Roberts family could not continue to control most of the voting stock. Second, if talks continued, Comcast would have to sign both a confidentiality and a standstill agreement, promising not to launch an unsolicited bid against AT&T or any of its parts.

"They won't accept those conditions," Noski told the board. "The voting shares are important to the family, and I doubt they'd agree to a standstill." Then he made a prediction: "In October, when we do the Broadband spin-off, they may try to disrupt it with a higher offer." He had the right idea, but Comcast wouldn't wait that long.

Noski called Brian to tell him how the board had responded. "You just ruined my weekend," Brian said, "but I'll think about it and get back to you."

When the Comcast deal team heard the board's conditions, they decided to move ahead with a public offer for Broadband. Soon there was a compelling reason to move quickly. To prepare for the tracking stock spin-off, Noski arranged for what is known as a beauty contest—a series of presentations by investment banks who are hoping to be hired as underwriters. The banks that were secretly advising Comcast could not be part of this event, which was scheduled for Monday morning, July 9, and their unexplained absence would constitute an announcement that something big was in the works. Now, suddenly, Brian was facing a deadline.

The deal team decided that on Sunday, July 8, 2001, Ralph and Brian would fax a formal offer to Mike Armstrong that would be made public the same day. On Monday, if AT&T's stock rose by a dollar or more, that would constitute a positive response from investors, which would presumably force the company to talk to Comcast. They might also hold an auction, but the team was willing to take that risk. "There was no guarantee we'd be successful," says Julian. "All we were looking for was the opportunity to try."

All weekend, Brian and the deal team tinkered with the letter to Armstrong, fine-tuning and second-guessing almost every phrase. Only the offering price was left blank as the group debated what the final number should be. On Saturday night, they all gathered at the Manhattan offices of Abernathy MacGregor, Comcast's public relations firm. Brian ripped a couple of pages from a yellow legal pad, tore them into pieces, and passed them out to the thirty or so people in the conference room—mostly bankers, with a sprinkling of Comcast executives, and asked them to estimate the likelihood that Comcast would end up with Broadband. The guesses tended to fall between 20 and 30 percent, with the bankers, who are normally optimistic about takeover attempts, submitting the lowest estimates. But everyone knew that AT&T might swat away the offer with little or no change in its stock price.

Brian wasn't deterred. "If we pull this off," he said, "it will change our company forever. And if we don't, we'll dust ourselves off and go on to something else." It was okay to fail, he was saying. But it wasn't okay to let the opportunity of a lifetime pass them by.

This was the biggest moment in Brian's career, and Aileen had come to New York to be with him. They had spent the previous night in Maine—the only part of a planned long weekend away that they were able to salvage—and had talked at length about whether the bid for Broadband was the right move, and what might happen if it succeeded—or failed. When Brian needs business advice, he goes to Ralph, and he and his father had discussed this plan in detail. But on really important decisions, he also consults with Aileen, and he was grateful that she could be with him at this critical moment in his business life—and Comcast's.

The plan was to fax the offer to Armstrong at four o'clock on Sunday afternoon, and to call him immediately as an act of courtesy and respect. But even huge transactions have to get the details right. Where, exactly, was Mike Armstrong going to be on the final afternoon of the Fourth of July weekend? At what number could he be reached, and how could they find that out without arousing suspicion? When these questions were finally answered, Ralph called Armstrong, who was at home in Connecticut.

Why Ralph? "Sometimes the senior statesman is the better spokesman," says Brian. There was another reason, too: when AT&T had offered Comcast two million subscribers to bow out of the Media-One auction, Armstrong had called Ralph, not Brian.

With general counsel Art Block sitting next to him, Ralph said, "Mike? It's Ralph Roberts. I wanted to let you know that tomorrow we're going to make an offer for your cable division. The details are in a letter we're faxing to you. I know this comes as a surprise, and I'm sure your first reaction is not a happy one, but we really hope you'll take a look at what we're offering. You've decided that this division doesn't belong with the rest of your company, and we think our plan is best for your shareholders. Our proposal will accelerate what you're already doing and will give you a better price. I hope that together we can make this work."

Armstrong was not pleased. "Can we talk about this privately?" he asked.

"I'm sorry, Mike, but we're going public with it tonight."

The letter to Armstrong, which was signed by both Ralph and Brian, stated that in return for Broadband's assets and its debt, Comcast would pay $58 billion in stock, a sum that valued the division "at a significant premium to your potential market valuation." Ralph and Brian addressed the issue of the voting shares by pointing out that multiclass structures were common in the cable industry, and that the value of Comcast's nonvoting shares had risen considerably over the years. "We are confident," they wrote, "that your shareholders would welcome our currency."

The real battle began the next morning. At this point, the only way to separate Broadband from AT&T was through pressure from investors. And that was a delicate maneuver. Comcast had to demonstrate that it could significantly improve the profitability of the Broadband systems, and that Comcast shares were a better investment for AT&T shareholders than the shares they already owned. But this argument had to be made without sounding arrogant or overly critical, because if the plan had any hope of succeeding, it would need the support of not only AT&T's shareholders but also of its board.

On Monday morning, as several investment banks were making their scheduled presentations to AT&T, Brian, Steve Burke, John Alchin, and other senior executives began meeting with fund managers and investors to make the case for the Comcast bid. In front of an audience that included his wife, Brian pointed out that Comcast had doubled in size over the past two years, and that Burke and his team had been able to improve margins almost immediately in the newly acquired systems. Burke then explained how, with Jones Intercable, Comcast had achieved a 25 percent increase in operating cash flow in one year, and that the gains had been even higher in the Lenfest systems. Again and again, Burke said, we have shown that we know how to do this.

Brian and Burke made presentations in other cities, too, including a quick trip to Herbert Allen's annual Sun Valley retreat for media moguls and Wall Street players. Because the schedule was already so full, and the Comcast bid so unexpected, the only time they could speak was at 6:30 a.m. And yet the room was packed, and the audience included Warren Buffett, Katharine Graham, Barry Diller, AOL Time Warner's Gerald Levin, Cox's Jim Kennedy, and Viacom's Mel Karmazin, who asked, "Why is this deal good for me? Why should I be happy about lower prices for programming?" It was a strange moment: Brian was making the case for Comcast's acquisition of Broadband to a group that included not only several members of the AT&T board, but two competing bidders—although nobody knew that yet.

Whatever the moguls thought, the investors' verdict was clear: Twenty-four hours after the Comcast offer, shares of AT&T closed up $1.98. By the end of the week they were up an additional $2.00, which was more than the deal team had dared to hope for. And three days after receiving the fax, Armstrong acknowledged that the Comcast proposal "recognizes some of the value we've created in AT&T Broadband. The question is whether it recognizes the right value." The deal team was delighted: it sounded as if the Comcast offer had turned into a negotiation.

At its July board meeting, the AT&T directors turned down Comcast's proposal. But the board instructed management to pursue and evaluate "all available options," a phrase that may have been intended to assure shareholders that although the company was rejecting the bid, it was not dismissing it. And now that Broadband was apparently in play, Noski started hearing from other potential bidders.

In August, when Brian called to make peace, Armstrong responded positively. This was a good sign—and far from inevitable. "When you punch someone in the nose," says Steve Burke, "the odds of their working with you are much lower."

In September lawyers from the two companies met to discuss a more congenial relationship. AT&T wanted Comcast to sign a confidentiality agreement before it could begin due diligence and participate in the "process," which was generally assumed to be an auction. Comcast asked to be treated like any other bidder, despite its unsolicited offer in July. Both sides got what they wanted.

The next step was a dinner for four—Brian, Ralph, Armstrong, and Noski, at an inn in Bernardsville, New Jersey, where Armstrong and Noski sometimes talked after work, and where there was little chance of being spotted by a reporter. This was the first time Brian and Armstrong had seen each other since January, and the first time the four of them had talked together. Noski, who was struck by the "impressive and unusual" relationship between Ralph and Brian, says the dinner was meant to clear the air, and it did: "Everybody said all the right things—and we meant them."

Over the next few weeks, interest in Broadband took on all the trappings of an auction, a three-way battle among AOL Time Warner, Cox, and Comcast. After reminding participants that the AT&T board still reserved the right not to sell the division, Noski called for the first round of bids. When they were submitted in early November, Noski told the bidders that none of the offers was high enough, and that final bids were due on December 16.

"We spent hours at AT&T's law firm," says Burke, "knowing that on other floors, other bidders were doing the same thing. Noski was playing us off against each other, and doing it brilliantly, making all of us feel that parts of our offers were special. But it's scary when the seller knows that you see this as the opportunity of a lifetime."

It got scarier. On Saturday, December 8, eight days before final bids were due, Brian, Ralph, and Burke had lunch with Armstrong and Noski at the Peninsula Hotel in New York. They agreed in advance that Ralph, Burke, and Noski would leave the room early to give Brian and Armstrong a few minutes alone. When the three of them went down to the lobby, Ralph told Noski, "Chuck, there are times in a company's history where you have to go for it, and this is one of those times. If you need a little more from us to beat out one of the other bidders, just let me know."

Burke was mortified. No! he wanted to yell. Don't say that! Don't tell him we're willing to overpay even more than we already are!

"Will you give us a chance to top the highest bid?" Ralph asked.

"You know I can't do that," Noski replied.

Noski said later that he didn't blame Ralph for asking for the last

bite of the apple, adding, "You'd be amazed at some of the proposi-
tions I received."

The AT&T board was scheduled to meet in New York on December 19 to review the bids and declare a winner, assuming there was
one. The night before, Brian was attending the QVC Christmas party
when Noski called the three bidders to let them know that their offers
were roughly the same.

"Do we have to improve our bid?" Brian asked.

"I can only tell you it's close," said Noski. Recalling what Ralph
had said in the hotel lobby, he added, "Listen to your father."

On the morning of the nineteenth, the *Wall Street Journal* reported
that offers for Broadband were still in flux, and that Cox, the smallest
of the bidders, was thought to be favored by AT&T's management.
Early that morning, just before Brian and his colleagues boarded the
train for New York, Noski called Brian: "I want to recommend you,
but something has happened with one of the other bids. You'll need
to increase your offer again."

On the train to New York, the deal team held a conference call to
discuss the new information. Because cell phone service was spotty,
the Comcast executives were forced to stand between cars, which
gave them both privacy and better reception. Should they, at this late
stage, come up with another billion dollars? After listening to the
arguments on both sides, Art Block spoke up. "I think we should
raise our bid. It's less than two percent of the total, and this is our one
chance to go for it. If we win, and it doesn't work out, it won't be because of the extra billion. But if we lose this deal because we stopped
here, we'll regret it for the rest of our lives."

For a moment there was silence on the line, which may have im-
plied consent. When the train pulled into Penn Station, Brian called
Noski from the escalator to Seventh Avenue. "We'll go higher," he
said, "but this is all I can give. Will that do it?"

"I don't know," said Noski. "If it's the high bid, I think Mike will
support it. But I want something else."

Brian groaned. Was there no end to this?

But Noski wasn't asking for money. Because there had been some acrimony in the press, he wanted to make sure that if Comcast was the high bidder, its advisors and spokespeople would not portray the outcome as a Comcast victory and an AT&T defeat. "If you win," he told Brian, "we'd like to position this as the coming together of two great companies." Brian gave his word.

Then he called Dennis Hersch, Comcast's lead lawyer in the deal, and asked him to fax a letter to Dick Katcher, his counterpart at Wachtell Lipton, which represented AT&T, officially increasing Comcast's bid. After calling Katcher to alert him that the letter was coming, Hersch hurried to his office to send it. It was still early and his assistant wasn't in yet; Hersch could never remember which of the firm's fax machines required the sender to insert the document face-down. Katcher called him a moment later: "Were you serious about the higher bid? I just received a blank page."

For the Comcast team, there was little to do but wait. Some of them gathered at Abernathy MacGregor, where rumors were flying, including a report that Cox had already won. At the St. Regis, Brian, Ralph, and several of their colleagues were waiting anxiously in Brian's crowded hotel room. The TV was tuned to CNBC, which was keeping a close watch on the auction, but there was nothing to report.

Brian spent part of the morning on the phone with Standard & Poor's and Moody's, the two major rating agencies, trying to make sure Comcast would retain its investment-grade status if it won the auction. Around one o'clock, the group went downstairs for lunch. Although they were in the midst of a multibillion dollar auction and had been to New York countless times, the Comcast executives were still shocked by the price of a modest lunch (soup, sandwiches, and Cokes) at one of the city's best hotels. "We kidded Brian about how expensive it was," says Ken Mikalauskas, "and how, if we bought Broadband, he could never afford to eat there again."

In the middle of the afternoon, just to break the tension, Larry Smith leaned down and surreptitiously dialed Brian's number on his cell phone. Brian ran to the phone, thinking it might be Noski, but it would be hours before he heard any real news.

Over at Wachtell Lipton, AT&T's board of directors had been scheduled to meet at 11:00 a.m. At 10:30, Armstrong and Noski made their decision: after reviewing the three bids with their last-minute emendations, they would recommend the Comcast offer, which came to $72 billion—24 percent higher than the bid the company had announced in July.

By now the other issues had been resolved. If the merger went through, the new company, known as AT&T Comcast, would be headquartered in Philadelphia with an executive office for Armstrong in New York. The new board would consist of twelve directors—five from each company plus two new members. Brian would be CEO, with Armstrong serving as the non-executive chairman. When it became clear that Armstrong would be named chairman, Brian had turned to his father and said, "Dad, how do you feel about that?"

"We have to do it if we want the deal."

"But if Mike's the chairman and I'm the CEO, what do you want to be called?"

"Call me Ralph," said Ralph.

The big issue for Ralph, the painful one, the one he really had to think about, was the multiple-vote class of voting stock, which the family had owned from the time the company went public in 1972. Over the years, these shares had given Comcast's leaders the freedom to run the business with a long-term horizon, with no real danger of an outsider swooping in with an unwanted takeover bid.

And here Ralph made a major concession. He went along with Brian, who had agreed that if the merger went through, the family's voting power in the combined company would be reduced from 87 to 33.3 percent, provided that this percentage could not be diluted by any future stock issuances. Ralph hated to do it, but he didn't want to lose the deal.

At the AT&T board meeting, there was some support for keeping Broadband, especially now that Bill Schleyer from Continental had been hired to run it. But if there was going to be a sale, the directors agreed that Comcast had made the best offer. "Comcast had a lifetime of experience," says Mike Cook, an AT&T board member, "and while we could project reaching their level of profitability, that day was a long way off."

At 5:45, Brian's phone rang. It was Mike Armstrong. After some preliminary comments, he said, "Are you doing anything tonight? Come over here. You won."

Brian had been sitting on the head end of his hotel bed, with Ralph and Art Block a few feet away. "When the call came in," Block recalls, "we didn't know whether this was a question or the news we were waiting for." When Brian said nothing and his face showed little expression, Ralph and Block wondered if another bidder had prevailed. Then, after about half a minute that must have felt like a week, Brian grinned and pumped his fist. "Finally," says Block, "he looked at us and realized we didn't know. He hung up the phone and said, 'Dad, we got it,' and they hugged."

A few years later, Ralph was asked if he remembered the moment when Brian hung up the phone and hugged him.

"Well," Ralph said, "he always hugs me."

It was finally over, and people would say later that both sides had won. "At the end of the day," says Steve Burke, "Mike Armstrong deserves a lot of credit. He did the right thing for his shareholders, although he didn't have to." Some executives in Armstrong's situation might have responded vindictively after Comcast's aggressive opening move, but the chairman of AT&T was not that type. One of his favorite expressions was "rise above it," a reminder to those around him to focus on the bigger, long-term objectives, especially when they were tempted to react emotionally.

Brian called the group at Abernathy to tell them the good news. Then he, Ralph, Julian, Art Block, Steve Burke, Larry Smith, John Alchin, and Bob Pick walked over to Wachtell Lipton at Sixth Avenue and 52nd, where the law firm's lobby was swarming with lawyers, bankers, and PR people. When Brian and Ralph walked in, a huge cheer went up, which was led by Mike Armstrong. "I've been in a lot of deals," says Brian, "and this was the only time I've heard cheering. It was a classy reception after a very difficult struggle." Hands were shaken, shoulders hugged, congratulations exchanged, champagne poured, and, most important, papers were signed. On another floor of the building, lawyers from Cox finally stopped working on their version of the agreement.

Brian and Armstrong drove over to CNBC to be interviewed about the biggest deal in the history of cable, and one of the largest in all of American business. Later that night, the Comcast team drank a toast in the lobby of the St. Regis. Exhausted, and facing a meeting with investors the next day, they filed into the elevator to go up to their rooms.

Ralph and Brian, who weren't sharing a room this time, happened to be staying on the same floor. "We got off the elevator, just the two of us," says Brian, "and walked down the hall together. We hadn't had a moment alone since the call from Mike Armstrong. When we got to my room, my dad stopped and looked at me. He had a tear in his eye, and so did I. He put his arms around me and said, 'This is a miracle. I'm so proud of you!'"

Back in Philadelphia, and all around the country, Comcast employees were feeling the very same way.

22

Making It Work

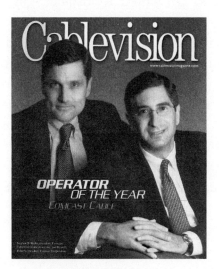

Steve Burke and Brian Roberts

As soon as the cheering died down, it was time to face reality. For all that Brian and his team had accomplished, the only thing they actually won was the right to buy a huge, troubled, and expensive cable division that hadn't originally been for sale. It was a victory, and a big one—but only if they could make the acquisition work. And this next battle looked to be even tougher.

"What concerned the board during the AT&T auction," says former board member Decker Anstrom, "was, what if the dog catches the car? If we succeed in buying Broadband, would we really be able to finance the acquisition and execute this huge integration?"

The board was persuaded, but many outside observers had doubts because the obstacles seemed so daunting. Broadband's margins were the lowest in the business. Its employees had grown distrustful of management. The TCI systems needed significant capital improvements. The industry was quickly becoming more complicated. No cable company had ever attempted an acquisition on this scale, and when it closed, Comcast would be facing a mountain of debt.

First came the challenge of raising enough money to pay for the loans that Comcast had agreed to assume. When the deal finally closed, which was expected to take about a year, the company would require $17 billion in financing. Although the money wouldn't be needed for a while, John Alchin asked Brian if the financial team should start lining it up right away. It wasn't an easy call, because securing such a large sum so far in advance was expensive and probably unnecessary. But the merger agreement made no allowances for financing problems, and who knew where the economy was headed?

Brian had learned long ago, from Ralph and Julian, to have money available even when he didn't need it, because it might not be available when he did. "My father's philosophy was, take the money when you can get it, even if it meant having extra cash on hand," he recalls. Brian followed that advice, and it was a good thing he did. Bank financing wasn't hard to arrange in early 2002, but a few months later, when WorldCom defaulted and Adelphia was in trouble, loans were considerably more expensive. And the window was closed for junk bonds at a time when Comcast's rating was only slightly above that level.

"The banks thought we were crazy to tie up all that money in advance," says Ken Mikalauskas. (For a monthly fee, a financial institution will commit to a loan before the money is actually paid out.) Alchin asked the lenders to leave their commitments outstanding for up to a year and a half, which was almost unheard of. Within weeks, he arranged all the loans Comcast would need, although the company's investment bankers had recommended against doing this so far in advance. One of them said later that at his firm's next management meeting, the recommendation that Comcast should delay its Broadband loans was cited as the worst advice the firm had ever given a client.

A million other details had to be attended to before the close, including making arrangements with the many municipalities whose cable systems would soon be part of Comcast. It was AT&T's responsibility to ensure that almost two thousand cities and towns approved the changeover, but Comcast's Sheila Willard and her team had to jump in often because municipalities wanted to hear from their new cable company, not their old one. Although most of the transfers went smoothly, some mayors, local officials, and town councils were skeptical; they had heard promises and assurances from cable operators before, and had learned not to trust them. "Ms. Willard," said one mayor, "I appreciate what you're saying, but I don't believe a word of it."

But Comcast has a history of fulfilling the commitments of the companies whose systems it acquires, even when those promises have been unrealistic or ill advised. In one Maryland system, the previous provider had agreed to set aside thirteen different channels for PEG (public, educational, and governmental) access, and although this arrangement made no sense, Comcast let it stand. "We honor promises we would never have made on our own," says Willard, who says this policy did wonders for her credibility.

Everyone knew that Comcast and AT&T had very different corporate cultures, and now these contrasts become more apparent. David Cohen, who joined Comcast as executive vice president a few months before the deal closed, saw that Broadband had something like fifty lawyers at its corporate headquarters, compared to ten at Comcast. One of us must be wrong, he concluded, and he didn't think it was Comcast. Broadband's corporate headquarters in Denver housed more than four thousand employees, while Comcast's had fewer than five hundred, and although Broadband had many more customers, the ratios were clearly out of balance.

There were reasons for these differences. AT&T had long functioned as a classic, centralized bureaucracy, and had used the same approach in the cable systems it had acquired. Comcast, meanwhile, had tried to preserve the decentralized, entrepreneurial culture of the cable industry. A former Broadband employee offered this analogy:

Imagine that you have to send a technician to do an installation on the moon, and he'll need to fill out the necessary paperwork while he's up there. To come up with a pen that functions in the lunar atmosphere, AT&T would build a gravity-free chamber and conduct all the necessary research on the physics and chemistry of the mission. Then they would test every pen on the market. The study would take six months and cost $10 million, but the tech would end up with the right pen for the job.

And at Comcast? They'd hand the guy a pencil and send him on his way.

Well before the deal closed, Ken Mikalauskas, Bill Dordelman, and three of their colleagues from Comcast's treasury group went to AT&T's corporate headquarters in Basking Ridge, New Jersey, to discuss several outstanding issues with their counterparts. The first item concerned a tax-driven deal, and Mikalauskas assumed that the assistant treasurer would explain it. Instead, three other executives came in to provide the details. The next topic was AT&T's leveraged lease portfolio, and two more employees were called in to explain it. For every new item, two or three additional people entered the room. "At Comcast," says Mikalauskas, "every treasury-related subject would have been explained by the five of us."

Initially, Comcast's leadership wasn't sure what to do about Broadband's headquarters and the many people who worked there. But when Mike Tallent flew to Denver for his first visit, he was reminded of the legend of the Gordian knot. When Alexander the Great was unable to unravel it, he solved the problem with one stroke of his sword.

"We've got to cut off the head," Tallent told Steve Burke, who agreed that Comcast should close down Denver and run its entire cable division from Philadelphia. During Tallent's early visits to Broadband headquarters, the executives he met described various marketing initiatives, but he wasn't impressed. "You're getting back only twenty cents on the dollar," he would say, "and every other cable company is getting back thirty-five to forty cents. Why is that?" But nobody could answer what Tallent calls "the most fundamental of all business questions."

Before he started reorganizing the company, Burke sought advice from his father and from his friend, banker Jamie Dimon, who both urged him to move quickly and openly. "The bigger the acquisition," they said, "the faster you have to go." Burke was already inclined to move fast. "We know there are rumors about layoffs," he said in a *Comcast Live* broadcast, "and some of these rumors are true." He explained that the company would be hiring additional people in the field because Broadband had relied heavily on outsourcing, but that many Denver employees would be losing their jobs. Before these lay-offs, David Cohen met with the governor of Colorado, the mayor of Denver, and a host of other state and local elected officials to explain why Comcast was doing this. The company retained four thousand system employees in Colorado and made Denver the headquarters for its new Western Division, which was headed by Brad Dusto.

With a workforce consisting almost entirely of former Broadband employees, Dusto met often with his new managers, asking them about Broadband and telling them about Comcast. He learned that they had grown accustomed to spending a lot of money early in the fiscal year, because they could never be sure that additional funds would be available. One manager had purchased 150 new trucks that were sitting there, unused, because if he hadn't bought them early, he risked not being able to buy them at all. They had learned to game the system because that was the way to survive.

These managers were pleasantly surprised that their new boss understood the work they did every day. In Salt Lake City, Dusto was given the standard executive tour, which normally ran fifteen minutes. But not this time. "We started at dispatch," he says, "and when I stopped to ask about the code for a new install, the rep was shocked that I knew what that was." That day, the executive tour took an hour and a half.

It was Steve Burke's job to "Comcastify" Broadband. This was the kind of challenge he relished, the one he had been planning for from the moment he arrived. This was why he had established Comcast University, which was already preparing younger executives for bigger jobs and was arranging Spirit of Comcast programs for managers from the field. Julie Bomgren, a former Broadband manager from Seattle, was one of many new employees who came to Philadelphia to meet the company's top executives. "I was impressed by the leaders telling their stories," she recalls, "not with PowerPoint or fancy presentations, but talking to us like real people, like we mattered." The Broadband integration was also why Burke had started *Comcast Live* and *Leadership Link*, and why he had developed the Credo, whose benefits were becoming clear as an urgent need developed to communicate the company's operating principles to tens of thousands of new employees.

To staff the many regions and systems that needed qualified managers, Burke spent much of his time moving executives around—or at least trying to. "You'd be shocked at how many people turned us down for promotions," he says. "If they didn't want to move because of the weather, I tried to persuade them. But if they didn't want to take their kids out of school, what could I say?"

His first strategic move was to abandon AT&T's telephone-centric approach and replace it with a major effort to win back some of the many cable subscribers who had drifted away. "Forget telephone," he said. "We'll come back to that later."

Burke ordered upgrades of the older Broadband physical plant to get it ready for digital video and high-speed Internet. This also paved the way for Comcast's digital telephone service, using a more advanced system than AT&T's outmoded circuit-switch technology.

A year or so later, Burke came to Brian and said, "I've been thinking about our new position as a leader, and I've been looking at what these digital boxes can do. We could start a video-on-demand service, but instead of showing only movies, we could have entertainment shows, sports, kids' programs, or almost anything. And we could make most of it free, like the Internet. Because we're the largest buyers of programming, maybe the programmers will give us the right to use some of their content this way, which will give us something that satellite doesn't have." Other cable operators were skeptical at first, but On Demand has become a huge part of the business.

Because he intended to hit the ground running (another favorite Burke-ism) the moment the AT&T systems turned over, he began working on the integration well before the deal closed. During the year between the end of the auction and the closing, Burke, Tallent, and their transition team visited every large Broadband system three times and each of the smaller ones twice. As the merger awaited government approval, the company sent a voice mail twice a month to all Broadband employees to keep them in the loop.

But getting this deal approved was far from automatic, especially at a time when Comcast still had only one employee in Washington. "The whole thing could have come apart," says David Cohen, who made sure everybody involved was up to speed, and who helped prepare Mike Armstrong and Brian for their Senate antitrust subcommittee appearances.

In the summer of 2002, Burke convened a series of meetings to review POPs, or Preliminary Operating Plans, which was as close as Comcast could come to actual budget meetings for systems it didn't yet own. The first time the Comcast team came in, local managers were understandably wary. "They just wanted to give us good news," says Tallent. But when they realized that the visitors wanted them to put aside the happy talk and tell the truth, most were relieved and eager to help. "Good news is not actionable," says Tallent. "It's a hundred times more useful to hear what's *not* working."

Brad Dusto had a similar experience in the Western Division. On his initial visits to Broadband systems, he would be handed a fifty-page presentation that contained nothing but good news, and managers would point to at least one area in which their operation was number one. But with so many different metrics, it wasn't hard to be the best at *something*. "What about the number of subscribers?" Dusto would ask. "What about cash flow? I can't help you until I hear the whole story. You won't be fired for making a bad decision, but you could be for trying to hide a problem. We're starting over, so let's look at the facts and figure out how to get better."

There were also some pleasant surprises. In New England, the most profitable of the AT&T regions, the Comcast team was impressed by the straight talk of GM Kevin Casey. "We've been number one in operating cash flow per subscriber," Casey told the visitors, "but by Comcast standards, we're near the bottom. Our goal is to make New England number one within Comcast as well."

Burke could see that Casey was somebody to watch. "We kept the guys who were honest with us," he says. "Managers get in trouble when they try to make themselves look good by hiding problems from their bosses. The quickest way for a company to die is to stop being honest about the business. Executives need to be able to say, 'I don't know,' or 'I screwed up.'" Burke was right about Kevin Casey: before long, his division was the most profitable one at Comcast.

Soon after the deal closed, Burke decided that he, Brian, and Ralph should visit the AT&T systems and meet *all* the employees—not just the executives and the managers who worked on budgets. In the early weeks of 2003, Comcast held about two dozen of these brand launches, as they were called, at sports arenas and other large facilities around the country. Most of the program consisted of regional management teams addressing their employees before the corporate leaders took the floor.

The San Francisco-area brand launch was held aboard the USS *Hornet*, an aircraft carrier anchored in the bay that had been part of the Pacific Fleet in World War II. As three thousand employees boarded the ship, they were greeted by union picketers handing out leaflets. After Ralph spoke about the family feeling he had tried to maintain over the years, and how Comcast would be the last cable company these employees would work for, the audience rose as one and gave him a standing ovation. And some of the union organizers, who had reportedly planned to heckle Ralph, asked him to sign their shirts.

Before the program began, Steve Burke had asked for information about the ship. When he addressed the group, he spoke about the *Hornet* with such authority that you might have thought he had served on it. At one point, however, he referred to it as a *boat*.

When he heard that, Ralph said to Brian what any navy veteran would have said: "It's not a boat, it's a *ship*." Brian urged him to point this out, and when it was Ralph's turn to speak, he said, "I have never had an opportunity before to correct Steve, because he's never been wrong, but Steve, this isn't a boat. This is a *ship*!" A big cheer went up from the many military veterans in the audience.

Everywhere Ralph went, employees were thrilled to see him. When he appeared in the Roy Wilkins Auditorium in the Twin Cities, the room erupted, although local executives had warned the visitors that Minnesotans are not very demonstrative. "They had seen Ralph on *Comcast Live*," says Rich Ruggiero, "and they couldn't believe he came out to visit them. It's so rare that a true American business icon is still in the mix."

"He gave people faith in the company," says Sandy Weicher, who attended the Chicago brand launch at McCormick Place. "No head of a cable company had ever addressed our employees, and some of them had worked for several operators."

It was like that everywhere: in Sacramento, California; at the speed-skating oval in Salt Lake City; the new football stadium in Foxborough, Massachusetts; the Rose Garden in Portland, Oregon; the Tacoma Dome in Washington; the Gwinnett Center in Atlanta; the Mellon Arena in Pittsburgh; the Natural History Museum of Los Angeles; and the University of Denver event center, where the cheers for Ralph were especially loud. "I have never seen people leap out of their chairs so fast to applaud someone," says Tracy Baumgartner, who helped organize half a dozen of these brand launches. At the end of the program, the Colorado employees gave their corporate visitors a parting gift—jerseys from the Colorado Avalanche hockey team. Oh no, Baumgartner was thinking, that's a mistake, because Comcast owns the Philadelphia Flyers. But when Ralph, Steve, and Brian put on their jerseys, "that gesture had extra meaning for those of us who knew," Baumgartner says. "They were telling the employees that we were all on the same team."

Years later, employees who attended these events still recall the excitement. "When Ralph appeared in Foxborough," says Jennifer Khoury, "it was like Elvis entered the room." At that event, says Kevin Casey, "Ralph essentially recruited three thousand employees.

They had a lot of anxiety about their new bosses, and he changed it all in about seven minutes."

Several years later, when Ralph was asked exactly what he told the new Comcast employees at the 2002 brand launches, he reached into his wallet and pulled out a well-folded page. Delighted at the opportunity to speak these words once more, he began:

We started by buying a cable system of 1,200 subscribers in Tupelo, Mississippi, the birthplace of Elvis Presley, and today we have 21 million plus—*and we still have Tupelo*. How did we get that way? We're good salespeople and we love our product, and people get caught up in it. We grow internally, and we make acquisitions.

How many people here have worked for more than one company? [A sea of hands would go up.] Well, we don't sell our systems. [Huge applause.] We're long-term players, and as I said, we still have Tupelo.

We have a family feeling in this company, and people can talk to one another and try to discuss their problems. We want everybody to talk. That's the way we get to know people. That's why we're here.

We also have high integrity, the way we run this company. You see newspaper stories about corporations doing bad things, but you should know that integrity keeps things going.

We have a family culture, which is hard to maintain when the company gets so big. How do you maintain that same culture? You do it by being warm and friendly. And instead of one big family, we have a lot of little families. If your boss won't listen to your ideas and you're up against a stone wall, give me a call.

To be successful, we have to maintain the cash flow, we have to meet the budgets, and keep our noses to the grindstone. If you do that, we'll all have a good time.

We're happy to be here, and we'll get to know each other a lot better. And by the way, if you have people in your own family who want to join the company, as I see it, nepotism is a good thing. And speaking of nepotism, here's Brian!

"We bet the company," said Steve Burke in 2004, when it was already clear, far sooner than even he had dared to hope, that the Broadband gamble had paid off. By every conceivable measure—cash flow, number of subscribers, progress of the rebuild, not to mention employee morale and the combining of very different cultures—Comcast's integration of Broadband was a home run.

"It went off like silk," says Glenn Jones. "Nobody else in the business could have done that, ahead of schedule and under budget." Jones wasn't the only cable operator hoping for a positive outcome; the whole industry wanted the Broadband integration to succeed. "When things don't go right," says Jones, "a lot of heat rises out of cities and into congressional delegations, and we all have to deal with the consequences."

The deal had closed on November 18, 2002, bringing a formal end to AT&T Broadband. Even its name disappeared, although it was supposed to survive in the combined company's new name, AT&T Comcast. But the chairmen of both companies now agreed that the combined entity should be known simply as Comcast.

"This will change us forever," Steve Burke told his executives. "You'll know within a few months whether you're cut out for big-company life, and you won't like all the changes. We'll do our best to preserve our culture, but we're going to become more bureaucratic."

As planned, Mike Armstrong became the non-executive chairman of the newer, bigger Comcast, but nobody knew how, or whether, that arrangement would work. According to the merger agreement, Brian, as CEO, held virtually all the power. But the plan did work, in no small measure because of David Cohen's efforts to help both Armstrong and the new directors who came over from AT&T get comfortable in a very different culture.

It also worked because of Armstrong. "Chuck Noski made the acquisition happen," says Brian, "but Mike had to want it to happen. He didn't like our approach, but he put his shareholders first, ahead of his own interests."

The first test of the newly created Office of the Chairman took place at a board meeting in New York right after the closing. Seven of the twelve directors were new to Comcast, including five who came over from AT&T. There was a potentially difficult moment when Steve Burke announced that only two high-level executives from AT&T's cable division, Kevin Casey and Dave Fellows, would be joining Comcast. However Armstrong may have felt, he responded by saying, "That's a great plan, Steve." And then, to reassure the former AT&T board members, he added, "Steve and I have already met to discuss this." With Armstrong's blessing, they were off and running.

Burke's presentation at that meeting was critical. "It was a delicate situation," says David Cohen. "Facing seven directors who had never met us as a management team, and who didn't know what they were getting into with this relatively unknown family-run company from Philadelphia, Steve explained, very diplomatically, why the Broadband management team had to go." Mike Cook, one of the former AT&T directors, told Cohen after the meeting that until Burke's presentation, he and the other directors hadn't fully understood the cable business—or how good Comcast's management really was.

If Steve Burke was the hero of the integration, Mike Armstrong's contribution was no less important. His early goal of combining video, Internet, and telephone was the right approach, but Broadband's version of what Comcast would later call the Triple Play had started too soon and was plagued by problems beyond his control. Even after Comcast ambushed him, he refused to hold a grudge. "Mike was a realist and a gentleman," says Brian. "He took the high bid, and the high road as well."

23

Programming the Future

Amy Banse

In the mid-1990s, Amy Banse considered herself fortunate to be working on the thirty-fifth floor of 1500 Market Street. Although her office was tiny, it was just down the hall from the company's leaders, which gave her plenty of exposure to Ralph, Brian, and the other senior executives. Over time, she says, "I wormed my way into the outer circle of the core."

Sometimes, when she walked by Brian's office, she saw his deal team gathered around the table—a group that typically included Larry Smith, Julian Brodsky, Bob Pick, John Alchin, Art Block, and, of course, Ralph. One morning in 1996, Banse, who was in the legal department, was invited to join them as they worked on the complicated and ultimately successful acquisition of the E! network, in which she played a major role. Just before the meeting began, Brian called Dennis Hersch at Davis Polk. "Okay, Dennis," he said on the speakerphone, "the gang's all here."

"And Amy, too," said Larry Smith.

Brian shot him a look of mock anger. "Like I said," he repeated, "we're all here."

Banse took that as a vote of confidence. She was the first woman to sit at the deal table, and she knew that her presence was a significant event in the company's history. The others knew it, too. "It's hard for a woman to fight her way through a male organization," Ralph says, "but Amy was determined, and I liked that."

Hanging on the wall over Brian's conference table was a small, colorful painting by Alexander Calder of men playing cards. *The Gamblers* had been a gift from Suzanne Roberts to her husband. To Banse, the title of the painting was a good description of the men sitting beneath it, who saw themselves as risk-takers with the skill, the boldness, and often the luck to get the deal done. They had earned that reputation, and they would earn it again on a bigger stage with the acquisition of AT&T Broadband.

Because Banse specialized in acquiring individual networks, she wasn't directly involved a few years later when Brian and his team embarked on two ventures that would have represented huge gambles on content, had they worked out. In the summer of 2003, Vivendi, the French media conglomerate, put a package of its assets on the market, including the USA Network, the Sci-Fi Channel, and Universal Studios, with its theme parks and its film and television libraries. Brian and Steve Burke were especially interested in the film library of four thousand titles, which could have powered several new cable channels. Burke wanted to start a horror network called Scream, an idea that would later come to life with a different name and a new format. But when the price soared to levels that seemed unreasonable, the gamblers folded their cards. The Vivendi assets went to NBC in a deal that created NBC Universal.

Soon another idea surfaced, an audacious plan that had been in the air for a couple of years—that Comcast should try to acquire The Walt Disney Company. Disney looked vulnerable in 2003. Its shares had tumbled and Roy Disney, Walt's brother and the company's closest link to its late founder, was feuding openly with CEO Michael Eisner and calling for his replacement. As Ralph puts it, "In a company whose leader is under assault, anything can happen."

Still, this was a long shot. Beyond the huge expense of such an acquisition, Disney wasn't just another media company. It was a beloved American institution, and an uninvited takeover attempt could lead to a serious public backlash. Even if Comcast could somehow pull it off, integrating Disney would be far more difficult than the recent merger with Broadband, which was close to a perfect fit.

On the other side of the ledger, here was an opportunity for Comcast to play catch-up in its continuing search for content by acquiring a lot of it in one gulp. And not just any content, but some of the best in the business. In addition to a major movie studio, Disney owned several valuable cable networks, including the Disney Channel. It also owned the enormously popular and lucrative ESPN, which was costing Comcast more than a billion dollars a year to carry.

Although Brian and his team had reason to think the Disney board would be receptive to an offer, they were misinformed. On February 9, 2004, when Brian placed a courtesy call to Michael Eisner to let him know Comcast was coming, Eisner responded with a cold and lawyerly statement that seemed to leave no room for discussion. The next day, when Comcast offered to buy the company for $54 billion in stock, the Disney directors dismissed the idea with no suggestion that a higher bid might lead to a different result.

This flat-out rejection was both a surprise and a disappointment. But the real shock was the negative reaction of some of Comcast's institutional shareholders, who concluded that if Brian and his team were pursuing a huge content company, they must be having doubts about their core business. Comcast shares fell sharply when the bid was announced, and it wasn't until late 2009, when the company announced an agreement to buy a majority interest in NBC Universal, that the lingering memory of the Disney offer finally faded from the minds of investors.

The deal team, which had anticipated any number of obstacles, was unprepared for the vehemence of the shareholders' response. To anyone in the cable industry, the rationale for the bid was self-evident: here was an opportunity to add Disney's treasure house of content to Comcast's newly enhanced distribution and technology. The bid for Disney wasn't a critique of cable; it was a *tribute* to cable. "When we bought Broadband," says Bob Pick, "we told the world we would now be able to acquire content for a bigger and better distribution system. By going after Disney, we were doing exactly what we had talked about."

There was some talk of a second, higher bid. "Our first offer was to let them know we were there," says Ralph, "and if there was any interest, we would have sweetened it considerably." But given the disheartening response, there was little point in going forward. Later, when asked to explain what went wrong, Ralph said, "We thought Mickey Mouse was waiting for us. We thought we were his piece of cheese, but we were wrong."

"The concept was right," says Brian. "We believe that distribution and content go together, and we can do much more with our technology if we own more content. Disney was a unique opportunity, and it made sense to go after it." For now, Comcast would keep on acquiring content the old-fashioned way: one channel at a time.

When cable was young, there was no content beyond broadcast television. And when the first cable channels were launched in the late 1970s, most operators continued spending their limited resources on distribution—especially during the frenetic race to expand into the nation's cities and suburbs. The first to invest in content was Time Inc., which acquired HBO and later added CNN and the rest of the Turner empire. The biggest enthusiast was TCI's John Malone. If we're paying these cable networks for the right to carry them, he asked, shouldn't we own some of them and participate in those revenues?

Ralph didn't disagree, but he had other priorities. Except for QVC, he kept Comcast focused on distribution: "I always felt that the more customers we had, the easier it would be to put on content."

Given the company's success, it was hard to argue with that decision. Viacom's Sumner Redstone had long preached that "content is king," and Julian liked to tease him at investor conferences: "Sumner," he would say, "on your birthday I'm going to send you two big buckets. Why don't you fill them with your content and try to get them to our customers?"

Although Comcast fared remarkably well by sticking to its knitting, Ralph and Julian both acknowledge that they could have made other choices. "If you were looking down on us from Mars," says Julian, "you'd probably say we should have put more emphasis on content. Certainly Brian and Steve felt that way." Brian still regrets passing up an opportunity to invest in the Discovery Channel, and Burke says, "You don't want to be ninety-five percent in a single business, no matter how good that business may be. And it's hard to find anything more synergetic with what we do than cable channels."

But by the time Burke joined Comcast in 1998, the content gold rush was over. For the next few years, the most compelling opportunities had shifted back to distribution.

Comcast owned little content when Amy Banse arrived in 1991, and nobody, including Banse, expected that she would play a role in changing that. She grew up outside Philadelphia, a middle child with two brothers. Her father, Robert, was general counsel and executive vice president of Merck during the pharmaceutical giant's heyday; her mother, Anne, was a homemaker. After graduating from Harvard, where she majored in social studies (a combination of government, economics, and social policy), Amy went to law school at Temple University. Business school might have been a better choice for someone with her entrepreneurial instincts, but she adored her father and hoped to end up, like him, as an in-house lawyer at a big corporation.

She was working at a large law firm when a recruiter told her about an opening at Comcast, a company she had never heard of. Stanley Wang hired her as the fourth member of his surprisingly small legal department, which consisted of himself, Art Block, and Tom Nathan. She was asked to help negotiate program affiliation agreements, and was soon working closely with Brian, who became one of her mentors.

Comcast in the early 1990s was an ideal environment for a talented young woman who believed in herself. "There was plenty to do," Banse recalls, "and the more they saw you accomplish, the more responsibility they gave you. When Brian saw me run with the ball, he told me to keep running." She ran right out of the law department and into the business arena.

In its early years, E! Entertainment Television was owned by a partnership between Time Warner and several cable companies, Comcast among them. After studying the partnership documents, Banse found a way that Comcast might be able to acquire a controlling interest in the network. It wouldn't be easy, but she thought it was possible, and Brian encouraged her to try. Although she had little experience in deal making, she was good at finding allies and working with her counterparts at other companies, and through a combination of hard work, persistence, and charm, she succeeded. Larry Smith, the consummate deal maker, says that Banse's work on acquiring E! was like turning straw into gold.

When E! became part of Comcast, Banse reminded Brian that it was time to put together a board, and to appoint someone to begin overseeing the network. "Why don't you do it?" he said. It was that casual.

Banse has been called "the softer side of Comcast," and although she is as driven and determined as her male colleagues, there is some truth to that phrase. Even in difficult negotiations, she refuses to see the situation as adversarial. She believes that women have an easier time building relationships and being flexible, and that they can compromise more easily than men. Women are often more adept at keeping a number of stakeholders happy, which is a real advantage in complicated, multiparty deals. "Even when you see the world differently," she says, "it's important that the other person feels you are united with them in their objectives."

As a high-achieving woman, Banse has had to fight some battles within the company, too. Once, when she asked for a raise, a colleague said, "Why? Don't you have a husband who works?" He said it with a smile, but he said it.

She recalls that comment with more regret than resentment. "That's the way things were," she says, "and not only at Comcast. If the wives of male executives worked outside the home, it was often for additional income. The men I worked with didn't go grocery shopping, and when they came home at night, their refrigerators were full and their dinners were made. They hadn't had much exposure to women in business."

Although her colleagues treated her well, Banse initially found their vocabulary intimidating. The executives around her spoke in what she calls "man-code," with colorful expressions, occasional insults, and what seemed like an endless array of sports metaphors. But the biggest challenge was getting used to their bluntness, to hearing expressions that women rarely used with one another. She had to learn that comments like "You're crazy," or "You don't know what you're talking about," meant nothing more than "I disagree." She had to train herself not to take it personally when one of her ideas was shot down or even dismissed, because that happened to everybody, she noticed, including Brian. And no matter how it sounded, the language these men used wasn't intended as hostile; it was actually a form of affection with people they knew well. She also realized that some of the toughest talkers, including Julian and Larry Smith, were the men who had mentored her and pushed her into becoming the company's first female corporate vice president.

When Banse finally became comfortable with man-code, she found it liberating: "Once you develop a thick skin, it's wonderful, because you know exactly where you stand. These comments aren't meant to demean anyone. They're just a kind of shorthand." As one of the highest-ranking women in the company, Banse often has to explain this to younger women. She advises them to adapt to a style that is gradually changing with the support of the company's leadership. Although she has no patience for the male-bashing she sometimes encounters among women in the corporate world, she believes that male executives have to do more to welcome women into corporate life.

Grace Killelea, senior vice president of talent and leadership initiatives, thinks about these issues every day. "What Amy experienced a few years ago is already different," she says, "because men have changed a lot." Women have to change, too, she says. When Killelea meets with college women who are considering careers in corporate America, she talks about adapting to the culture. "If you were living in Mexico," she tells them, "you'd learn Spanish. And if you're working in a corporation, you have to learn its language and understand its currency." She tells younger women that they might have to ask for assignments, rather than waiting for opportunities to come their way. This takes assertiveness, along with the realization that sometimes the answer will be no.

Killelea says that women who have played on a sports team in high school or college are often more successful in corporate life. "Everyone wants people who can get the job done," she says. "Most leaders don't care who carries the ball into the end zone. They just care that it gets there. The leaders of this company are looking for more female executives. Are we where we need to be? No. Are we headed in the right direction? Yes. Will it take time to get there? Definitely."

In 2011, in a move into another predominantly male part of the company, Amy Banse was named managing director of Comcast Ventures, the company's venture capital fund that invests in, among other areas, digital media, e-commerce, and entertainment.

As an accountant at Deloitte & Touche, Cathy Avgiris was used to meetings where she was the only woman in the room. She came to Comcast in 1992, and as an honors graduate of Mike Tallent University she served as a kind of divisional CFO in the Northeast before the company had divisions. When Comcast launched its high-speed Internet business, Avgiris became its CFO. In 2002, when the Broadband acquisition closed, Tallent wanted to make her a division president, but for family reasons she couldn't leave Philadelphia. "In that case," he said, "why don't you figure out this phone business that we've inherited from AT&T."

Circuit-switch technology was rapidly becoming obsolete, and Avgiris was asked to head up the company's rollout of its digital telephone service. She also manages Comcast's high-speed Internet service, the nation's largest, and leads its wireless initiatives.

Marlene Dooner, who grew up in a Spanish-speaking home in San Juan, Puerto Rico, came to Philadelphia to attend a small Jesuit university, where she majored in French and economics. She then joined Provident National Bank and worked in its corporate lending department, where her clients included a number of communications companies, including Comcast. A woman she knew at the company was head of Investor Relations. "I'm having a baby," she told Dooner, "and I'm leaving to become a full-time mother. Why don't you apply for my position? It takes a lot of the same skills as banking."

Dooner got the job, which consists mostly of communicating the company's financial story to lenders and investors. At the bank, her focus was on debt and risk, and she paid close attention to the borrower's financial history; at Comcast, her focus is on institutional equity investors, and on the company's prospects for growth. But both positions require high-level financial analysis and depend on long-term relationships.

When Dooner arrived in 1995, Comcast consisted of cable, the cellular phone business, and QVC. QVC and cellular are gone, but today the company also includes Internet, telephone, and an outstanding collection of content, and in addition to being much bigger and far more visible, Comcast is on much firmer ground. "When I started," she says, "we did as many presentations to high-yield debt conferences as to equity groups." These days, of course, high-yield debt is no longer part of the company's financing. Either way, Dooner must tell the company's story as accurately as possible, resisting any temptation to make the picture look rosier than it actually is.

Amy Smith doesn't work out of the corporate office, but as head of the cable division's Freedom Region, which is made up of metropolitan Philadelphia and all of New Jersey, she was certainly visible to the company's leaders. She grew up in Roanoke, Virginia, and was part of the first class of women to be admitted to Washington and Lee University, where the men outnumbered their female counterparts by about ten to one, a ratio she describes as "a beautiful thing."

In 1994, after a couple of years at a small cable operation, Smith was hired as the business manager of Comcast's system in Charleston, South Carolina. She helped manage a system in Florida, and when Comcast ended up with Suburban Cable as part of the MediaOne settlement, she ran systems in New Jersey and central Pennsylvania. Before long she was heading up what she calls the "mother ship region," and did much to improve it. "It's easy enough to spend money fixing plant or headends," she says, "but the key to turning things around is to engage the hearts and souls of people who deal directly with customers. It's all about employee engagement." It must have been the right approach. "This region wasn't always in the top echelon," says Dave Watson, "but it is now." In 2011, Smith assumed responsibility for an even larger region covering most of Florida.

E!, which until the NBC Universal transaction was the most widely viewed cable channel in the Comcast portfolio, began in 1987 as Movietime, which consisted mostly of trailers that the studios were happy to provide for free. Available in only eight million homes and on the air just a few hours a day, Movietime was run by executives from HBO who believed it could be made into something bigger and better when they found the right person to head it.

In 1989 they brought in Lee Masters, who had recently been successful at MTV, and asked him to transform Movietime into a kind of CNN about Hollywood, with twenty-four hours a day of entertainment news. It was a daunting assignment, but Masters thought it was possible. "HBO was hugely supportive," he recalls, "and very patient—much more than I was."

A few months into his tenure, HBO changed the network's name to Entertainment Television, or ETV. When Masters hired a production and marketing team to develop a logo, they came up with a single letter with a punctuation mark.

"E!? You've got to be kidding. Where's the rest of it?"

"We thought the other letters were unnecessary," he was told.

Masters couldn't believe it. He knew all about the power of names, having changed his own name from Jarl Mohn because it was hard to remember and even harder to pronounce. (He has since reclaimed it.) He had spent all this money on a logo for ETV, and they wanted to call it E!? He hated it! He imagined himself trying to make phone calls: "This is Lee Masters from E!" And the other person would ask, "From *where*? How do you spell that?"

Which is exactly what happened. But he wasn't on the phone very much, because he and his team were busy discussing new program ideas. One was called *Talk Soup*, because Masters thought it would be fun to show outrageous segments from TV talk shows with a funny host to introduce them. When his staff greeted the suggestion with silence, he challenged them to do better with the same small budget. "Even I didn't think it was a great idea," says Masters, "but we had a hole to fill, and it was cheap to produce." *Talk Soup*, hosted by Greg Kinnear, became a big hit. So did E!'s red-carpet coverage of the major Hollywood awards shows, which Movietime had been doing back when nobody was watching. Masters brought in TV cameras for Howard Stern's enormously popular radio show. By the time Comcast bought the network, E! was firmly on the map.

When Masters left, Mindy Herman grew the business to the next level. She was followed by Ted Harbert, the former president of ABC Entertainment and the head of NBC Studios, who has given E! additional spark and variety. "We're not curing cancer here," he says. "We're about entertainment and pop culture, and we try to have a good time with it."

Now that Amy Banse was serving as Comcast's unofficial content manager, Brian named her to the board of the Golf Channel, which was started in 1991 by Joe Gibbs, a cable entrepreneur in Alabama. After enlisting Arnold Palmer as an investor, Gibbs, with Palmer's help, set out to find additional partners among cable companies. Most operators were cool to the idea, but Tim Neher, the number two man at Continental Cablevision, was willing to make a modest bet, and he invited his friend and occasional golfing partner Brian Roberts, with whom he had served on the Turner board, to join him. When Brian agreed that Comcast would put $15 million in the Golf Channel, Neher lined up three more operators to invest. ("If Brian hadn't come in," he says, "I wouldn't have called them.") In a move reminiscent of Ralph's request when he went to work for Pioneer, Brian asked for, and received, a promise that if Continental were ever acquired, Comcast would have the right to buy its interest in the venture. In 1996, when Continental was sold to US West to create MediaOne, Brian exercised his option. He and Banse then put the wheels into motion to buy out the other partners.

"One reason I put Amy on the board," says Brian, "is that she knew nothing about golf. She could look at the channel in strictly business terms." Several years after she and Brian persuaded Fox to invest in the Golf Channel, Banse started talking to Jeff Shell, Fox's representative on the board, about a complicated deal in which Comcast would buy out Fox's share.

Comcast paid dearly for Fox's piece of the Golf Channel, which not everyone viewed as a good idea. "I didn't think there was enough of an audience for a whole channel devoted to golf," says Larry Smith, "but Brian was hell-bent on doing it, and he was right." Of all the Comcast channels—in fact, of all *cable* channels—Golf has the most passionate audience and the most desirable demographics. Although its viewers are a much older audience than advertisers normally pursue, they're an affluent group; the channel ranks first among cable networks in both household income and home value.

The final step was for Comcast to buy out the founders. Because Arnold Palmer preferred to complete the transaction in person, the papers were signed at his house in Latrobe, in western Pennsylvania. In the fall of 1998, Brian, Ralph, and Banse flew in for a friendly visit that included a lunch of sloppy joes served at the kitchen table by Winnie Palmer, Arnold's wife. When it was time to sign the papers, Palmer looked into Brian's eyes and asked, "Will you take care of my baby?" Brian assured him the channel would be in good hands, and Palmer agreed to continue appearing on it. "I was especially pleased to sell to Comcast," he says, "and I'm more and more pleased all the time."

Ralph and Palmer made an instant connection. Almost thirty years earlier, Palmer had won the annual Hickok Award from Ralph's former competitor in the men's accessories business, and when Ralph spotted the familiar diamond-studded gold buckle in a display case, they began to reminisce. Palmer had been close with his own father, and it meant a lot to him to be doing business with this father and son.

When the paperwork was done, Palmer turned to Brian and said, "Great. Let's play some golf."

They played next door at Palmer's course, a former country club where his father had been the grounds superintendent. Brian played exceptionally well, shooting the best nine holes of his life and finishing one stroke under par, with his father and Banse as witnesses. Even Palmer was impressed. "Brian's quite good," he said years later. "He could be very good if he spent more time playing golf, but he's already working pretty hard."

Arnold Palmer played like Arnold Palmer. On one of the final holes, with a dead tree blocking his path to the green and a second tree directly behind it, he approached the ball, hitched up his pants, and announced, "Under, over, and around."

"He was in the woods," Brian says, "and he hit that ball under the limb of the first tree and over the top of the next one. Somehow, it hooked hard and landed on the green. It was the greatest shot I've ever seen."

"Want to play another nine?" Palmer asked when they were done.

"Absolutely not," said Brian, who knew a good ending when he saw one.

Comcast and Fox were minority partners in other channels as well, including Speedvision, which covered auto racing, and Outdoor Life, which focused on hunting, fishing, and other active pursuits as well as the Tour de France bicycle race. "If you sell us your piece of Speedvision," Jeff Shell told Banse, "we'll sell you our piece of Outdoor

Life." In 2006 Outdoor Life, which was a Comcast network, was rebranded as Versus and featured the National Hockey League, along with IndyCar racing, bicycle racing, college football, and professional bull riding. In 2012 Versus was rebranded as NBC Sports Network.

G4, one of the smaller Comcast networks, was born when Charles Hirschhorn, a former Disney executive, reached Steve Burke in his car while Burke was driving home from work. "I have an idea for a cable channel," he said.

Burke winced. "In my job," he says, "that's the phrase you least want to hear. You get it constantly, and it's usually a silly idea."

"Make it quick," said Burke, "because I'm almost home."

"MTV for video games," said Hirschhorn.

"Hold on," said Burke. "I'm pulling over."

Amy Banse got G4 off the ground. She then partnered with Echo-Star to acquire TechTV, a small channel that covered technology and the Internet. TechTV became part of G4, which is now focused more on technology than on games.

Amy Banse was all too familiar with Steve Burke's complaint about the nonstop barrage of programming ideas; when she ran the programming portfolio, the calls never stopped. She came to think of it as the tinker-tailor-soldier-sailor parade, because it sometimes seemed that just about every living American was convinced that his or her passionate interest should become a new cable channel. Among the more serious ideas Banse considered, sometimes in more than one incarnation, were the Traffic Channel, the Air and Space Channel, the Real Estate Channel, the Car Channel, the Boat Channel, the Horticultural Channel, and the Women's Sports Channel.

These calls only increased in 2004, when the *Wall Street Journal* ran a prominent story about Comcast's portfolio of channels. In what must have seemed like her worst nightmare, the headline read, "Want to Start a TV Channel? See Amy Banse."

One of the callers was Gary Knell, the president and CEO of Sesame Workshop, which used to be known as Children's Television Workshop. Knell's group had owned 50 percent of Noggin, a cable channel for kids, but had recently sold its stake to raise money for the rights to those Muppets who appear exclusively on *Sesame Street*. With a huge backlog of *Sesame Street* episodes and no place to show them, he was looking for a distribution partner.

He had called the right person. A few years earlier, Banse had been home on maternity leave with a toddler and a newborn. As she was feeding her infant daughter, her son started screaming for *Thomas the Tank Engine*. Flipping through the DVDs scattered around the playroom, Banse wondered, Why isn't anyone planning to put shows for very young children on demand? On-demand programming hadn't even started yet, but to Banse, the future was already here.

Back at work, she decided to do something about making quality programming for very young children more available to viewers. Talks with Disney and Nickelodeon led nowhere, but eventually she put together a new channel with three unlikely partners—two nonprofits, Sesame Workshop and PBS; and HIT Entertainment, an English company that owned *Barney and Friends*, *Fraggle Rock*, and *Thomas the Tank Engine*. The result was PBS Kids Sprout, more commonly known as Sprout, which began in 2005 as an on-demand service—the first television channel ever to start that way. Preschoolers watch TV differently from other people, and it's not uncommon for a three-year-old to watch the same episode again and again, which isn't possible on a linear channel.

Sprout On Demand was followed six months later by a twenty-four-hour linear channel of short program segments that track a child's daily schedule from breakfast to bedtime, with a limited amount of advertising, all of it directed at parents. Why a twenty-four-hour channel for viewers who go to bed early? "Sometimes kids wake up in the middle of the night with a bad dream or an earache," says Sprout's president, Sandy Wax, "and parents appreciate that we're always there when they need us."

Wax, who grew up in Towson, Maryland, had dreamed of becoming a marine biologist. While working as a lab technician, she started earning her MBA at night, and when she walked into a marketing research class, she knew she had found her calling. She was hired by the Discovery Channel, and then joined The Disney Channel as vice president of research, where she worked on the company's strategy for preschool kids. She moved to SoapNet, another Disney channel, as head of programming. In 2005, when a recruiter told her that Comcast was looking for someone to run Sprout, she applied for the job. Under her leadership, Sprout became more successful—and more quickly—than anyone had anticipated.

"Sprout was one of Amy's big coups," says Larry Smith. "It was almost impossible to do this with four companies—two of them commercial and two nonprofits. I would have given up." Despite some skepticism among her colleagues about the viability of a network geared exclusively to small children and their parents and caregivers, Sprout's many grateful viewers have proven the naysayers wrong.

TV One, another new network, was born in 2002, and Banse traces its genesis to Steve Burke's idea of launching a channel for African American adults. Burke won't take credit except to say that he was aware that Viacom's BET (Black Entertainment Television) was showing mostly music videos. "A second channel was in the air," he says. "I pushed Brian a little, but Amy made it happen."

"Steve came to me after AT&T," Brian recalls. "Now that we're the largest operator," he remembers Burke saying, "we have the opportunity to show that we're not just about making money. Why don't we develop a different kind of African American channel with a different tone and a different aspiration?"

After meeting with several possible partners, Banse recommended Cathy Hughes, a single mother who, with her son, Alfred Liggins, had turned a small Washington, D.C., radio station into the largest minority-owned media company in the country. They struck Banse as a partnership that would fit well with Comcast, and she thought Brian and Ralph would like teaming up with a mother who worked closely with her son. "We have never been in cable TV," Liggins told her, "but we know how to program." In recommending them, Banse was choosing character and talent over experience.

Because Banse was happier as an entrepreneur than as a manager, there came a point when she, Burke, and Brian agreed that it was time to bring in an experienced content executive to oversee the company's growing portfolio. Jeff Shell had a reputation for making things happen at Fox, and a history of working harmoniously with Amy Banse and her colleagues. A native of Los Angeles with a Harvard MBA, he had been at Disney in the early 1990s before moving to Rupert Murdoch's News Corp. as head of business development for Fox Television, where he started a string of Fox-branded regional sports networks and worked with a variety of cable channels in which Fox had an interest. In 2002 Murdoch asked him to run Gemstar/TV Guide, which had been hit with a scandal; Shell's job was to clean it up. When Steve Burke called in late 2004 to see if Shell would become Comcast's head of programming, Shell said yes. His work at Gemstar was done, and his wife had family in Philadelphia.

When Burke hired Shell, he told colleagues that he liked to bring in executives who not only had a vision but were able to execute it. Another factor in Shell's favor was his extensive experience with regional sports channels, an area of growing interest for Comcast, which had been quietly building up its own regional sports portfolio. That part of the business began in 1996, when Pat Croce, the former conditioning coach of the Philadelphia 76ers, asked the team's owner, Harold Katz, if he could buy an interest in the franchise. Katz dismissed the idea, but Croce kept after him until Katz gave him a thirty-day option to see if he could raise the money.

In urgent need of a partner, Croce turned to Ron Rubin, a Philadelphia real estate developer. Rubin had just read that New York's Cablevision had acquired two of the city's sports teams, the Knicks and the Rangers, to secure the local TV rights to their games. "I knew cable companies were looking for content," he says, "and there's no better content than sports, because every game is different."

He was tempted to call Ralph Roberts right away, but first he contacted his friend Ed Snider, who had owned the Philadelphia Flyers hockey team since its inception and who also owned the Spectrum, where both the Flyers and the 76ers played. Snider had no plans to leave; he was building a new arena that would later be known as the Wells Fargo Center. But when Ron Rubin asked if he might be interested in selling control of the whole package to Comcast, Snider said that at the right price, he might consider it. Only then did Rubin call Ralph.

Although Ralph has no interest in sports, he was well aware of the passion of Philadelphia fans. When Rubin said that Comcast might be able to buy both the 76ers and the Flyers, which would make it possible for the company to launch a sports channel in its hometown, Ralph and Brian asked Art Block and Bob Pick to investigate.

Less than a month later, amid great secrecy and some late-night drama, Comcast became the majority owner of both teams and both arenas. But Brian, who supported the transaction, was concerned that as the president and future CEO of Comcast in a sports-crazy city, he and his family could end up with far more attention than they wanted.

During a heart-to-heart talk with her husband, Aileen Roberts supported a solution that was already being discussed—that Brian should ask Ed Snider and his company, Spectacor, to remain involved, and that Snider should be chairman and controlling partner of the company and the executive face of the two teams. Snider, who was ambivalent about leaving a job he loved and was concerned about the fate of his employees, including his close associates, Peter Luukko, Sandy Lipstein, and Phil Weinberg, was delighted to stay on, and he and his company have been an important part of Comcast ever since. "Our cultures meshed right away," says Luukko, president of Comcast Spectacor. "This is by far the best partnership we've ever been in." And because Snider had once started a sports and movie channel, his expertise was helpful in launching Comcast SportsNet, headed by Jack Williams, which soon added the Philadelphia Phillies to its lineup to go with the 76ers and the Flyers. (In the fall of 2011, the 76ers were acquired by a new ownership group.)

Comcast went on to develop sports networks in a number of cities, with the early ones negotiated by Brian and Banse until Jeff Shell took over the process. His adjustment wasn't easy. Although he knew that Comcast had long ago positioned itself at one end of the distribution-content spectrum, he hadn't realized how deep that culture ran. The company was obviously serious about expanding its content offerings, but Shell, who thinks of himself as a TV guy rather than a cable guy, noticed that many of his fellow executives didn't watch much television or show much interest in popular culture. Shell, whom Sam Schwartz calls "a twenty-four-hour media machine," and who claims that he had to fight to get a television in his office, found this surprising in a media company. As a former Fox executive who had spent most of his time in Los Angeles, he was now in a very different environment.

When he wanted to sign *American Idol* host Ryan Seacrest to be the face of E!, some of his new colleagues didn't recognize the name. But they trusted Shell, who hired Seacrest in a move that everyone came to applaud. The first time Brian met Seacrest, at a rehearsal for Brian's 2008 keynote address to the Consumer Electronics Show in Las Vegas, the two of them put their cell phones on the same table. Half an hour later, Brian accidentally picked up the wrong one. He realized his mistake when he noticed that instead of the usual text messages from Steve Burke and David Cohen, he was suddenly hearing from Britney Spears and Paris Hilton.

As president of the Comcast Programming Group, Shell began streamlining the content division and cutting costs. He consolidated the entertainment channels under Ted Harbert, who ran the Comcast Entertainment Group in Los Angeles, which included E!, G4, Style (an offshoot of E! with a focus on fashion), and FEARnet (which started as an on-demand channel specializing in horror movies and other frightening fare). Shell put the advertising sales of all the Comcast networks under Dave Cassaro, who had previously worked at Fox and E!

He brought big changes to Versus, broadening its offerings from niche sports like bull riding and the Tour de France to more popular fare, such as college football and especially NHL hockey, which really put Versus on the map.

Shell is known for his bold style. "When Jeff came," says Steve Burke, "he said we were dramatically underinvesting in some of our networks, and that a couple of them might have to go backwards before they got bigger. It took courage to come into a new company and say that, but he was right." Like Amy Banse, Shell pushes the company in directions his colleagues sometimes resist. And yet, says Sprout partner Gary Knell, "he's willing to listen, and he can admit when he's wrong, although he isn't wrong very often."

In 2007 Shell brought in Jon Litner to run the Comcast Sports Group of regional sports channels, each one headed by a GM who reports to Litner. A former catcher on the Yale baseball team, Litner had been at ABC Sports, where he was in charge of *Monday Night Football*, and where one of his bosses had been Steve Burke. After five years as chief operating officer of the National Hockey League, he returned to television to head up SportsNet New York, in which Comcast is a founding partner. "When we hired Jon to run the Mets channel," says Burke, "we were already thinking of him as a candidate to run our sports business."

Although the sports networks are profitable, there's also a strategic advantage for the company to maintain a vigorous local-content sports programming arm, which provides promotional opportunities, branding, and the kind of goodwill that is difficult to acquire in other ways. "There's an insatiable appetite for sports, particularly in big markets," says Litner, "and nothing means more to a fan than his home team." Litner considers himself fortunate, because his job allows him to root for quite a few of them—from the Boston Celtics to the San Francisco Giants, from the Oakland A's to the New York Mets, and from the South Side of Chicago (the White Sox) to the North Side (the Cubs), along with the Bulls and the Black Hawks. Just about every night of the year, Jon Litner has something to cheer about.

24

The Volunteer

David Cohen

"In a few months I won't be here very much," Steve Burke told Brian early in 2002. When the AT&T deal closed in the fall, Burke would be visiting Broadband systems around the country as he headed up the integration of tens of thousands of new Comcast employees. "When there's a crisis," he continued, "and there'll be more of them when we're bigger, I won't be around to help. A problem will come up in Chicago or San Francisco, or a politician will attack us, and we'll need to respond. We're moving onto a more public stage with more external pressures—the press, public policy, the FCC, and so on."

Brian nodded. He had been through so many acquisitions that it was easy to forget that this one was different, that its sheer size would change the company irrevocably. Although Comcast was about to become the industry leader, it still had the culture of a much smaller organization.

"It would be great to find one senior person to handle it all," Burke said. "David Cohen wants his firm to handle crisis management, but I think we should try to get David himself." Cohen, one of the most respected and well-connected attorneys in Philadelphia, was chairman of Ballard Spahr Andrews & Ingersoll, a high-profile corporate law firm. He and Brian had worked together when Mayor Ed Rendell asked them to co-chair a committee tasked with trying to bring one of the two major political parties to Philadelphia for its 2000 political convention. Together with Karen Buchholz, the president of the committee and a future Comcast employee, they succeeded in landing the Republicans.

Brian had enjoyed working with Cohen, and one moment from their partnership still made him smile. Early on, when a delegation of Republicans came to tour the city, the transit system was on strike. Brian had just driven his kids to school, and the traffic was terrible. When he saw that he couldn't possibly be on time to meet the visitors, he called Cohen to let him know.

"Where are you, exactly?" Cohen asked.

"Five minutes later," Brian recalls, "eight police motorcycles surrounded my car and the waters parted." He arrived on schedule, having just witnessed a dramatic demonstration of David Cohen's ability to get things done.

Cohen still did legal work, and Comcast was one of his clients. When Brian and Steve Burke asked him to help resolve a potentially acrimonious programming and carriage dispute with Disney over ABC and ESPN by leading the team that was working on the problem, Comcast gave him an office and a voice-mail account as if he worked there. But it was hard to imagine that he would leave his law firm for a corporate job. "We'll never get David," Brian said. "Not in a million years."

"It's worth a try," said Burke. "Do you mind if I talk to him?"

Brian didn't mind. He had hired Burke in part because Burke

thinks big. If Steve wanted to invest an hour in a long shot, he wasn't going to argue.

The next morning, Burke called Cohen to ask if he could come over to see him.

"When?"

"Today."

Cohen was free at four o'clock, but the call made him nervous. *This can't be good*, he thought. *The Comcast guys never come over here. We must have screwed up.*

Later that day, in Cohen's office, after a moment of small talk about the AT&T Broadband acquisition, Burke began by saying, "You've been doing a wonderful job for us, David, and you've helped us in so many ways . . ." Cohen wasn't really listening. He was waiting for the *but*, and it came soon enough: "But for all your good advice, you've neglected to tell us that the best thing for our company is for you to come over and join us. With your talent and experience in government and administration, you're the missing piece we need. Besides, you've done everything you can possibly do in this city. Now you'll have a chance to play on a national stage."

Cohen, who is awfully good at anticipating the future, hadn't seen this coming. He had spent most of his career practicing law, which is what he had wanted to do ever since he was a boy in central New Jersey, the oldest of three children and the son of a Bulova watch salesman who eventually put in close to sixty years—sixty years!—at the company.

At Swarthmore College, where Cohen had triple-majored in history, economics, and political science, he was the editor of the school paper, which is where he met Rhonda Resnick, the editor just before him, whom he would soon marry. In the summer after his sophomore year, he interned in Washington for Congressman James Scheuer, a Democrat who represented Brooklyn and Queens. When Cohen graduated, Scheuer brought him back as the youngest chief of staff on Capitol Hill.

A year later, he enrolled at the University of Pennsylvania Law

School, where he served as executive editor of the *Law Review*. In class he was known for reading (and remembering) everything—not just the cases, but the footnotes as well, to the point where some of his fellow students referred to him as Chief Justice Cohen.

One of his professors, Arthur Makadon, saw in Cohen "an uncanny sense of reality, an ability to see the world as it actually is, combined with extreme intelligence." Makadon, the hiring partner at Ballard Spahr, recruited his student to the firm, where he quickly became a star. Cohen once tracked down the only published book on an obscure area of insurance, studied it, interviewed the author, and found a near-perfect defense for the claim in question, which led to a highly favorable settlement instead of the bankruptcy his client had feared. "He was great at figuring out and then brokering a solution to complex problems," says his mentor and friend Helen Pudlin. "Whenever David was in charge, there was a successful resolution."

One morning, Cohen was in Pudlin's office when the dean of Penn Law School called to ask if she would teach a course in appellate advocacy. When Cohen heard her say she didn't have time to organize the curriculum, he volunteered to prepare all the materials she would need. "He really meant it," Pudlin says. And then he really did it.

Cohen, who made partner in record time, was known around Ballard as COE—chief of everything. He generated so much work that the firm hired two secretaries to keep up with him.

But as much as he loved the law, he also loved politics. When his friend Ed Rendell was elected mayor in 1991, Cohen, who had served as his campaign manager, resigned from Ballard to become the new mayor's chief of staff—a title that doesn't begin to describe his long hours and myriad involvements in the city's political and economic life. (Cohen's role is chronicled in *A Prayer for the City*, by Buzz Bissinger.) In 1997, after almost six years at City Hall, he was recruited back to Ballard Spahr—this time as its chairman.

When Steve Burke came to see him five years later, Cohen was perfectly happy at Ballard, where Rhonda, too, had been a partner, and where they had many friends. Burke knew he had already left the firm once, and that for a man as loyal as Cohen, once was a lot. "If you have no interest in coming," he said, "we'll certainly understand. But if you'd like to consider this, you should talk with Brian."

A couple of days later, in Brian's office, Cohen pulled out a sheet of paper enumerating the pros and cons of moving to Comcast. At the top of the list was the fact that he already liked and respected the company's senior leadership, starting with Ralph, whom he had known since the 1980s through their common interest in civic philanthropy.

When Brian saw the list, he started laughing. He then showed Cohen his own list, from what he imagined as Cohen's perspective. They were already on the same page, and they would soon be working together.

Burke's bold bet had paid off. "When Steve wanted to approach David," says Brian, "I couldn't imagine he would come. And when he did, Steve wasn't like some people in his position, who would have said, 'and he should report to me.' His attitude was, 'Hire David if you can, he's terrific, he'll help us all.'"

Cohen's colleagues at the law firm were shocked that their chairman was leaving for a job in which he would report to someone else, but Brian's collaborative management style had reassured him on that point. Rhonda, too, was stunned; she had left Ballard a couple of years earlier and jokes that maybe her husband just didn't like being there without her. But he was ready for a new challenge, especially one where his insatiable civic idealism could be expressed in a corporate environment.

When David Cohen came to Comcast in the summer of 2002, it wasn't clear exactly what he would be doing, or even what his title would be. In government he would have been chief of staff, but that wasn't quite right, so he and Brian settled on executive vice president. In addition to advising Brian, Cohen would be doing administrative work that Larry Smith preferred not to do, public relations tasks that John Alchin didn't enjoy, and about a thousand other things.

When Arthur Makadon learned that his former student was leaving Ballard, he left a cryptic, four-word message on Brian's voice mail:

"You have no idea." Brian still wonders about the rest of that sentence. Was it, "You have no idea how much this hurts? How amazing this guy is? How much your life will change when he starts working with you?"

"Most people still have no idea," Brian says. "David works behind the scenes, where he's often invisible. His range is enormous: No problem is too big, no detail too small. He'll give me great advice on policy, and the next moment he's arranging just the right entertainment for John Alchin's retirement dinner."

One of Cohen's first assignments was to help facilitate the Broadband integration at the highest levels, and he quickly established a good rapport with former AT&T CEO Mike Armstrong. And with five AT&T directors moving over to the Comcast board and two independent members coming in, it was Cohen's job to welcome them and bring them all up to speed. "At board meetings," says one former director, "David did everything but park the cars."

Mike Cook, another former AT&T director who now chairs the Audit Committee, says, "Maybe other organizations have their own David Cohens and I just never met them, but I doubt it. There are companies where, if you don't ask just the right question, you won't learn much. But David always tells us what we need to know."

When people ask Cohen what, exactly, he does at Comcast, he likes to mention the boy in the old Life Cereal TV commercials, about whom the other kids would say, as some people remember it, "Let's give it to Mikey. He'll eat anything!" With his seemingly unlimited capacity for work, Cohen volunteers for even the least appealing duties, such as showing up at events nobody else wants to attend, or meeting with disgruntled shareholders and other critics. "His shoulders are so broad," says Ralph, "you can give him any task and he steps right into it."

Cohen's new colleagues were amazed at how much he was able to accomplish. He works cheerfully: the more there is on his plate, the happier he seems to be. Watching him in action, those around him are often reminded of the adage: if you want something done, ask the busiest person you know. "Just looking at a week of his schedule is enough to scare you," says Jennifer Paternostro, his longtime assistant.

His responsibilities fall into three general areas. First, he's in charge of the company's communications, public policy, community investment, and political functions, including Comcast's relationship with elected officials and regulators. Second, he has taken over many of the administrative functions that Larry Smith and Stanley Wang used to handle, especially those that pertain to the internal functioning and governance of the corporation and the oversight of its legal function. Finally, he helps the senior officers, and especially Brian, think through the strategic direction of the company.

Cohen likes to bring people from different parts of the organization into the same room—sometimes a physical room, sometimes a virtual one—to make sure everyone knows what his or her counterparts are doing. "That didn't matter as much before AT&T," he says, "but now that we're the biggest cable provider, anything, in any of our systems, could end up on the front page of the *New York Times*. All our functions were in silos, and while I'm all for silos, I think they should be only waist high, so you can see what's going on in the other silos."

He knows when it's time for Brian to make a decision, and he'll offer a well-considered opinion as to what it should be. But he describes his advisory role in more modest terms, as "helping other people be more effective." He has a knack for clearing away administrative underbrush so his colleagues can focus on what they do best. "David is not without an ego," says Steve Burke, "but it's in the service of—well, of *service*."

Cohen is more visible on public policy issues. He understands how government works, and he knows how to make the company's case in terms that politicians will understand. On visits to Washington he will schedule meetings all day long, and he seems to have a connection to almost everyone he sees. If he doesn't already have a relationship with a politician or staffer, he'll make sure to form one. He's especially good at staying in touch. "They won't always remember who they ran into," he says, "but they'll remember the people who follow up."

What makes Cohen an effective advocate, a colleague says, is that he gives credence to the other side. "What they're saying is not altogether wrong," he will tell a government official, "but let's examine that idea more closely." Politicians respond well to someone who is well informed on almost every topic and can be reasonably objective about both sides of an issue.

Before coming to Comcast, Cohen, who has long been active in community affairs, told Brian he wanted to continue his extensive volunteer work on the boards of local philanthropies, civic organizations, and nonprofit groups, and that he hoped to raise Comcast's image in the community. Ralph had always encouraged local systems to help people in need, and now, as the company was growing into its new role as a media powerhouse, Brian knew that Cohen would help him take corporate giving and volunteering to the next level. "David has an agenda," he says. "He wants philanthropy to be a bigger part of our identity, which is one of the reasons we wanted him."

Cohen wasn't the only one who was eager to move in that direction. Right after the Broadband deal closed, Steve Burke's uncle, the former CEO of Johnson & Johnson who was now chairman of the Partnership for a Drug-Free America, asked Burke if Comcast could donate advertising spots for his organization's public-service announcements. Burke immediately agreed, and in 2004, Dave Watson strengthened that connection by joining the Partnership board. To date, Comcast has aired over $100 million worth of public-service announcements for the group.

A few years earlier, Brian and Aileen Roberts had brought the company into another new venture. Their youngest daughter, who was then in preschool, had become aware of the city's homeless problem, and she told her mother she wanted to build a house for everybody. "You can't ignore a comment like that," says Aileen. In 1998, on the Saturday morning after Thanksgiving, the whole family went to visit Sister Mary Scullion, an activist who took them to

Judson Street in one of the city's poorest neighborhoods. Sister Mary and a colleague ran Project H.O.M.E. (Housing, Opportunities for Employment, Medical Care, Education), a group that enables homeless and low-income residents of Philadelphia to break the cycle of homelessness and poverty. Sister Mary, who likes to say that "none of us are home until all of us are home," has an extraordinary record as an advocate for the homeless. She has been the prime mover behind the dramatic decrease in the city's homeless population, and her organization has become a model for dozens of other communities.

As the family toured the area and saw the various components of Project H.O.M.E.—the houses, the gardens, the community center, and the women's shelter, Sister Mary pointed to an empty lot and said, "and this is where I want to build our technology center. It will take years before computers in the classroom will mean much in this neighborhood."

Brian and Aileen looked at each other, and each knew what the other was thinking. "I've always wondered how you can give computers to schools that don't have the resources to fix the machines or train the teachers," Aileen says. "You have to support that kind of gift, and Brian understood that. As soon as we heard *technology center*—bingo!"

Even before David Cohen came to Comcast, he tried to facilitate this relationship and make it happen. He and Sister Mary were already friends, despite the fact that they had first met when she was demonstrating in front of his office in City Hall and Cohen had her arrested. She had also sued the city, and although Cohen testified as the city's lead witness, he didn't hold that against her. He respected her and thought most of her claims had merit.

With Cohen and Steve Burke driving the project, and in partnership with the Honickman Learning Center, Comcast built the country's largest neighborhood technology center, with classrooms, teachers, and more than two hundred Internet-connected computers. The building, which is now an anchor for the community, houses a charter school, various after-school programs, and adult digital literacy classes, as well as a recording studio and a neighborhood newspaper, both run by kids. In 2007 Cohen arranged for the Comcast board to have dinner at the new Comcast Technology Labs, which tied in perfectly with that day's agenda—a review of the company's community investment strategy.

But what about the rest of the country? Shortly after Cohen arrived, Ralph gave him a chart showing that most of the Comcast Foundation's giving was confined to the Philadelphia area. But most of the customers lived elsewhere, and Ralph thought the company's charitable contributions should reflect that diversity.

So did Cohen, who decided to build on what Ralph had started long ago. United Way used to prepare TV commercials for some of the agencies it supported, with space for a local cable manager to go on the air and say something supportive about one group or another. Comcast had been active in that effort, and Ralph made sure that GMs around the country had a discretionary fund to support other worthy communal causes as well.

Cohen was a longtime fan of United Way who became active in the organization when he was at City Hall. He joined the board of the Philadelphia chapter, and during three years as its chairman, he transformed the group from a fund-raising federation into more of a community impact organization. As soon as he came to Comcast, he and Brian teamed up to co-chair the local campaign, and they have continued to visit the city's business leaders to encourage their companies' participation in United Way.

Cohen has had considerable success in making United Way a higher priority for Comcasters around the country. In 2001, the year before he arrived, the employees gave approximately half a million dollars; by 2011 their contributions had grown to more than $5 million. Comcast now has one of the top fifty United Way campaigns in the country.

Comcasters in Michigan have been especially responsive. In 2007, when Cohen called for a 40 percent participation for the company as a whole, which was a big step up from the 23 percent level of the previous year, Michigan employees, led by David Buhl, set their own goal of 50 percent—and reached it. Michigan is a special case, because its economy was suffering well before the 2008 stock market crash and the collapse of the domestic auto industry. "The sensitivity of our Michigan employees is as high as anywhere I've ever worked," says Bill Connors, the Central Division president.

The head of a technical operations hub told Buhl that his technicians would be happy to participate if the company made it easy to contribute. So during their lunch break, the techs who agreed to make a contribution—which is normally done through a regular payroll deduction that can be as low as a dollar per paycheck—merely had to sign their names. The HR team handled the paperwork, and every tech who signed up received two hot dogs and a Coke. Other hubs and offices organized rallies, brought in speakers, held lotteries, and gave away candy.

Christopher Pugh was a manager at a call center in Plymouth, not far from Detroit. Call center employees are on the phone constantly, and not every interaction is pleasant. They must be aware of so many details and policies that when their shift is over, many of them just want to be left alone. But Pugh wasn't deterred. He believed Michigan's 50 percent goal was still too low, and he wanted to shoot for 80. Unlike most of his colleagues, he didn't use speakers, incentives, or anything else. He just sent an e-mail to every employee, announcing that he was the man to see about United Way, and that if you didn't come to him, he would go looking for you.

Pugh canvassed the halls, bathrooms, break rooms, and parking lots, talking about United Way and explaining that most of the money went to help people who lived nearby. "I was born with the gift of gab," he says. "I could sell dust to a rock." When the campaign was over, the Plymouth call center had generated contributions from over 80 percent of its employees.

In Ann Arbor, administrative assistant Amy Radel put up posters, held meetings, and dropped literature and candy on every desk. Her boss, David Williams, announced that every employee who contributed to United Way could wear jeans for a week, which was surprisingly effective.

United Way is just one of Cohen's community investment projects. Under his leadership, the company has created relationships with several national organizations, including One Economy (a highly regarded digital literacy program), City Year, the Urban League, Big Brothers Big Sisters, Boys and Girls Clubs, Teach for America, and NCLR (formerly known as National Council of La Raza), which works to improve opportunities for Hispanic Americans. The company's scholarship program has also been strengthened and simplified. To replace dozens of different arrangements around the country, Cohen encouraged the expansion of Comcast Leaders and Achievers, which awards one-time education grants of a thousand dollars to high school students who are catalysts for positive change in their communities. Each year, the scholarship winners are featured in local newspapers and television news broadcasts.

Of all the community events in which the company participates, Comcast Cares Day is easily the most popular. It began as part of Philadelphia Cares Day, an annual program of service in which the city's residents join together to clean and paint local schools and playgrounds. In 1996, when Joe Waz, who later became president of the Comcast Foundation, asked for volunteers, Comcast sent its first team of about two hundred corporate and cable employees, including Ralph, Brian, Julian, and Dave Watson. "Home Depot had a big turnout," Waz recalls, "and early on our goal was to get as many people as they did."

When Steve Burke attended his first Philadelphia Cares Day, his reaction was, This is great! Why don't we do this nationally? "Many of our employees wanted to help out in their communities," he says, "and it's so much easier when it's all planned out for you and you can participate with your colleagues."

After Burke organized a company-wide conference to get it going, the first Comcast Cares Day was held in 2001. "Steve recognized that this program was not only an investment in the communities we serve, but was also good for business," says Diane Tuppeny-Hess, who worked for Waz in public affairs and organized teams of employees each year to participate. "It gave us the opportunity to invite mayors and other local leaders to join us and get to know us."

Every year, the company's top executives fan out to a wide array of Comcast Cares Day projects, and Ralph has been especially visible, just as he was with Philadelphia Cares Day. Back then, in the fall of 1997, he joined a group of volunteers who were fixing up Germantown High School—his first visit there in the sixty years since he graduated. The neighborhood had declined considerably and the school had metal detectors. Brian accompanied his father and brought along his three children. Their grandfather, in jeans and a T-shirt, spent almost five hours painting walls and greeting volunteers, students, and teachers, who welcomed him back, showed him around, and presented him with a school jacket. "But the important thing," Ralph says, "is that we had volunteers from every Comcast entity in the city working with me, and with each other. These events are great for employee morale."

On Comcast Cares Day in 2005, when Ralph was eighty-five, he and a group from the corporate office traveled to Irvington, one of the most economically challenged and crime-ridden towns in northern New Jersey. When the Philadelphia bus arrived and Ralph got out, two hundred employee volunteers screamed with excitement and took pictures with their cell phones. But it wasn't only Comcasters who were happy to see the company's founder. As Ralph was raking leaves in a park that had formerly been a vacant lot, a group of residents came over to thank him. "Mr. Roberts," one of them said, "it's just incredible that you are here today. Nobody ever comes to Irvington."

As always, he was an active participant. "He was working so hard in the garden that I was afraid he might dislocate his shoulder," says Kate Noel, who smiled when she noticed his trademark bow tie peeking out from under his Comcast Cares Day T-shirt. In addition to planting a garden and fixing up a community center, the volunteers removed graffiti from surrounding buildings; built a playground; cleaned, painted, and restocked a food pantry; and provided lunch at a nearby community center, where Ralph was one of the servers. At the end of the day, he presented a check for $25,000 to the Association for the Advancement of Inner City Communities.

After Steve Burke got Comcast Cares Day off the ground, David Cohen took it to the next level—building it up from five thousand volunteers across the country to more than sixty thousand in 2010, and almost seventy thousand in the spring of 2011, when they worked on 659 projects in 40 states.

In Grand Rapids, Michigan, volunteers have bagged groceries in a food bank. In Broward County, Florida, employees improved the local Boys and Girls Club, which is right across from their office, painting every room in the building, planting a vegetable garden, and putting up new bleachers. In Grants, New Mexico, a tiny system with only six employees, Comcast Cares Day is a huge event; virtually the whole town turns out, usually to fix up one of the local schools.

The list goes on and on. "We have fun dreaming up the T-shirt design each year," says Brian. "One year, my daughter suggested that we make it look like a rock tour, with a list of all the cities and towns. It was a great idea, but we couldn't begin to fit them all on one shirt."

In Denver, in 2006, hundreds of Comcasters helped out at Project Homeless Connect, a daylong event where homeless people are matched up with representatives from dozens of social service organizations that offer training programs, job opportunities, and medical care. "Normally," says Steve Stainbrook, who was then vice president of technical operations for the West Division, "if someone has a problem with the courts, they'd have to go to the courthouse to find out where they stand. It can take all day to find the right office, but we had someone from the court system who could assist them. This project is a way to help people without making them run all over town, which can be very difficult if you don't have a car."

Stainbrook was assigned to help a man who had just been released from prison for a drug offense. John was on his way from New Mexico to Montana, but had stopped in Denver to look for work after running out of money. Because he wasn't a Colorado resident, there wasn't much that Project Homeless Connect could do for him, so Stainbrook found a bus to Montana and paid for John's ticket with his own credit card.

This wasn't a random act of kindness. Seventeen years earlier,

Stainbrook himself had been homeless and living on food stamps, and he still remembered how it felt to take a few coins from his pocket and scrape together enough for a small order of fries for dinner. All he wanted was an opportunity to work, and he had been fortunate enough to find it in the cable industry.

"Comcast's participation was a tipping point for us," says Jamie Van Leeuwen, the director of Project Homeless Connect. "After they got involved, so did the University of Denver, and then other companies, and all of our major sports teams. Comcast still makes a donation every year."

In the summer of 2006, when Comcast took over some of the Adelphia systems, Comcast Cares Day activities for that year had already been planned. Some former Adelphia employees in Vermont were unhappy not to be part of these efforts. The organizers of Comcast Cares Day hadn't wanted to rush them, but when the employees insisted on participating, they were welcomed. The Burlington group fixed up a youth office for after-school activities, and the Rutland office organized a food drive.

In West Palm Beach, Florida, four hundred employees who had just come over from Adelphia visited a local elementary school, where they painted every room, scrubbed the place down, installed new cabinets, and provided musical instruments for the students. "It was a great team-building exercise for our people," says Rebecca Tilleson, former regional vice president of HR for the West Palm Region, "and a wonderful introduction to Comcast. A lot of companies don't have a good experience coming through an acquisition, but being part of this program made it easier for us."

David Cohen, who often talks about "connecting the dots," likes the way Comcast Cares Day intersects with different segments of the corporation, including public affairs, government affairs, investor relations, and public relations. Along with the rest of the corporate leadership, he knows that these days of service probably do as much for the volunteers as for the communities they are helping.

At Cohen's first Comcast Cares Day, he joined a group of employees at the YMCA in Chester, a struggling community not far from the Philadelphia airport, where the group repainted a mural and installed a high-speed data lab for after-school programs and adult education. During the day, the head of the Y told Cohen that her immediate priority was to get the roof repaired. Cohen had already arranged to give the organization a check from the Comcast Foundation, and when the time came to present it, he said, "You now have $20,000 toward your roof repair project." He then called the head of the roofers' union and a contractor to make sure that amount would do the job.

Cohen loves to talk about Comcast Cares Day, and a few weeks later he was describing his Chester visit to a group of former Broadband employees at a Spirit of Comcast program. At the end of the session, a young woman came up to him with tears in her eyes. "Mr. Cohen," she said, "I work in Virginia now, but I grew up in Chester, and I can't tell you how important the Y was to our family. It was the only safe haven in the city, and I don't know how we would have survived without it. To be working for a company that is helping the Chester Y—that means the world to me."

David Cohen didn't invent Comcast Cares Day, and many other employees have worked hard to make it so successful, but his energy and commitment to this and other community service programs have helped transform the company. "He leads by example," says Karen Buchholz. "He asks a lot from people, but he'll never ask you to do something he wouldn't do himself."

Even with an overflowing schedule, he enjoys the relentless chaos of the job, which reminds him of his old days at City Hall. He compares his ever-changing agenda to swimming in high surf: "A big wave comes in, you run and dive into it, or you jump over it, and just as you're catching your breath, here comes another big one. It's constant."

But the man who thrives on work wouldn't have it any other way. "I can't imagine not being productive all the time," he says. "My idea of hell is sitting at my desk with nothing to do."

25

Going Up

Stanley Wang and Karen Buchholz; Comcast Center

Looking ahead to a new century, Willard Rouse decided it was time for another big project in Center City Philadelphia. More than ten years had passed since the celebrated developer and his colleagues at Liberty Property Trust had put up One Liberty Place, the city's tallest building. It almost became Comcast's new home in 1989 until Ralph changed his mind when he saw the reflective glass in the windows.

Now Rouse had his eye on the property that Comcast had moved to instead. One Meridian Plaza, across the street from the south side of City Hall, had been destroyed by the terrible office fire of 1991. But it took years before the building was finally demolished, and its burned-out hulk had long loomed over the neighborhood as a sad, unsightly symbol of urban distress. That site was a parking lot, but some people, including Ralph, thought of it as the best undeveloped commercial location in the area.

Because the property was too small for a skyscraper, Rouse and his associate, John Gattuso, asked the prominent New York architect Robert A.M. Stern to design what Gattuso calls a petite and precious office tower. But when legal problems arose over the purchase of the land, Rouse backed off, leaving the project with an architect and a plan, but no place to build.

Across the street from the Meridian site, at 1500 Market, Brian Roberts was wondering how long Comcast could remain in its current location. The company, which had been there since 1994, had been growing so fast that its space in the building had more than doubled, leaving Comcast headquarters with offices in two towers served by five separate elevator banks, and a variety of noncontiguous floors that Gattuso calls "the real-estate version of Swiss cheese."

When David Cohen joined the company in 2002, the question of when, where, and even whether to move the corporate office was one of the first things Brian asked him to focus on. They explored several options, including relocating to the suburbs or the old Philadelphia Navy Yard, and Cohen generated and fielded informal inquiries from officials in both New Jersey and Delaware. After the AT&T deal closed, the mayor of Denver asked Brian and Cohen to consider moving the corporate office to his city, where Comcast had plenty of available space now that the old Broadband headquarters was empty. But Brian and Ralph were committed to Philadelphia.

Before long, Liberty found another location for its new building: where the old Sheraton Hotel had been, at 17th Street and John F. Kennedy Boulevard, which was now a parking lot above Suburban Station, the city's commuter rail center. Together with Robert Stern and the Olin Partnership, a leading landscape architecture firm, Rouse and his colleagues began planning a speculative office development that would include a public square and be known as One Pennsylvania Plaza.

Would this be a good home for Comcast? Initially both Ralph and Brian were skeptical, because although the planned building was only four blocks from the company's current headquarters, it felt a little remote. Rouse and Gattuso were not surprised by this reaction. To longtime Philadelphians, the compact area from City Hall to Broad and Chestnut had always represented the heart of the city. "In Los Angeles," says Gattuso, "they measure in miles. In New York they measure in blocks. In Philadelphia they measure in yards."

As professional developers, the Liberty team could see that the core of the city had started moving west. David Cohen saw the same thing. The offices of his former law firm had moved westward and were now in the BNY Mellon Center (formerly the Mellon Bank Center) just east of 18th Street. The land at 17th and JFK was like the hole of a doughnut, and if you filled that hole with an exciting new building, you would be creating a new core for Center City in a spot that was already surrounded by the Four Seasons Hotel, the Bell Atlantic building, Liberty Place, the Mellon Center, the Blue Cross headquarters' building, and the main branch of the Free Library of Philadelphia.

The new site began to grow on Ralph and Brian. Brian was pleased that the land was big enough for two buildings; he was thinking about a permanent headquarters with room for expansion, and he liked the idea of a vertical campus. And for the majority of the corporate workforce, who rode to work on public transit, an office right on top of the train station would be awfully convenient, especially in bad weather.

By the time Brian, David Cohen, and Liberty Property Trust began talking in earnest about Comcast's becoming the lead tenant, the architect and the developer had agreed that the building would be made of Kasota stone, a warm, golden material that had been used to great effect in the Philadelphia Museum of Art. But Brian, who had been looking closely at corporate headquarters in several European and Asian cities, preferred a more contemporary look. "When I asked myself what I really wanted," he recalls, "the words that came to mind were *progressive*, *cool*, *elegant*, and *hip*, but also *understated* and *unostentatious*." He knew this would be a difficult balance, but he wanted to try.

He was hoping the company would end up in a glass building, and maybe a taller tower than the the Liberty team was planning, although he and Ralph wanted to avoid anything extravagant. Brian believed—and Ralph felt this even more strongly—that the new tower should be a prominent part of the city's skyline. Stern had no objection to designing a taller building, although with Comcast intending to occupy only 40 percent of it, the executives at Liberty worried about flooding the rental market with more office space than the city could absorb. But a higher building didn't have to contain more usable space—not if the ceilings were raised from nine feet to eleven or thirteen, which was unusual, but not unthinkable.

That was fine with Stern, because higher ceilings brought in more natural light. It wasn't the height of the building that concerned him, or even the material it was made of. Stern, who was also dean of the Yale School of Architecture, had become interested in "sustainable" or "higher performance" buildings before *green* became the term of choice. He and Liberty had recently worked together on a small, sustainable office building in Allentown, Pennsylvania, which served as a kind of warm-up to this one.

Everyone was pleased that the new location over the commuter rail station would not only replace a parking lot but also encourage even more employees to leave their cars at home. "If you're interested in a high-performance building," Gattuso says, "you don't abandon the city's existing infrastructure. You reinforce it and try to give it new life. Years from now, people will know that this building helped propel Philadelphia toward embracing sustainability."

And, indeed, in the spring of 2009, the building that became Comcast Center was awarded LEED CS Gold Certification from the U.S. Green Building Council—the tallest building in the country to have earned that honor. The citation mentioned a 40 percent reduction in water usage from that of a typical office building, plaza shading that creates a 70 percent reduction in the heat-island effect, a curtain-wall glass coating that reduces the amount of energy needed for air conditioning, and the effect of a remarkable amount of natural light, diminishing the need for artificial illumination.

As late as November 2004, Comcast was still considering other locations. Just after Brian, David Cohen, and Steve Burke toured the Navy Yard, an option that would have allowed for significant tax advantages and would have returned Ralph to the site of his military service during World War II, Gattuso made a final pitch for the Liberty site: "You know," he said, "Chrysler built a new headquarters in Michigan in 1998 and nobody mentions it. But Walter Chrysler built the Chrysler Building in New York back in 1930, and people still talk about it."

At that stage, the leaders of Comcast were more concerned with economics. A few months earlier, they were hoping to have the Liberty site designated as a Keystone Opportunity Zone, which would have provided tax benefits that made the lease much more affordable. The legislation, which was controversial, made it through the city council, and it passed the state Senate in Harrisburg in the early hours of July 4. But the House adjourned without voting on the measure, which was equivalent to turning it down.

At a meeting with John Gattuso and Bill Hankowsky, who took over as CEO of Liberty after the 2003 death of Willard Rouse, Cohen laid out the situation. "We all have an idea of what the governor might be prepared to do," he told them, "but for us to go ahead, we'll need a better deal from you." This was a critical moment, says Gattuso: "Everything could have spun apart, but David kept it together and allowed the deal to move forward in a new structure."

After a series of meetings between Comcast and Liberty during the final days of 2004, which included a brief intermission on December 24 when everybody on both teams rushed off to complete their Christmas shopping, the two sides finally reached an agreement. On Sunday, January 2, 2005, Cohen and Hankowsky signed the lease for a glass building that had yet to be built and would be known as Comcast Center. The company was planning to occupy only 40 percent of it, but three years later, when it was time to move in, Comcast had taken 90 percent of the available space.

As the building went up, Cohen kept an eye on costs. Every time Brian expressed a preference to the architects and designers, they always said yes, but as Cohen points out, "Nobody ever comes back to talk about the price. That was my job." The budget was exceeded a few times, but Cohen's bias, and Brian's, too, was to try to limit those overruns to the building's more public spaces, such as the lobby, the employee dining area, the conference center, and the floor that would be occupied by Comcast University.

As always, Cohen had many other items on his plate, and he needed a senior deputy who could coordinate this huge and complicated project. Fortunately, Brian had already hired someone who loved difficult assignments. Karen Buchholz had started her career in politics, working for Senator John Heinz before she was hired as membership director of the Pyramid Club, a private dining club at the top of the Mellon Center. She then worked for Spectacor, selling corporate suites for the city's new arena with the help of Mayor Rendell. Rendell and Cohen were so impressed with Buchholz that they asked her to head up the effort to bring a national political convention to Philadelphia, where she worked closely with Cohen and Brian Roberts. Soon after the convention, Brian brought her to Comcast as the company's first head of corporate communications.

In 2004, when Buchholz was vice president of administration, she told Cohen that if the company was moving to another site, or ended up building a new home, she would love to be involved. Cohen was pleased to hear it. "Karen is unbelievably organized," he says, "with the ability to keep a thousand balls in the air."

For the next few years, her days were a whirlwind of phone calls, meetings, crises, and resolutions. Working closely with project manager Chris Warth, she kept track of what every department needed and where each segment of the company would be housed. In a job that was stressful even on good days, some of her most difficult moments came when she had to tell the Liberty team that floors that were already built would have to be changed, but with no adjustment in the schedule. There was a firm deadline: the expiration of Comcast's leases at 1500 Market Street. "The one thing you can't buy is time," says Buchholz. "Fortunately, I love pressure."

She also worked closely with Stanley Wang, who, in his capacity as executive vice president for law and administration, had been actively involved in looking for a new location. Although he was semiretired by the time the new building was going up, "Stanley was my sounding board for everything," Buchholz says. "He had tremendous institutional knowledge, and although he wasn't always vocal, he was decisive. His comments often changed the direction of the meeting. It took over a year to negotiate the lease, but he had a knack for relaxing the room and reminding us that even difficult work can be enjoyable."

Wang was extending the legacy of his good friend Dan Aaron. "He was adamant that we shouldn't create a culture that differentiated between executives and more junior employees," Buchholz says. "He made sure there was no executive dining room, and that even in the private dining areas there would be no servers. He was a big proponent of the fitness center, and saw to it that both the gym and the café were subsidized, so any employee in the building could enjoy them."

"Stanley worked hard to understand the infrastructure of the building," says David Binswanger, Comcast's tenant representative. "How would the mail get from the loading docks to the floors? How, exactly, was food in the café going to end up in the serving area? And he was adamant about putting in a big bike rack. Whenever I walk by Comcast Center and see all those bicycles lined up, I know that somewhere, Stanley is smiling."

Buchholz led a high-level team that consisted of Comcast executives and some of the professionals who were most involved in the project. But with so many experts in the same room, not all of whom were accustomed to playing nicely with others, the initial months were often difficult. With no time to lose, Buchholz brought in a facilitator for an all-day retreat. "The whole team made fun of me," she says, recalling a rare moment of early unanimity. "They told me they were not going to hug or sing 'Kumbaya,' but we got everything out in the open and made a commitment to work together more effectively." To help the process run more smoothly, she came up with a rule: if you couldn't solve a problem within three e-mails, you had to use the phone or set up a meeting. "E-mails are curt," she says. "They often sound rude, sometimes even intentionally. With smart people on a tight schedule, you can often accomplish more by picking up the phone or arranging a meeting, even if it takes a little longer."

"Karen is the reason it ran smoothly," says John Gattuso. "She created a great team environment, and when she didn't know something, she asked the right questions. She's a terrific communicator, which is even more valuable than experience."

Ralph, meanwhile, was actively involved behind the scenes, especially when it came to his twin passions—architecture and design. "Years ago, when we built our house in Elkins Park," says Suzanne, "he would sit with the architects for hours. He loved the whole process. He would whistle and hum, and I'd say, 'You should have been an architect.'"

But this was Brian's baby, and here, as with everything they worked on together, Ralph expressed his views without imposing them. "When he had something to say," says Bill Hankowsky, "he'd whisper to Brian without interrupting the meeting or taking the floor. He seemed to be saying, 'This is your project, but I'm happy to tell you what I think.'"

Ralph would have chosen a traditional and warmer look with plenty of wood, but he understood that Brian wanted a more contemporary feel, and he was pleased that Comcast had long outgrown the stage where a staid, conservative appearance would have reassured bankers and other lenders. "We didn't need the building to appear solid," he says, "because the company was solid. And although I initially objected to the high ceilings, which seemed impractical, I've come to enjoy them."

His excitement was apparent to everyone who worked on the building. When a large mock-up was constructed on the plaza in front of the construction site, Ralph climbed the steep stairs to examine the different kinds of glass being considered, returning a few hours later to see the same views after sunset. He wanted to ensure that the employees would enjoy wonderful views, while the exterior retained the shimmering effect that would make the building stand out.

Ralph was in his mid-eighties, but being around the construction site made him feel younger. Architect Graham Wyatt took him to the top of the building while it was still unfinished. "These are dangerous places," Wyatt says, "and here was this older man, slightly frail, on top of this huge tower in a construction elevator, totally undaunted. There were no finished walls or floors, but Ralph was as excited as a kid."

His biggest influence was on the upper part of the tower. In a meeting with the construction team, Ralph, who found the initial plan a bit staid, started doodling on a yellow pad, drawing slightly tapered versions of the higher floors. The current design, he said softly, was boxy. He raised his hands in the air, demonstrated a gentle tapering, and asked, "Why can't we do *this*?"

The others liked the idea, and here, too, Stern was flexible; in the months ahead, the architect and his team kept coming up with variations for Ralph to consider. "The tapering idea enhances the verticality and leads your eye up," says Stern. "We had some great conversations that went beyond problem solving."

Ralph was equally attentive to the building's interior. He and Buchholz flew to Chicago where, at the Merchandise Mart, they examined dozens of desks and chairs. Ralph tested every chair the only way he could—by sitting in it. "Our employees would be spending a lot of time in the building," he says, "so they might as well have a good seat."

From the start, Brian wanted a state-of-the-art, bright and open dining area that would serve as the nerve center of Comcast's new home and a daily meeting place for employees. Most companies put their cafeterias in the basement or on a low floor, but Brian thought the Comcast dining area—the word *cafeteria* was never used—should be high up, with marvelous views of the city. "He wanted every employee, no matter what floor they worked on, to have some of that beauty in their day," says Ralph, with obvious approval. The dining area would take up two floors, the forty-third and forty-fourth, with a stairway connecting them. "I've never seen that before," says Keith Rosen of Gensler, the architectural firm that designed many of the tower's interiors. "It's a real investment in the employees."

Brian had done his homework. During a trip to California, he and Steve Burke had had dinner at Google in a dining room Brian describes as "green, healthy, casual, and fun." In Manhattan he admired the variety, quality, and simplicity of the offerings at Davis Polk, Comcast's law firm. In Philadelphia, after visiting the dining room at the law firm headed by longtime board member Sheldon Bonovitz, who had named it Morris's after one of the firm's founders, Brian thought it would be a nice touch to call the Comcast dining area Ralph's Café. Everyone loved the idea, with the predictable exception of the man whose name would be on it. But when Brian said, "Trust me, Dad," he accepted the honor and soon came to enjoy it.

Ralph's is a magnificent space with huge windows and intoxicating views; it sits directly across from the elegant Pyramid Club on the fifty-second floor of the Mellon Center, which has long been known for its panoramic vistas of Philadelphia and beyond. The café's interior, designed by Karen Daroff, is equally striking. "We wanted it to be soothing and in harmony with the outdoors," she says, "with aqua, gray, taupe, and water imagery to give you the feeling of being up in the clouds, which in fact you are."

The effect is breathtaking. In the summer of 2008, Comcast hosted a late-afternoon reception at Ralph's for the National Governors Association. "Amazing," one of the governors told David Cohen as he gazed around the room. "How often do you use this facility?"

"Every day."

"Really? You have events like this every day?"

"Actually," Cohen said proudly, "this is where our employees have lunch."

The employees have embraced it. "These days," says Bret Perkins, "it's not hard to get people to meet me for breakfast." Perkins likes to sit on the east side, facing the Delaware River, because "it's serene in the morning, with the sun coming up as you watch the sparkling city return to life."

Comcasters enjoy the food, too—the quality as well as the range of offerings. They also appreciate the variety of seating arrangements. But above all they speak of the social and business benefits of Ralph's, and how even a five-minute conversation with someone from another part of the company can make a big difference in their day. "You're always running into someone you've been meaning to call," says Joe Waz, "and Ralph's provides a lot of cross-pollination." Marlene Dooner moved to Comcast Center just before the café opened, when the building felt to her like a body that didn't yet have a soul. But now, even on days when she picks up lunch and eats at her desk, she often ends up having a brief, impromptu meeting with someone she runs into at Ralph's.

Comcast University's Dan Gallagher enjoys walking into a place where he knows so many people; for all its beauty, Ralph's feels as comfortable as his old college cafeteria. At many other companies, says chief marketing officer Peter Intermaggio, working from home has become an accepted part of the culture, but at Comcast, people prefer to meet and interact in person. Ralph's makes that easier, he says, calling the café "a bit of a throwback to old-school values, when you did business face-to-face and shook hands with the other person."

Whatever the cost of building Ralph's, says Steve Burke, it was a great investment—for not only morale, but also productivity: "At lunch, maybe a thousand people aren't going to spend ten or fifteen minutes walking to and from a restaurant or waiting to be served." Initially, Burke didn't think a new building could have a major impact on the company's culture. Now he says, "I was wrong."

When Comcasters say that "everyone goes to Ralph's," they mean not only that the dining area attracts a high percentage of employees, but that it draws people from all levels of the company. "We like to

think that everyone here is part of the same team, with no prima donnas who eat in a more exclusive setting," said Stanley Wang, who had
planned to hold his retirement party at Ralph's, but who didn't live to
see that day.

The top executives may not have their own dining room, but they
do enjoy an elegant setting on the building's highest floors. Early on,
when somebody wondered aloud whether there would be any notice-
able difference in the views between the fifty-second and fifty-fifth
floors, David Cohen said he didn't think so, because all of these floors
would be higher than any other building in town. But Cohen, being
Cohen, didn't want to rely on assumptions—not even his own. "I'll
go up there and look," said the man who enjoys volunteering for unpopular missions. In the winter of 2006 there was no "there" yet, so
Cohen, accompanied by John Spitz from Liberty, went up in a bucket
attached to a crane, which is known as a man-basket, to check the
views from floors that hadn't yet been built. After they were strapped
into a special safety harness and began ascending into the freezing,
windy sky, Cohen turned to Spitz and shouted, "By the way, what
good is the harness if the bucket comes off?" Spitz explained that
the harness was there in case the wind blew the bucket upside down.
"But if the bucket comes off," he added, "we're dead." Aha, thought
Cohen, so *that's* why I had to sign a release. The other thing Cohen
learned on his soaring adventure was that just as he had guessed, there
was no discernible difference in the views from the various floors at
the top of the building. But now he knew for sure.

The height of the tower raised an unusual concern for the city's
many sports fans. For years there had been a gentleman's agreement
that no building in Philadelphia could exceed the height of the hat on
the massive, 27-ton statue of Pennsylvania's founder, William Penn,
on the top of City Hall. That accord had been broken with the building of One Liberty Place, which some residents believe was punished
by a curse: in the twenty years since William Penn was slighted, none
of the city's four major sports teams had won a championship. In
an attempt to end the Curse of Billy Penn, David Cohen suggested
that at the topping-off ceremony for what was now the city's tallest

building, a miniature version of the statue could be embedded at the top of the tower to appease the founder's spirit. The replica can't be seen, but everyone knows it's there, 975 feet above the ground. This was in 2007. A year later, the Philadelphia Phillies won the World Series.

Back on earth, the plaza in front of the building features a handsome fountain that is lit up at night and a large outdoor café with a kitchen embedded in a clear glass cube. The visitor who enters the building finds herself in a 120-foot atrium, looking up at a dramatic installation by the artist Jonathan Borofsky. *Humanity in Motion* consists of ten figures of various ages, races, and styles, each one walking across a different angled horizontal beam to convey the idea that every individual has a unique path that he or she must follow. In a whimsical touch, Borofsky added two figures on the floor, an African American father and his young son, who are looking up at the elevated pedestrians striding purposefully above the many commuters, employees, and visitors who are, in fact, doing the same thing down below.

But something was still missing. As the building was going up, Brian had dinner with the architect and designer Edwin Schlossberg, who looked at the plans and offered some advice. "I love what Stern is doing," he said, "but when you put your name on the building, it will change from being your office to being your home. And as with any new home, you'll want it to reflect who you are."

For the interior end of the lobby, between the security desk and the elevators, Schlossberg suggested a stunning, high-definition video screen. Brian loved it: What better symbol could there be for Comcast than a world-class screen, 83 feet wide and 25 feet high, that uses an advanced form of high definition with five times the resolution of the finest HD televisions? When it was unveiled at the official opening of Comcast Center in 2008, the images were so clear and vivid that many of the guests were certain that the figures moving on the wall in front of them were live, human dancers.

The obvious thing to do with this fantastic equipment was to promote the company, either by showing the best of cable television or by portraying all the things Comcast does. Instead, at Steve Burke's suggestion, Brian commissioned a series of short videos—scenes of both technology and nature, many of which were created by the acclaimed film and television producer David Niles. To avoid repeating programs, Niles arranged to show the images in computer-generated sequences that allow even daily visitors to experience something new every time. In reality, nothing is projected onto the screen. What visitors see are 30 million tiny lightbulbs turning on and off.

The videos are a gift from Comcast to the people of Philadelphia, and all day long, from six in the morning until midnight, tourists and residents alike flock to the lobby to enjoy the spectacle. "Doesn't it make you feel like you're in Tokyo, or someplace bigger, more technologically savvy?" said an early visitor. This was exactly the response Brian was hoping for. At the Panasonic building in Osaka, Japan, he had watched an employee tap a wall, which caused a video to spring to life; then, merely by waving her hand, she had sent that same image to another spot on the wall. He was inspired to offer something equally exciting in the company's new home, and he did: the Comcast Center screen soon joined the Liberty Bell, Independence Hall, and the Rocky statue as one of the city's must-see places.

During the 2008 holiday season, at the start of every hour between Thanksgiving and New Year's Day, the screen featured an eighteen-minute, high-tech, twenty-first-century incarnation of the old John Wanamaker Christmas Light Show, a long-standing and beloved Philadelphia tradition that ran for years in the city's most famous department store and continues now at Macy's. Over a hundred thousand people saw the first Comcast Holiday Spectacular, and Ralph liked to go down to the lobby for the sheer pleasure of watching all the visitors, many of them schoolchildren, enjoy the show. There were times when the place was so packed that it was difficult for employees to get in and out of the building. The holiday show became an annual event. In 2009, when the program was shown in 3-D, the company distributed more than 120,000 3-D glasses that were handed out by attendants in white gloves, holding red satchels. In 2011, more than 200,000 visitors watched the latest edition of the Holiday Spectacular.

The giant screen impresses even those who see it every day. "When I get off the train and come into the lobby," says Mary Cassidy, "I can't believe I work here. And when the people on the screen are clapping, I feel as if they're greeting me." Art Block says, "It puts a smile on your face to know that your company is putting a smile on the faces of so many people—and it makes you feel special to have a pass to go behind the scenes." Bill Dordelman takes that image a step further. Crossing the threshold in front of the commuters and tourists reminds him of the mysterious cornfield in *Field of Dreams*, which Ray Kinsella (played by Kevin Costner) can only wonder about as the ghostly ballplayers go in and out.

Employees have noticed something else about crossing from the public lobby into the private area. "It makes such a difference when the security guards wish you a good morning and say good-night," says Susan Honness. "They know you by name and treat you with respect. Coming or going, they make you feel welcome."

Well before the building opened, John Gattuso, Ralph, and Brian had agreed that employees and visitors alike should feel as if they were entering a five-star hotel, rather than just another office building. "We can teach security," says Liberty's Jim Birch, "but we can't teach people to be nice. So we started with employees who had a predisposition to provide customer service, and put together a team that was hospitality based." The security ambassadors, as they're known, worked with a Disney trainer and benefited from instruction by experts at two of the city's best hotels.

Employees moved into Comcast Center on eighteen successive Mondays, starting in December 2007. As each new cohort arrived, they were greeted at the door by Ralph, Brian, David Cohen, and Karen Buchholz. In the early weeks, the builders were still adding the finishing touches when suddenly, recalls Bernice McCann, "it stopped being a construction project and sprang to life as a commercial office building." McCann was part of a team of greeters who showed up every Monday morning to welcome another group. They wore big black buttons with an orange question mark and the words *ASK ME* in white letters, but there wasn't much to ask. By the time employees moved in, their names were on the doors, their furniture was ready, and their phones and computers were already working.

"The great thing about this place is that you never have to leave," says Ashton White, referring to the café, the coffee bar on the sixth floor, the third-floor fitness center with its portrait of Stanley Wang to honor all he did to make the building a success, and The Market at Comcast Center—an upscale food court one level below the atrium, on the way to the trains, where commuters can pick up a snack or even shop for dinner on their way home.

Above all, employees rave about the amazing views and the abundance of sunlight. When Dan Gallagher returned to 1500 Market Street for a meeting, he was struck by how dark and dull the building seemed, although he hadn't experienced it that way when he worked there. The company's new home, he says, feels like moving up to the main floor after you've been living in the basement.

The view can be startling, and so can your proximity to the sky—especially when a helicopter buzzes right past your window, close enough to see the pilot's face. "It's remarkable to watch a day unfold," says Jennifer Khoury, "from the morning sunrise to the changing sky of late afternoon. And then suddenly it's night, with the whole city lit up below."

The delicate balance that Brian had been striving for has been realized. "There's a bit of wow in here," says Bill Stemper, the head of business services, "but it's tastefully done." Dave Watson calls it "special without being *too* special."

The employees seem delighted to be working in a building that was so clearly constructed with them in mind. On nights and weekends they bring friends and families to show them the interior spaces. Comcast Center has already been a valuable recruiting tool, especially for young computer programmers who think first of Silicon Valley or New York, or younger engineers who might be attracted to companies like Google or Facebook. "Philadelphia isn't on their radar," Bill Dordelman says, "but when they see this place, with the café and that screen, the idea of moving here seems a lot more appealing."

Early in 2008, a woman came up to David Cohen at a party and said, "My neighbor's daughter works in the new Comcast building, and she loves her view."

"What's her name?" Cohen asked.

"Oh, you wouldn't know her," the woman said. "She's just a billing clerk."

Cohen couldn't have been happier. "That's exactly what we were hoping for," he says. "She loves the view although she's on a relatively low floor and doesn't have an outside office."

At the opening ceremony on June 6, 2008, John Gattuso paid tribute to the visionary Willard Rouse and told the invited audience that on a clear day, you could see the ocean from the top of the tower. Ralph acknowledged the thousands of construction workers who had built Comcast Center piece by piece and thanked Brian for his leadership. Brian saluted his father for his passion and unwavering optimism, and he described the new video screen as a once-in-a-lifetime opportunity for Comcast to show its gratitude to the city of Philadelphia. Then he smiled and said, "Welcome to our new house of dreams."

26

Elder Statesman

Oil Portrait of Ralph Roberts by Nelson Shanks

Not long ago, Ralph and David Cohen were on their way to lunch at Ralph's Café. As the elevator stopped at various floors, employees got in and greeted the company's founder, who responded warmly to each of them. When they were alone again, he turned to Cohen and said wistfully, "You know, there was a time when I knew everyone's name."

"Ralph," said Cohen, "the important thing is that they all know who you are."

Just as Comcast became a different company after the AT&T acquisition, Ralph became a different kind of leader. He was eighty-two when the Broadband deal closed in 2002, and his role has continued to evolve. The slow, gradual transition that began officially in 1990, when Brian became president, is still unfolding, as Ralph manages the graceful dance of stepping back a little more every year while continuing to be present and visible. On important decisions and initiatives, Brian and his colleagues make a point of keeping him informed. They still value his advice, but these days he is more likely to offer it privately.

The man who started out in 1963 with a small cable system in Tupelo finds it hard to believe how much, and how fast, his company has grown. When the Broadband deal closed, Ralph and Steve Burke were examining some figures, including the total number of Comcast employees, which came to around 68,000. "It must be a typo," Ralph said. "We can't possibly have that many people." But the number was correct, and by late 2011 Comcast had more than 125,000 employees.

Although Ralph isn't the type to hold forth about his business philosophy, or even to explain why Comcast has prospered, he once told Burke that a big part of his success "is the result of holding my tongue." He has always been able to exercise restraint, both at home and at work, but in his later years he has ventured a little further down that road. In important meetings he often says little. This is partly due to problems with his vocal cords, which sometimes make it difficult to talk. He has also experienced some hearing loss, which makes him reluctant to speak, because he doesn't want to repeat what somebody else may have said. There is a modesty in that reserve: many men in his position would insist on speaking anyway.

But even when he doesn't say much, he communicates a great deal. When employees see him, either at Comcast Center or on visits to the field, he is a living symbol of the company's values and a reminder of how successful businessmen used to carry themselves. "Ralph represents a more modest era," says Kate Noel, "when business leaders didn't put themselves on display. He comes from a world where showboating is unimaginable."

His courtesy is a nod to the vanishing art of being a gentleman. He is chivalrous, holding doors for women and stepping back to let others go first. He acknowledges every gift, every note, and every card he receives, to the point where sometimes, says his longtime assistant

Joan French, "it feels like we are saying thank you even for thank-you notes."

In spontaneous encounters, he retains his energetic sociability. "He loves walking the city," says French, who adds that Ralph will often mention the people who have stopped him on the street or the conversations he's had with complete strangers. Many of them are customers, and if they mention a problem or a complaint, he asks for their phone number and makes sure they'll hear from someone who can help.

He has long been able to joke about aging. A few years earlier, at a cable convention, Ralph and E!'s Lee Masters were walking the floor together. Masters, who loves gadgets, watched as Ralph took a small black item from his pocket, tapped it lightly, and put it back. Masters asked Ralph what it was.

"You don't have one of these?" Ralph said. He handed it to Masters and said, "Have a look, but don't press any buttons." Masters examined the device but couldn't find any hint as to what it might be. Finally, Ralph put him out of his misery: "It's a hearing aid."

"He was happy to tell me," says Masters, "but he wanted to have a little fun with me first."

If he has complaints about getting older, he doesn't share them, preferring to focus on the many blessings in his life. He likes to say that he intends to stay active "as long as I'm vertical." He is proud of his age: when Karen Buchholz told him she was going to a celebration for her in-laws' fiftieth wedding anniversary, Ralph laughed and said, "Ah, they're just kids."

His own marriage, dating from 1942, continues to make him happy. In nicer weather, he and Suzanne like to spend long weekends at their horse farm in Chester County, where they are sometimes joined by assorted children, grandchildren, and friends. (Ralph had hoped to live there, but Suzanne thought they should split their time between the farm and their Center City apartment.) For years he loved riding horses, building on a skill he had learned as a boy in New Rochelle, and participating enthusiastically in fox hunts—the kind, he hastens to point out, where the fox is chased but not killed. But after a couple of falls in his late seventies, he and the horses agreed to an amicable separation.

He loves the farm, especially the replication of an antique house that was constructed from scratch, "from the basement to the roof," he says proudly. He and Suzanne decided to build it when they couldn't find exactly what they wanted (or more accurately, what Ralph wanted), which was an authentic eighteenth-century farmhouse on a beautiful piece of land. Except for modern amenities like electricity, running water, banisters on the stairs, and a couple of well-hidden television screens, their weekend home is an accurate reproduction of a house from the Federal era. Ralph loves antiques and has an appreciation for old-world craftsmanship. Some people go to another place to relax; he likes to visit another era.

When the house was finished, Ralph and Suzanne started collecting objects from before 1750—paintings, drawings, silverware, dishes, and pottery. They used to attend antique shows to look for items that seem appropriate for the farm. Ralph loves being there so much that whenever they travel and find themselves in a beautiful spot, he will turn to Suzanne and ask, "Do you think this beats the farm?"

Although he spends less time in the office than he used to, he is more conspicuous than ever at Comcast Center, where his impact seems to grow by the month. "He adds another dimension now," says Larry Smith. "People feel good when they see him, which is great for morale." When he speaks, either to a visiting group or to employees around the country, he generates real excitement. What he offers isn't exactly charisma; he's never been a spellbinding orator. It's his genuineness and his warmth that people respond to again and again.

"We see him as a pioneer and a visionary," says Bill Stemper, "and he provides a natural inspiration even when he doesn't say a word. With Ralph, there's no veneer. It's pure hardwood. What you see on the surface goes all the way through."

He represents integrity, and some Comcasters have been known to ask themselves, in difficult situations, "What would Ralph do?"

These days, says David Cohen, one of Ralph's roles "is to remind us that a corporation can have a heart, a soul, and a set of values."

"He's a national treasure," says Grace Killelea. "Our DNA, the core of who we are, comes from Ralph, and our employees adore him. We live in a culture where businessmen in their eighties, the captains of industry, aren't so visible anymore. Think of all the CEOs who have gone to jail or were involved in scandals, and then look at Ralph."

His knack for connecting with the workforce hasn't diminished with age. In June 2007 the Houston Region held a brand launch for 2,300 new Comcasters who had recently come over from Time Warner Cable. Brian introduced Ralph, who received the usual rousing reception and standing ovation. He began by saying that Brian had told him on the plane that he shouldn't be too formal in his remarks, that he should loosen up a bit because this was Texas, after all. And then Ralph did something nobody at the company had ever seen him do before: he untied his bow tie and removed it. The employees, who knew he was doing this for them and having a little fun at his own expense, roared their approval.

A month later, in July, the South Division of Comcast University held its annual four-day meeting in Naples, Florida. Sandie Zeigler, who ran the event, wanted to ask Ralph to address the group. "You can invite him," her boss said, "but he's eighty-seven, so don't expect him to make the trip." The morning after Zeigler sent Ralph an e-mail, he accepted, but she decided to keep his visit a surprise. As Ralph waited in the wings, Dan Gallagher from the home office told a hundred and fifty Comcast University employees about a class he had taught recently back in Philadelphia. The group needed a break, Gallagher said, so he took them out for a walk around the block. They came to a hot dog stand. "And who do you think we ran into, buying a hot dog?" he asked.

"Ralph!" said the audience, answering as one. Gallagher had counted on that.

Just then the side door opened and Ralph entered the room. "Does anyone have a hot dog?" he asked.

The employees were on their feet, yelling and clapping, although some of them weren't buying it. Why would Ralph Roberts, at his age, be coming to Florida in the heat of the summer? But they went along with the gag and welcomed what they believed was a very convincing impersonator.

When the conference was over, Zeigler started receiving e-mails about the unexpected visitor. John Underhill from Little Rock wrote: "Mr. Roberts walking into that room was like me walking on the moon, something I have dreamed about but thought would never happen. In all my life I have never been so speechless." Cecile Carroll from West Palm Beach wrote: "The tears welled up and the goose bumps just flowed through my body. I looked around the room and saw that I wasn't the only one feeling that way."

Ralph doesn't mind speaking, but he would just as soon be listening and learning. In the winter of 2006, when he and Suzanne were vacationing with friends in Sarasota, Florida, he looked up the number of the local Comcast office in the phone book and asked the customer service agent who answered if she would please get a message to Steve Dvoskin, the regional vice president. It was a Sunday, and when Dvoskin heard that Ralph Roberts was looking for him, he worried that something was terribly wrong. When he returned the call, Ralph told him he would like to visit the office.

"It's Sunday," said Dvoskin. "Did you mean today, or would you rather come tomorrow?"

"Would it be all right if I came tomorrow?"

Dvoskin couldn't quite believe it. You're the founder of the company, he wanted to say. You can do whatever you want.

On Monday Ralph spent hours talking with the employees, many of whom asked to have their picture taken with him. If he saw a family photograph on someone's desk, he would ask that person to tell him about it. He still loves to spend time with the frontline workers who deal directly with the customers, and he stayed at the office until Suzanne finally called and said, "Can somebody get Ralph back to the hotel?"

He is so popular with the ladies that Bob Pick calls him "the Tom

Jones of cable." Not long ago, on Comcast Cares Day, Pick watched in amazement as employees at all levels, women and men alike, flocked to Ralph, lining up to shake his hand or pose for a picture with him.

He travels less these days, which is why he can often be found in the Comcast Center video studio, taping greetings and other messages for conferences and meetings. "He's a perfectionist," says internal communications director Mary Beth Casey. "After a perfectly good take, he'll say, 'I was awful. Let's do it again.'" He is very conscious of how he comes across, and he's especially concerned that anyone might think he is talking down to his audience, although nobody has ever thought that he was.

Above all, he wants to be personal. At one taping, when Ralph was asked to deliver a message on the same topic that would be shown at four different meetings, he insisted on shooting four separate versions, one for each group. He's always willing to do more, and to try another take if there's a chance of making it better.

He likes to tinker with the script to make sure he sounds like himself. "He doesn't just say what we suggest," says Amy Riley, who works on his video appearances. As he has always done, Ralph speaks simply and conversationally, and goes out of his way to avoid jargon or even acronyms.

He has always fretted over his bigger speeches. In the days leading up to a speaking engagement, says Joan French, "that's about all we do. He'll take a professionally written speech and make it his own." And whether it's a full speech or a brief greeting, live or on tape, he invariably returns to his favorite topic—the feeling of belonging to a family.

He is surprisingly strong and vigorous for his age. In 2003, shortly after Kerry Knott joined the company's government affairs office in Washington, Ralph came to town for a lobbying program called Comcast in the Capital. "We were amazed at his energy," says Knott, who accompanied Ralph to a dozen meetings in a single day at various office buildings on Capitol Hill. After dinner a few people went back to the office to plan the next day's schedule, and Ralph asked if he could join them. As Knott puts it, "Nobody minds working until midnight if the founder is there with them."

And he never seems to tire of meeting new people. Every evening during the 2000 Republican National Convention in Philadelphia, Ralph would go over to public policy executive Jim Coltharp in the Comcast suite at the convention hall and ask, "Jim, when can we go to the parties?"

He shows up at tough times, too. When Hurricane Katrina struck in 2005, Ralph flew to Mississippi to meet with employees in Hattiesburg, which was especially hard hit. The mayor was in tears as he told Ralph that the community had been devastated, and that the first thing he had seen after the storm was a Comcast truck, whose driver got out and asked, "How can I help?" In Meridian, every single employee wanted a picture with Ralph, who signed shirts, hats, and pieces of paper. Ralph thanked them all for working so hard to help restore essential services to the city.

"He's indefatigable," says Julian. "Twenty or thirty years ago he told me he wanted to live to a hundred. On his eighty-ninth birthday, I sent him an e-mail reminding him that he was only eleven years from his short-term goal."

In March 2008, at Comcast's quadrennial management conference in Arizona, just before his eighty-eighth birthday, Ralph refused even to consider not showing up, although he was so sick with the flu that he had to be hospitalized during the event. When he wasn't in the hospital, he attended every session. Although the speakers included Oprah Winfrey, banker Jamie Dimon, General Colin Powell, and Ted Turner, the conference couldn't end without an appearance by the company's founder. As the four-day program was ending, Ralph dragged himself to the podium, looking so tired and weak that many in the audience feared they might never see him again.

But even then he conveyed his characteristic optimism. "The future is incredibly bright," he told the group. "I've seen good times and bad times. Good times get better. Bad times pass away." He ended by saying, "See you in four years. Get back to work!" A few weeks later, at the annual cable conference in New Orleans, he was at the bar with Julian at two in the morning, looking as strong and as fit as ever.

A few months later, near the end of 2008, he tripped while playing tennis and broke his hip, which led to an emergency hip replacement. "That was hard for him," says Aileen Roberts, "because he's always been the caregiver, never the recipient." But he recovered quickly and returned to the office a few weeks later, walking with a cane, which made him look even more like a classic Philadelphia gentleman. In the spring of 2009, he was traveling around the country again, meeting with groups of employees to promote the company's new Credo, and although he looked a little frail, he seemed to be even sharper than before. "He's made his peace with being older," says Aileen. "These are bonus years, and he's thankful for every day."

Ralph remains what he has always been: a happy warrior. Although he doesn't seek attention, he has no trouble enjoying it. An interviewer once asked him to explain why a thousand employees had just greeted him with a standing ovation.

"Darned if I know," said Ralph, who then gave a more serious answer: "I think they sense that I believe what I preach, that they're part of my family and I'm part of theirs. It sounds corny, but it's true. I like the people at Comcast, and I respect them, and I hope they know how much they mean to me."

27

A New Beginning

Brian Williams, Ralph Roberts, and Steve Burke

Do content and distribution belong together? Even as other media companies were moving to separate the two, Brian Roberts and Steve Burke continued to see them as natural partners that strengthened and enhanced each other. As Burke puts it, "The best businesses in entertainment are cable channels, because they have a dual revenue stream. If we weren't trying to figure out how to get bigger in that area, we wouldn't be doing our job."

Comcast had tried to build up its content portfolio in 2003, when Vivendi auctioned off a package of its media assets, and again in 2004, with the pursuit of Disney. When neither effort succeeded, the search for content continued.

Well before Vivendi and Disney, Ralph and Brian had been interested in NBC. Bob Wright, who headed the company from 1986 (when GE bought it from RCA) until 2007, was president of Cox in the early 1980s. Back then, when cable networks were in their infancy, he and Ralph had talked about investing together in Bravo and several regional sports channels. Years later, when Wright was running NBC, Ralph and Brian went to see him to let him know that if GE ever considered selling, Comcast would be interested. Although Wright thought that made sense, it wasn't his call. All he could tell his visitors was that CEO Jack Welch seemed to have no interest in a sale.

Brian remained patient. In 2001, when Jeff Immelt succeeded Welch as head of GE, Brian and Steve Burke paid him a visit. (Burke and Immelt had been classmates at Harvard Business School.) When they raised the possibility of acquiring NBC, Immelt said he had no plans to sell the company. Undeterred, Brian called Immelt from time to time to remind him of his interest. Only when GE outbid Comcast and the other contenders for Vivendi Universal Entertainment in 2003, and merged its assets with NBC to create NBC Universal, did Brian stop calling—but only for a while.

When he resumed, he found that on one or two occasions, Immelt seemed open to exploring the idea. Years earlier, Brian's inability to buy MediaOne turned out to be a blessing in disguise when Comcast ended up with all their subscribers, plus a great many more, in the AT&T deal. Was it possible that a similar scenario was unfolding here, with NBC becoming even more attractive—and possibly more available—in its new, expanded form?

When Michael Angelakis came to Comcast in 2007, the new CFO and his team started thinking about how the company could expand in directions other than cable distribution, where there wasn't much room left to grow. They identified three areas that seemed especially appropriate for new investments: wireless, business services, and content. As an initial effort to become more active in wireless, Comcast, together with Time Warner Cable, Google, Intel, and Bright House Networks, teamed up with Sprint to invest in Clearwire, a wireless data service provider. The company also beefed up its new business services division under Bill Stemper, who had previously been at Cox. But when it came to content, Angelakis and his colleagues knew that the only way to make significant progress was through a major acquisition.

And there weren't many ways to do that. Time Warner owned some wonderful assets, including HBO, Cinemax, and the former Turner properties—CNN, TBS, Turner Classic Movies, and Cartoon Network. But Time Warner had just spun off Time Warner Cable to focus on content, so that option was out. There was National Amusements, Sumner Redstone's company, which controlled both CBS and Viacom (which owned MTV, Nickelodeon, Showtime, and other properties), but Redstone, who is known for the phrase "content is king," had no interest in selling.

Disney, whose assets included the ABC television network, ESPN, and The Disney Channel, had already rejected a Comcast bid. Rupert Murdoch had recently purchased Dow Jones, which owned the *Wall Street Journal*, so he seemed to be a buyer of content, rather than a seller, which presumably ruled out Fox and his other media properties. The Scripps properties included Food Network, Home & Garden Television, and the Travel Channel, but this was a smaller package than Comcast had in mind, and it wasn't for sale.

That left NBC Universal, and as Brian had been told repeatedly, it wasn't for sale, either. But that was before the economic earthquake of 2008. With GE's stock falling sharply and its credit arm, GE Capital, caught in the financial turmoil, a consensus was growing that Jeff Immelt might decide to shore up his company's balance sheet by selling its programming assets and concentrating on its core industrial businesses.

In addition to Universal Studios and its theme parks, and the NBC television network, with its prestigious news division and its legacy of great sitcoms, these properties included the highly successful USA Network, whose offerings were so broad and so popular that it sometimes resembled a conventional broadcast network. NBC Universal's other holdings included Telemundo, the country's second-largest Spanish-language broadcast network, as well as Bravo, CNBC, MSNBC, Syfy (formerly the Sci-Fi Channel), Oxygen, and interests in both The Weather Channel and A&E.

In early March 2009, Brian and Angelakis were in New York for a wide-ranging conversation at JPMorgan Chase with investment banker Jimmy Lee and Jamie Dimon, the bank's CEO. (Dimon, too, had been a business school classmate of Steve Burke's, and Burke has been on the board of JPMorgan Chase since 2003.) The recession had worsened, and March was an abysmal month for the American economy. With the stock market about to hit a twelve-year low, the conversation began with an assessment of the financial meltdown.

When the talk turned to Comcast, Jimmy Lee asked, as a number of other bankers had also been asking Brian, "Have you thought about trying to buy NBC?"

"We've been thinking about it for years," said Brian, who added that he had been talking regularly to Jeff Immelt but hadn't made much progress.

"I'm having breakfast with him tomorrow at our media conference," Lee said. "Would you like me to bring this up?"

Brian said yes. And Lee called him the next day to say that Immelt was interested in talking.

This was good news, but Brian was cautious. He had learned the hard way that conversations that begin with one potential buyer often end up as an auction with several bidders, which was a scenario he was determined to avoid. It had happened most recently with his pursuit of AT&T Broadband, although that may have been unavoidable after Comcast's bold approach.

"I'd like Jeff to be talking only to us," Brian told Lee. "I'd like to hear from him that this will be a monogamous conversation." It was a bold request, but he had little to lose by making it. In addition to avoiding an auction, Brian wanted to prevent a leak, especially early on, before anyone knew if a deal was even possible. GE had recently reversed its stated intention to sell its credit card division, and letting go of NBC Universal, if it happened at all, would not be easy. It would be embarrassing if a leak occurred and there was no deal.

A day later Brian was in the lobby of a hotel in Baltimore, where his younger daughter was playing in a squash tournament, when Immelt called. After assuring Brian that he would talk only to Comcast, Immelt made a request of his own. Because he, too, was concerned about leaks, he asked Brian to tell as few people as possible that the two companies would be talking. Brian, of course, was more than happy to make that pledge.

The first meeting took place a few days later, when Immelt came to the Four Seasons Hotel in Philadelphia with GE's CFO Keith Sherin, and Pam Daley, GE's primary corporate development officer, to talk with Brian and Angelakis. Among other things, Immelt said that if GE were to sell NBC Universal, the price would be $30 billion, a number that struck their hosts as rather high.

"We can't do it," Angelakis told Brian after the meeting. "We can't raise that kind of money in this economy." And even if they could, he added, such a large expenditure was too risky. "What we should be discussing with them," he said, "is some kind of joint venture."

Brian had been thinking the same thing. As much as he wanted NBC Universal to be part of Comcast, he wasn't about to bet the company.

The conversation continued in April at Angelakis's home in suburban Philadelphia, where Keith Sherin, Pam Daley, and Jimmy Lee met with Angelakis, Bob Pick, and Steve Burke. Although Lee was working for GE, Brian didn't send a banker; both sides trusted Lee, and the smaller the group, the easier it was to protect the secret. "This was as tight a circle as we've ever had," says Art Block, one of several senior Comcast executives who wasn't yet in the loop.

In the early stages of a secret deal, the various parties are often referred to by alphabetically appropriate code names. In Project Crimson, as the potential acquisition of NBC Universal was known at Comcast—it was named for the fact that Burke, Immelt, and Dimon had all been together at Harvard—Comcast was Crimson, GE was Green, NBC Universal was Navy, Telemundo was Teal, and Vivendi, which still owned 20 percent of NBC Universal, was known as Violet. Initially, GE insiders referred to the potential deal as Project

Enterprise and used initials for individual companies, but they soon adopted the names that Comcast was using.

It quickly became clear that this conversation would be enormously complicated. "There were so many issues," says GE's Keith Sherin. "What's the structure? What's the valuation? What's the governance? And if Comcast is buying only part of a joint venture, how do we get out later, and at what price?"

At the April meeting, Sherin brought a summary of the NBC Universal companies, and the Comcast executives signed a nondisclosure agreement. The Philadelphians asked questions and the visitors answered them, although not with the degree of detail that Comcast would have liked. "A lot of the answers were housed inside NBC Universal," says Angelakis, and for months, because of the high level of confidentiality, nobody there knew the division might be sold. The way GE was structured, there was little public information about its programming assets, so due diligence would have to wait.

The Comcast team had in mind a joint venture to which GE would contribute all of NBC Universal, and Comcast would contribute its own programming assets (including E!, the Golf Channel, Versus, Style, G4, and its regional sports networks, along with Fandango and DailyCandy from Comcast Interactive Media), plus enough cash to give Comcast a 51 percent ownership share. Over time, Comcast would be able to buy out GE's 49 percent interest.

The meeting at Angelakis's house was followed by an unsettled period, when it sometimes seemed to the Comcast team that the other side had lost interest. "GE was going through some big ups and downs," says Brian, "and the negotiations started to yo-yo as well." He brought in Morgan Stanley banker Paul Taubman, who had advised Comcast on other large transactions. Later on, GE hired Gene Sykes of Goldman Sachs, who was especially helpful in the company's dealings with Vivendi.

This was a big and complex transaction, and the principals, who operated in very different worlds, didn't know each other well. Not surprisingly, both sides were nervous. "We didn't want to start a process we couldn't finish," says Keith Sherin, "and we knew there would be pressure from Comcast shareholders when the word got out." As spring turned into summer, Jimmy Lee suggested that Ralph, in his role as Comcast's founder and elder statesman, might want to assure Jeff Immelt in a face-to-face conversation that his company had every intention of completing the deal.

In early July Brian was in Israel for his fifth appearance at the Maccabiah Games, this time with his younger daughter, a member of the junior girls' squash team. While he was away, Ralph and Steve Burke flew to Sun Valley, Idaho, for the annual Allen & Company media conference, which Immelt was also attending. "He was aware that many deals don't get concluded," says Ralph, "and he wanted some reassurance from the father of the groom that we wouldn't let this opportunity slip through our fingers."

Even in Idaho, the two sides had to meet covertly. Jeff Zucker, the head of NBC Universal, who was also at the conference, was still not aware that GE was talking to Comcast about the future of his company. This was no small achievement: although two major corporations were discussing a huge media deal, the secret ultimately held for almost six months.

Immelt and Jimmy Lee were waiting in a condo near the golf course when Ralph and Burke arrived. Immelt was dressed informally in a polo shirt; Ralph, as always, appeared in a bow tie. "Jeff," he told Immelt, "I've done a lot of deals in my life. Every deal has its time, and this is the time for this deal." Recalling that conversation later, Ralph said, "it's easy to sell something when you know it's true."

In late July, back at the Four Seasons in Philadelphia, the GE team made clear that the $30 billion valuation for their content assets was nonnegotiable, and that they needed some protection from Comcast with regard to the back end. But they were flexible on several other points, including the idea of a joint venture and the valuation of the Comcast assets that would go into the new company. And if the value of the joint venture appreciated over the next few years, they were willing for Comcast to receive a higher share of that increase in exchange for its willingness to value GE's remaining shares at a small market premium. In the event that the joint venture could not raise the necessary financing to buy out GE, Comcast agreed to commit a certain amount of its own capital to purchase those shares.

It was an elegant solution, but there were still unanswered questions. Which company should manage the new venture, and what rights would the minority partner have? When, and under what terms, could GE sell its remaining stake in NBC Universal? And how would the partners arrive at a price for the 49 percent share that Comcast would acquire a few years down the road?

These complicated issues were not easily resolved. The talks didn't end, exactly, but for a while they seemed dead. The Comcast team started working on creative solutions that might get the process back on track.

Then Angelakis engaged in some shuttle diplomacy. As it happened, he and Immelt both had vacation homes in South Carolina, and on his next visit, they played golf together. "Although Keith Sherin was the negotiator," says Angelakis, "it was important to float our new ideas to Jeff to see how he responded." Immelt, who clearly wanted to do the deal, encouraged Angelakis to put those ideas on paper and show them to Sherin. Back in Philadelphia, Angelakis, Brian, Bob Pick, and Paul Taubman, with suggestions by board member Sheldon Bonovitz, drew up a revised proposal that they hoped would be acceptable to GE.

"Let's take another stab at it," Angelakis told Sherin on the phone. "I'd like to show you a few ideas I discussed with Jeff."

It was August, and Sherin, who was vacationing on Cape Cod, invited Angelakis to visit him there. Angelakis flew to Hyannis and drove to Sherin's house in Chatham, where they sat together and went through Comcast's latest proposal, a three-page document that outlined potential solutions to five major issues. "This is constructive," Sherin said. After a little horse-trading, he added, "I think we could do this." They drove to dinner in separate cars so each of them could consult with his boss.

Brian was at Jake's, a Philadelphia restaurant, when his cell phone rang. "Here's what we worked out," Angelakis said. "I think we should take it if we can."

Brian listened to the details and quickly agreed. "Mike's visit saved the deal," he says.

Three days later, on the night of August 13, Immelt and Sherin had a phone conversation with Brian and Angelakis. With no lawyers or bankers on the call, the four principals ironed out the major terms of the agreement. Now a few more executives at both companies were let in on the secret.

By the end of August, the broad outlines were clear. GE's programming assets would be valued at $30 billon, and Comcast's at $7.25 billion. Because GE was planning to borrow $9 billion against its assets and to withdraw that amount from the joint venture, Comcast had to put up only $6.5 billion in cash, in addition to its programming assets, for a 51 percent share of the new NBC Universal.

When the deal closed, Comcast would manage the new company. Over the next seven years, NBC Universal would have the primary obligation to purchase GE's stake, with Comcast having a secondary obligation to invest up to $5.75 billion to assist it in doing so, if that became necessary. But if the new NBC Universal performed well enough, it would generate enough cash that Comcast would not have to invest any additional funds. This structure provided strength and flexibility for Comcast—a point that wasn't lost on the investment community.

Throughout these months, a big, unresolved issue had been looming over the talks: Vivendi still owned 20 percent of NBC Universal and had the right to veto a deal. Unless Vivendi and GE could agree on a price at which GE could acquire Vivendi's stake, Immelt would be forced to take the company public. "This is our problem, not yours," he assured Brian. "No matter what price we work out with Vivendi, it won't affect *our* deal." Brian appreciated that commitment, which wasn't something a deal maker could take for granted.

On the Tuesday before Thanksgiving, Immelt and Sherin flew to Paris, where they negotiated a price with Vivendi and returned home in time for the holiday. Until then, the very real possibility of an IPO had given GE a reason to begin exploring valuations of the various NBC Universal companies without arousing suspicion that a private sale was in the works.

In most deals, due diligence is conducted early on. Here, because of the danger of leaks, it didn't begin until the fall. The extra caution was warranted: on September 30, 2009, news of the deal broke on TheWrap.com, an entertainment news website.

As the process moved forward, some of the negotiations proved difficult, especially in the late innings. "As deals come to their end," Jimmy Lee says, "small things can take on an exaggerated importance."

All during these talks, relations remained cordial among the four men at the top—Brian, Angelakis, Immelt, and Sherin. There were, however, some rough moments a level or two down. As Bob Pick describes it, "GE is like an eight-hundred-pound gorilla that's used to getting its way, and here they ran into a five-hundred-pound gorilla that pushes back." It wasn't always pretty, and it certainly wasn't easy, but the deal got done. "As tough-minded as we are," says Art Block, "we are also practical, and we know how to compromise. There's a goal to reach, and we try to remember that the other side often has a valid point—one that we would be making in their situation."

When problems came up that the teams were unable to resolve, the Group of Four settled them. At one point Sherin returned to Angelakis's house, where they resolved several outstanding issues at the kitchen table. There were more of these issues than Pick and Block would have liked, but, as Block notes, "They were just as frustrated with us."

"Often," says Paul Taubman, "the larger the deal, the simpler it is, but not here. And because it involved NBC, there was so much public interest that we were negotiating in a fishbowl."

Even the end was difficult. On December 2, 2009, the final night of negotiations, Bob Pick was leading the Comcast team at the law offices of Davis Polk. In the wee hours of the morning, the remaining details took so long to resolve that Pick was forced to delay the planned 6:00 a.m. press release until the remaining tax issues were settled. "We've worked all night before," says Pick, "but never like this."

Comcast's leaders didn't get much sleep, either. Brian and Burke kept calling and texting to see if the deal was finally done. "It's a binary event," says Burke. "If the deal gets signed, the rest of your life is changed." There were times that night when he wondered if that was ever going to happen.

If it did, his life would change dramatically. After running Comcast's cable division for eleven years, Burke was ready for a new challenge. Before joining Comcast, he was slated to become president of ABC, and almost everything else in his background pointed to the same conclusion: Steve Burke was the ideal person to run the new, expanded NBC Universal—which, when the deal finally closed, would be known as NBCUniversal.

The cable division would need a new president, and Brian had a candidate in mind. As a board member of the National Cable & Telecommunications Association, he had come to know and respect Neil Smit, the CEO of Charter Communications, the nation's fourth-largest cable company. Charter, which was based in St. Louis with customers in twenty-five states, had been burdened with a crushing debt load and serious operational problems, and in 2005 they brought in Smit to turn things around. He did it by guiding the company through a structured bankruptcy, hiring a new team of senior people, and paying special attention to customer service.

"I wanted a change agent," Brian says. "I was also looking for an operator and a leader. Neil had learned the cable business and he understood the Internet. He struck me as smart, decisive, disciplined, and fair."

Smit, who grew up on a Connecticut farm, attended Duke University on an ROTC scholarship. When he graduated in 1980, he joined the Navy SEALs, the elite special operations force. He was a SEAL for six years, where he formed the first counterterrorist team and rose to the rank of lieutenant commander. Navy SEALs are known for their emphasis on teamwork, and Smit offers a vivid description of what that really means: "On a long run in the sand, if you're out in front and you don't go back to help the guy who's trailing behind, and put him on your shoulders, if necessary, then you aren't doing your job. If everybody isn't performing together, you need to help the person who's struggling."

After the navy, and a degree from Tufts University's Fletcher School of Law and Diplomacy, he joined a crisis management company, where he specialized in kidnap negotiations. Then came a stint at Pillsbury, where he worked on security, insurance, and business services. After turning around Pillsbury's Mexican operation, followed by an assignment in Argentina, he took a job with the Latin American division of Nabisco.

In 2000 he joined America Online, where he held a number of positions before going over to Charter. When Brian and Steve Burke invited Neil and Barbara Smit to Philadelphia to talk about his moving to Comcast, Barbara encouraged her husband to take the job. "Once your ego gets over no longer being CEO of a seven-billion-dollar company," she told him, "I think you'll like it here." He didn't need much persuading. "I found a can-do attitude and a spirit of innovation," he says. "These are smart people with good values."

The feeling seems to be mutual. "Neil is one of the most effective operating leaders I've ever known," says Dave Watson. "He makes sure people have the right focus and the right resources to get the job done, and he clears out the impediments. He's relentless on execution: he'll give you the responsibility to get it done, and he'll hold you responsible for the results." Amy Smith, who heads the company's Florida Region, says that Smit "has clearly found our pain points and is determined to fix them."

Smit reorganized the technology side of the company and stepped on the gas. He moves quickly. "That sounds good," he'll say after being briefed on a project. "Now, instead of doing it in six months, do it in three."

From the start, Brian and the executive team knew that reaching an agreement with GE was only the first step. Acquiring control of NBC Universal would also require the approval of the government, specifically, the Justice Department and the FCC. A decade earlier, Comcast's acquisition of AT&T Broadband, a classic horizontal merger and a bigger deal than this one (in dollar terms), had taken more than a year to receive regulatory approval, although relatively few conditions had been imposed. This transaction was largely a vertical one: a company whose primary business was distribution was merging with a content company. But although there were fewer antitrust issues, this deal would be closely scrutinized for other reasons.

In part because of concerns about consolidation and the potential removal of disparate voices, media transactions tend to generate significant attention and commentary from a variety of third parties. And because one of the media's favorite subjects is the media, the approval process would generate a great deal of coverage. With the added novelty of a cable company acquiring a broadcast network, consumer groups and other advocacy organizations would also be eager to weigh in.

Moreover, this would be the first major corporate transaction to be considered during the Obama Administration, when not only the White House but also the House and Senate were in Democratic hands. The approval process would likely have been considerably easier had it occurred a year or two earlier.

On an intellectual level, everyone at Comcast understood what was coming, even if it was difficult to imagine the full extent of the gathering storm. Joe Waz, who was responsible for the company's public policy activities, sent a memo to his colleagues noting that this transaction would attract far more attention and opposition than anything they had experienced. Even so, Waz believed that with sufficient preparation and intelligent planning, the deal would go through.

The effort to secure the government's approval was led by David Cohen, Joe Waz, and two executives in the company's Washington, D.C., office. Melissa Maxfield, who headed Comcast's federal legislative affairs team and formerly worked for Senator Tom Daschle, was responsible for the legislative side of the effort. Although Congress had no role in the approval process, both the House and the Senate would be holding public hearings on the merger, and their goodwill (or at least the absence of organized and sustained opposition) would be hugely important. Kathy Zachem had joined Comcast from a Washington, D.C., telecommunications law firm that she had co-founded. With her extensive experience, she was the ideal person to represent the company at both the FCC and the Justice Department.

Because of the enormity of the task they were facing, the Comcast team decided to try something that is rarely done in this situation. Instead of waiting for the FCC to impose conditions on the deal, the company announced a set of voluntary conditions that it promised to honor. Initially, not everybody at Comcast agreed with this approach: Why make commitments in advance, some executives asked, if the government was only going to add to them later?

"This will be a battle from Day One," David Cohen explained. "If we're proactive, and we take the first step, we won't be playing defense. We can control the conversation by showing that we under-stand the likely concerns and are responsive to them. By making clear that we 'get it,' we can create a sense of momentum that the transac-tion will be approved—that it's only a question of when, and with what reasonable conditions."

On December 3, 2009, when the deal was announced, Comcast released a five-page memo promising, among other things:

- that the NBC television network, along with the local stations it owned and operated, would continue to be free, over-the-air channels, and would not become cable networks;
- that the network and its stations would expand their ongoing commitments to local programming, including news and public affairs;
- that Comcast would respect the independence of NBC's news and public affairs programming; and
- that new, independent networks would be added to the Comcast channel lineup.

Later in the process, Comcast and NBC Universal made addi-tional, voluntary, "social" commitments, promising to run public service announcements on childhood obesity and other issues, to improve parental controls, and to help bridge the digital divide by launching a unique broadband adoption program for low-income families. The company was also able to negotiate fair and reasonable conditions in three substantive areas—net neutrality, program access, and online video.

The voluntary commitments proved to be highly effective. Another major factor in getting the transaction approved was the company's decision to encourage its allies to speak up in support of the merger. Comcast had built up a lot of goodwill through its various community involvements; and at Congressional hearings, and in front of the FCC, many individuals and organizations were happy to return the favor by describing their experiences with the company. This outpouring contributed to a generally positive Congressional reaction, and letters of support for the transaction were ultimately signed by more than two hundred members of Congress.

Although Ralph did not testify at the various House and Senate hearings, he attended all the Washington hearings. Sitting just behind Brian, he was a prominent and visible presence. Again and again, elected officials used some of their allotted time to recognize him, and to comment on his reputation, his integrity, and his contributions to the national economy.

Early in 2011 the FCC approved the transaction by a 4-1 vote. The Justice Department also entered into a consent decree with Comcast. While the approvals were long and detailed, they addressed the same issues that Cohen and Waz had identified at the start of the process. And although the conditions were significant, they were not overly restrictive.

The day before the deal was announced, Brian decided to give Jeff Immelt a gift to commemorate the historic transaction. To prepare for their joint meetings with the press, the top executives from both companies were scheduled to gather at 5:00 p.m. in an NBC conference room at Rockefeller Center. That morning, Brian asked Paul Taubman to suggest a suitable present.

Taubman wasn't expecting this. Gifts are normally exchanged at the closing, when everyone involved has had months to think about what might be appropriate. But Brian knew how difficult it had been for Immelt to part with NBC Universal, and he wanted to express his appreciation for both the process and the result.

At first, he and Taubman discussed a gift that might incorporate the iconic NBC chimes, and Taubman suggested an antique music box that played those three famous notes. It was a fine idea, but it would have taken months to arrange. Taubman then suggested that they find some special item from 1926, the year the National Broadcasting Company (NBC) was founded by its three corporate owners—RCA, Westinghouse, and General Electric. They considered a bottle of wine before one of Taubman's colleagues came up with a better idea: an uncirculated 1926 twenty-dollar gold piece, known as the Saint-Gaudens double eagle, which is considered an especially beautiful example of classic American currency. Taubman's team scrambled to find one in the next couple of hours, and then to provide an appropriate gift wrapping.

That evening, at the conclusion of the session in which Brian, Ralph, Burke, Angelakis, and Cohen coordinated their statements with their GE counterparts, Brian turned to Immelt and said, "Jeff, there's one more thing. On the eve of a special and historic day for our company, I'd like to give you a little gift to mark this occasion. GE has been a great owner, first of NBC, and then of NBC Universal, and I promise you that we will be good stewards of the company. And because GE was one of the three founding partners of the network in 1926, I'd like to present you with this gold coin from that year."

It was an emotional moment, and some of the participants were a little choked up. Immelt was genuinely touched, and slightly embarrassed that he had nothing for Brian. "How about an NBC hat?" he joked.

"Don't worry about that," said Brian. "You've given us the best possible gift."

• • •

Although Brian and Immelt were deeply involved, the deal was really done by their chief financial officers. "Mike Angelakis puts the *private* in private equity," says Brian of the man who came from a private equity firm and still prefers to operate behind the scenes. "But everyone involved in this transaction knows how it happened."

"Just as AT&T Broadband was mostly Brian," says Steve Burke, "this deal was mostly Mike. He had a great relationship with Keith Sherin, and Brian trusted him." Sherin calls his negotiating partner "a constructive problem solver who pays close attention to what the other side needs." Others who worked on this deal with Angelakis point to his low-key, thoughtful style, his unusual combination of caution and creativity, and his ability to defuse tense situations with a disarming charm.

"In the AT&T deal," says Brian, "because of the synergy, money got it done. This deal was about persistence, trust, and creativity, and Mike provided all three. He and I were teammates in Comcast's Super Bowl, although we had no season to build on, or even a practice. But it was as if we had been doing this all our lives."

The fifty-fifth floor of Comcast Center houses the offices of the company's retired senior executives, which is why Julian refers to it as Jurassic Park. Of Angelakis's three predecessors, only Julian, as a director of the corporation, had been aware of the negotiations with GE. The day after the announcement, he, Larry Smith, and John Alchin ran into one another outside Smith's office. "The three of us sat down together," Julian recalls. "John and Larry, who had just learned about the deal, were in awe of how well constructed it was, and I felt the same way. This was the fulfillment of a strategy that was crying for fulfillment." Alchin adds: "We loved that the company wasn't using its shares to pay for the acquisition. All of us appreciated what Mike had created." The investment community had a similar response: when the deal was announced, Comcast shares rose for seven consecutive days, which had never happened after the announcement of an acquisition. (To be sure, the stock had been hammered hard when word of the deal first leaked.)

• • •

Early on the morning of December 3, just moments after the press release went out announcing the deal, Brian and Steve Burke arrived at 30 Rockefeller Plaza for a series of meetings and interviews. On their way in, they passed the Rockefeller Center Christmas tree. It was scheduled to be illuminated in just a few minutes, which struck them as a good omen. That morning, as they hurried into the building to be interviewed on CNBC, the weight of what they had just accomplished hit Burke hard: "It felt like we were standing in the center of the world." He and Brian, together with the two Jeffs—GE's Immelt and NBC Universal's Zucker—met with an audience of NBC Universal executives and on-air talent in an event that was seen by employees around the world.

It was Brian's idea for Ralph to appear at the end of the session to greet the NBC Universal employees. "It wasn't so much what he said," Burke recalls, "as the way Brian talked about him." As the meeting drew to a close, Brian told the group, "For me there's an even bigger reason I'm here, and that's my father." When Ralph stepped out in a dark suit and his trademark bow tie, he was greeted with a prolonged standing ovation. "That spontaneous eruption was something visceral," Brian recalls. "The employees were proud of their company's heritage, and you could feel that pride. And they seemed to have a real understanding of what Ralph had created."

Ralph spoke emotionally about his journey—and Comcast's. Then he invited the NBC Universal employees to become part of that journey in the years ahead. "I hope we can make your future, your career, better than you ever imagined possible," he told the group. "I'm thrilled that at eighty-nine I'm still vertical," and, when the laughter subsided, "to be part of this historic day."

"Today," said the man who had started out in the media business by buying a little cable system in Tupelo, Mississippi, "today we begin all over again."

The Values of Comcast

A Virtual Conversation

Two visitors, who prefer to remain anonymous, enjoy the 2009 3-D Comcast Holiday Spectacular.

The Value of a Family Culture

Ralph: How do you maintain a family culture when the company is so big? By being warm and friendly. Instead of one big family, we have a lot of smaller ones, and I urge employees to get to know the people in their own part of the company. That's your immediate family. Be kind, do favors, and offer help to those who may be having problems.

Brian: My father never wanted to work for a large corporation. When Comcast kept growing, he had to make it the kind of company he did want to work for.

Melanie Penna: When I feel overwhelmed in the morning and my kids are crying, at least I'm going off to my second family.

Rebecca Tilleson (no longer with Comcast): I don't see most companies even claiming to be a family, but when people here use that word, they mean it. And when you mention Ralph's name, they smile.

Tina Waters: As an African American woman, I have peers in other companies who don't feel respected. But here I feel like part of the family. These are people I would choose to spend time with even if I didn't work here.

Pat Donovan (retired): Ralph would always consider what effect a decision would have on the frontline people and their families. Although the leadership wanted to satisfy both customers and stockholders, they were always considerate of employees.

ACCESSIBLE LEADERS

Dan Aaron (deceased): Time and again I reminded the Comcast staff, don't be shackled by a chain of command. Everyone in this company is at your disposal at any time, from Ralph on down.

Joan French (retired): Employees from all over the country feel comfortable sending e-mails and letters directly to Ralph and Brian.

Joe Waz (now a consultant to Comcast): At AT&T it was Mr. Armstrong. At Comcast it's Ralph and Brian.

Lucille Fital: I have friends in other companies who know what their CEOs look like only from seeing their pictures in magazines. Our offices have glass walls and our executives wander the halls.

Maria Carriere (no longer with Comcast): The employees appreciate that you don't have to go through special procedures to have access to our leaders.

Salaam Coleman Smith (Style Network): When I arrived, I expected to find the corporate equivalent of a huge city. But it felt more like a small, friendly town where it was easy to meet the top people.

Beth Bacha (NJ): I've worked in companies where there were memos circulated about how to address senior executives. I once received a memo saying that when a corporate leader finished speaking, it would be appropriate to give him a standing ovation. When Ralph gets one, it's because that's how people feel about him.

Dawn Stagliano (FL): If the head of my previous company had ever shown up, I wouldn't have dared to introduce myself. But the culture here gives you the opportunity to do that.

Jeff Gibson: On the final day of Comcast University's year-long Executive Leadership Forum (ELF) training, the six teams reported their findings and recommendations to the top leaders in the company. It was incredible to me that they spent a couple of hours listening to what we came up with, and then took action on some of our recommendations.

THE FAMILY SPIRIT

Dave Watson: I often tell people, quoting Ralph, that if somebody at work is having an issue or needs help, it's your obligation to give them a hand. We look out for each other.

Bob Victor: If someone stumbles, you pick them up and make sure they're okay. It's the opposite of a cutthroat culture.

Cathy Avgiris: We're a very big small company.

Jennifer Daley: I had been with the company six months when I was invited to Ralph's seventy-fifth birthday party. Everyone in the building was invited, which surprised me. It made me feel that they value everyone who works here.

Ray Child (UT): When I was nominated for some public relations awards, I received a handwritten note from Brad Dusto, our division president. Considering the number of employees in the West Division, I was amazed and pleased that he knew who I was.

Mike Molinaro (NBCUniversal): When potential employees ask me to describe our culture, I say we're like an extended family getting together for dinner. Everyone is in the kitchen, and there may be arguments or even angry words, but by the end of the evening, the meal is on the table and we're all together.

Rodrigo Lopez (UT): Ralph spoke at the graduation dinner of my ELF class and said some nice things about Steve Burke. Then he said,

"If I could have another son, it would be Steve." When Steve ran up and hugged him, Ralph said, "But I'm not raising your allowance!" Brian, who was at my table, grabbed a dinner roll, threw it at Steve, and hit him in the head, as if to say, "Hey, wait a minute, that's *my* dad." Everyone laughed, and that little scene seemed to embody the company's family spirit.

YOUR FIRST FAMILY

Dan Aaron: I always took the position that family responsibility came first. I was keenly aware that a solid family life helped sustain a dedicated employee.

Dave Cassaro (no longer with Comcast): Family trumps business here, and people are happy and more productive because of it.

Payne Brown (no longer with Comcast): The leadership is incredibly grounded. I once heard Steve say, "For those of you who think that work is the most important thing in your life, you have your priorities wrong." That's what I mean by *grounded*.

Ernie Pighini: I came from public accounting, where you felt like you were on a treadmill. At Comcast you work hard, but you are entitled to a family life.

Charisse Lillie: Although our people work very hard, we try to make sure they can still have a life. We try not to wrench them away on evenings and weekends if we don't have to.

The Value of Integrity

Ralph: In a big company you need certain fundamentals to believe in. Around here, everyone knows that integrity comes first.

Bern Gallagher (retired): Integrity isn't just about big things. If Ralph said he would be somewhere at a certain time, you could bank on it. And it made no difference who the other person was. To Ralph, everyone was important.

Sharon Ingram (retired): We were told that our word was our bond. There was no such thing as saying one thing and doing another.

Ed Breen (former director): When I was with Motorola, we always knew that at Comcast we could do business with a handshake and get the contract done later.

Brad Dusto: When potential employees come to us from companies that had ethical issues, we say, "You won't be asked to do those things here, and in fact, doing them will get you fired."

Michael Sovern (former director): The commitment to integrity is almost palpable.

THE SPECIAL INTEGRITY OF NUMBERS

Julian: A lie in any language is a lie, and numbers are just another language. They're either truthful or they're not.

Marlene Dooner: When we worked together on annual reports, Julian showed a mania for accuracy and perfectionism. He didn't believe in adjectives and was careful to avoid hype. We would always understate and underpromise.

Ernie Pighini: We are fastidious about finances.

Neil Smit: There's real financial rigor here. People understand both the numbers and the dynamics behind the numbers.

Larry Salva: Sometimes there is more than one way to present information, and we try not to color the story or make it into something it's not. We look for the right answer, not necessarily the best answer to present.

The Value of Being Entrepreneurial

Ralph: I used to tell our people, "It's okay to make mistakes. I make them every day because I'm doing too much, too fast. We all are. But let's learn from our mistakes and try to make sure they're not too big."

D'Arcy Rudnay: I'm able to try things without putting every idea through a long bureaucratic chain. You don't get smacked down for taking risks.

Rick Germano: There's a saying around here that it's better to ask for forgiveness than permission. You'll get in trouble for lack of integrity, not for taking a risk.

Gene Shatlock: In Tallahassee, in my first GM job, I saw that people didn't do much on weekends beyond watching football games and visiting the mall, so I pitched the idea of opening a cable store in the mall, and it was approved. When it wasn't profitable, we closed it. There were no recriminations.

Jon Gorchow (no longer with Comcast): I was told early on that no good idea goes unfunded. And nobody has ever said to me, "That's a great idea. Too bad we can't do it." If you come up with a proposal that moves the needle, we'll find a way to get it done.

Fehmi Zeko (banker): They're a great company to bring ideas to because they're bright and can move quickly. Nothing is too crazy to consider, but they can be tough on any idea that isn't well thought out.

Julian: Sometimes the best deals are those you don't do.

Brian: Or the ones you didn't plan on doing, like the cell phone business. We hadn't intended to go in that direction, but when it came our way, Ralph grabbed it.

HIRING GREAT PEOPLE

Tom Baxter (retired): Ralph always went out of his way to hire the best people he could find.

Howard Fischer (executive recruiter): If a company has a couple of high performers and a bunch of laggards, there will be discontent. But when you have high performers seeded everywhere, they motivate each other to greater levels of accomplishment.

Len Rozek (WA): When you have very smart people looking at your work, it motivates you to do your very best because you're being pushed.

Tony Werner: Even though we're a large, publicly traded company, the senior executives care as if they were the owners. That's the way cable used to be.

GETTING IT DONE

Charisse Lillie: We don't like to say that something can't be done. People here are always trying to figure out how we *can* get it done.

Jaye Gamble (no longer with Comcast): We have a bias for action.

Ray Celona: We hire people with a can-do spirit, who don't need much direction.

Bill Stemper: There's an exciting, competitive spirit here that says no challenge is too big.

Jeff Shell (NBCUniversal): We do aggressive things in a cautious way. Things are carefully debated before they're done, but they are done.

FAST AND FLEXIBLE

Joe Waz: It's a company with great freedom of communication and movement.

Josh Steiner (consultant): I'm impressed by the speed of decision making at Comcast, which is refreshing and unusual.

Bill Kettleson (NJ): The company's rapid pace is not for the faint of heart.

Doug Gaston: For a big company, we are relatively nimble. We can respond quickly when the situation changes, and we don't need a big committee to make a decision.

Bill Wright (no longer with Comcast): I have been amazed at how fast the company can pivot and head off in a new direction.

Dave Juliano: But everything we do is about building value for the long term.

FINANCIAL FOCUS

Brian: As a child of the Depression, Ralph taught me to keep cash on hand for unexpected circumstances, which was very helpful when credit dried up, as it did in the fall of 2008.

Bill Wright: When I first came to Comcast, I couldn't believe the level of detail in the budget process.

Bill Connors (GA): There's a clear expectation. It's not, "Try your best to hit your numbers;" it's, "Deliver the numbers."

Scott Tenney (IN): When I worked at corporate, Steve Burke held a meeting where he showed a slide listing every market's basic sub and cash-flow performance. Only four markets missed both targets, and all four were getting new GMs. Steve didn't say that was the reason, but I'm sure it was. It's a demanding culture.

BUSINESS SOLUTIONS

Ralph: We don't want the other person to walk away unhappy. Most of the people I've done business with over the years have remained my friends.

Bob Pick: We are known as tough negotiators, but we don't beat the other guy down.

Joe Collins (director): Comcast doesn't make many enemies, which is unusual in this business. They play hard, but by an honorable set of rules.

Julian: Over the years we've had a remarkable lack of litigation. We always felt there was a negotiable or business solution.

Stanley Wang (deceased): That comes from Ralph, who believes there's a business solution to any problem. It was seen as a kind of failure if we had to litigate. One way we have avoided litigation is to examine every word before we sign an agreement. This goes back to the first lawyer Comcast ever had, Bernie Eskin from Wolf Block, who advised us, "Unless a seventh grader can understand the contract, don't sign it."

Art Block: There are financial costs to litigation, and human costs, too. We don't like to make enemies, especially in an industry that's full of ongoing relationships. There is almost always a business solution.

The Value of Ideas

Ralph: Everyone has a right to speak, and everyone does. As a result, we've got a closely knit group who are probably right in most of their decisions. We make them collectively.

Brian: My father welcomes different points of view. He never surrounded himself with yes-men or shrinking violets. He has always had strong-minded and smart people in his inner circle, and if they didn't agree, that was fine.

Jeff Shell: At my previous company, everyone deferred to the CEO. Here we make decisions through big, open debates.

Decker Anstrom (former director): Brian doesn't mind being challenged, and when he hears a better idea, he'll change his mind. Think how empowering that is for the executives.

Mike Tallent (retired): We operated not by rank, but by persuasion. There was a constant, ongoing conversation that began in 1963 and is still going strong.

Art Block: Loyalty counts, but ideas count more.

Dave Watson: We are encouraged to introduce ideas and debate them in the same way the company's founders did.

Bob Clasen (retired): We used to joke that everything was second-guessed, including the second-guessers.

Bill Stemper: There are companies where the higher your pay grade, the better your idea. But here a good idea can come from anyone at any level.

Howard Fischer: It's a meritocracy.

CONFLICT, COURAGE, CANDOR

Dave Scott: Ralph told me early on not to give up if I had a good idea, even if I couldn't get anyone to listen.

Marlene Dooner: If you have a different view, people want to hear it.

Rick Germano: When I came to Comcast, I noticed that the leaders wanted to know what you thought. They didn't want to miss opportunities.

Fehmi Zeko: My colleagues and I have gone to many pitch sessions at Comcast, and they'll debate among themselves in front of us. It's encouraged by Brian, who will sometimes prompt it. They challenge each other openly. It's unusual and effective, and they tend to make good decisions.

Mike Tallent: Some people tell you only good news: everything is great and no action needs to be taken. We encouraged people to bring us problems so we could address them.

Tom Baxter: At Comcast they don't shoot the messenger.

Gabrielle Ingram (no longer with Comcast): Typically, the higher up you get in an organization, the less candid the executives are. That's not true here.

Art Block: The way to be respected is to speak your mind, which takes courage and strength of personality.

Brad Dusto: At the first senior management meeting I attended, the conversation was all over the place. I thought I had joined a really dysfunctional family, with no direction or consensus. But out in the hallway, where people were friendly, Mike Tallent told me, "This is how we make decisions. We toss out ideas, focus on some, and disregard others. Just watch." I started to see that the company wanted to hear many voices. Over time, people began to change their minds until a consensus was reached.

Mike Tallent: When that happened, Ralph would smile, and we'd leave knowing what the decision was.

Marlene Dooner: It's true consensus building, rather than pretending we all agree and calling it consensus. It takes longer and it's more frustrating, but when you get there, it feels worth it.

LOSING THE ARGUMENT

Art Block: When we vote on whether to make an acquisition, and it's nine to one in favor, Brian wants to know who said no, and why. And that person will tell him.

Mark Coblitz: At some companies, if your idea loses, *you* lose, and you might not get the next promotion. Here, if you take a position that isn't adopted, you don't lose face or reputation. You merely lose the argument.

John Ridall (retired): You won't be punished for disagreeing, or for saying, "I don't think that will work in my division."

Scott Tenney: There's room for dissent, but once the decision is made, you get in line and execute.

Adam Miller (NBCUniversal): There is often vehement disagreement, but it's honest and respectful, and not personal. It's a process that makes people want to join Comcast and stay there, or partner with the company, or serve as advisors.

The Value of Modesty

Jim Cramer (CNBC): I had Brian and Steve Burke multiple times on my show, and every time I'd failed to catch the bravado and machismo that had to lurk beneath their simple white shirts, plain ties, and indistinguishable blend-in suits. Even close up, they lack the bravado I've seen in every single media player from miles away. The Robertses and Burke just don't carry themselves like moguls.

Brian Mossor (no longer with Comcast): I attended a talk where Brian and Steve explained how Comcast had integrated the employees from AT&T. The room was packed, and I was sitting behind two CEOs from major pharmaceutical companies. One of them leaned over to the other and said, "Those are two of the most humble people I've ever seen. They don't even want to take credit for the amazing thing they accomplished. I'd be happy if we could achieve something like that between departments!"

Grace Killelea: Our modesty has helped to preserve our culture and keep our core values intact.

Bill Dordelman: Part of the culture of modesty is that we're in Philadelphia.

Troy Fitzhugh (no longer with Comcast): We have some of the greatest executives in the business, but many people have never heard their names because they quietly do their jobs.

Beth Arnholt: There are no titles on the office doors, which is unusual.

Dawn Stagliano: People will pitch in to do whatever needs to be done. Nobody feels that anything is beneath them.

Filemon Lopez (FL): Egomaniacs don't do well here. Every now and then one sneaks in, but they don't last.

Scott Tenney: At AT&T we had a lot of PowerPoint presentations, but not here. We are encouraged to get to the heart of the argument.

MATERIAL MODESTY

Stanley Wang: Before we moved into Comcast Center, our executive dining room was the food court across the street.

Sheila Willard: AT&T had executive dining rooms even in the divisions. There was a separation that doesn't exist here.

Steve Burke: My office at ABC was three times the size of my office at Comcast.

Jim Cramer: Ralph Roberts still won't take a chauffeured limousine. He goes for the van and sits in the front.

Sharon Ingram: In 1990, when Ralph was seventy, we had to beg him to get a driver, which he saw as too fancy. He finally agreed, but there were conditions: the driver couldn't wear a uniform, and the car had to be a minivan, because other people might be going to and from the airport.

THE RELATIVE ABSENCE OF POLITICS

John Alchin (retired): When I came here, the most pleasant surprise was the complete lack of a political environment, with none of the infighting I had seen in the banking world.

Sam Schwartz: The stability represented by Ralph and Brian explains why Comcast is less political than other companies. People here play fewer games.

Paul Taubman (banker): There doesn't seem to be any infighting, factions, or politics.

A TEAM APPROACH

Ralph: We have no prima donnas here.

Brian: I sometimes see us as a law firm with a number of partners. I'm the managing partner, but everyone gets a vote.

Matt Bond (NBCUniversal): The culture at Comcast is collaborative and action-oriented. It's team-oriented in the sense of a unity of purpose around one thing: winning.

Tom Nathan: I tell our government affairs people to think of their job in terms of a zone defense: When the ball is in your area, it's your job to step out and take responsibility for it. But you're not alone; there's a team behind you. And when the action moves into someone else's zone, you've got to be prepared to assist *them.*

Peter Intermaggio: The culture here is the opposite of a command-and-control environment.

The Value of a Happy Workplace

Ralph: At the dinner table, Suzanne and I used to encourage our kids to go into whatever field gave them the greatest amount of happiness. And at Comcast I've often said, "If you're unhappy in your job, look for something else within the company." I've always told our HR people that their job is to let the employees know that we care about them and want them to be happy.

Dan Aaron: I had my own agenda for our company, which my associates shared, that work could be a joy as well as a challenge.

Bob Clasen: At Comcast I found happy people leading happy lives.

Jan Iannacci: When I came to Comcast in 1989, I felt the difference right away. There was an easiness I wasn't used to, and I wondered, Could it be true? I kept waiting for reality to kick in.

D'Arcy Rudnay: When I got here, people said such positive things about the company, their bosses, and each other, that I thought it was because I was new. But I've been here a few years now, and they're still saying these things.

Buck Dopp (retired): When I came here from Storer, I noticed that people had a good sense of humor. They tell jokes about themselves, and they're down-to-earth and real.

Bob Smith (PA): From the start, Ralph has embraced people from the many companies we have acquired over the years. We're a company of immigrants.

Bernice McCann: When people are happy, they treat other people well. You can't share what you don't have.

Mike Casillo (no longer with Comcast): From the day I arrived, I had the sense that if you contribute, you'll be rewarded.

Michael Angelakis: There are no screamers here, no people who are especially difficult. We care a lot about employees being happy.

Lisa Birmingham (VT): I've never worked for a company that spends so much energy on employee development and satisfaction. The question here isn't just what have you done for the company. It's also, what have you done for yourself?

Tina Waters: I laugh as hard at work as I do at home.

Brian: Every one of us could be working somewhere else, but we all choose to work here. There's something unique about the spirit of Comcast, and it's Ralph's gift to us all.

Barbara Gehrig (retired): We're constantly asking employees to tell us how to get better, and they take us up on it.

Tom Baxter: A company has to decide whether its employees are assets or liabilities. At Comcast we saw them as assets, but many companies don't.

Kevin Casey (NH): I feel that I have a personal stake in this company. I like the people I work with, what they stand for, and how we go about creating a great company.

Janet Turpen (WA): What I like best about working here is that we're allowed to think. In my previous cable job, the corporate leadership did the thinking for us.

Al Peddrick (retired): There aren't many companies where the CEO comes in to talk to you about treating the employees properly, as Ralph did. Ever since Tupelo, people here have felt that this was a good place to work.

A LOCAL FORCE FOR GOOD

Brian: The idea of volunteering comes from Ralph, who decided early on that we should be giving something back in local communities.

Barbara Lukens (retired): The individual systems were expected to provide services to the local community, especially donating free time for public service announcements from the United Way.

Dave Breidinger (PA): Ralph recognized early on that it was our relationships with the communities that allowed us to do business in those places. We have always been a company with strong local connections.

Dan Gallagher: In our leadership training programs, we stress the importance of representing Comcast in the participants' home communities. Every year, when they visit Philadelphia, we bring about fifty high-potential managers from across the country to Children's Hospital, where they read books to the kids. It's our way of emphasizing that being a good corporate leader includes civic responsibilities. We then ask these managers to initiate their own community service projects for employees back home.

Steve Burke: Comcast Cares is both a great family day and a great day for Comcast as a family. Each year, there's a real buzz in the company after we hold it. People feel great about themselves, and about the company they work for.

A Final Word

I was hoping this book would be completed by my ninetieth birthday in 2010, but as often happens in life, things took a little longer than we expected. And I didn't want to rush, because it's been so enjoyable working with Bill Novak and telling him about my early years, my first jobs, and the growth of Comcast. The more we talked, the longer that story became. New chapters of our improbable journey kept unfolding, and Bill didn't want to miss anything.

But there's something we almost missed. There's a certain someone who means the world to me, and this book wouldn't be complete without my saying a little more about Suzanne. After all, I didn't get to where I am today without her. We've been married for nearly seventy years, and during that time she has also been my closest friend and my inspiration, especially when it comes to public service.

When we met, Suzanne had already started her acting career. During World War II, she appeared in a series of plays that encouraged audiences to buy war bonds and donate blood. When the war ended, she started acting in dramas that dealt with social problems ranging from racism to alcoholism. Over the next few decades she appeared in so many productions, and played so many roles, that it sometimes felt as if I were married to a hundred different women.

When Suzanne noticed a lack of television programming for older Americans, she created a two-time Emmy Award-winning show, *Seeking Solutions with Suzanne.* The program, which runs in both five-minute and half-hour formats, explores topics of interest to seniors, ranging from medical and legal issues to self-enrichment and the arts.

She has also been a public-service leader within our family. I'll never forget the day in 1970 when she turned to me and said, "Ralph, every year we take the kids away on a nice vacation. This year, why don't we do something that will benefit other people?"

We spent that summer on a Navajo reservation in New Mexico, where each of us, including our youngest children, was able to make a contribution. Suzanne volunteered at the local hospital, where she developed a technique for communicating with hostile and withdrawn patients. When we came home, she began working with troubled children in Philadelphia.

I'm only scratching the surface here, but you can see why I'm so proud of her. I'm also proud of our children, their husbands and wives, and our wonderful grandchildren. Both my life and my career have been shaped and enriched by a loving, supportive family.

How fortunate I am to have built Comcast together with so many great people—tens of thousands of you. We have accomplished so much together since that first little community antenna television system in Mississippi, and we've done it with intelligence, hard work, and imagination. I'm even prouder that through the years we have retained our reputation for integrity.

My only regret is that there aren't enough pages in this book to mention everyone who has helped Comcast become what it is today. Call me old-fashioned, but I still think of us as all belonging to one family, even if that family is now bigger than we ever imagined.

So with Bill's permission, I want to dedicate this book to every single member of the Comcast family—past, present, and future. I can't thank you enough for helping us achieve this incredible dream.